CONSTITUTION-MAKER: SELECTED WRITINGS OF SIR IVOR JENNINGS

CONSTITUTION-MAKER: SELECTED WRITINGS OF SIR IVOR JENNINGS

edited by
H. KUMARASINGHAM

CAMDEN FIFTH SERIES
Volume 46

CAMBRIDGE
UNIVERSITY PRESS

FOR THE ROYAL HISTORICAL SOCIETY
University College London, Gower Street, London WC1 6BT
2014

Published by the Press Syndicate of the University of Cambridge
UPH, Shaftesbury Road, Cambridge CB2 8RU, United Kingdom
32 Avenue of the Americas, New York, NY 10013-2473, USA
477 Williamstown Road, Port Melbourne, VIC 3207, Australia
C/Orense, 4, Planta 13, 28020 Madrid, Spain
Lower Ground Floor, Nautica Building, The Water Club,
Beach Road, Granger Bay, 8005 Cape Town, South Africa

First published 2014

A catalogue record for this book is available from the British Library

ISBN 9781107091115 hardback

SUBSCRIPTIONS. The serial publications of the Royal Historical Society, *Royal Historical Society Transactions* (ISSN 0080-4401) and Camden Fifth Series (ISSN 0960-1163) volumes, may be purchased together on annual subscription. The 2014 subscription price, which includes print and electronic access (but not VAT), is £153 (US $255 in the USA, Canada, and Mexico) and includes Camden Fifth Series, volumes 45 and 46 and Transactions Sixth Series, volume 24 (published in December). The electronic-only price available to institutional subscribers is £132 (US $220 in the USA, Canada, and Mexico). Japanese prices are available from Kinokuniya Company Ltd, P.O. Box 55, Chitose, Tokyo 156, Japan. EU subscribers (outside the UK) who are not registered for VAT should add VAT at their country's rate. VAT registered subscribers should provide their VAT registration number. Prices include delivery by air.

Subscription orders, which must be accompanied by payment, may be sent to a bookseller, subscription agent, or direct to the publisher: Cambridge University Press, UPH, Shaftesbury Road, Cambridge CB2 8BS, UK; or in the USA, Canada, and Mexico: Cambridge University Press, Journals Fulfillment Department, 100 Brook Hill Drive, West Nyack, New York, 10994-2133, USA.

SINGLE VOLUMES AND BACK VOLUMES. A list of Royal Historical Society volumes available from Cambridge University Press may be obtained from the Humanities Marketing Department at the address above.

Printed in the UK by Bell & Bain Ltd.

CONTENTS

ACKNOWLEDGEMENTS

My first and most appropriate acknowledgement is to Mrs Shirley Watson for giving me permission to edit the papers of her father, which I first examined in the Institute of Commonwealth Studies Library (then located at 28 Russell Square) in July 2005. I am so grateful to Mrs Watson for her generous hospitality in discussing her formidable father, illuminating me with family tales, beckoning memorabilia, and rare photographs, and enlightening me on several points of her father's career and life. As Jennings' only surviving child she, along with her son, Michael Watson, and daughter, Rebecca Caine, has been gracious enough to provide me with the support I needed to complete this task without ever seeking to control it.

The Institute of Commonwealth Studies, as the custodian of the papers, has also been entirely encouraging of my labours. Its director, Professor Philip Murphy, librarian, David Clover, and the Emeka Anyaoku Professor Emeritus of Commonwealth Studies, James Manor, have been supportive and knowledgeable backers of this project, facilitating its progress at every stage. It is a privilege to be a Senior Research Fellow in such a welcoming and erudite environment. Philip and Dr Donal Lowry were also especially helpful with the complexities of the Federation of Rhodesia and Nyasaland.

To Professors Arthur Burns and Emma Griffin at the Royal Historical Society I record my appreciation for backing this volume to be part of the prestigious Camden Series with Cambridge University Press, and thanks to Emma and to Hester Higton in particular for their editorial help. Professors Martin Loughlin and Linda Mulcahy at the Law Department of the London School of Economics have been generous and enthusiastic patrons of this project on Jennings. Without them and the LSE's Legal Biography Project the transcription and copying of the papers would have been impossible and my task obdurately harder. Jonathan Harrison and his team at Senate House Library special collections have always been wonderful in their professionalism and I am so appreciative of how they did everything to make my work easier in using the papers. Tim Livsey made an excellent job of the unenviable labour of deciphering Jennings' appalling handwriting.

Emeritus Professors Anthony Bradley and Chris Himsworth have not only shared their memories of Jennings and his legacy but have also been good enough to advise on thorny legal questions beyond my ability; for this last assistance Dr John Allison is also added with many thanks. Professor Sir Christopher Bayly and the Smuts Managers at the University of Cambridge have, by electing me in 2013 to the Smuts Fellowship in Commonwealth Studies, provided me with the time, resources, and stimulating conditions at the Centre for South Asian Studies to carry out this demanding responsibility.

Professor Vernon Bogdanor has been an exceptionally kind mentor and has uncomplainingly allowed me to pick his lucid mind for many facts and concerns. I am in the debt of my friend Dr Peter Catterall for his advice and guidance over how to edit historical papers. His first-class editing of Harold Macmillan's diaries is the model I have attempted to emulate and I hope that this volume meets his high standards. My deepest intellectual and practical debts are to my colleagues Dr Mara Malagodi and Dr Asanga Welikala. They have kept me going with their expertise, sustenance, and friendship and it is no exaggeration to say that without them this volume would be the poorer. Any errors are mine, but any praise will be shared with the above.

To my parents, who were born in the age of Jennings and grew up in his wake, I am indebted for so much, including this book. Finally, Karolina and Maks, thank you for tolerating Sir Ivor Jennings in our home – though I'm not sure he's moving out quite yet!

H. Kumarasingham,
October 2014

INTRODUCTION

'We have the advice of the greatest living authority on Constitutional Law regarding the British Commonwealth – Dr Jennings', proclaimed the Leader of the Ceylon Senate in December 1947 in a parliamentary debate on the future constitutional design of the island.[1] So in thrall to William Ivor Jennings was the powerful and soon to be first prime minister of independent Ceylon, D.S. Senanayake, that in the same debate it was contemptuously suggested that his initials stood for 'Dominion Status Senanayake', a form of independence that Jennings advocated as Senanayake's pervasive and persuasive adviser.[2] Senanayake was never in doubt as to the value of Jennings and publicly expressed his gratitude by delivering to the Englishman a knighthood, on his advice, for services to Ceylon, less than six months later in the King's 1948 Birthday Honours List.

Ivor Jennings was born in Bristol on 16 May 1903. He had a remarkable career stretching across the world as a constitutional scholar in the heyday of decolonization before his death in Cambridge at just sixty-two on 19 December 1965.[3] After studying mathematics and law, he obtained a first-class degree for the law tripos in 1924–1925 while at St Catharine's College, Cambridge. After a short time as a law lecturer at the University of Leeds, he went to the London School of Economics (LSE) in 1929, where he rose to become Reader in English Law. While at the LSE, Jennings published some of his most famous and influential works, including *The Law and the Constitution* (1933), *Cabinet Government* (1936), and *Parliament* (1939).

After just over ten years at the LSE and a visiting professorship (in political science) at the University of British Columbia, Jennings accepted a job in Ceylon, becoming the first vice-chancellor of the University of Ceylon once full university status was achieved in 1942

[1] *Parliamentary Debates (Hansard)*, Ceylon Senate, vol. 1, p. 172, 2 December 1947. The speaker was Sir Oliver Goonetilleke.

[2] *Ibid.*, p. 174.

[3] For greater detail regarding information on Jennings and his background, see his autobiography, posthumously edited and introduced by H.A.I. Goonetilleke, *The Road to Peradeniya: an autobiography* (Colombo, 2005), and, especially concerning his public law contributions, A.W. Bradley, 'Sir William Ivor Jennings: a centennial paper', *Modern Law Review*, 67, no. 5 (September 2004), pp. 716–733.

(it had previously been a college with affiliation to the University of London). With characteristic ambition and formidable brio, he spearheaded the university's move in 1952 to its new site in Peradeniya.[4] Jennings proved himself an adroit administrator and he moved from Ceylon back to Cambridge to become Master of Trinity Hall, a position that he held until his death, along with a term as the university's vice-chancellor (1961–1963) when that position rotated among the college heads.

Further academic and professional honours came his way. He was made a King's Counsel in 1949, and was elected a fellow of the British Academy in 1955. He delivered the 1949 Waynflete lectures at Magdalen College, Oxford, on the Commonwealth in Asia (later published as a book in 1951). In 1950 he held a visiting professorship at the Australian National University. He was Chairman of the Royal Commission on Common Land from 1955 to 1958. In 1958 he delivered a lecture series on 'Problems of the new Commonwealth' at Duke University (published as a book the same year) and was also made a bencher of Gray's Inn. Finally, he was appointed to the prestigious Downing Professorship in the Laws of England at Cambridge in 1962.

Jennings contributed significant international advice to universities and higher education institutions in Ceylon, Hong Kong, India, Jamaica, Kuwait, Malta, Malaya, and Uganda. Meanwhile, his publishing endeavours matched his professional ones. In addition to the books mentioned above (which have since seen multiple updated editions), came such works as *The British Constitution* (1941), *The British Commonwealth of Nations* (1948), *The Constitution of Ceylon* (1949), *Constitutional Laws of the Commonwealth* (1952), *The Queen's Government* (1954), *The Approach to Self-government* (1956), *Constitutional Problems in Pakistan* (1957), and *Party Politics* (3 vols, 1960–1962). These editions were accompanied by an almost endless succession of critical articles in leading international journals of multiple disciplines, covering subjects as diverse as English housing legislation, emergency regulations during wartime, constitutional interpretation in Canada, utilitarianism, and prime ministerial removals.[5]

[4] For Jennings' time at Peradeniya see his posthumously published *The Kandy Road*, edited and introduced by H.A.I. Goonetilleke (Peradeniya, 1993).

[5] Ivor Jennings, 'Courts and administrative law: the experience of English housing legislation', *Harvard Law Review*, 49, no. 3 (January 1936), pp. 426–454; *idem*, 'The Emergency Powers (Defence) (No. 2) Act, 1940', *Modern Law Review*, 4, no. 2 (October 1940), pp. 132–136; *idem*, 'Constitutional interpretation: the experience of Canada', *Harvard Law Review*, 51, no. 1 (1937), pp. 1–39; *idem*, 'A plea for utilitarianism', *Modern Law Review*, 2, no. 1 (June 1938), pp. 22–35; *idem*, 'Removal of a premier', *Cambridge Law Review*, 21, no. 2 (November 1963), pp. 169–172.

An international constitutional authority

The above description points to a substantial and prodigious academic career. However, this does not reveal the full influence of this Cambridge public law don. Ivor Jennings commanded critical attention as an adviser beyond Britain to nations mostly of the Commonwealth, especially those emerging from imperial rule. From at least Easter 1938, when he gave advice to a Canadian Royal Commission on dominion–provincial relations, until his death, Jennings was one of the most sought-after constitutional experts in the world. He advised on great and small issues alike, and, at least as viewed from his papers, his advice was requested on specific constitutional, parliamentary, political, and legal issues by Canada, Ceylon, Cyprus, Eritrea, Gambia, Ghana, Gibraltar, Malaya, the Maldives, Malta, Nepal, New Zealand, Nigeria, Pakistan, Rhodesia and Nyasaland, Singapore, South Africa, and Sudan. The degree of involvement in the countries ranged from being a member of the Reid Commission responsible for drafting a constitution for the Federation of Malaya, through acting as unofficial adviser to D.S. Senanayake, producing memoranda on financial issues in western Nigeria, functioning as a paid advocate in a fundamentally important case for Pakistani democracy, and giving an opinion on the advisability of South Africa becoming a republic, to providing private advice solicited by the Governor-General of New Zealand on what to do in the event of a hung parliament.

Such a varied and topical agenda allowed Jennings an opportunity to engage and contribute beyond the limited confines of academic scholarship. Perhaps surprisingly, but no doubt excitingly for him, he readily and more often than not strayed beyond narrow terms of reference or questions of law. This allowed him to generate personal judgments on all manner of issues, especially political questions. As he remarked, for example, in his autobiography, about his fourteen years in Ceylon, 'though I have often been consulted by the Government of Ceylon on matters within my field of study, I remember only one occasion on which I was asked to advise on "the law"'.[6] As the selected documents will show, Jennings engaged in political realities (and expediencies) when dealing with the array of questions put before him and did not let academic niceties or legal minutiae restrict the expanse of his assessments or the style of his analysis.

When discussing British constitutional issues Jennings was and is still regularly cited, even if only in criticism or in reference to his

[6]Jennings, *Road to Peradeniya*, p. 70. The question was on martial law in the event of a Japanese invasion of the island, and was raised at Easter 1942, not long after he arrived.

constitutional authority. He remains on the reading list of many constitution-related courses and is supposedly read by the Prince of Wales and Buckingham Palace.[7] Lord Butler of Brockwell, who held the constitutionally omniscient role of Cabinet Secretary from 1988 to 1998, revealed in retirement that Jennings was someone 'on whom I was brought up', a sentiment that was probably shared by that generation of Oxbridge civil service panjandrums.[8] The Commonwealth scholar D.A. Low despaired that the works of Jennings were not at hand at Yarralumla[9] before Sir John Kerr sacked Gough Whitlam as Australia's prime minister in 1975,[10] though they were used by the solicitor-general, Maurice Byers, to comprehend the Crown's powers during this infamous crisis.[11]

The British journalist and political historian Peter Hennessy mockingly described Michael Heseltine as giving an impression of being a 'Jermyn Street Sir Ivor Jennings' on account of his appearance on *Panorama*, where he ponderously explained his dramatic resignation on constitutional grounds from the Thatcher Cabinet in January 1986.[12] In 2007, Anthony King included Jennings in his 'Canonical Sextet' next to Walter Bagehot, A.V. Dicey, Sidney Low, Leo Amery, and Harold Laski as authors who 'define[d] for the British, over a long period of years, what their uncodified constitution was and what it meant'.[13] Martin Loughlin credits Jennings as one of the pioneers of the 'functionalist' method and approach to public law, which, rather than viewing law and politics as separate, compartmentalized entities, understood these fields as intimately connected and complementary, and sought to reinforce the view that the constitution is merely 'an object of description' that could only be properly understood by an analytical study of how critical state institutions actually functioned.[14] David E. Smith believes, with comparable application to other countries, that selective reference to scholars such as Jennings in

[7] D.A. Low, 'United Kingdom', in David Butler and D.A. Low (eds), *Sovereigns and Surrogates: constitutional heads of state in the Commonwealth* (London, 1991), p. 15.

[8] Lord Butler of Brockwell, review of Nevil Johnson, *Reshaping the British Constitution: essays in political interpretation*, *English Historical Review*, 121, no. 490 (February 2006), p. 265.

[9] The Governor-General of Australia's official residence in Canberra.

[10] D.A. Low, 'Introduction: Buckingham Palace and the Westminster model', in D.A. Low (ed.), *Constitutional Heads and Political Crises: Commonwealth episodes, 1945–85* (London, 1988), p. 18.

[11] Paul Kelly, *November 1975: the inside story of Australia's greatest political crisis* (Sydney, 1995), pp. 212–213.

[12] Peter Hennessy, 'Mottram's law and the efficiency of cabinet government', *Political Quarterly*, 57, no. 2 (April 1986), p. 137.

[13] Anthony King, *The British Constitution* (Oxford, 2007), p. 15.

[14] Martin Loughlin, *The British Constitution: a very short introduction* (Oxford, 2013), p. 37, and Martin Loughlin, *Public Law and Political Theory* (Oxford, 1992), pp. 167–176.

Canada is done to employ his arguments on British practices for local objectives.[15] Dennis Kavanagh, in a recent well-regarded collection devoted to British politics, places Jennings as one of the 'founding fathers of British political science'.[16]

Sir Roy Welensky happily interpreted a 1960 opinion from Jennings to mean that, constitutionally speaking, the politically complex 1953 Federation of Rhodesia and Nyasaland he led was essentially 'indestructible' (though it was, in fact, ultimately doomed). The Monckton Commission's ideas on any secession were supposedly 'unsound' according to Jennings, which was music to Welensky's ears.[17] The historian Joseph Fernando persuasively reasons that the Malaysian constitution was effectively drafted by one man – Ivor Jennings;[18] while A.G. Noorani and Allen McGrath strongly claim that Jennings had a not insubstantial role in the demise of democracy in Pakistan before the advent of military rule in 1958.[19] Even today, his name is seldom out of the Sri Lankan newspapers, either in commendation or condemnation.[20] Few would disagree with Asanga Welikala's assessment that Jennings' role must get 'the weight it deserves' in the constitutional set-up of independent Ceylon.[21]

Historical influence

For historians of Britain, empire, decolonization, and Commonwealth, the benefits of examining Jennings and his work are threefold. First, Jennings is particularly useful for his guidance on the existence of conventions. He asked three questions: were there any precedents for these conventions; did the actors in those precedents believe they were bound by them; and what was the reason behind such conventions?[22]

[15] David E. Smith, *The Invisible Crown: the first principle of Canadian government* (Toronto, 2013), p. 18.

[16] Dennis Kavanagh, 'Antecedents', in Matthew Flinders, Andrew Gamble, Colin Hay, and Michael Kenny (eds), *The Oxford Handbook of British Politics* (Oxford, 2009), pp. 29–30.

[17] J.R.T. Wood, *The Welensky Papers: a history of the Federation of Rhodesia and Nyasaland* (Durban, 1983), pp. 838 and 842.

[18] Joseph Fernando, 'Sir Ivor Jennings and the Malayan Constitution', *Journal of Imperial and Commonwealth History*, 34, no. 4 (2006), pp. 577–597.

[19] A.G. Noorani, 'Court martial: the great betrayal', *Dawn*, 27 October and 1 November 2008; Allen McGrath, *The Destruction of Pakistan's Democracy* (Karachi, 1996).

[20] A recent article by Rajan Philips gives a good overview of the issues: 'From Jennings to Geneva: Sri Lanka's tortuous decline', *The Island*, 15 March 2014.

[21] Asanga Welikala, 'The failure of Jennings' constitutional experiment in Ceylon: how "procedural entrenchment" led to constitutional revolution', in Asanga Welikala (ed.), *The Sri Lankan Republic at 40: reflections on constitutional history, theory and practice* (Colombo, 2012), p. 194.

[22] Ivor Jennings, *The Law and the Constitution*, 5th edition (London, 1959), p. 136.

Though there are limitations to this assessment as identified by scholars including Turpin and Tomkins in their recent edition of *British Government and the Constitution*,[23] the 'tripartite specification' of testing the establishment of conventions has nonetheless been utilized by British and Commonwealth courts, including in a case from 2012 investigating the constitutional influence of the Prince of Wales.[24] Jennings' analysis of the observance of conventions, as Bradley and Ewing acknowledge, was in favour of political realities over legal shibboleths.[25] Conventions were, as Jennings famously proclaimed in *Law and the Constitution*, 'the flesh which clothes the dry bones of the law'.[26] The documents selected in this volume clearly show his predilection for 'the flesh'.

Secondly, an area of particular interest for imperial and political historians is Jennings' observance of the Crown and Cabinet and their political prerogatives. His work has clearly aged; in particular, his conception of party government and parliament is, as Bogdanor argues, 'out of date'.[27] Nonetheless, as Brazier notes, despite the separation from events, Jennings' work has historical value. Its utility is its inventory and deployment of constitutional precedents from at least the seventeenth century.[28] In fact, arguably Jennings' most preferred source for his writings were historical – the memoirs of political and constitutional practitioners. Waiting for a train in York he bought for 5 shillings the reminiscences of Sir Almeric Fitzroy, the Clerk of the Privy Council from 1898 to 1923, and thus began his massive thirst for historical precedents and ideas: 'From it I discovered the immense volume of Constitutional Law which was not in the books but which yet regulated the whole practice of government. I went round to the best second-hand bookshop in Leeds next day and ransacked it for political biographies.'[29]

Cabinet Government is clearly a work that relies on these biographies. Echoing Loughlin's comment above about Jennings being descriptive and practical, Herman Finer, the eminent scholar of government, commented in his review of the 1936 first edition: 'As a result of Dr Jennings' work, there is a code available for Prime Ministers

[23] Colin Turpin and Adam Tomkins, *British Government and the Constitution*, 7th edition (Cambridge, 2011).

[24] Geoffrey Marshall, *Constitutional Conventions: the rules and forms of political accountability* (Oxford, 1986), p. 10; *Evans v. Information Commissioner* [2013] UKUT 313 (AAC) (18 September 2012).

[25] A.W. Bradley and K.D. Ewing, *Constitutional and Administrative Law*, 15th edition (Harlow, 2011), p. 24.

[26] Jennings, *Law and the Constitution*, p. 81.

[27] Vernon Bogdanor, *The Coalition and the Constitution* (Oxford, 2011), p. 142.

[28] Rodney Brazier, *Constitutional Practice: the foundations of British government*, 3rd edition (Oxford, 1999), pp. 3–4.

[29] Jennings, *Road to Peradeniya*, p. 69.

and Ministers, the Crown and the people – a veritable treasury for constitutional lawyers and political scientists.'[30] Jennings harnessed examples from courtiers and counsellors around sovereigns including Queen Victoria and George V to assert judgements on less than clear-cut topics such as the personal prerogatives of the Crown to dissolve Parliament, refuse assent, and sack ministers, and the exercise of patronage.[31] For Jennings, the Queen and her realms and responsibilities could never be treated as an academic legalistic case to 'be read like metaphysics', however great the temptation.[32] In his view these powers were important. The renowned Canadian constitutional expert Eugene Forsey was convinced that Jennings believed that even the perceptive Bagehot had 'certainly underestimated the real power of the Crown'.[33] Even in republican India, Jennings' work on the Crown and the historical precedents that he disseminated were cited, for example, by the attorney-general and other Indian constitutional luminaries to diminish the political aspirations of the president vis-à-vis the prime minister and Cabinet in 1951.[34]

The third area where Jennings was arguably at his most influential was in the shaping of constitutions in the Commonwealth and beyond, owing to his being the most physically and intellectually available expert on constitution-making during the high tide of decolonization of the British Empire. As a study of democracy and responsible government in Asia and the Pacific concluded, individuals such as 'Ivor Jennings' were 'important at the inception of Westminster', as the British system is heavily reliant on the first two of Jennings' contributions outlined above – conventions and the powerful personalities who exercise them.[35] Jennings was seen as the man who could get things done. He was even supposedly sought by a movement that wanted Natal to secede from South Africa in the 1960s.[36] Related to this broader point is the fact that Jennings was also the authority who directly drafted (or at least recommended to the states he advised) a Westminster constitutional system – a system readily exported,

[30] Bradley, 'Sir William Ivor Jennings', p. 716.

[31] Ivor Jennings, *Cabinet Government*, 3rd edition (Cambridge, 1959), pp. 394–450.

[32] Ivor Jennings, *The Queen's Government* (London, 1954), p. 37.

[33] Eugene Forsey, *The Royal Power of Dissolution of Parliament in the British Commonwealth* (Toronto, 1943), p. 109.

[34] H. Kumarasingham, *A Political Legacy of the British Empire: power and the parliamentary system in post-colonial India and Sri Lanka* (London, 2013), p. 83.

[35] Haig Patapan and John Wanna, 'The Westminster legacy: conclusion', in Haig Patapan, John Wanna, and Patrick Weller (eds), *Westminster Legacies: democracy and responsible government in Asia and the Pacific* (Sydney, 2005), p. 255.

[36] *The Times*, 10 October 1960.

easily manipulated, and evasive of comprehensive description.[37] As he commented in *The Approach to Self-government*, 'wherever Britain has ruled, her constitutional ideas prevail, and [. . .] our [Britain's] task is eased because we have to adapt those ideas to local conditions'.[38] Jennings, as I have argued elsewhere, was seen, and saw himself, as a spiritual guide and guru advocating 'Eastminster', an experiment of the Westminster-derived model in Asia, for territories emerging from British rule in the region.[39]

Jennings functioned in an era of elites, both British and indigenous, and operated if not at their behest then comfortably from their verandas. This gives a certain understanding to his famous statement that the 'people cannot decide until someone decides who are the people'.[40] Jennings advised and was employed by those who made those decisions and he was their expert. As Andrew Harding argues about Jennings in Malaya, though he was the 'dominant intellectual force in the drafting process', recognized for his 'unique blend of academic brilliance, leadership, practical wisdom, and sheer hard work', the method of constitution-making by experts was 'surprising' compared to the elected Indian Constituent Assembly only a few years earlier.[41] Although Jennings consulted, travelled, and read widely, and was an adviser to assemblies, his preferred method was cloistered hard work following a perceived or real legal brief. As his obituary in *The Times* noted, 'he never spared himself' and operated with 'unusual powers of clear thinking, concentration [and] logical analysis'. Perhaps this was due to his having little time for anything but work: the dedicated don recorded his only recreation as 'books'.[42] Though frequently mentioned in the press either as author or subject, his inclination and skills tended to lend themselves to private rather than public constitutional assignations.

While he was not their creature, the sultans and the Savile Row-suited could expect a sympathetic ear, as Jennings often looked to traditional rulers and the surrounding elites as a substitute for perceived democratic deficits, in the hope that they might eventually conform to British ideals. In Nepal, for example, Mara Malagodi reflects that 'Jennings was convinced that a modified Westminster

[37] H. Kumarasingham, 'Exporting executive accountability: Westminster legacies of executive power', *Parliamentary Affairs*, 66, no. 3 (2013), pp. 579–596.

[38] Jennings, *Approach to Self-government*, p. 20–21.

[39] Kumarasingham, *Political Legacy of the British Empire*; H. Kumarasingham, 'Constitution making and decolonisation in the Eastminsters', in H. Kumarasingham (ed.), *Constitution Making in Asia: decolonisation and state-building in the aftermath of the British empire* (London, 2015).

[40] Jennings, *Approach to Self-government*, p. 56.

[41] Andrew Harding, *The Constitution of Malaysia: a contextual analysis* (Oxford, 2012), p. 31.

[42] *The Times*, 20 December 1965.

model would be easy to transplant in Nepal assuming that the Nepali constitutional edifice would revolve around the principles of constitutional monarchy as expounded in the UK.'[43] This is not to say that he was always appreciated. The Governor of Ceylon, Sir Andrew Caldecott, told London in 1944 that, 'however great an authority on the British constitution', Jennings had limited knowledge of Ceylon and was 'not a legal draftsman'.[44] Meanwhile, the formidable Kenneth Roberts-Wray, legal adviser at the Colonial Office, thought in late 1945 that Jennings' draft for Ceylon 'would be quite useless as a Constitution' and 'must be started *de novo*', which did not happen.[45]

As a scholar of English public law, Jennings is still quoted, critiqued, and drawn upon by public law scholars. His famous critique of Dicey having too narrow and conservative a view of the constitution is still utilized.[46] He encouraged generations of his students and colleagues to look beyond narrow legal definitions. As the principled public law scholar John Griffith explained, recalling lectures by his old teacher at the LSE from decades before, 'He taught me to see the important distinction between definition and description'.[47] This was a clear Jennings axiom, which he employed constantly in practice with his constitution-making and advice. It sometimes put him at odds with legal doctrines and their associated luminaries, but it also helped promote a career beyond the legal–academic parapet. Perhaps most prominently, Jennings' place in public law was illustrated by a special centenary issue of the *Modern Law Review* in September 2004, entitled 'Sir Ivor Jennings and the development of public law'. The articles in this special issue of a journal for which Jennings had been a regular contributor and editor covered many areas, including Cabinet, Parliament, public law as a discipline, his academic career, and his major English law publications.[48]

As Loughlin commented in his introduction, the issue served not to celebrate Jennings' career but instead to assess his significance

[43] Mara Malagodi, 'Constitutional developments in a Himalayan kingdom: the experience of Nepal', in Sunil Khilnani, Vikram Raghavan, and Arun K. Thiruvengadam (eds), *Comparative Constitutionalism in South Asia* (New Delhi, 2013), p. 93.

[44] Sir Andrew Caldecott to G.E.J. Gent, 6 February 1944, CO 54/986/5/1, no. 104, in K.M. de Silva (ed.), *Sri Lanka, Part I: the Second World War and the Soulbury Commission 1939–1945*, British Documents on the End of Empire, Series B, vol. II (London, 1997), p. 282.

[45] Note by J.B. Sidebotham, 14 November 1945, CO 54/986/6/4, in K.M. de Silva (ed.), *Sri Lanka, Part II: towards independence 1945–1948*, British Documents on the End of Empire, Series B, vol. II (London, 1997), p. 164.

[46] For example, see J.W.F. Allison, 'Editor's introduction', in A.V. Dicey, *The Law of the Constitution*, vol. I, The Oxford Edition of Dicey (Oxford, 2013), p. xxviii.

[47] John Griffith, 'A pilgrim's progress', *Journal of Law and Society*, 22, no. 3 (September 1995), p. 411.

[48] See *Modern Law Review*, 67, no. 5 (September 2004).

and 'contribution to the development of public law scholarship' for so long. The authors of the core legal textbook *Constitutional and Administrative Law*, A.W. Bradley and K.D. Ewing, respectively describe Jennings' personal and professional contributions to the law and his lasting reminder that an understanding of social and economic factors is essential to explain constitutions.[49] Adam Tomkins delivered to Jennings the accolade of giving public law scholars two reasons to be grateful for his 'pioneering work':

> The first arises through his efforts in bringing detailed analysis of political institutions into the mainstream of British public law research. All public lawyers who have written about Parliament or about the institutions of government have Jennings to thank for demonstrating that these topics rightly belong at the heart of public law scholarship. The second reason lies in Jennings' successful endeavours in showing that public law scholarship could consist of something other than the mere application of private law technique to the worlds of politics and government.[50]

Beyond Britain and law

The special issue made no claim to cover all of Jennings' work and openly admitted the gap of his toils over constitution-making in the Commonwealth. Even his entry in the *Oxford Dictionary of National Biography* devotes just one sentence to his role as an international constitutional adviser.[51] Perhaps part of the reason is that the extent of Jennings' international roles were often recognized by few in Britain; even abroad his precise contribution was rarely known beyond a small circle of indigenous and British official elites. It is interesting to note that he was never directly honoured by the British state. Instead he was knighted first in 1948, as mentioned above, on the recommendation of the Ceylonese, and a KBE followed in 1955 on the advice of 'Her Majesty's Pakistani Ministers' for his role as 'Constitutional Adviser to the Government [of Pakistan]'.[52] Even his appointment to the Reid Commission on the Malayan Constitution a year later was almost rejected by senior officials within the Commonwealth Relations and Colonial Offices, who thought Jennings '"a bit of an advertiser", apt to

[49] Bradley, 'Sir William Ivor Jennings'; K.D. Ewing, 'The law and the constitution: manifesto of the Progressive Party', *Modern Law Review*, 67, no. 5 (September 2004), p. 751.

[50] Adam Tomkins, 'Talking in fictions: Jennings on Parliament', *Modern Law Review*, 67, no. 5 (September 2004), p. 786.

[51] W.A. Robson, 'Sir (William) Ivor Jennings (1903–65)', revised, *Oxford Dictionary of National Biography* (Oxford, 2004).

[52] *London Gazette* (Supplement), issue 40501, 3 June 1955.

throw his weight about and perhaps somewhat lacking in tact'. Only the personal representations of the Malayan leader Tunku Abdul Rahman, who had been a friend of Jennings' since their time as students at St Catharine's College, Cambridge, ensured his selection. He remained 'unpopular' with British officials.[53] Perhaps this was the reason for Jennings' conspicuous absence in the first wave of Caribbean decolonization, starting in August 1962 with Jamaica and Trinidad and Tobago. This was the case despite his former student and the future Governor-General and President, Sir Ellis Clarke, being one of the key constitutional players in Trinidad and Tobago's politics.[54]

Jennings spent approximately half his career in Britain and the other half overseas. This naturally affected his interests, capabilities, and reputation. The Master's Lodge at Trinity Hall was a regular meeting place for figures from around the world seeking his advice.[55] When overseas, apart from meeting the leading locals, he would more often than not spend time with British diplomatic and colonial officers and they with him. In Nepal, for example, he and the British ambassador shared a 'sense of desolation' in not being able to hear the result of the 1958 University Boat Race between Cambridge and Oxford as their radio 'faded out'.[56] His peripatetic career and multiple relationships with indigenous and British elites bolstered the scope of a man otherwise isolated by habit and inclination. His experience of both worlds did not necessarily make him a natural fit in either, but it did foster his impressive range of experience. Locals and Britons sought information on the other from a man who dealt with both. Held in high esteem as a constitutional authority by many, he was also seen less positively by others as a superior Svengali not given to suffering fools.

In a similar manner, he has been characterized recently as having two sides: an 'occidental Jennings' and an 'oriental Jennings',[57] which neatly differentiates the two separate avenues of scholarly interest in his work and influence. The Orient had certainly affected him. Following his return to a British academic post in 1955 after a gap of almost fifteen years, his forays back into writing British constitutional

[53] Charles O.H. Parkinson, *Bills of Rights and Decolonization: the emergence of domestic human rights instruments in Britain's overseas territories* (Oxford, 2007), p. 80.

[54] Ellis Clarke, 'West Indies', in Butler and Low, *Sovereigns and Surrogates*, p. 172.

[55] For example, Jennings' daughter Shirley Watson remembers several distinguished visitors to the Lodge, including Jomo Kenyatta and Hastings Banda.

[56] Jennings, *Road to Peradeniya*, p. 245.

[57] Mara Malagodi, 'The oriental Jennings: an archival investigation into Sir Ivor Jennings' constitutional legacy in South Asia', *Legal Information Management*, 14, no. 1 (March 2014), pp. 33–37.

scholarship were judged by W.A. Robson to be without the 'freshness and originality which had marked his earlier work', owing to his long absence, and his 1960–1962 *Party Politics* 'was a mistake'.[58] Meanwhile, a recent study on the Westminster system in the settler countries has argued that Jennings was too occidental and that 'none of his principles is concerned with the wider Commonwealth'.[59] This opinion was not shared by the elites in the oriental 'Eastminsters', who employed him precisely because of his knowledge of the wider Commonwealth, his appreciation of their political agenda, and his ability to navigate the corridors of both Whitehall and Government House.

There were limits to oriental Jennings' deviations from the Occident. His qualms about the Westminster model's suitability outside of Britain did not translate to an eagerness to advocate other foreign models and innovations such as bills of rights.[60] There were clearly tensions between these facets of Jennings' academic personality. However, neither occidental or oriental Jennings, thus far, has been properly exposed, since for both avatars he carefully cultivated an academic and professional appearance that allowed his books and lectures to do the explaining. While his 'flood of authorship' was legendary,[61] even his pieces covering countries or issues where he was acutely involved would hardly ever reveal anything about his own often critical role, beyond fleeting personal observations or comedic relief. Though K.M. de Silva believes that Jennings' absence from his writings on Ceylon were 'uncharacteristically modest',[62] this was also the case for other countries in which he was involved. Jennings, perhaps for scholarly or personal reasons, left himself out of the analysis.[63] This volume seeks to put him back in.

Constitution-making matters

Though Jennings held academic law positions such as the Downing Chair in the Laws of England at Cambridge, he robustly believed it absurd to be restricted by one discipline. He wrote that 'boundaries between academic subjects are very artificial', and his remark that

[58] Robson, 'Sir Ivor Jennings'.

[59] R.A.W. Rhodes, John Wanna, and Patrick Weller, *Comparing Westminster* (Oxford, 2009), p. 6.

[60] See Parkinson, *Bills of Rights and Decolonization*.

[61] Bradley, 'Sir William Ivor Jennings', p. 722.

[62] De Silva, 'Introduction', in *Sri Lanka, Part I*, p. lxxi.

[63] For example, in *Constitutional Problems in Pakistan* (Cambridge, 1957), which examines key legal and constitutional issues in Pakistan after independence, there is almost no detail of what Jennings actually witnessed first-hand and was tasked to provide.

he was sometimes accusingly labelled 'not a lawyer' illustrates a frustration at academic narrowness.[64] Indeed, it may surprise legal scholars that in his autobiography he constantly refers to himself as a political scientist.[65] Whatever else, he fervently believed that, regardless of one's academic background, constitutions mattered and affected everyone. In particular, he believed in the intrinsic value of the British constitution – though he was mindful of its defects. In *The British Commonwealth of Nations*, the first sentence of a chapter (appropriately titled 'Where the sun never sets') expresses the following opinion: 'Whatever be their defects, the British people have a remarkable capacity for constitutional innovation. They make no attempt to force governments into a rigid classification; on the contrary, they adapt institutions to suit the environment.'[66]

Jennings could have been describing himself. He was responsible for taking the abstract principles and curious institutions of Britain to places far removed from the comfort of the Master's Lodge. Despite warning 'that every country must have a Constitution to suit itself, a Constitution made to measure, not one bought off the rack',[67] he was suggesting constitutional designs from British material. This is what his clients wanted; observing one exchange with members of the Constituent Assembly of Pakistan and their British predilections, he saw parallels with the barons at Merton in 1236 and their pronouncement '*nolumus leges Angliae mutare*' – 'we do not want to change the laws of England'.[68] To Jennings, the fact that even the local critics of the British constitution, as he observed in Ceylon, depended on books written by British intellectuals such as Harold Laski, G.D.H. Cole, and D.N. Pritt belied their anti-British rhetoric.[69] In his own writings and actions, Jennings admitted his preferences for the intrinsic merit in Britain's constitutional heritage and approach:

> There is method in this peculiarly British – or it may be Commonwealth – fondness for the ambiguity in politics, for it avoids debate over words which disguise unessential differences, allows the dead past ample time to bury its dead, and permits generations yet unborn to build new Jerusalems in their own pleasant style. It is hardly an exaggeration to say that the British constitution and the British Commonwealth have survived the storms of centuries because

[64] Jennings, *Road to Peradeniya*, p. 69.
[65] See, for example *ibid.*, p. 105.
[66] Ivor Jennings, *The British Commonwealth of Nations*, 4th edition (London, 1961), p. 11.
[67] Jennings, *Approach to Self-government*, p. 2.
[68] *Ibid.*, p. 12.
[69] Ivor Jennings, *The Commonwealth in Asia* (Oxford, 1951), p. 61.

> they took no thought for the morrow but bent to every wind that blew strongly enough.[70]

With this ethos Jennings set to work as an adviser and constitution-maker across the world, frequently exemplifying the message above with various consequences. As the anthropologist Maxwell Owusu reminds us, Jennings had major reservations about the successful implementation of democracy, in spite of his role as constitutional adviser to states seeking just that. He confessed as much in one of his last books, *Democracy in Africa*:

> the essential problem of African democracy is [. . .] the essential problem of democracy everywhere – and it is wise to remember that only a few countries in the world have really made a success of it. Democracy has succeeded in Northwestern Europe and in a few countries outside Europe because it has become entwined in the traditions of the people.[71]

Perhaps to counter the above apprehensions, Jennings created new traditions and precedents like a 'slot machine' and, powerfully, he had the power to explain and justify them, which he candidly admitted:

> we have a series of precedents so vast that hardly anyone, and perhaps no one, knows all of them. Nevertheless, they are tucked away in one's memory or at least accessible in the books. When a member of a Drafting Committee or Constituent Assembly asks a question about the means to overcome a local difficulty, it is as if he puts a coin in a slot machine. Out pops a precedent; perhaps not exactly in point, but near enough to suggest a line of development.[72]

With his range and reputation, Ivor Jennings would be one of the most influential constitution-makers the world has ever seen.

Selected documents

The documents in this book are drawn exclusively from the papers held at the Institute of Commonwealth Studies, University of London, which were purchased from Lady Jennings in 1983. The collection is a vast one and this volume does not include them all. Material related to Jennings' multiple educational and administrative duties across the world have been entirely excluded, as have papers narrowly covering specific legal cases and statutes. The papers selected concentrate

[70] Ivor Jennings, *Constitutional Laws of the Commonwealth, Volume 1: the monarchies* (Oxford, 1957), pp. 1–2.

[71] Ivor Jennings, *Democracy in Africa* (Cambridge, 1963), pp. 68–69, cited in Maxwell Owusu, 'Democracy and Africa: a view from the village', *Journal of Modern African Studies*, 30, no. 3 (1992), pp. 381–382.

[72] Jennings, *Approach to Self-government*, p. 23.

instead on three main sources: diaries, memoranda, and private impressions of subjects that he knew well through his international constitutional roles and academic expertise. As editor I have followed two rules in making my selection: first, the material has not been published elsewhere (to the best of my knowledge); second, Jennings had to have had a personal involvement or expertise in the subject he was writing about. The first rule was made primarily because some of his books are still in print and his important published works are still available in most libraries. The material in this introduction consciously cites Jennings' important published works so that the reader can be aware of them when reading the documents selected and consult them for further reading. The second rule was established to weed out the massive range of topics on which Jennings wrote and instead to concentrate on the subjects he knew best and on which he had a privileged perspective to comment.

Owing to my objective to keep as wide a selection of documents from varied cases as possible, I have not included everything from the two countries with which Jennings was most heavily involved – Ceylon and Pakistan, both of which he wrote on extensively. However, I am planning two separate collections covering these countries.[73] The London School of Economics and the Institute of Commonwealth Studies are also currently establishing a website on Ivor Jennings, which will initially be administered by Dr Mara Malagodi and me.

As the contents page indicates, I have divided the book into country sections for ease of reference and have a large section at the end covering Jennings' impressions on constitution-making, South Asian prime ministers, and the Magna Carta in the Commonwealth. Despite the structure of the volume, I would encourage the reader to consult the index for countries and names, since Jennings more often than not draws on examples from further case studies to illuminate others. For legal case references, unless otherwise noted, I have not reproduced the original citations of various printed case reports as used by Jennings, but the system of neutral citation that has been adopted across the Commonwealth since 2001. This is to facilitate universal access, especially via online resources such as the case and statute databases of the Commonwealth Legal Information Institute (www.commonlii.org) or the British and Irish Legal Information Institute (www.bailii.org).

[73] For Ceylon, this will include a previously unpublished and candid manuscript, which Jennings entitled 'Donoughmore to Independence: a contribution to the constitutional history of Ceylon, 1931–1948'. The proposed Pakistan volume will include material related to his controversial role in the mid-1950s advising the Constituent Assembly on drawing up a new constitution and later advising the Governor-General of Pakistan in the *Tamizuddin Khan* case.

Readers will notice that some words are missing and occasional individuals named in the text left unidentified. Jennings' near indecipherable handwriting and the difficulty despite strenuous research of finding all the minor figures he came across made this a regrettable reality. I have generally left the documents in the style and format Jennings wrote them and have not corrected anything except clear accidental mistakes. Jennings occasionally used different spellings for names of places and people. In order to achieve consistency I have standardized all names to reflect the version he either used the most or the one that he employed in his published works.

Yash Ghai, a prominent public law professor and 'constitution-maker' in his own right, looked back at the 'glamorous' era when Ivor Jennings could write constitutions from the 'splendour of a vice-chancellor's lodge' compared with the modern-day life of a constitution-maker who 'rubs shoulders with soldiers and rebels with AK-47s, self-confessed killers while roughing it in small towns, putting himself or herself at considerable security risk'.[74] Though it is true that Jennings rarely roughed it with the partisans and protestors, he had to perform as adviser-extempore in fluid and complex constitutional situations where the domestic situation was often fraught with political tension and desolate of precedent. As one learned and general overview of the task comments, the field of constitution-making still 'retains a frontier quality' and often lacks 'systematic empirical evidence' to expose the perspective and context of the constitution-makers and their process.[75]

Jennings operated at the 'frontier', and the documents in this volume will go some way towards rectifying the current lack of detailed first-hand observations of constitution-making, since they hold a treasure chest of information on the subject from a wide field of cases. Thus, in A3 we see Jennings advising the unsure prime minister of Ceylon, Dudley Senanayake, how to sack his capricious cousin and eventual successor, Sir John Kotelawala. In A4 we read his predictions for constitutional monarchy in Ceylon and in B1 the need for Ethiopia to become one under Haile Selassie. Meanwhile, in C1 and E1 respectively Jennings inserts his political judgments in the Mediterranean to justify the retention of Gibraltar as a British fortress and the overlooked idea of integrating Malta with the United Kingdom.

[74] Yash Ghai, 'A journey around constitutions: reflections on contemporary constitutions', *South African Law Journal*, 122, no. 4 (2005), p. 805.

[75] Tom Ginsburg, Zachary Elkins, and Justin Blount, 'Does the process of constitution-making matter?', *Annual Review of Law and Social Sciences*, 5 (2009), p. 202.

In F1 and H1 Jennings offers the Nepali king and the Pakistani governor-general the institutional machinery to display a façade of democracy while maintaining the tools associated with absolute monarchy, such as the power to suspend the constitution. We learn in D1 of his frustrations working with his fellow commissioners in Malaya and the intriguing idea in D2 to keep the Queen on in Penang and Malacca after independence in the Federation of Malaya. In another federation, that of Rhodesia and Nyasaland, he gives ultimately vain legal reasons for its future existence in I1, despite the political realities of the 'Wind of Change' era. In H3 we see Jennings advising a solution to the Kashmir quagmire. South Africa in K1 is supplied with the positives and negatives of leaving the Commonwealth and the political perils of its 'euphemistically' separate development policy for Black South Africans.

Jennings warns Lord Cobham not to do a 'Byng' as Governor-General of New Zealand in the event of an electoral dead heat. He mercilessly parodies all and sundry at constitutional conferences in London on Rhodesia and Singapore in I2 and J1. In L2 he seeks to pre-empt the disintegration of Sudan by advocating a scheme that would give a degree of autonomy to Juba. In M3, meanwhile, he unleashes his inner voice by confiding what he really thinks of the South Asian prime ministers he has encountered. In M4 we follow the mythical 'Wilkins' and his journeys as a constitutional draftsman. The final document, M6, investigates problems and promises of the Magna Carta in the Commonwealth, including an admission that bills of rights could be useful for certain states. While not a Damascene conversion, it is a noticeable change for a man who otherwise throughout his career advised against such protective instruments as an unnecessary encumbrance.

Though many of the issues, events, and constitutions that Jennings addresses in this volume have themselves disappeared (though many have not, especially the issues), this does not equate to their irrelevance. In fact a closer examination may expose the roots of contemporary concerns and directions.

Jennings stated in the preface to the first edition of *Parliament* in 1939 that his method in writing it was to try to give 'description and analysis and not criticism', and that he tried to 'suppress [his] own views' in the book.[76] Though it is not clear that he succeeded in these objectives, they are, nonetheless, also mine for this volume. I have endeavoured to allow only Jennings' voice to be heard throughout these pages, as this book is neither a biography nor an argumentative judgement of

[76] Jennings, *Parliament*, 1st edition (Cambridge, 1939), pp. xi–xii, n. 2, cited in Tomkins, 'Talking in fictions', p. 774.

his actions. As editor I have tried to evade the enticing lure to critique Jennings so that this volume can be a tool for scholars seeking Jennings directly and not my version or assessment of his life and work.[77] However, I do fiercely advocate his importance and significance, which this volume illustrates. It is my hope that *Constitution-maker* will become a resource for scholars in Britain and across the world to understand analytically the impact of Jennings and the political context in which he was working, in order to undertake much-needed full appraisals of the multiple areas and issues that he influenced. As editor, nothing would please me more than if this volume were used for constitutional scholars critically to examine not only Jennings and his legacy but also the trials of democracy and state-building, which never cease.

[77] Such a critique will be attempted in H. Kumarasingham (ed.), *Constitution-making in Asia: decolonization and state-building in the aftermath of the British Empire* (London, 2015).

SECTION A: CEYLON

Jennings was in Ceylon from 1941 to 1955, serving from 1942 as the first vice-chancellor of the University of Ceylon. During his time on the island he acted as the informal but highly influential and well-known adviser to D.S. Senanayake and other leading Ceylonese figures. Ceylon was the official name of the country until 1972, when it became a republic and was renamed as Sri Lanka. Apart from the published books and articles that he wrote about Ceylon, Jennings also produced a manuscript, never published during his lifetime, of his personal involvement in Ceylon's path to independence. This will be part of a collection entitled *Sir Ivor Jennings and the Constitutional Development of Ceylon: selected writings*, ed. H. Kumarasingham (Colombo, 2015).

1. 'Anecdotes of D.S.', *c.*1952

Those of us who worked with D.S.[1] ought to put our recollections in writing, for they will soon be forgotten. Only a few weeks ago Sir Oliver Goonetilleke[2] reminded me of an incident in Bandarawela, narrated below, which has passed out of my memory until he recalled it.

It soon ceased to be a secret that the "Minister's Draft", which ultimately formed the basis of the new Constitution, was being worked out in Civil Defence Headquarters in Union Place. A newspaper columnist painted an imaginary picture of the scene. D.S. was walking up and down dictating to stenographers. Sir Oliver was lying in a chaise longue with hands folded on his stomach. The constitutional expert was sitting by, interminably smoking, and putting in a word here and there. Only one detail of that picture was accurate. These meetings usually took place after sundown, when D.S. had finished

[1]Don Stephen Senanayake, commonly referred to as 'D.S.'. First Prime Minister of Ceylon, 1948–1952; founder-leader of the United National Party (UNP).

[2]Sir Oliver Ernest Goonetilleke, leading Ceylon administrator and minister, who was a friend and colleague of Jennings; Governor-General, 1954–1962. Often referred to as 'O.E.G.'.

at the Ministry of Agriculture and Lands and I had finished at the [*illegible*]. Sir Oliver was seated bolt upright at his desk, sipping a glass of water, and with the fan racing full speed immediately over his head. D.S. sat opposite him, drinking a cup of unsweetened black coffee. I sat in a G.O.H.[3] Chair, out of the range of the fan, "interminably smoking" and supplying a "smokescreen". There were no stenographers. The story of the stenographers showed that the picture was imaginary, for D.S. could not dictate.

On the rare occasions on which a stenographer was called in, D.S. began "I mean to say, what I want to say is, as a matter of fact . . . " and then left Sir Oliver and me to do the job. In fact, though, a stenographer was rarely used. It was much better I let D.S. tell his story in his own way and then go away to think out how to put it into writing. It could then be read to him the next day and amended to suit his views.

The "sundowner" much impressed D.S. though himself a teetotaller, he was always tolerant of other people's opinions and habits, and he considered that, if I liked a "sundowner" I ought to have one. As soon as D.S. received the proof copy of the Soulbury Report[4] in August, 1945, Dr David de Silva[5] phoned. I was at [*illegible*]. "The Boss" wanted me at once, and would I bring a bag to stay at least a week? I took the next train, collected the report from the Boss, and took it to Dr de Silva's bedroom. On the table was a full bottle of whisky. Now, a bottle of whisky was unprocurable in London in 1945, and I had not had a "sundowner" for four months. Naturally I enquired where the bottle came from. I discovered that D.S. had made friends with the barman of his hotel and asked his advice. The barman had pointed out that the only way to get a bottle of whisky was to buy all the drinks in his bottle across the counter. D.S. did so, and so that bottle cost something like £5. It was a gross extravagance – which came out of his own pocket – and I would have stopped it had I known. Nevertheless, the story is worth the telling as an example of his tolerance and generosity.

There was an occasion on which D.S. undertook to drink alcohol and another occasion on which he did. Nearly every evening when we were in London he had official guests, with whom a little propaganda was injected by his staff. On one such occasion he was due to learn from the Secretary of State what was the decision of the British cabinet

[3] Government-owned housing.

[4] Britain appointed the Soulbury Commission in 1944 to recommend constitutional reforms for Ceylon. The Commission's report laid the foundations for the first constitution of Ceylon. The head of the Commission was Herwald Ramsbotham, Baron (later Viscount) Soulbury. He later served as Governor-General of Ceylon, 1949–1954.

[5] A friend of both Jennings and D.S. Senanayake.

on his application for independence. The staff was eager to know the result but knew that nothing could be said while guests were present. It was therefore arranged that if its answer was favourable he should, on returning, order a glass of sherry – an act which he would not do without motive aforethought. When he came in we watched him breathlessly. He looked at us with a grin and called a waiter to him. "Bring me," he said, "a glass of water".

The second occasion was on the 11th November 1947. The decision to confer independence had been reached and all the documents had to be agreed by the Ceylon Cabinet. It was learned, however, that some slight amendments to the Ceylon Independence Bill were required. They were said to be unimportant and it was necessary that approval should be expressed forthwith because, if the Bill was not passed within the next month it would have to be postponed until the New Year. The Cabinet therefore agreed that if the Prime Minister were satisfied he should have authority to sign. We assembled at Queen's House[6] at 9 p.m. that evening, but they were long in coming through. Just before 11 p.m. Mr Mulhall[7] brought in the decoded telegram. Sir Alan Rose[8] and I at once explained that the amendments had nothing to do with Ceylon. They were amendments to the United Kingdom legislation necessitated by the fact that Ceylon was ceasing to be a colony. D.S. agreed to sign. The formulation being completed, Sir Henry Moore[9] invited us into the dining-room, where the champagne was on ice, to drink to "Independent Lanka". It was explained to D.S. that by the constitutional convention this toast had to be drunk, at least on the first occasion, in champagne, and so he tried a little. He pronounced it to be poor stuff, not up to the standard of sweet toddy.

It was a few months earlier that he committed his one indiscretion in a public speech. He knew from Sir Oliver Goonetilleke, who was in London, that a telegram offering independence was being drafted. Since this was the termination of 35 years of political work, the news was much on his mind, and in a speech in Sinhalese, in a small village near Negombo, when he thought that no reporters were present, he said that in a few days he hoped to make a most important announcement. There was a reporter present and the statement got in the headlines. D.S. was most embarrassed, especially by the question of his political friends, some of whom did not even know that negotiations

[6]The official Colombo residence of the Governor (and, after independence, Governor-General) of Ceylon.

[7]Official Secretary to the Governor (and later Governor-General) of Ceylon.

[8]Legal officer in Ceylon; Attorney-General, 1947–1951; Chief Justice, 1951–1955.

[9]Sir Henry Monck-Mason Moore, Governor of Ceylon, 1944–1948; Governor-General of Ceylon, 1948–1949.

were going on. He got out of it very nicely. "I am going to announce" he said, "Dudley's[10] engagement to be married".

There were some amusing incidents during the drafting of the Constitution of 1946, and they illustrate Mr Senanayake's particularity. He wanted the Constitution drafted in his way and not in Sir Robert Drayton's,[11] because this Constitution was to be the platform from which he could demand Independence. The person responsible was the Secretary of State for the Colonies, and he asked Sir Barclay Nihill[12] to make the preliminary draft. Sir Barclay would of course consult Sir Robert. My job was to see that Sir Robert took his pound of flesh but not a drop of blood. The last edition of the Senanayake draft had been sent to Sir Henry Moore, and so much of it had received the approval of the Soulbury Commission that huge chunks had to be inserted. Nevertheless, Sir Robert Drayton and Sir Barclay Nihill, with Mr B.P. Peiris,[13] spent Christmas at Nuwara Eliya working on a new draft. D.S. insisted that he and I should see it. We started out with no less than 88 suggestions. Sir Barclay and I went to Temple Trees[14] and dealt with all but the more important amendments, and then D.S. came in to discuss the substantial points of difference. Sir Henry Moore who was in Nuwara Eliya, was anxious to take part in the discussions, and D.S. agreed: indeed he may have suggested it.

Sir Henry, again supported by D.S., was anxious to have me present, so as to have legal opinion on both sides. Sir Robert Drayton objected that I had no official status, and Sir Henry had to agree. What is more, by accident or design, (probably the former), the conference was fixed for a week-end when I should be in India, bringing my wife from Bombay. D.S. was not to be defeated by such an arrangement. My wife and I flew back by air. We were met in Colombo by D.S., who took us straight to the Senanayake bungalow in Nuwara Eliya, where a small staff had been assembled. A list of objections had been made and D.S. was briefed on each of them. So long as one did not wrap up the law in verbiage, he got a point very quickly. In fact, he had once acted in a case. He had accompanied a friend to a Magistrate's Court where the friend was charged with some offence. The Magistrate apparently mistook D.S. for another and asked D.S. for his opinion. D.S. took the bait and spoke at length. As he said when he told the story: "It's useful not to be a lawyer, I got the man off."

[10] Dudley Shelton Senanayake, eldest son of D.S. Senanayake; UNP Prime Minister of Ceylon, 1952–1953, 1960, 1965–1970.

[11] Chief Secretary of Ceylon, 1942–1947.

[12] Legal Secretary of Ceylon, 1945–1947.

[13] Legal draftsman in the Ceylon civil service; later Cabinet secretary.

[14] The official residence of the Prime Minister of Ceylon.

The idea was that, as soon as the conference was over, Sir Barclay should fly to London with the draft. By one of those remarkable coincidences which he attributes to his horoscope, Sir Oliver Goonetilleke was on leave in London. What is more, Mr L.M.D. de Silva[15] was also in London and was available for consultation. D.S. insisted that Sir Oliver be consulted about all changes to the draft. The procedure was as follows. D.S. had a complete brief on each question. He noted on it whether Sir Robert and Sir Barclay had agreed, disagreed or reserved a question. He then came back to the bungalow and gave me the full story, which I promptly wrote out and sent to Sir Oliver by air. Sir Oliver's job was to see that an agreed change was not altered and to argue any point which the Officers of State had refused to concede. Actually, the Secretary of State and his advisers were much readier to concede changes than the Officers of State, and indeed he had a wide discretion. Sir Oliver was thus able considerably to improve the draft.

In spite of these precautions, D.S. had insisted that his approval should be sought to the final draft. Before it arrived, Sir Oliver was back in Ceylon. The Governor was in Nuwara Eliya and I was in Bandarawela, and so D.S. and Sir Oliver drove up to Bandarawela with the text so that we could discuss it before they went on to Nuwara Eliya. They did not arrive until 9 p.m. and so we adjourned to my room, where the discussions went on until nearly midnight. Next door was a European, probably a planter. He soon came in to complain, very politely, that we were keeping him awake. We tried to moderate our voices, but he was in again after 15 minutes, and this time he was more vehement. When he came in a third time he was quite angry. We apologised, but we could not tell him that the first Prime Minister was settling the lines of the Constitution.

The turning point in the negotiations was the debate in which the State Council approved the White Paper by 51 votes to 3. Oddly enough the most difficult job was to draft a suitable motion. It had to be an outright acceptance so as to pledge H.M.G. On the other hand it had to be an acceptance which expressed disappointment and asked for more. That sounds easy, but the difficulty about drafting is that when an idea is in one's head, it is difficult to remove. When we went in Sir Oliver's house I had two drafts and A.G. Ranasinghe[16] had one. We tried various combinations, but after two hours we still had no satisfactory resolution. At that stage somebody remembered that Sir Barclay had a draft, and so we adjourned to the Galle Face

[15] A prominent Ceylonese jurist and former solicitor-general.

[16] Senior Ceylon civil servant; later Cabinet secretary.

Hotel, where at last a combination of Sir Barclay's and Ranasinhe's was accepted.

2. 'Notes on the formation of a new Government, March 1952'

D.S. Senanayake had a stroke while horse riding on the morning of Friday, 21st March 1952. He fell heavily and cracked his skull. He died on Saturday, 22nd March, at 3.30 p.m.

The Governor-General, Lord Soulbury had gone on leave and in fact arrived in England on the 22 March. The Chief Justice, Sir Alan Rose, was O.A.G.[17] Sir Alan phoned me on Saturday morning and asked me to return to Colombo from Peradeniya. We learned of the death from Claire,[18] whose car we stopped on the way down. I dined with Sir Alan that night, Sir Oliver Goonetilleke being the only other guest.

Before he left, Lord Soulbury had asked Mr D.S. Senanayake who he considered ought to be his successor if he died while Lord Soulbury was away. D.S. replied that he hoped his son would succeed him. Lord Soulbury had told this to Sir Alan and had added that if the need did arise he (Lord Soulbury) would like to be recalled.

Sir Alan had sent a warning message as soon as the accident occurred. He had then sent a second message announcing the death and stating the political position. He had arranged for Lord Soulbury to telephone between 8 p.m. and 9 p.m.

Even before D.S. died the political manoeuvres started. Sir John Kotelawala,[19] who was Leader of the House and the only Minister who had been in office since 1936, thought that the succession fell to him. Sir Oliver agreed with him at first, and pressed Sir Alan to appoint Sir John. It was at this stage that Sir Alan phoned for me. I expressed the opinion that, apart from Lord Soulbury's request, it was the duty of the O.A.G. to inform the G.G. and give him an opportunity of returning to take charge of the situation. I was prepared, if need be, to give this opinion in writing. Sir Alan did not in any case want to take a decision because it would embarrass him in his position as C.J. if he were responsible for a split in the U.N.P.[20]

In the interval between the call to me at 1 p.m. and my arrival at 7.30 p.m. the position had changed. The opposition to Sir John had

[17] Officer administering the Government.
[18] Claire Dewing, Jennings' elder daughter.
[19] Sir John Kotelawala, nephew of D.S. Senanayake and UNP Prime Minister, 1953–1956.
[20] The United National Party (UNP) was founded by D.S. Senanayake in 1946.

made its strength felt, and there was a growing volume of support for Dudley Senanayake. O.E.G. had therefore changed his opinion that an immediate appointment was desirable. Lord Soulbury telephoned soon after 8 p.m. He stated that he was leaving England on the evening of the 24th March and would arrive in Ceylon at 1.30 p.m. on the 26th March.

Sir Alan called a meeting of Ministers to Queen's House on the morning of the 23rd. He explained that Lord Soulbury had requested him to recall Lord Soulbury in the event of a vacancy in the office of Prime Minister, and that Lord Soulbury would be returning on Wednesday afternoon. Until then he did not propose to make any appointment to the office of Prime Minister.

Before the meeting on the 23rd, J.R. Jayewardene,[21] Minister of Finance, phoned to ask my opinion of the propriety of the summons. I explained that the death of the Prime Minister did not in itself affect the Ministers. They remained in office, but their offices were at the disposal of the new Prime Minister, so that he could supersede them if he wished. There was therefore no constitutional objection to a meeting of the Ministers, whether summoned by the Governor-General or by one of the Ministers. It should not, however, be treated as a Cabinet meeting.

During the next two days opinion crystallized against Sir John Kotelawala. I am told that 37 members, supporters of the U.N.P., sent a memorial to the Governor-General advising the appointment of Dudley Senanayake. The European members sent a separate memorial in the same sense. It was known too, that the Opposition preferred Dudley.

Lord Soulbury arrived at 1.30 p.m. on the 26th March and was met by Sir Alan. They drove straight to Queen's House, and Sir Alan stayed to lunch. Dudley was summoned at 1.55 p.m. Sir Alan phoned me at 2.15 p.m. to ask whether the Governor-General could appoint a Prime Minister then and there, or whether he had to commission a Prime Minister and send him away to see if he could form a Government. I said that the latter was the usual practice, but that there was no particular reason for it, and that in view of local conditions it was better to appoint the Prime Minister there and then. Lord Soulbury took over at this point and I explained the position to him. It appears that Dudley was with him. He went at once to the meeting of Ministers and came back in ten minutes to accept the appointment.

[21] Junius Richard Jayewardene, senior UNP minister; Prime Minister, 1977–1978; Executive President of Sri Lanka, 1978–1989. Often referred to as 'J.R.'.

3. Note of proposal to dismiss Sir John Kotelawala, 15 September 1952

On Tuesday, 9th October 1952, I was summoned from Peradeniya and saw the Prime Minister at Temple Trees before 10 a.m. He explained to me that Sir John Kotelawala, Minister of Transport and Works, had written (or on his behalf had had written) a diary of the formation of the government under the title "The Premiership Stakes in 1952". It had been shown to several people, and a copy got into the hands of [*illegible*], an opposition weekly, which had published it. It contained false and defamatory material relating to the Governor-General, the Chief Justice, Members of the Cabinet, Parliamentary Secretaries, and Members of Parliament. The Prime Minister had therefore written to Sir John, who was in New York, asking for his resignation. Sir John had cabled that he was returning for consultations and in fact he was expected on the 10th October. The Prime Minister asked what I thought of the situation and whether a Minister could be dismissed on such grounds.

I asked if there was any doubt that Sir John was responsible for this document. The P.M. replied that Sir John himself had shown it to several people. I asked what would happen if Sir John denied the association. The P.M. replied that Sir John would have to deny not only his association with the document but also the allegations in the document.

I said that I had no doubt that a Minister could be dismissed. (I had already advised Lord Soulbury in this sense. He put it as a hypothetical case, though of course he knew that I knew why the question was asked.) The usual practice was for a Minister to resign when his resignation was sought, but a Minister held his office at the pleasure of the Queen, and if he refused to resign there was no need for the P.M. to resign and reform his government. It would be enough for him to write to the Minister something in the form:

> "I have advised the Governor-General that Her Majesty should be pleased to dispense with your services as Minister of Transport and Works. The Governor-General has considered my advice and accordingly I have to inform you that it is no longer Her Majesty's pleasure that you be employed as Minister of Transport and Works."

The P.M. said that the U.N. Parliamentary Party would perhaps wish to be consulted in the matter – he gave the impression that the Party would want Sir John dismissed even if Sir John gave satisfactory assurances. I stated emphatically that in my opinion the P.M. should not allow such a discussion. His attitude should be that if the Parliamentary Party did not want him as P.M. he would resign, but that so long as he was Prime Minister he would exercise the prerogatives of his office. If he once gave way on a point of that kind we should have not Cabinet Government but Consensus Government. The P.M. said that he had already taken that line on two previous occasions. He had refused to allow the Party to discuss the composition of the Cabinet or to discuss whether a particular person should or should not be a Minister. He entirely agreed with my point of view. He had never wanted to be Prime Minister and he had fully determined to retire from politics when his father died, but he had agreed to serve under pressure from the U.N.P. members.

The real question for him was whether Sir John would be a bigger nuisance outside the Cabinet than he was inside. It was Sir John who had forced Banda[22] out of the Cabinet. His faction had tried to keep the party together. Also, Sir John was incapable of keeping his mouth shut. He went along to the Orient Club and gossiped about all that went on in the Cabinet. He lacked a sense of judgement (perhaps my phrase and not his, but it is what he meant). I offered my services if they were needed, pointing out that there were usually two ways of saying the same thing. I then left.

On the 11th the newspapers published a statement by Sir John, issued by the Information Office from Temple Trees, to the effect that he had no connection with the document, that he disassociated himself from it, and that the Prime Minister had accepted these assurances.

I do not think the matter will end here. The Ministers concerned, especially J.R. Jayewardene ("Dirty Dick"), + the U.N.P. members will not be satisfied. The Opposition is apparently considering raising the attacks on the members of the House as a breach of privilege.

4. 'The Queen of Ceylon', *c.* 1953

When the consequences of India's becoming a republic were under discussion by the Prime Ministers in 1949,[23] Mr D.S. Senanayake remarked that he spoke for the oldest monarchy in the

[22] Solomon West Ridgeway Dias Bandaranaike, Sri Lanka Freedom Party (SLFP) Prime Minister, 1956–1959.

[23] Not long after independence in August 1947, India had formally announced its intention to become a republic, but its desire to remain in the Commonwealth. At the 1949 Commonwealth Prime Ministers' Meeting, the 'London Declaration' allowed republics to be members of the Commonwealth, which had hitherto been made up only of Dominions, which held the British monarch as head of state. The meeting also created a new role for George VI as 'the symbol of the free association of its member nations, and as such Head of the Commonwealth', which is now held by his daughter by consent of all Commonwealth

Commonwealth. His claim rested on the theory that the Sovereign held the Kingdom of Kandy under the Kandyan Convention[24] and that the Kandyan Kingdom was the successor of the ancient Sinhalese kingdoms. Possibly if claims had been critically examined there would have been other claimants, for many monarchies have been fused into the present royal line: but no doubt what Mr Senanayake meant was that a country which had been a monarchy for nearly 2,500 years would require notice of any question relating to its abolition.

The Indian decision was an odd mixture of sentiment and reason like the monarchy itself. It would have been wholly logical if the Constituent Assembly had wished to give substantive powers to the Head of the State: for one would not give such powers to a hereditary monarch. In fact, though, it did not. It reproduced the British Constitution with almost perfect fidelity replacing the monarch by an elected President. It would have been equally logical if India like Burma[25] had wished to dissociate itself from the Commonwealth. Again it did not. The Government of India stated that it wished to remain within the Commonwealth and suggested that, in relation to India, the monarch be "Head of the Commonwealth". Except in matters of pure form, India differs in no respect from the other members of the Commonwealth.

The main consequence of the change of form was that India had to invent some device for securing a Head of the State.[26] Its success will of course depend not on the nature of the device but on the manner in which it is operated. At the first election the electoral college was dominated by the Congress[27] and accepted the candidate nominated by the Prime Minister. In other words, the person who would have been appointed Governor-General was elected President. This may not always happen, however. In future there may be a contest on political lines, with the result that the President may be a partisan elected by partisans, like the President of the United States – but the President of the United States is elected to carry out a policy and not to act as an impartial and ceremonial Head of the State. Moreover, the President of India and the Prime Minster of India may

members. The office of Head of the Commonwealth has no constitutional powers over any member state.

[24] An agreement between the Kandyan nobles and the British in March 1815 that replaced the Kandyan monarchy with the British one and completed British rule over the whole island.

[25] Burma became an independent republic in January 1948 and did not seek membership of the Commonwealth.

[26] The Indian President is elected by the Electoral College, consisting of members of both houses of Parliament and of the state legislatures.

[27] Indian National Congress, a leading Indian political party, founded in 1885.

be drawn from parties in opposition to each other, for the electoral college is so weighted that it need not contain the same majority as the House of the People.[28] Even more dangerous I think, is the fact that the President has been given powers comparable to those of the Queen. In Britain (and in Canada, Australia and New Zealand) those powers are exercised according to well-settled constitutional conventions. In India Dr Rajendra Prasad[29] is applying the same conventions. It need not be so. Indeed some Indian lawyers draw from the fact that the monarchy has been abolished the conclusion that the President's powers are substantive powers and that the monarchical conventions of Britain do not apply.

If a future President of India is antagonistic to his Government and refuses to act on its advice, what happens? There seems to be no remedy except a constitutional amendment. The President cannot be impeached except for a breach of law; and he will have broken no law. It is remarkable that in Ceylon care was taken to see that both the Sovereign and the Governor-General were required to observe the conventions. India has no such requirement: and yet in Ceylon the Governor-General can be recalled by the Queen on the advice of the Ceylon Government, while in India nobody can get rid of a President who sticks to the letter of the law and refuses to observe the conventions.

These considerations suggest that the Constituent Assembly, swayed by the emotional release which independence brought after nearly fifty years of conflict, abolished the monarchy without adequate discussion of the consequences. The case against monarchy as a constitutional device is now untenable. The case against the monarchy on social grounds, which was put by the Radical Movement in the nineteenth century and by a minority group in the Labour Movement in the present century, has disappeared in Britain through the caution of George V and George VI and their advisers. Whether it has disappeared in Ceylon is not a question on which I am entitled to an opinion. Social conditions are in fact changing rapidly in this country – a fact which is probably more obvious to a detached observer like me than to a Ceylonese who lives in them and has his ideas moulded by them. Monarchy is certainly a very adaptable instrument, and I see no reason why it should fail to adapt itself to the changing conditions.

Constitutional lawyers are not always safe guides because they have to emphasise formal rules. Off the record they sometimes realise the truth of Mr Bumble's proposition: "If the law supposes that … the

[28] Also known as the Lok Sabha.

[29] First President of India, 1950–1962.

law is a ass – a idiot".[30] Nevertheless the aspect of monarchy has changed in Ceylon since 1948.

When territory is annexed to the Crown, whether by settlement, cession or conquest, the main principles of English constitutional law apply. When the maritime Provinces were ceded by the Treaty of Amiens in 1802 and the Kandyan Provinces ceded by the Kandyan Convention in 1815 the people of Ceylon became subjects of George III, his heirs and successors according to law, with exactly the same rights and duties (unless the written law made a distinction, which it rarely did) as Englishmen and Scotsmen. This did not imply that Ceylon had forthwith the same system of government as the United Kingdom, though it did imply that in the United Kingdom a British subject from Ceylon had (and still has) the same rights and duties as a British subject from England. In Ceylon, as elsewhere, the Crown set up a local legislature which provided only gradually for Ceylonese participation, and which was for all practicable purposes under the control of the Government of the United Kingdom.

This control was weakened in 1931[31] and abolished in 1948.[32] As in Canada, Australia, New Zealand and South Africa, the formal relationship with the Crown remained unaltered. Indeed, it became closer, both as a matter of fact and as a matter of law, because, the Government of the United Kingdom having been removed as an intermediary, the Crown appeared directly in the Constitution. A Governor represents the Crown, but he also represents the Government of the United Kingdom. Since 1948 the Governor-General represents the Crown, while the Government of the United Kingdom, like other Governments, is represented diplomatically by the High Commissioner. In matters affecting Ceylon the Queen is advised direct, either through the Governor-General or by personal advice given in London. The Government of the United Kingdom like the Government of the United States or the Government of the U.S.S.R., has nothing whatever to do with the matter.

As I have said, English constitutional law is part of the law of Ceylon, subject however to the Constitution and to any local legislation.

The Queen succeeded in February 1952 by virtue of the Act of Settlement, 1701, as amended by His Majesty's Declaration of Abdication Act, 1936. These are Acts of the Parliament of the United Kingdom (or, in the case of the Act of Settlement, of England) which

[30] Quoted from Charles Dickens' *Oliver Twist*.

[31] The Statute of Westminster (1931) confirmed that Dominion parliaments, upon ratification, were independent legislatures and discontinued the imperial parliament's ability to legislate for them without consent.

[32] Ceylon became an independent Commonwealth realm in February 1948.

are part of the law of Ceylon, and therefore they may be repealed or amended by the Parliament of Ceylon in accordance with the Ceylon Independence Act, 1947. No doubt the succession would be changed, if at all, by agreement among the Commonwealth countries but an Act of the Parliament of Ceylon would be needed and, legally speaking, there is nothing to stop it establishing a different line of succession on its own account. Hence, when the Queen was proclaimed in February 1952 it was correctly claimed that she had succeeded by "our law", i.e. the law of Ceylon.

On the other hand, though Canada proclaimed Elizabeth II as "Queen of Canada", Ceylon did not proclaim her as "Queen of Ceylon". In relation to Ceylon the Queen acts on Ceylon advice just as, in relation to Canada, she acts on Canadian advice. In fact, therefore, she was both "Queen of Canada" and "Queen of Ceylon"; but Ceylon did not say so because, as a legal proposition, the statement was incorrect. Since the Act of Union with Scotland the royal style and titles have been governed by Act of the Parliament of the United Kingdom. The latest of them was the Royal and Parliamentary Titles Act, 1927, which applied to Canada as to Ceylon. Hence the Queen's title was "Queen of Great Britain, Ireland and the British Dominions beyond the Seas" etc. That title could be changed in relation to Canada by Act of the Dominion Parliament, and in relation to Ceylon by Act of the Parliament of Ceylon: but until that was done it was wrong to describe the Queen officially as "Queen of Canada" or as "Queen of Ceylon".

The Queen's titles were discussed by the Commonwealth Prime Ministers at their meeting in December 1952. Separate titles, containing a common element, were then agreed upon. It then became necessary for each of the Commonwealth countries (except India) to pass legislation which in effect amended the Royal and Parliamentary Titles Act, 1927. This was done in Ceylon by the Royal Titles Act, 1953. Hence one of the titles by which the Queen is being proclaimed at the Coronation is "Queen of Ceylon and of her other realms and territories, Head of the Commonwealth". In this respect, of course, she is being advised by the Government of Ceylon.

The reader may think this a long rigmarole about a title. He must however remember that the monarchy lies in the realm of sentiment and emotion, which are important. In Ceylon sentiment and emotion attach to Sri Lanka, a personage which is not the less real for being entirely mythical. The older generation of educated Ceylonese was brought up in the nationalist conflict against colonial rule and therefore its extreme wing seems to an Englishman (whose forbears [*sic*] got rid of colonial rulers about 800 years ago by the simple process of providing them with English wives and making their children English) to be almost chauvinist. We have to have a national culture, national languages, national medicine, national costume, a national flag, a national anthem, national music and national dancing, while some would like to have a national religion and a national university, though as the very name implies a national university is like cold steam or hot ice. These emotions are easily understood, and only occasionally do they become excessive. They are in fact being tempered among the new generation, where nationalist "leftism" (if one may coin a word out of a Ceylonism) has a wide appeal.

[T]hus, Ceylon has a nationalism within the monarchy rather different in texture from that of Canada, 40 per cent of whose people trace their descent from the United Kingdom. Thirty years ago King George V and his advisers thought out the consequences of the new Commonwealth and adapted the monarchy accordingly. It will be the task of Queen Elizabeth II to work out the consequences of the independence of India, Pakistan and Ceylon.

5. Notes on the royal visit to Ceylon, 1954

Local opinion seems to be exaggerating the success of the Royal Visit. The Queen was surrounded by friendly V.I.Ps., and huge well-disposed crowds turned out, often in most uncomfortable positions, to see her. There has not been a single report of any unfriendly action. Nevertheless one must remember that all the tamashas were boycotted by two important groups.

(1.) The Swadeshi Movement[33]

This name is given because the movement is entirely unorganized and therefore it has no name. Its characteristic is rejection of western ideas. Upon analysis, of course, one finds Aristotle, Christian morality, liberty, equality, fraternity and all the rest. They have learned a lot from the West and forgotten only that it came from the West. Nevertheless, there is conscious rejection of what is consciously western. English must be superseded by Swabasha;[34] western music must be superseded by Indian music; western art by eastern art; western drama by Sanskrit drama; western clothes by Swadeshi; western philosophy by Indian philosophy; and so on. We have to develop "our ancient culture" and our inspiration must come from India, whence it always has come.

[33] This refers to South Asian independence movements from the late nineteenth century that drew upon South Asian culture.

[34] A term that refers to use of indigenous languages.

It is an intellectual movement which is particularly strong among the Sinhalese in the Faculty of Oriental Studies; and my recollection is that not one of the younger Sinhalese in that Faculty attended the Opening of the University. If one could get an agreed statement from them, it would probably claim that the contacts with European countries since 1505 have been destructive of Sinhalese culture, that British ideas have been particularly destructive because they have infiltrated so deeply, that the "brown sahibs" who surrounded the Queen were traitors to their own culture, and that to have a British monarch at all is foolish.

If this affected only the University it would be unimportant, but the University is merely the English-speaking spearhead of the whole Swabasha movement, which spreads through the schools (especially the Swabasha schools) and the Swabasha press: the latter is becoming more and more important. It is not merely Swabasha; in the realm of ideas it is also at least superficially, Swadeshi.

My impression is that at University level it is not organically connected with politics, and certainly none of our Swabasha enthusiasts take an active part in politics. Nevertheless, it is at the lower levels such an important section of opinion that all political parties have to pay attention to it.

(2.) The Political Opposition.

The boycott carried out by the Opposition did not concern only the Members of Parliament. Those members of the University staff who are known to be members of the Sri Lanka Freedom Party,[35] the Lanka Sam Samaja Party,[36] and the Communist Party stayed away from the University function. The press poked fun at Opposition politicians who, so to speak, satisfied their curiosity by peeping through the blinds: but it would be wrong to assume that the boycott was a mere vote-catching political demonstration. The monarchy and the Commonwealth have not been "sold" to large sections of the English-speaking middle class. The Queen is not their Queen and they do not want to belong to the Commonwealth.

2. It is difficult to estimate the effect of the Royal Visit on the United National Party. Sir Oliver Goonetilleke used the opportunity to promote the Prime Minister[37] to the rank of Maharajah of Sri Lanka. Whether this had any effect on the general population I do not know, but I very much doubt it. Unlike D.S. Senanayake and Dudley Senanayake, the Prime Minister has little influence in the villages.

[35] Founded by S.W.R.D. Bandaranaike in 1951, as noted above.
[36] Leftist party founded in 1935 and often referred to as the LSSP.
[37] Sir John Kotelawala.

His pujas at the Dalada Maligawa do not make him a Buddhist as the Senanayakes are Buddhists. His sherwani and his Privy Council uniform become him far better than a morning coat and the same uniform became D.S. Senanayake: but this merely showed that D.S. was "one of us" who was called to higher things, while Sir John is a "brown sahib" who pretends to be one of us because he is Prime Minister. Sir Oliver's influence ceases where his arm cannot stretch; and he has never succeeded in embracing more than the couple of lakhs of the English-speaking official class. The difficulty is that the Senanayakes have no successors. The Members of Parliament are proctors, schoolmasters, and the like who had Senanayake support. Most of them have too little local influence to be elected by Kotelawala support, which has no influence outside a couple of North Western Province constituencies. In 1952 a great many people voted for D.S. Senanayake, though he was dead. Will anybody vote for Sir John Kotelawala in 1957?[38]

3. I think the Queen caught the imagination of the ordinary man in the areas where she could be seen. The antagonism to the white face is, I believe, limited to the middle class. The villager and the bungalow servant are not supporters of the Swabasha nationalists. They approved of their English civil servants because, though remote, they were just and they had no uncles and nephews.[39] They do not always approve of the gentlemen from Moratuwa and the University of Ceylon who are sent to govern them. Indeed university graduates sometimes say that they can do very little because the villager is so caste-conscious; the English had no caste. Nor is the urban or suburban worker of the west coast, who votes L.S.S.P., very different. He is more politically conscious; he thinks he can better his lot either by political action or by trade union action (the two are really the same): but he is not a Swabasha nationalist, a republican or a Marxist. Swabasha nationalism, republicanism and Marxism are middle-class movements. Indeed they are in large measure (using English terms) lower middle-class movements. In large measure they are a reaction against the dominance of the England-educated who superseded the European. This must not be carried too far. All the Opposition leaders – S.W.R.D. Bandaranaike, N.M. Perera,[40] Colvin R. de Silva, S.A. Wickremasinghe and P.G.B. Keuneman[41] – were

[38]The election was actually held in 1956. The SLFP under Bandaranaike won a landslide.

[39]The abbreviation UNP was satirically said to stand for Uncle Nephew Party on account of the multiple kinship ties within the party.

[40]LSSP leader and Leader of the Opposition.

[41]De Silva, Wickremasinghe, and Keuneman were all major Leftist leaders and members of the Ceylon House of Representatives.

England-educated: but politically they cash in on the lower middle-class, the clerks and the teachers among the English-educated, the teachers and the vedaralas[42] among the Sinhalese-educated.

4. All parties in Britain have to be monarchist because they would lose votes if they were not. The Opposition parties in Ceylon need not be monarchist because the ordinary voter does not regard monarchy as relevant. The Queen does not belong to him or he to the Queen. The Ceylonese child does not – or at least has not in the past – acquire at home and at school the personal loyalty which the English or Scottish child acquires. Indeed he could not in many cases, because the Governor of Ceylon, though the representative of the monarch, was the representative of the United Kingdom Government also, "British imperialism". Since his teachers, and possibly his parents also, were advocates of "freedom", the child tended to be antagonistic to "British imperialism" and therefore to the King's representative. This may be changing. The most significant of the Colombo pandals was the rather shoddy one in Thurstan Road: "We the children of Lanka, welcome our Queen". It was put up by the Education Department and so it was not a spontaneous expression of loyalty; but it was an indication that loyalty to the Queen is being taught. This was not so in the past. Indeed, the wartime propaganda from Britain, which stressed loyalty to the monarch, was a hindrance to our propaganda in Ceylon. The change must not be exaggerated. Many of the teachers are among the strongest and most influential supporters of the Opposition groups. It is, however, possible to foresee a change in a generation if the position of the monarchy can somehow be consolidated.

5. The conversion of India and (presumably) Pakistan to republicanism makes the position in Ceylon more difficult. Little Ceylon has to strut among her greater neighbours. A Ceylonese Governor-General had to be nominated because it was infra dig for the representatives of Asian nations to be received by an Englishman on behalf of Sri Lanka. Sir Oliver promoted the Prime Minister during the Queen's visit not merely to catch votes for the U.N.P. but also because he did not want Lord Soulbury to be too prominent. Sir Oliver as Governor-General will be *plus royaliste que la Reine*. Indeed he has already told his Permanent Secretary that the standards of Queen's House must be maintained. It is true that he will be the U.N.P.'s principal propagandist: but he will also be a propagandist for royalty more effective than any English successor of Lord Soulbury could possibly be. On the other hand, if the Government found it

[42] Indigenously trained physicians.

politically expedient to create a republic Sir Oliver would find it expedient to become President.

6. The Queen could exercise a very great influence – as the recent visit has demonstrated – if she could pay frequent visits. Visits by other members of the Royal Family, as we have seen from the visits of the Duke of Gloucester and the Duchess of Kent, have nothing like the same influence. They are useful; and they would be even more useful with Sir Oliver as Governor-General because he would play them up. Even so, the Queen is the Queen and the others are mere delegates. On the other hand, it is clear that the Queen's visits must be rare and fleeting. Possibly more use could be made of royal messages. Could not the Queen have a Ceylonese equerry who would be prominent on Commonwealth occasions and who could draft messages of congratulation and condolence? For instance, there should be a personal message from the Queen, read by the Governor-General, on every celebration of Independence. Also, it must be noted that everybody in Ceylon wants what is still called an 'Imperial honour'. The Order used for this purpose is usually the Order of the British Empire, which is singularly inappropriate. Should not a special Order be created for Ceylon as the Order of Sri Lanka with the Governor-General as Grand Master and with a Registry in Ceylon? The Governor-General himself should always be a G.C.V.O. rather than a G.C.M.G.,[43] which savours of 'colonialism', while the Royal Victorian Order is personally associated with the Queen.

7. These are minor matters; but they have to be dealt with because the major problem has no ready solution. One cannot even guarantee that the U.N.P. will hold together until 1957. The S.L.F.P. is of small importance, the L.S.S.P. has lost strength lately; the 'common front' is still a small minority movement. Nevertheless, the U.N.P. may lose most of the west-coast seats from Colombo South to Hambantota, all seats in the Northern Province, and some seats elsewhere. Unless it remains in power it will not get Independent support. It is therefore possible to envisage a 'common front' Government with S.W.R.D. as Prime Minister. More likely is a split in the U.N.P.; for Sir John's handling of his colleagues is not likely to be very tactful, especially if all this adulation goes to his head. There is already the nucleus

[43] British imperial honours – GCMG: Knight Grand Cross of the Order of St Michael and St George; GCVO: Knight Grand Cross of the Royal Victorian Order. The latter is given at the discretion of the Sovereign, while the former is given on the advice of the Prime Minister.

of an Opposition – not only Bandaranaike but also Ponnambalam[44] and Sir Lalitha Rajapakse.[45] Both would be monarchists. But if (say) J.R. Jayewardene broke away it is possible to imagine a quite strong republican Opposition supported (against the U.N.P.) by the L.S.S.P., the Communists, and the Indians.

8. Hence though the Queen's visit has helped to strengthen monarchy and ties with the Commonwealth, the future is far from secure. A republic needs a two-thirds majority in the House of Representatives, which is difficult to obtain. Hence the problem would arise not in 1957 but in 1962. If things could be kept going until 1977 all should be well: but this cannot be guaranteed.

[44]G.G. Ponnambalan, former Cabinet minister and Tamil Congress Leader. Often referred to as 'G.G.'.

[45]Former Cabinet minister.

SECTION B: ETHIOPIA

The British had administered Eritrea as a mandate territory since taking it from the Italians during the Second World War. The Allied powers sent a commission of enquiry in 1947 to investigate Eritrea's position, but could not agree on a way forward. The United Nations then sent its own commission in 1950, which reported back to the General Assembly in its report 390(v) of 2 December 1950. Its first recommendation was that 'Eritrea shall constitute an autonomous unit federated with Ethiopia under the sovereignty of the Ethiopian Crown'. Jennings was asked by British diplomats and UN officials for his opinion on the legal and constitutional practicality of this recommendation in 1951.

1. Letter to the United Nations Commissioner in Eritrea, 3 December 1951

1. The question which we discussed on 29 November was whether the Commissioner had the legal power to include the Emperor of Ethiopia[1] or his representative as part of one or more of the institutions (especially the Executive) of Eritrea. I had not considered the question to be of great importance because, as a matter of practical politics it would not seem desirable to give him one or more substantive powers. You explained, however, that it was of great practical importance because you had for six months rejected all such claims from the Emperor on the purely legal ground that you had not the power under the resolution to assent to any of them. I have therefore studied the question again, and I regret to say that I feel bound to repeat my opinion that some form of constitutional monarchy, as practised in the democratic countries of Western Europe and the British Commonwealth, is not inconsistent with the resolution as it stands.
2. I must, however, also repeat my opinion (for what it is worth) that any such arrangement would probably be undesirable, for the reason which you have yourself given, namely that the Emperor of Ethiopia knows nothing of constitutional monarchy and has no desire to be

[1] Haile Selassie I, Emperor of Ethiopia, 1930–1974.

a constitutional monarch, but on the contrary is anxious to have substantive powers of control over Eritrea. It is therefore more than probable that if he were given the formal powers of a constitutional monarch he would in fact use those powers in undemocratic ways, and so would interfere with the autonomy of Eritrea in breach of the letter as well as the spirit of the resolution. One could contemplate giving him some powers as a constitutional monarch only if they were rigidly defined, were placed under strict judicial control, and were necessary in order to secure the Emperor's assent to other provisions which he disliked.

3. I must also add that I am in complete disagreement with the views expressed by the Vice Minister of Foreign Affairs for Ethiopia in document A/AC.44/SR.72 of 6 November 1951,[2] which I have now had the opportunity of reading. His claim is not that the Commissioner has power to include a representative of the Emperor in the Eritrean Executive but that the Emperor has a right to such a place in accordance with the resolution as he interprets it. I am unable to accept that interpretation.

. . . .

I agree that it is easier to resist suggestions from Ethiopia by asserting that they are illegal than to resist them by saying that they might lead to encroachments which would be illegal. On the other hand, the resolution as I interpret it gives you a wider discretion to make formal concessions which satisfy the Emperor's amour-propre without giving him substantial powers. For instance, the following are possible:

(1) Laws could be made by the Assembly of Eritrea "in the name of the Emperor".
(2) The Executive could be styled "His Imperial Majesty's Government in Eritrea" and executive acts done in his name.
(3) "The judicial power shall be exercised by the courts. Decrees and judgments shall be executed in the name of the Emperor" (cf. Belgian Constitution, Art. 30[3]).
(4) There could be a Governor-General to whom petitions would be presented, who would represent the Emperor at the opening of the Assembly, and read "the Emperor's Speech".

These are indicated as possibilities, not suggested as desirable. Incidentally they might teach the Emperor (and his people) the ways of democracy.

[2] Not included.
[3] The 1831 Constitution of Belgium.

I. The Resolution[4]

1. Paragraph 1 of the resolution prescribes that Eritrea shall constitute an autonomous unit federated with Ethiopia under the Sovereignty of the Ethiopian Crown.

The fact that two countries have the same King or Emperor does not imply that the one or the other is not autonomous. On the contrary, they may both be fully sovereign States in the sense of international law. The personal unions supply examples, and so does the British Commonwealth. I have lived all my life under the sovereignty of the British Crown, but I have lived in six sovereign States, namely, the United Kingdom, Canada, Australia, India, Pakistan and Ceylon. When India became a republic in 1950 it did not in any way enlarge its sovereign status, which was fully ensured from 1947 to 1950 while the King-Emperor was part of the Constitution of India,[5] as he still is part of the Constitution of Pakistan.[6]

2. Nor is it impossible for the same monarch to be at once Head of a Federation and Head of an "autonomous unit". There are three federal Constitutions in the British Commonwealth in which this is so, Canada, Australia and Pakistan. It was so in India between 1947 and 1950, and even now the President of India appoints the Governor of the States. On page 13 of the document A/AC.44/SR.70 of 30 October 1951, the Commissioner twice quotes the example of Canada in support of his thesis, but the example in fact supports mine; for the Executive of the Dominion is appointed by the Governor-General, who is appointed by the King, and the Executive of a Province is appointed by the Lieutenant-Governor, who is appointed by the Governor-General. It has been specifically held by the Privy Council that the powers of the Governor-General over the Lieutenant-Governors do not give the Provinces "a subordinate position".[7] It is therefore possible for the Emperor of Ethiopia or his representative to be part of, or to appoint, the Executive of Eritrea without affecting the "autonomy" of Eritrea or destroying the federal character of the Constitution.

[4]For the full text, see Resolution 390(v) of the UN General Assembly of 2 December 1950: 'Eritrea: Report of the United Nations Commission for Eritrea'. See also the introductory paragraph of this chapter.

[5]India was an independent realm within the Commonwealth from 1947 to 1950 and the King (not King-Emperor as Jennings states, as this title ceased to exist on Indian independence in August 1947) was represented in New Delhi by a Governor-General.

[6]Pakistan was an independent realm within the Commonwealth until 1956.

[7]See *The Liquidators of the Maritime Bank of Canada v. The Receiver General of New Brunswick (Canada)* [1892] UKPC 34 (2 July 1892).

3. Paragraph 2 of the Resolution says that the Eritrean Government shall possess legislative, executive and judicial powers in the field of domestic affairs. In my memorandum of 25 November 1951[8] I agreed that, when this is read with paragraph 3, it becomes clear that the powers are exclusive. But this does not mean that the Emperor, or his representative, may not take part in the legislative, executive or even judicial powers. I need take only the example given by the Commissioner himself, that of Canada. The legislature of a Canadian Province is the Lieutenant-Governor and the Legislative Assembly; the Executive of a Province is appointed by the Lieutenant-Governor; the judges of the Provincial courts are appointed by the Governor-General. As I have said, the Governor-General is appointed by the King, and the Lieutenant-Governors are appointed by the Governor-General. In Australia both the Governor-General and the Governors are appointed by the King.

4. Paragraph 12 says that the Constitution of Eritrea shall be based on the principles of democratic government. The Commissioner very properly places great emphasis on this provision, and it may be that my learned colleagues from France and the United States regard republicanism and democracy as identical. My view is that some republics are not democratic and some monarchies are. That view would, I think, be shared by all my colleagues from Norway, Sweden, Denmark, the Netherlands, Belgium and the British Commonwealth. If, then, it is possible for a monarchy to be democratic, it is theoretically possible for the Emperor or his representatives to take part in a democratic government of Eritrea.

II. The Commissioner's Argument[9]

There is very little with which I disagree in the Commissioner's formal statement given in the Appendix to document A/AC.44/SR.70 of 30 October 1951. I have mentioned already the references to Canada in paragraphs 14 and 15, which support my view, and not his, and I should make minor reservations to paragraphs 18, 38 and 51. My serious disagreement, however, is only over paragraph 13. I therefore set out his statements and my comments in parallel columns:

[8] Not found in the Jennings Papers.

[9] Commissioner's formal statement not found.

Statement	Comment
1. If the Eritrean Executive were to be appointed by the Emperor or by the representative of the Emperor, it would not in fact be a fully representative Eritrean Executive, which would be contrary to the provision that Eritrea should constitute an autonomous unit.	1. In nearly all the countries which operate Cabinet Government the Cabinet (or the Prime Minister) is appointed by the Head of the State. In many of these countries the Head of the State is a monarch. Is it contended that those countries have not a fully representative Executive or that they are not autonomous? If the Emperor of Ethiopia appoints an Eritrean Cabinet which has the confidence of the Eritrean Assembly, I cannot agree that the Executive is not fully representative or that Eritrea loses its autonomy.
2. In the opinion of the Commissioner, paragraph 2 of the resolutions which lays down that Eritrea shall possess legislative, executive and judicial powers in the field of domestic affairs, is clear. According to its terms, a Government which did not emanate from the people could not be considered as an Eritrean Government based on democratic principles, as laid down in paragraph 12 of the resolution.	2. The argument seems to be that a Government which is appointed by a monarch or a Governor-General does not emanate from the people and could not be regarded as a Government based on democratic principles. Therefore the Governments of Norway, Sweden, Denmark, the Netherlands, Belgium and the British Commonwealth do not emanate from the people and are not based on democratic principles. Their representatives in the General Assembly of the United Nations would I fear, express some doubt about this argument.
3. The Commissioner therefore feels that the text of paragraphs 1 and 2 excludes the possibility of appointment or nomination of the Eritrean Executive by the Emperor of Ethiopia.	3. I can find nothing in the two paragraphs which prevents the Commissioner from recommending a Cabinet system of government, or from recommending that the Cabinet or the Prime Minister be appointed or nominated by the Emperor or his representative.

4. If the Ethiopian Government is of the view that the Government of Eritrea shall derive from the Emperor, then the Commissioner considers that a different text should have been drafted at Lake Success.	4. I agree: but if the Emperor of Ethiopia were given power to appoint a Cabinet according to well-known democratic principles, no change of the text would be needed.

III. Reply to the Vice-Minister of Foreign Affairs[10]

(This reply is limited to the points raised above and does not deal, for instance, with the question of official languages).

1. In paragraph 7 the Vice-Minister translates "the sovereignty of the Ethiopian Crown" as "the supreme authority of the Crown". The interpretation is very understandable, for when the theory of sovereignty was elaborated by such theorists as Bodin and Hobbes[11] it did in fact mean "supreme power" or "supreme authority". A similar meaning is given by British lawyers when they refer to "the sovereignty of Parliament" or by other European lawyers when they refer to "the sovereignty of the people". As a result of the constitutional disputes of the seventeenth and eighteenth centuries, however, other meanings became permissible. Thus, a "Sovereign State" in international law is not a State which has supreme power according to international law, but a State which has full personality according to international law. If the State is represented in international affairs by an Emperor or a King, then the Emperor or the King is often spoken of as "the Sovereign".

2. A similar usage is often followed in constitutional law: thus, though English lawyers speak of "the Sovereignty of Parliament", they often refer to the King as "the Sovereign". Examples may be taken about at random. Thus, in Duff Development Company v. Kelantan (1924)[12] the House of Lords was asked to define the status of the State of Kelantan, which was under the protection of the British Crown. The British Government then stated that "the King did not exercise or claim any rights of sovereignty over Kelantan". This did not mean that if Kelantan had been British territory the King would have been able to claim "supreme authority", but only that Kelantan was

[10] Minister's statement not found.

[11] Jean Bodin, sixteenth-century French jurist and philosopher; Thomas Hobbes, seventeenth-century English political philosopher and author of the seminal text *Leviathan* on the state's role.

[12] *Duff Development Company, Ltd. v. The Government of Kelantan and Another* [1924] A.C. 797.

not British territory. Again, in the Engineer's Case (1920)[13] the High Court of Australia drew attention to "the common sovereignty of all parts of the British Empire". This did not mean that the King had supreme authority over all parts of the Empire, but only that all parts of the Empire owed allegiance to the same King. Australia was not merely "autonomous"; it was an independent country, and indeed a member of the League of Nations, but it was under the "sovereignty" of the British Crown in the narrower sense of that term. As the Balfour Declaration[14] said in 1926, Britain and the Dominions were "autonomous communities ... united by a common allegiance to the Crown". Allegiance is the obverse of sovereignty. The Declaration might therefore have said, with equal accuracy, "autonomous communities ... united under the sovereignty of the Crown".

3. It is plain that in the resolution the word "sovereignty" is not used in the sense of "supreme authority"; for, if it were, Eritrea would not be 'an autonomous unit"; the Eritrean Government would not have the exclusive legislative, executive and judicial powers in the field of domestic affairs contemplated by paragraphs 1 and 2; the provision of human rights and fundamental liberties in paragraph 7 would be useless; and, above all, the Constitution of Eritrea would not be "based on the principles of democratic government" as required by paragraph 12.

4. In paragraph 5 of the memorandum reference is made to the "right of the Crown to designate the Head of the local Executive". There is no provision in the resolution conferring any such right. The form of the Executive is clearly a matter for the Commissioner and the Eritrean Assembly, in accordance with the provisions of paragraph 12 of the resolution and subject to paragraph 13 of that resolution. Paragraph 7 of the memorandum assumes that the Federal Act and the Constitution would be ratified by the Emperor in a single act and instrument. There would seem to be no objection to this arrangement, but it is not the case that the act and instrument would provide for the transfer of power, because such transfer is to be effected by the British Administration in accordance with paragraph 14 of the resolution. Nor is there any provision in the resolution for the appointment of Executives by the Emperor. Such a right might follow from "supreme

[13] *Amalgamated Society of Engineers v. Adelaide Steamship Co. Ltd.* [1920] 28 CLR 129.

[14] The Balfour Declaration, made at the 1926 Imperial conference, established the principle that the Dominions were 'autonomous communities within the British Empire, equal in status, in no way subordinate one to another in any aspect of their domestic or external affairs, though united by a common allegiance to the Crown, and freely associated as members of the British Commonwealth of Nations'. This laid the basis for the Statute of Westminster (1931).

authority", but it does not follow from "sovereignty" as expressed in the resolution.

5. Certain other reasons are given for the exercise by the Crown of powers not conferred by the Federal Act. These are:

1. To protect federal jurisdiction from abuse by the local (i.e. Eritrean) Government. It is certainly necessary to provide such protection, but it is also necessary to protect the Eritrean jurisdiction from abuse by the federal Government. These problems arise in every federation, and they are solved by giving jurisdiction to the Court.
2) To discharge the obligation of protecting minority rights entrusted to the Federal Government. No such obligation is entrusted to the Federal Government. Both the Federal Government and the Eritrean Government must ensure the enjoyment of human rights and fundamental liberties in accordance with paragraph 7 of the resolution and it will be the duty of the Courts to ensure that the provisions of that paragraph are observed by both Governments.

2. Letter to the United Nations Commissioner in Eritrea, 4 December 1951

So far as can be judged from the documents, the opinion which Your Excellency has expressed to the Ethiopian Government is that the Ethiopian institutions of government, with the additions contemplated by paragraph 5 of the resolution of the General Assembly, will become the federal institutions, but that it is legally impossible for the Emperor or his representative to be given any place in the institutions of Eritrea.

On the other hand, the Ethiopian Government contends not only that the institutions of Ethiopia will become the federal institutions, but also that the Emperor will have the right to appoint the Executive Government of Eritrea. Indeed, the Vice-Minister of Foreign Affairs for Ethiopia speaks of the "supreme authority" of the Emperor in Eritrea.

2. I regret that I find it difficult to accept either interpretation. The argument that the Emperor will have "supreme authority" must clearly be rejected: for if that were the case Eritrea would not be an autonomous unit as required by paragraph 1; the distribution of powers contemplated by paragraphs 2 and 3 would be irrelevant; and the Constitution of Eritrea would not be "based on the principles of democratic government" as required by paragraph 12. On the other hand, there is nothing in these paragraphs to prevent the establishment of constitutional monarchy in Eritrea. Such an arrangement is not necessitated by the resolution, but it would not be inconsistent with it

if it were thought to be a suitable form of government for Eritrea. Certainly the Emperor has no "right" to appoint the Executive of Eritrea, but I can find nothing in the resolution to prevent the establishment of a Cabinet system in Eritrea or to forbid the conferment on the Emperor or on his representative of the normal prerogatives of a constitutional monarch.

3. The opinion that the institutions of Ethiopia, with the additions contemplated by paragraph 5, will become the federal institutions, is based on the fact that the General Assembly has made no provision for the enactment of a Federal Constitution. It is contemplated by paragraphs 13 and 14 that the Federal Act and the Constitution of Eritrea will come into operation when the necessary approvals have been given and ratifications effected. Nothing is said about the approval of a Federal Constitution. These are strong arguments. Nevertheless, the resolution implies that there will be federal laws. Attention should be drawn to the following points:

1. Eritrea is to be an autonomous unit federated with Ethiopia. According to the ordinary meaning of language, this would imply that both Eritrea and Ethiopia were to be States or Provinces of a Federation.
2. Paragraph 3 makes a precise division of powers between the Eritrean Government and the Federal Government, not between the Eritrean Government and the Ethiopian Government acting as Federal Government.
3. Paragraph 3 refers to "federal functions and services" and distinguishes them from what paragraph 2 calls "domestic affairs". There must therefore be federal laws to regulate federal functions and services.
4. Paragraph 3 refers to "uniform taxes" to meet the expenses of "federal functions and services". Therefore there must be a federal budget distinct from the Ethiopian budget, and federal taxation laws distinct from Ethiopian taxation laws.
5. Paragraph 5 requires a law, which must clearly be a federal law, giving participation in the federal institutions to citizens of Eritrea.
6. Paragraph 6(d) refers specifically to "federal laws" governing federal nationality, and generally the paragraph requires a federal law to determine who shall be federal nationals, in addition to those specifically provided for by sub-paragraphs (a), (b), and (d).
7. The division of powers in paragraph 3, the limitation on legislative power in paragraph 4, and the provision of "human rights and fundamental liberties" (which apply both to the Federal Government and to Eritrea) in paragraph 7, all require the establishment of a Federal Supreme Court.

4. It is possible to imagine a system in which the Emperor of Ethiopia was the federal authority, but in that case the use of the terms "federation" and "federal" seems to be inappropriate. The relationship would be more like that between the United Kingdom (of Great Britain and Northern Ireland) and Northern Ireland than like a federation. It would give the Emperor substantial powers over Eritrea which are not implied in the phrase "the sovereignty of the Ethiopian Crown" and which he does not possess at present. It is difficult, too, to see how the autonomy of Eritrea could be protected in such circumstances. One would therefore like to see in the resolution some phrase which justified such an interpretation. There is, however, no such phrase. Accordingly, though I cannot say that the interpretation accepted both by Your Excellency and by the Government of Ethiopia is incorrect, I must express considerable doubt about it.

5. My opinion may be summarised as follows:

1. The resolution does not give the Emperor "supreme authority" in Eritrea.
2. The resolution does not give the Emperor a right to appoint the Executive of Eritrea.
3. There is nothing in the resolution to exclude the possibility of a constitutional monarchy in Eritrea.
4. There is nothing in the resolution to justify the assumption that the Ethiopian authorities, enlarged in accordance with paragraph 5, would become the federal authorities; and it would seem that a Federal Constitution, for which no provision has been made, would be required.

SECTION C: GIBRALTAR

The following is an undated opinion of Jennings from around 1965 on Gibraltar's 'right to self-determination'. It is not clear who specifically sought this opinion. In 1963–1964 the United Nations Special Committee on Decolonization examined the case of Gibraltar at Spain's request.

1. 'Status of Gibraltar', *c.*1965

I have been asked for an opinion on certain contentions said to have been put forward by the Spanish Government in relation to Gibraltar. For the purposes of this opinion I assume that the present Spanish Government is recognised as the de jure Government of Spain, and that no question arises as to the succession to the rights and obligations under the Treaty of Utrecht, 1713.[1]

2. The "town and garrison" of Gibraltar became one of Her Majesty's dominions by conquest in 1704. Neither for the purposes of English law nor for the purposes of international law was there need for a treaty of cession. The "town and garrison" has been governed under the royal prerogative since 1704, when Prince George of Hesse Darmstadt[2] was appointed Governor and Major-General Shrimpton Lieutenant-Governor. In 1706 the Earl of Portmore[3] became Governor, and he continued in office until 1720, no constitutional change being necessitated by the Treaty of Utrecht. In accordance with common law principles going back to Calvin's Case (1608),[4] those inhabitants of the "town and garrison" who chose to remain under the jurisdiction of the Crown of England became in 1704 English subjects, though in

[1]The treaty established after the War of the Spanish Succession resulting from the death of Charles II of Spain in 1700. Among other details affecting the balance of power in Europe, the Treaty of Utrecht ceded control of Gibraltar from Spain to Britain.

[2]Military commander in the service of the Habsburgs.

[3]The Scottish general David Colyear, Earl of Portmore. Portmore officially became Governor in 1713.

[4]*Calvin's Case* (1608) 7 Co. Rep. 1.

1707 they became British subjects.[5] Under the British Nationality Act, 1948, the native inhabitants of Gibraltar are both British subjects and citizens of the United Kingdom and Colonies.

3. It was, however, the practice of English and British Governments to secure ratifications of wartime annexations by appropriate provisions in the treaties of peace. There were two reasons for doing so. The first was that in the 17th and 18th centuries colonial territories could be made the subject of international bargaining: e.g. limitations in Gibraltar and Minorca could be accepted in return for limitations on Spanish jurisdiction in South America. The second reason was that, while an annexation based on conquest was a good title both in English law and in international law, it was not necessarily effective in the law of the country from which the colony had been conquered. For instance, though an inhabitant of Gibraltar became an English subject in 1704, his new nationality was not necessarily recognised in Spain until the Rock was formally ceded in 1713. In English law the cession had no effect whatsoever, for it makes no difference whether Gibraltar is described as a conquered colony or as a ceded colony. It was, and still is, governed under the royal prerogative. It was a Crown colony whose "constitution" was the Governor's Commission until, late in the 19th century, the practice was developed of putting the instrument of government into letters patent or orders in council, under which the Governor was empowered to act by his Commission, though subject to any Instructions that he might receive from the Crown. Gibraltar is still a Crown colony governed under the royal prerogative. The instrument of government is an order in council the Gibraltar (Constitution) Order, 1964.[6] Gibraltar is one of the colonies with representative legislatures, as defined by the Colonial Laws Validity Act, 1865.[7] Because of the rule laid down in Campbell v. Hall (1774),[8] that if the Crown has granted a representative legislature it cannot subsequently derogate from its grant unless it has reserved a power of legislation, the Order provides in section 9, that the Queen shall continue to have "full power to make laws . . . for the peace, order and good government of Gibraltar". As has often been observed by the Judicial Committee of the Privy Council, this is a plenary legislative power, subject of course to the limits of the royal prerogative and

[5] The change occurred after the Acts of Union, 1707, which created Great Britain through the union of Scotland and England.

[6] This delivered further internal self-government and was objected to by Spain.

[7] This Act confirmed that legislation passed in colonial legislatures had full effect unless 'repugnant' and in contradiction to any Act of the British Parliament that covered the colony.

[8] *Campbell v. Hall* [1774] EngR 5; 1774 1 Cowp 204; 98 ER 1045.

to any Acts of the Parliament of the United Kingdom extending to Gibraltar as part of its law.

4. From the point of view of English law, therefore, there has been no fundamental change in the constitutional status of Gibraltar. Nor has there been any such change for the purposes of international law. Though the Treaty of Utrecht had no effect in English law, it imposed obligations in relation to Gibraltar under international law. Internationally, however, the Government of the United Kingdom is still responsible for acts done in Gibraltar, whether they are done by the United Kingdom Government or by the Government of Gibraltar.

5. Article 10 of the Treaty of Utrecht states that "the Catholic King does hereby, for himself, his heirs and successors, yield to the Crown of Great Britain the full and entire propriety of the town and castle of Gibraltar, together with the port, fortifications, and forts thereunto belonging; and he gives up the said propriety to be held and enjoyed absolutely with all manner of right for ever, without any impediment whatsoever".

There can be no real doubt about the meaning of this provision. "Propriety" is an eighteenth century word, often used in British treaties, and meaning "sovereignty" or "dominion". Gibraltar had been one of the dominions of the Crown of England and Great Britain since 1704. By this provision the Catholic King renounced his claim to sovereignty and recognized the Queen's title to "the town and castle . . . ".

The "town and castle" is a comprehensive description of the territory held by the Crown of Great Britain in 1713. It cannot be read as "the town" and "the castle" because there is no provision in the Treaty of Utrecht or elsewhere for the surrender of any territory not included in "the town" or "the castle". The phrase generally used in English documents, until recently, was "the town and garrison". Here "garrison" means a fortified place, and it is a better description than "castle" because, even in the 18th century, a castle had defensive outworks. (For the same reason, the island of Malta was sometimes described as a "fortress"). I concur entirely with the joint opinion expressed by the law officers, Sir John Campbell and Sir R. M. Rolfe, in 1838. They were asked how far the courts established in Gibraltar were entitled to take cognizance of offences committed on any portion of the territory outside the gates of the garrison. They replied (W. Forsyth, Q.C., Cases and Opinions on Constitutional Law, 1869, pp. 244–45[9]) as follows:

[9] William Forsyth, *Cases and Opinions on Constitutional Law: and various points of English jurisprudence, collected and digested from official documents and other sources; with notes* (London, 1869).

> "We entertain no doubt whatever that the courts established in Gibraltar are entitled to take cognizance of offences committed on any portion of the territory between the gates of the garrison and the extremity of the English lines. This territory is clearly held in full sovereignty by the English Crown, and is included in the charters establishing courts with jurisdiction over the garrison and territory of Gibraltar . . . Even under the strictest interpretation of the Treaty of Utrecht, this ground, which is indisputably necessary for the occupation and defence of the fortress, is to be considered part of the fortress of Gibraltar; and by our exercising jurisdiction over it there is no pretence for saying that we assume any territorial jurisdiction over or open any communication with the surrounding country, against the stipulations of the treaty. To gain the object desired by the Governor, as to the ground between the fortress and the British lines, there appears to us to be no occasion whatever for any new treaty with Spain, or any new charter from the Crown".

The isthmus was, of course, captured in 1704, since the naval force landed there. I believe that I am right in saying, too, that the port is outside the gates. The territory had been annexed in 1704 and the Treaty merely confirmed the annexation.

The words "together with the port, fortifications, and forts thereunto belonging" were no doubt added out of abundant caution. Gibraltar had been acquired as a fortress and a naval base guarding the entrance to the Mediterranean. It was being used as such, in conjunction with Minorca, dealt with in article 11, in 1713. The express reference to the port and the fortress resulted in a recognition by the Catholic King that Gibraltar was not to be demilitarised.

6. The second sentence of article 10 imposes no direct obligation on the Queen of Great Britain. It is a statement of intent by the Spanish King in relation to his own territory and leads to an acceptance by him, in the third sentence, of an obligation to allow, on the conditions specified, the purchase of provisions and other necessaries in the territory remaining under his control. Though the language is tortuous, it is plain that the Spanish King was concerned with the possibility of goods being smuggled through Gibraltar into Spanish territory. Indirectly there is an obligation on Her Majesty's Government not to seek territorial jurisdiction outside the British territory nor to encourage the fraudulent importation of goods into Spanish territory. On the other hand, the importation of goods from Spanish territory into Gibraltar is authorised both by land and by sea for the use of the garrison – which here means Her Majesty's forces – the inhabitants, and the ships in the harbour. "Imported by Gibraltar" means imported through (the Latin per) Gibraltar into

Spanish territory; if any such goods be fraudulently imported into Spain, the goods may be forfeited and the persons concerned may be punished by the Spanish authorities.

7. Apart from the implied obligations mentioned in the preceding paragraph, the obligations accepted by Her Britannic Majesty under article 10 were as follows:

(1) Not to authorise Jews or Moors to reside in the town of Gibraltar;
(2) Not to allow Moorish ships of war to shelter in the harbour of Gibraltar, in such manner as to obstruct communications between Spain and Ceuta or to allow incursions against the coast of Spain;
(3) To allow Roman Catholic inhabitants of the town of Gibraltar the free exercise of their religion; and
(4) "In case it shall hereafter seem meet to the Crown of Great Britain to grant, sell, or by any means to alienate therefrom the propriety of the said town of Gibraltar, it is hereby agreed and concluded that the preference of having the same shall always be given to the Crown of Spain before any others."

8. I have been asked to advise about the fourth point only. Strictly interpreted, it applies only when it seems proper to the Crown of Great Britain – which now means the Crown of the United Kingdom – to alienate the "propriety" i.e. the sovereignty or dominion. Two points are to be noticed. First, it is now generally held that the Crown cannot alienate territory except under the authority of an Act of Parliament. Partly, at least, this arises because an alienation of territory deprives persons of British nationality, which is now determined by statute and not by common law. The second point is that a constitutional change within the Commonwealth does not result in the alienation of territory unless the country concerned becomes a republic, which again would need an Act of Parliament, i.e. either an Independence Act or a Consequential Provisions Act. The appropriate formula is to be found in the Burma Independence Act, 1947, the Ireland Act, 1949, and later statutes, ". . . shall cease to be part of Her Majesty's dominions". The formula is not employed where a country becomes independent within the Commonwealth but retains the monarchy. Thus, Canada, Australia, New Zealand, Ceylon, Sierra Leone and Malawi remain parts of Her Majesty's dominions. The formula employed in the later Independence Acts (beginning with Ceylon in 1947) is "Her Majesty's Government shall have no responsibility for the government of . . . ". Here the responsibility for advising the Queen is transferred, but the Queen's sovereignty, propriety or dominion is not transferred. If this interpretation of the Treaty is correct, and I believe that it is, no constitutional change in Gibraltar would cause the last sentence of article 10 to take effect unless an Act of the Parliament of the United Kingdom deprived the Queen of her dominion over Gibraltar, or

authorised her to release the inhabitants from their allegiance to her and she exercised the power.

On the other hand, it might be argued that the Treaty of Utrecht was signed by a Queen who was under no constitutional obligation to act according to the advice given her by her Ministers, and that in international law references to the Queen of Great Britain should now be read as references to the Government of the United Kingdom. This is essentially a matter for an international lawyer; but if the doctrine rebus sic stantibus[10] is applied in this way, consideration would also have to be given to the fact that the sentence refers to what is now a particularly obnoxious aspect of "colonialism", as practised in the 18th century, under which a territory and its inhabitants could be granted, sold or otherwise alienated without consultation with the inhabitants. My own view, for what it is worth, is that an international court would be unlikely to hold that a transfer of power from the Government of the United Kingdom to a responsible Government of Gibraltar brought in the obligation, but that the sentence was designed to prevent the Crown of Great Britain from transferring sovereignty to the King of France or some other potentate without first offering Gibraltar to the Crown of Spain.

9. I have been asked a hypothetical question about the grant to Gibraltar of the "right of self-determination". I am not quite clear what the question means. It would theoretically be possible for the Parliament of the United Kingdom to confer power on the Legislative Council of Gibraltar, or on some other body representing the people of the territory, to produce such Constitution as they thought fit. Virtually, this was done by the Indian Independence Act, 1947. It might even go further and authorise the representatives of the people to negotiate with the Government of some other country, say Spain or France, for the inclusion of Gibraltar in the territory under its control. On a mere Constitutional change I have already said something in the preceding paragraph. A proposal to transfer sovereignty to the French Republic would no doubt import the last sentence of article 10.

This is not, however, the normal method of carrying out the wishes of the inhabitants. (There were unusual conditions in British India). Normally there are discussions between the representatives of the Government of the United Kingdom and the representatives of the people of the territory. The conclusion, whatever it is, is put into effect by legislation of the Parliament of the United Kingdom. It is at this stage, before the necessary Bill is introduced into the House of

[10] 'Things standing thus': a legal principle that treaties lose effect when conditions have fundamentally changed.

Commons, that consideration would have to be given to the effect of the last sentence of article 10.

10. Subject to what has been said above, my conclusions are as follows:

(1) The "town and castle of Gibraltar" or the "city and garrison of Gibraltar" includes all the territory occupied and controlled in the name of the Crown of England, Great Britain or the United Kingdom since 1704.

(2) The Gibraltar (Constitution) Order, 1964, involves no breach of the obligations of Her Britannic Majesty under article 10 of the Treaty of Utrecht and does not impose on her any obligation to surrender the territory to the King of Spain.

(3) Further constitutional development in Gibraltar would not raise any question under the Treaty unless it were proposed to introduce legislation providing that Gibraltar should cease to be one of the dominions of the Crown. I should, however, prefer to see the opinion of an international lawyer if it were proposed to confer independence, within or without the Commonwealth, on Gibraltar.

SECTION D: MALAYA

Jennings records in his notes that the future Malayan Prime Minister, Tunku Abdul Rahman, a contemporary of his from St Catharine's College, Cambridge, asked him informally (and later formally through the Colonial Secretary) in February 1956 whether he would join the Malayan Constitutional Commission. The five-member Commission, drawn from the Commonwealth, was headed by Lord Reid and became known as the Reid Commission. The Commission was formally tasked by the Queen and the Malayan Rulers to recommend a constitution for an independent Malaya, following agreements in London in early 1956 between representatives of the British Government, the Malayan Rulers, and local political parties. The independent Federation of Malaya came into being on 31 August 1957. The Reid Report was published as *Report of the Federation of Malaya Constitutional Commission 1957*, Cmnd 330 (London, 1957).

1. The 'Malayan Saga': diary from the Reid Commission, 1956–1957

Thursday, 21st June 1956, Kuala Lumpur

Lord Reid[1] left England by sea on the 9th May, or thereabouts, and arrived in K.L.[2] on the 31st May. He was accompanied by Lady Reid, who refuses to travel by air and who is therefore going to be something of a nuisance. Hall,[3] the Secretary, came out by air in time to meet Lord Reid – he refused a pressing invitation to go in the same ship. Len[4] and I left on the 12th June and arrived on the 14th. Sheikh Abdul Hamid[5] had left Karachi a couple of days earlier, was

[1] William Reid, Baron Reid. British Lord of Appeal in Ordinary and former Solicitor-General of Scotland.

[2] Kuala Lumpur.

[3] H.P. Hall, Secretary to the Commission.

[4] Helena, Lady Jennings (his wife).

[5] Justice Abdul Hamid was a Pakistani judge who had also been Secretary to the Law Ministry of West Pakistan; a member of the Commission.

in Singapore on the 14th, and came to K.L. on the 15th. Sir William McKell[6] reached Singapore on the 16th and K.L. on the 18th. Our Indian colleague was not appointed until the 19th + has not yet arrived.

Lord and Lady Reid refused to stay in a chalet, like the rest of us, but insisted on having a house. It was not ready for them when they arrived, and they were invited to stay at King's House, which they refused to do, perhaps rather brusquely. The rest of us are housed – with Keith Henderson, the Assistant Secretary from the M.C.S.[7] and Mrs Stephenson, the stenographer, in very comfortable chalets in Lake View Road. We are well fed at a mess in another chalet. Lord Reid's theory is that he can entertain better in a house, and no doubt it is correct; but it does mean that the rest of us see a great deal of each other and very little of Lord Reid. He was eventually given a furnished house temporarily and is moving in today. He has seen each of us individually at coffee or tea, and we have had meetings on three mornings this week. We have also seen H.E. (MacGillivray[8]) individually, while Hamid and I called upon the Tunku[9] for tea (and drinks).

Kuala Lumpur, Monday 25th June 1956

Our Indian colleague, Mallick or Malik[10] (I have not seen the name in print) is due to arrive on the 29th, + we leave for Johor Bahru on the 2nd of July. Lord (or Lady) Reid had arranged to go to Johor by train "to see the country". I at once spoke up and said that train journeys bored me and that I preferred to travel by air. The result is that all of us (except McKell who is going by car and Lord and Lady Reid) are going to Singapore by air + will go to Johor Bahru by car on the 3rd. I think most of us are spending the night of the 5th in Singapore + returning by air on the 6th; while Lord + Lady Reid will return by the night train.

[6] Sir William McKell came from Australia, where he had been the Labor Premier of New South Wales and Governor-General, 1947–1953; a member of the Commission.

[7] Malayan Civil Service.

[8] Sir Donald MacGillivray, the last British High Commissioner in Malaya. The office of High Commissioner was the highest British position in the Colonial Administration of Malaya.

[9] Tunku Abdul Rahman, United Malays National Organisation politician; Chief Minister of the Malayan Federation from 1955; Prime Minister, 1957–1970. He was often referred to as 'the Tunku', which is a Malayan title of nobility.

[10] Justice B. Malik, a member of the Reid Commission, had been Chief Justice of the Allahabad High Court in India.

There has also been some conflict over the length of our stay here. Lord (or Lady) Reid has decided to stay until the Report is completed, though he is willing to allow any of us to spend a couple of weeks elsewhere – he (or she) is thinking of a visit to Hong Kong. He told Hall that he did not intend to spend the winter in England. Abdul Hamid + I are clear that we must have a library at hand; and anyhow there is at present no justification whatever for Trinity Hall and the R.C. on Common Land[11] being deprived of my services for three months. McKell is not so positive, but thinks we ought to leave Malaya. Lady Reid's anxiety to preserve Lord Reid's health and strength is commendable: but such questions as we are discussing ought to be settled on principle. I have already cancelled my brief for the Nigerian Constitutional Conference, and so I stood to gain nothing personally by going home. Lord Reid is also proving difficult in other directions. So far, we have met almost nobody, because nobody is doing the organisation which O.E.G.[12] undertook for the Soulbury Commission. Accordingly, Hall arranged a cocktail party at the Chief Secretary's on Friday, when we met some senior officials, and had persuaded James to enable us to meet some Chinese next Friday. Lord Reid took exception to the latter because he had not met the Chinese Ministers, and anyhow he objects to cocktail parties. I tried to keep the Friday engagement going, but Lord Reid was adamant, and eventually Hall decided to drop the idea. On the other hand, I said plainly that I liked cocktail parties because we did meet people, and one invitation led to another. What the deuce is the good of our sitting in our chalets reading papers, when the Malayans are all around us? The difficulty, of course, is the shyness of the Malays; but ought this to stop us from meeting Chinese, Indians + Ceylonese? What Lord Reid is doing with his time I do not know, for Hamid and I are doing all the work, while McKell [is] lunching + dining with all the Australians. I suspect that much of the trouble stems from Lady Reid, who is the eminence grise of the Commission. Anyhow Lord Reid invited McKell to tea tonight: presumably he intends to talk him over. Perhaps he forgets that McKell represents Australian Labour [*sic*], and anyhow we Asians have a majority, if only Mallick (or Malik) will play.

The Canadian has dropped out. He wanted to bring a wife and five children. In the [*illegible*], difficulties were raised, especially as he is not so very eminent. He has now withdrawn on "medical grounds", and we have been informed, unofficially, that Canada does not intend to

[11] Jennings was also chairing the Royal Commission on Common Land.

[12] Sir Oliver E. Goonetilleke. See p. 19, n. 2.

replace him owing to the delay involved. We shall therefore be fully constituted on Friday, when the Indian turns up.

K.L. Friday, 29th June.

What a crafty old man he his! We worked out a programme of visits to the States and Settlements and gave it to the press. We – McKell, Hamid and I – had some suspicion that Reid was trying to spin it out, and we left for later decision whether it should end on Sept. 8th or Sept. 15th. A slight modification of the second visit, to the west coast, proved to be necessary – it had to be Perak, Kedah, Perlis and Penang instead of Perak, Penang, Kedah and Perlis – but this caused no difficulty. This morning Lord Reid said that he had been thinking it over, and perhaps a few days between Perlis and Penang would be helpful. We had some discussion about duties, but made no difficulty about meeting Reid's point, McKell very clearly saying that this would not affect the date on which we finished taking evidence. At lunch today, Hall told us that Reid had lengthened the Perak–Kedah–Perlis trip by two days, and extended from three days to five days the interval between Perlis and Penang, with the consequence that we should almost certainly have no time to take K.L. evidence, which would be much the most important, until after the return from the east coast on Sept. 8th or 15th. In other words he had (without consulting his colleagues) sought to put us in the position of lengthening the taking of evidence perhaps by as much as two weeks!

We discussed the matter at lunch and asked Henderson to hold up action until we met again tomorrow. Since he is due to go to Johor on Sunday (1st July), Henderson was reluctant, but finally decided that he should come with me to see Lord Reid this evening. I had given Lord Reid a note showing my engagements in October, November and December and making it plain that I could not stay in Malaya until Christmas, without referring the matter to the P.M. to decide whether I should resign from the Malayan Commission or from the Common Land Commission. Lord Reid had (after going home + presumably consulting Lady Reid) phoned for me to go out to his house this evening to talk things over "informally".

We spent no less time than two hours on the west coast towns, Lord Reid using all the tricks of the small town lawyer. For instance, at one point he went off on an irrelevancy for 30 minutes, coming back eventually to the point in which I was plainly striking. Eventually I agreed to one extra day in the Perak–Kedah–Perlis tour, an extra night at Maxwell's Hill on the ground that Lord Reid was an old man and could not put up with the bother of both unpacking and packing for one night only! We should, however, leave for Penang on the 1st (instead of 31st as decided by the Commission and 5th as decided by Lord Reid). Having lost the point, Lord Reid proceeded to hammer his chair for Henderson's benefit, saying that this must be done and that must be done. Henderson kept his [*illegible*] admirably, but was extremely angry about it nevertheless.

That left 30 minutes for my little business, but anyhow I was on solid ground and refused to give way. He demanded to leave the question open until early August, but it is quite plain that he has no intention of giving way. He intended to stay in Malaya until Christmas, and I would guess – though in this I have no evidence – that he intends to plead exhaustion at the end of it, to ask the Lord Chancellor for leave, and so avoid going back to Europe until the spring.

Only Henderson was in to dinner (the others had gone to the Chinese dinner which Lord Reid had refused to attend and from which accordingly I was excluded so as not to make it a rebellion) and got some amusement out of it. They really are an incredible couple, with a truly magnificent effrontery. They have not only mutually appropriated one of the cars, but are now trying to appropriate Majid, our A.S.P.[13] liaison officer, as their own A.D.C.[14] They are having special notepaper printed – they cannot use office paper like the rest of us – with the coronet of a life peer. Last night we had a buffet dinner at King's House[15] to meet the Rulers. At the end our cars were the last to be drawn up. Lady Reid was fuming, said it was a deliberate insult, and so forth.

All this is extremely petty, but clearly the Reids are on the make. My only concern is to get the job done quickly so as to get on with another job. I find the constant appeal to his age rather distasteful. McKell is at least as old, but he makes no song + dance about it. Malik arrived tonight, but I have not seen him yet. No doubt he was tired after his long journey – he has come right through – and wanted a quick dinner and a long sleep.

K.L. Wednesday, 18th July 1956.

We have done astonishingly little in the last three weeks. We had a useful three days in Johor, when we really did get down to brass tacks. McKell, Len + I stayed with the B.A.,[16] A.S. Sommerville, who was not only a pleasant host but also told us a great deal about the problems of the country. Lady Reid managed to put her foot into it at a dinner on the night of the 3rd. Sitting next to the B.A., she pointed out that the

[13] Assistant superintendent of police.
[14] Aide-de-camp.
[15] The official residence of the British High Commissioner.
[16] British agent.

card marking her place should have shown "The Lady Reid" and not "Lady Reid". The B.A. was furious; but I consoled him the next day by pointing out that the Tunku Mahkota[17] made the same blunder.

The whole party except Lord + Lady Reid (who returned by train on the night of the 5th) and Henderson (who returned by car the same day) stayed the week-end in Singapore, mostly shopping, though Len + I had lunch with the Commissioner-General (Sir Robert Scott[18]) + C.S. (Goode[19]) dined with Jumabhoy[20] (Minister of Commerce – Hamid + Malik were also present). We saw something of Selangor State Administration on the 9th. On the 10th the whole party went to inspect a rubber estate + had lunch with our host (Campbell). Afterwards we went down the Selangor River by launch + had tea with the D.O.[21] at Kuala Selangor. It was an interesting trip, marred by one incident only. Mrs Stephenson was taking a photograph of us on the launch when Lord + Lady Reid (who had stayed below while we jolly sailor boys were sitting up aloft) came up. Naturally, Mrs S. included Lord + Lady Reid in the next photograph. Lady Reid remarked to Hamid that she objected to being photographed without her permission. Afterwards Lady Reid made the same remark to Mrs S., + told Hall that she thought "the staff" were taking part in too many outings.

Since our return from Johor, Lord + Lady Reid have entertained McKell, Hamid + Malik to lunch or dinner. The idea was, evidently, to talk them into staying in Malaysia, or alternatively moving to India (Bangalore + Ootacamund were discussed). Malik dined on the night of the 12th whereupon Lord Reid raised the question at our meeting on the 13th. He asked me immediately before the meeting whether I would have any objection to the question being discussed. I replied, of course, that I had not: and as a matter of fact I had prepared a list of dates so as to be able to present my case if need be. It is, however, a little distressing to find oneself believing that Lord Reid raised this question without notice because it enabled him to think out his tactics + prevented me from doing so. Anyhow the tactics failed. It was agreed tentatively – Lord Reid refused to take anything like a firm decision – that we should leave by the S.S. Victoria on the 1st October + stay either at Geneva or on the French Riviera. This would enable us to discuss the lines of our report on board ship. We would complete our

[17] The Crown Prince of Johor.

[18] British Commissioner-General of South-East Asia.

[19] (Later Sir) William Goode, Chief Secretary of Singapore, 1953–1957; Governor of Singapore, 1957–1959.

[20] J.M. Jumabhoy, Labour Front Singaporean Cabinet Minister.

[21] District officer.

report and then return to Malaya for the signature. On the latter point McKell supported Lord Reid, though the rest of us thought it a waste of time. Nevertheless, Lord Reid was not defeated. He asked Henderson to ascertain whether accommodation was available on the ship + asked Hall to prepare an estimate of cost + ascertain whether the Federation Government objected to our going outside the sterling area.

What is more, Lord Reid saw Watherston[22] on the 14th, though he did not tell us he was going to do so; nor has he (so far) reported back to us. In point of fact, W. did his best to persuade Lord Reid that there was no need for us to come back. I am told, in fact, that the whole question is being raised in Ex. Co.[23] this evening (this is being written at 4 a.m. on the 18th – "this evening" means the evening of the 17th).

Meanwhile, Lord Reid dropped a bombshell this (17th) morning. He has, without consulting us, informed the C.O.[24] that Hall is inefficient and that for personal reasons he, Lord Reid, finds it impossible to work with him; and accordingly that another secretary must be sent out. The rest of us (we discussed it at lunch) had no evidence of inefficiency, and we were not told what were the personal reasons. Naturally we could not take exception to what had been done: we were not asked for our opinion and anyhow we were faced by a fait accompli. We have not discussed it with Hall, nor has Hall discussed it with any of us; but I stated at lunch that if the C.O. asked for my view – and I would tell Hall that I was ready to be invited – I would say what I could in his favour. Obviously failure to work with a Commission would mar Hall's chances of promotion.

K.L., Friday 3rd August 1956.

We left for Ipoh by train on the 19th July and stayed there until the 22nd – Len and I with A.G. Argent, State Financial Officer. We dined with the B.A. (Ballock) on the 21st – I had stayed with them when he was a comparatively junior officer in Ipoh in 1947. On the 22nd we went by road to Kuala Kangsar, where we inspected the Malay College and had lunch with the Sultan of Perak. Then to Taiping by road where we had tea with the D.O. Then up Maxwell's Hill, when Lord + Lady Reid could be persuaded to get into the land-rover. He had imagined a sort of limousine, and he cannot be persuaded even now that he travelled in a land-rover and not a jeep. To climb 4000 feet in 20 minutes, even in the most comfortable conditions, is no joke. Moreover, there was a fairly steep walk at the Box. In the end Lady

[22] (Later Sir) David Watherston, Chief Secretary of Malaya, 1952–1957.
[23] Executive Council.
[24] Colonial Office.

Reid almost collapsed, and they demanded not to go down to Taiping next day. Malik, who stayed with them, but who created a furore by getting "lost" in his room (Lord Reid did not know he had arrived) also stayed [*sic*]. McKell and Hamid were very uncomfortable in Hugh Dow's + decided not to come back next day. In the end only Len + I, Hall and Mrs Stephenson went down and up next day, while McKell, Hamid + I [*sic*] did the honours for the Commission in Taiping next day. This was an advantage, for we did it better than Lord Reid (who is an inefficient chairman) could have done it.

We moved on to the Alor Setar by road on the 24th. Lady Reid was quite ill, + went straight to bed when she got to the B.A.s at Alor Setar. She stayed in bed until the 26th, when she went down to lunch and dined with the B.A. When the B.A.'s wife went in to introduce the doctor, Lady Reid remarked "I don't want to see any books, please leave the room". She also asked for lemon sole, with the result that the B.A.'s wife had to drive to the cold store and then get her cook back from the Istana,[25] since he had been borrowed by the Sultan of Kedah. We stayed with Hill and his wife + were very comfortable.

At Alor Setar the dispute between Lord Reid + Hall came to a head. Lord Reid was angry over Maxwell's Hill (though he had insisted upon it), but anyhow Hall had been uncooperative generally, + there were times when they bit each other's noses off. Lord Reid consulted each of us separately, + we agreed that Hall had better be replaced. Hall was exceedingly angry + threatened that all four (Hall, Henderson, Majid + Mrs Stephenson) would resign. In the end Hall phoned Watherston (Chief Secretary) + asked permission to go home. Lord Reid let him go, but he turned up in K.L. when we returned. The rest of us discussed the matter afterwards + found that none of us had got on very well with Hall. We are of course a difficult Commission + to meet the needs of five of us, with two wives, is no easy matter. On the other hand, Henderson managed to live with us, though Hall did not. Lord Reid said he was always surly; McKell said he always had "a chip on the shoulder"; my remark was that he thought the Commission would be an excellent body if there were no Commissioners. Possibly he was too senior an officer. As he said himself, if he had been on tour by himself he would always have stayed with the B.A.; going round with us he was simply part of "the staff". He tended to think that, as representative of the C.O., he should give instructions to, or at least guide, us; we actually gave him instructions. Each of us had minor grievances against him, too trivial to be mentioned to anybody until we expressed opinions about Lord Reid's actions, when we told each other. I suppose there is some difference between this commission

[25] Palace.

and the R.C. on Common Land. We are being paid for the job, though at nothing like professional rates, whereas the R.C.C.L.[26] are giving their services to H.M. and therefore have to be treated with considerable deference by the representatives of H.M.G.[27] With Hall it seemed to be rather more than lack of deference. Henderson said that we all expected individual attention, and that is perhaps true; but quite often Hall's response to a request was a [*illegible*]. We could have carried on, however, if a first-class row had not developed between Hall and Lord Reid.

On the 27th July we went on to Kangar by road, where Hamid, Len + I stayed with J. Haner, the B.A., in pretty rough conditions, though hospitality made up for deficiencies in accommodation. McKell + Malik were at the Resthouse, but never took a meal there apart from breakfast, because Mrs H. filled the only gap in our public functions, took us all to the Seremban traders, etc. Indeed, we thoroughly enjoyed both Kedah + Perlis. We returned to Alor Setar by road on the 29th + thence to K.L. by air. Hall, to our surprise, met us at the airport. Watherston had told him to stay around until he and McGillivray had talked the matter over with Lord Reid. Hall left on the 1st August. Henderson has been acting Sec., with an M.C.S. officer as acting asst. sec.

On Tuesday, 31st July [1956], we drove to Seremban + back, without Lord + Lady Reid, Lord Reid having a cold (probably collected on Maxwell's Hill). It was a pleasant journey, and not too heavy a day. For the rest of the week we have been taking evidence from officials. On the working of the present Constn.[28] we are beginning to see daylight, though as yet we have no formulated ideas on the new arrangements.

<u>K.L. Sunday 12th August.</u> We have all settled down and there have been no major incidents on the Penang tour, where the Reids stayed with the Judge, McKell + Malik with the Resident (Bingham) and Len + I with the President of the Municipal Council (Cunningham-Brown): Hamid was housed with Sir T. Ariff, a prominent Malay. There was some sort of a row – Hamid says he was asked to share a room with another guest and to share a bathroom with five others – and Hamid left for the hotel, where he was joined by Mrs + Miss Hamid. The rest of us were very comfortable + our relations among ourselves + with the staff have been cordial.

For the time being, at least, our problems have been solved. Hall has gone, though the C.O. seems to be taking his view and there is some

[26] Royal Commission on Common Land.
[27] Her Majesty's Government.
[28] Constitution.

polite but rather frigid correspondence going on which I have not seen. One Laird, of the M.C.S.,[29] is to be our secretary, and Henderson has been acting. Mrs Stephenson has been (or is about to be) paid off and sent home. She was a buddy of Hall's and was supposed to be our private secretary, though Hall introduced her to Lord Reid as "my private secretary"; and, in fact, when we applied for her services we were snubbed. Since Hall had handed over all arrangements to Henderson, Mrs S. had little to do except to come to functions with us, where she managed to annoy Len as well as Lady Reid by being "pushy". Henderson himself suggested that she should be paid off + this was agreed. I hope we can move into her chalet. Henderson, Hall and Mrs S. took the three best chalets and sorted out the furniture to suit themselves. McKell has now moved into Hall's and Malik into McKell's.

Meanwhile Majid has been pretty well devoted to the Reids, while a [*illegible*] named Henry has taken over the tours from Henderson. We had a temporary asst. sec. last week, but he will be unnecessary when we have Laird as sec.

Lady Reid is still hankering after Hong Kong – I suggested that she go by herself when Len goes to Canberra on the 6th October but she said that "Scott" could not look after himself. (Actually, he is much more amenable when he is not under discipline. When we were dining with the M.C.A.[30] in Penang on the 10th she got up from her table, walked across to his, and told him audibly not to "drink too much". Afterwards she said to me that she hoped he did not say too much, because they had been "plying him with drink all the evening". After a Chinese had read us a paper and we were talking she came up and said "Come along, Scott, we must go home now". This is not henpecking but lionessing.) We have, however, compromised. The Reids are staying until the 1st November and are then leaving on the "Asia" with McKell + Malik. Len will leave for Canberra on the 6th October and will join us in Europe. I leave for Cambridge on the 26th October + Hamid (who will take his family to Karachi) will join me early in November. The arrangement was that we should meet in Rome (I suggested Geneva but the Reids preferred Rome) on the 21st November; but Hall has been at the C.O. + Malta has been suggested as a compromise. We have replied that we are willing to go to Malta if the C.O. insists, but would prefer Rome, + anyhow Malta would make things more difficult for me. The C.O. also says it wants the Report by December, when the S. of S.[31] meets the Tunku.

[29] E.O. Laird of the Malayan Civil Service.
[30] Malayan Chinese Association.
[31] Secretary of State.

This is clearly an afterthought suggested by Hall who had (as I think correctly) strong views about the suggestion that we return to K.L. to present the report. Actually I think that proposal is dead. Though Lady Reid has not given up hopes of Hong Kong, the Tunku would not play. The Reids had him to dinner + plied him with brandy; but he was cagy + said that he did not mind where the report was signed. Nothing further has been said about returning, + anyhow I shall plead other engagements. Possibly our discussions in Rome (or Malta) will be prolonged, for we do very little at conferences except listen to Lord Reid's speeches; but I do not mind staying in Rome (or even Malta) for most of the winter, provided that I can make frequent visits to England – though it could be said to be a waste of public money.

Anyhow, with the date fixed for my return to Cambridge, I have not quarrelled with the changes of programme, though I have expressed the hope that we could spend a full month in taking decisions before Hamid + I leave. I have even agreed, reluctantly, to a week-end on Fraser's Hill.

Sat. 8th September 1956, Kuala Lumpur.

In the end, only Malik went to Fraser's Hill with Lord and Lady Reid yesterday, though Majid is in attendance. They have three cars only – leaving the Austin and a hired car with the McKells and us. The Austin broke down this morning, + so we have only the hired car, which will presumably take us to Port Dixon for the week-end. The McKells will therefore have to use a taxi, if they can find one. They are going to Penang by the night train. The Hamids have slipped off somewhere – possibly to Singapore – without telling us where.

As a Commission, we have done very little since we returned from Penang. We have completed the taking of evidence because, in the end, there was little that mattered. The Chinese organisations of all kinds used a standard formula, with some variations of detail, based on the need for "equality" and "justice", while the Malays (of whom there were few) say this is their country + that if they give anything at all to the Chinese it will be because of their kindness and generosity. We are having communal [*illegible*] for the Rulers next week, go to Kelantan and Trengganu in the following week, and receive the [*illegible*] which will be the [*illegible*] document, on our return.

Meanwhile some of us (Hamid + I especially, though Malik + McKell have also done some work) have got down to brass tacks + are having concerns. We are upset by Lawson's[32] argument – in

[32] Rulers' Counsel, Neil Lawson QC.

instructions from the Rulers – that self-government in the States can be postponed at the will of the Rulers until the States are "ready" for it.

Rome 20th January 1957

I left K.L. on the 26th October and, in spite of the riots, Singapore on the 27th, + owing to the Suez troubles,[33] we were delayed at Karachi until the 28th, got through Cairo on the 29th + returned to England that evening. Hamid had gone to Karachi the day before. The others were delayed in K.L. by the riots in Singapore, but got away on the "Asia" on the 2nd November. Malik + the McKells disembarked at Bombay and arrived in Rome about the 22nd November. Henderson disembarked at Karachi and flew straight to Rome. The Reids and Laird went round the Cape and reached Rome on the 8th December, having compiled a large part of the first draft of the Report.

On the way home I had put the various drafts together and filled up most of the gaps. Claire began typing further notes, and on the 2nd November I was able to give the First Draft to the Press. They did a magnificent job and let me have copies on the 5th. Hamid not having arrived, I did some rapid corrections, sent the Second Draft to the Press on the 7th, + received copies back on the 9th. Hamid had arrived on the night of the 7th + he spent the next week in going through the Second Draft at his rather leisurely pace.

In the following week we went through his corrections. It took us rather a time because he seldom began work before 11 a.m., knocked off from 1 p.m. to 2.15 p.m., + finished at 4.30 p.m. However, we finished about the 22nd November and he left soon afterwards for sight-seeing in London, Paris, Berne and Geneva, arriving in Rome about the 9th December. I saw the Third Draft through the Press, and Claire, Helena and I left by train on the 9th December, arriving on the 10th. Helena had returned from Canberra a couple of weeks before.

The Third Draft was not entirely agreed. We differed on almost 20 points, none of them of first-class importance, + I suggested that they be left to the Commission to settle. We had, however, produced an agreed draft of the most contentious provisions on Malay Reservations and Malay Quotas. Our relations were very happy, and I think Hamid enjoyed Cambridge in general and Trinity Hall in particular. He struck

[33] Britain, France, and Israel occupied the Suez canal through military action in October 1956.

up a particular friendship with Louis Clarke and T. Ellis Lewis,[34] an odd combination.

In Rome we began consideration of the Third Draft on the 12th December, in the hope of finishing it before I went to England, for the Royal Commission on Common Land, on the 7th January. We got on quite well up to Christmas. Laird and Henderson then went to spend Christmas with their families in England. Accordingly, Helena, Claire + I went to Malta, the McKells to Tanzania, and Malik and Hamid to Spain. On our return I was given a sitting room, which helped enormously. I had been doing all the drafting in a small bedroom in the Eden Hotel, which was difficult because I could not work in the small room without waking Helena. After Christmas, however, Hamid turned cantankerous. There were several difficulties. First, we were working from 9 a.m. to 5 p.m. at [*illegible*]., with a break for lunch; and this gave Hamid no time for exercise. In Cambridge he walked for an hour every morning, had breakfast at 10 a.m., then had his bath, and started work at 11 a.m. In Rome he ate a very large dinner + took no exercise in the morning. Very soon he was not sleeping well. Another difficulty, though he never mentioned it, was that on nearly all points the Commission agreed with me, or produced a compromise which I could accept, and accordingly I did all the drafting. He argued at great length on points which he thought to be points of principle, whereas we thought them trivial. Owing to his background, he thinks of federalism in terms of the Government of India Act, and the India and Pakistan Constitutions. Many of the precedents are of course not relevant to Malaya, and anyhow we did not think that we were bound by any drafting principles except those laid down by the Terms of Reference. Consequently, when he raised objections to a draft he was usually overruled by 4 to 1. He particularly took exception to criticism by Malik. There is no doubt that Malik is out of his intellectual environment. He is rather a stupid fellow, third class in ability and fourth in imagination. When he gets a point, therefore, he sticks to it with a pertinacity which equals Hamid's. I was Hamid's superior in Karachi and anyhow I try to treat him with special courtesy when we differ: but (quite rightly) he does not regard Malik as his intellectual superior or even as his equal, and he thought Malik objected because he disliked Muslims – which is, I believe, not true. Possibly, too, he was annoyed by the way in which Lord Reid supports Malik. Malik has made himself pleasant to Lady Reid – the rest of us find it difficult to do so – and Lord Reid is therefore prejudiced in Malik's favour. Accordingly, Hamid does not blame Lord Reid or me, but blames Malik, quite unjustifiably.

[34] Fellows of Trinity Hall.

Lord Reid himself has done a lot of work on the drafts and his criticisms are always acute. He is unfortunately prejudiced by an emotional sympathy with the Rulers; but he might not unreasonably complain that McKell and I have an emotional antipathy to the Rulers. I must confess that I have no very high opinion [of] Tunkus, except Abdul Rahman, who is noteworthy for his plain common sense. On these matters McKell supports me and I support him. Nevertheless, Lord Reid has been a most effective critic of my drafts, which have generally been improved by him. His draft Report, too, is very sensible, and I have not found much in it to criticise – though I have not done very much on the Report, because my main job has been to produce the Draft Constitution.

McKell is a Q.C. but no longer [practises], but he is too honest a person to claim that he is. His prejudices generally accord with mine, but in two respects he seems to me to have gone too far. First, he does not allow sufficiently for the enormous lack of personnel in Malaya, + therefore applies his democratic principles with too close an adherence to his Australian experience. Secondly, he has been too much impressed with economic problems and therefore has tried to make us lay down policy instead of letting us arrange political institutions so that the Malayans can determine policy. On the other hand, he is always ready for a sensible compromise, and I was able to meet him by National Development Plans (invented by me to meet McKell's very sensible observations) and by giving some unnecessary emphasis to some of his proposals about soil conservation and so forth. The Report may be thought to be a bit unbalanced, but it does show (on McKell's insistence) that we realise the fundamental economic problems.

Lord Reid appears likely to dissent on two points and McKell on two others. Malik + I, apparently, will not dissent. Exactly what Hamid will do I do not know. Claire has typed a long screed for him, which he has not yet allowed us to see; but fortunately Claire kept a copy in her drawer, and Lord Reid now has it. The only point of political importance on which Hamid dissents is on Malay Quotas. He has thrown overboard the compromise which I accepted in Cambridge + has produced a memorandum which will start a row in Malaya because it is really a criticism not only of the Alliance[35] but even of our terms of reference. Hamid has no political nous. He lives in a world of his own in which practical problems do not intrude. His paper on Malay Quotas which we have seen really suggests – though

[35] The political coalition that represented the three main political organizations (and communities): the United Malays National Organisation, the Malayan Chinese Association, and the Malayan Indian Congress.

he does not seem to realise it – that the whole business of granting independence to Malaya is absurd. If he believes his own statements he ought to have resigned months ago.

The rest of us, nevertheless, must go on. We plan to finish consideration of the Fourth Draft on Tuesday next, 22nd January, in order that I may do the cleaning up and send the text to England on the 24th. I should have gone myself on the 22nd in order to preside over the Royal Commission of Common Land, but at Lord Reid's request I have cabled to ask the vice-chairman to take over. We are not sitting on the 23rd and 24th so as to give Hamid time to amend his numerous dissenting notes – extending, I think to about 25 typed pages. He does not realise that, the more he dissents, the less attention will be paid to his observations. I have written a note on this dissent on Malay Quotas, but I do not propose that it be published. I merely hope to make [him] qualify his general, and often extreme statements: but the real solution is to make him dissent as often as possible so that nobody will pay attention to him.

Rome, 2nd February 1957.

When we met on the 21st January, we decided to give way to Hamid over Malay Quotas. Thereafter we got through quickly + finished on the morning of the 22nd. Claire + I spent a hectic day and a half getting the Draft Constitution straight, and it was sent off by the pilot of a B.O.A.C. plane on the 24th.

Hamid had another version of his dissent typed, + this time we insisted on getting copies, which we took home on the 25th. It was a shocker. Out of 26 criticisms of the Draft Constitution, 11 had never been mentioned to the Commission. He attacked us for giving preference to citizens of the U.K. (Art. 15). He threw overboard the compromises on Malay Reservations and Malay Quotas and insisted that the Yang and the Rulers must have discretionary powers to protect the Malays. He justified this part by reference to the Alliance, but mainly by a series of inflammatory appeals to racial prejudice which might even have started riots. He produced a demand for making Islam the State religion which he had emphatically condemned when we had considered the matter in October. On "Provincial Autonomy" he had twelve verbose papers, full of errors and misquotations which helped his argument and of dogmatic statements which nobody could justify. Then came a mass of detailed criticisms, some sensible, some stupid. A second version, equally bad, was circulated on the 28th.

On the 29th we had a meeting to consider this document. For the whole morning Lord Reid kept up the pressure, trying to persuade Hamid to cut out the worst bits. Hamid said he felt like a prisoner in the dock, but he was not really giving way. He admitted that on special positions of the Malays he was breaking an agreement with us, but he thought we ought to follow the Alliance, whose Memorandum he had since read. This was not true, actually; he was preparing his memo all the week and, I feel reasonably sure, had the most dangerous paragraphs in the paper which Claire had typed before he accepted our compromise, but he argued rather incautiously. The difference was that, while he was regarding himself as a hero and a martyr in the interests of the poor Malays, he was using crooked, or at least [*illegible*], methods. If we tried to treat him as a crook, his sense of dignity was affronted + we made him more obstinate and extreme. A good example was a phrase at the beginning which said in effect that he had failed to convince his learned colleagues. In eleven matters, including all except one of the politically controversial matters, he had not even tried. In relation to special positions, we had accepted his drafts, with minor modifications to which he had agreed. State religion he had not even mentioned after the meeting in October when he condemned the concept. His reply was that he was at that stage trying to convince, and the Report was not complete until it was signed. If necessary he was willing to sit for another month to improve the Draft Constitution. Hence when the Report appeared, he really will have tried to convince.

We thought we had made some impression during the morning, + therefore decided not to continue to press him during the afternoon, but I was to see him on the 30th to get some of the errors of fact and law removed. Hamid would then revise his Note and we would discuss it again. I did not raise the controversial issues with him on the 30th. I dealt especially with his Part II on "Provincial autonomy", trying to get him to explain his novel theory of federalism more clearly (in order that it might be plain to the reader that it was an idea invented by Hamid), to cut out the errors and misquotations (which were numerous) and generally to clean up a rather dirty piece of work. I did make some impression on him, though he did not accept all my suggestions and in particular he did not seriously cut down the enormous length of this Part.

Hamid had a "rough draft" of his revised note ready on the 1st February. I was allowed a copy because I was leaving for London on the 3rd. Lord Reid was given a copy by Laird without Hamid's permission. The new draft was better, but the worst purple patches had not been removed. At dinner I told Hamid that I was going to draft a violent attack on him as our draft reply to his Note, and that I was going to do it in defence of the people of Malaya, of the Federation Government, and in particular of my friend Tunku Abdul Rahman. Nevertheless, he was to remember that he was my brother, and that if he ever came to England he must come to see me at Trinity Hall.

Hamid seems to have been struck with this, for having been upstairs he came down again, sat with us in the lounge, and asked if he could see me in the morning to find out exactly what I meant. I told him then and there what I meant. His note was based on the theory that so long as the Malays were in power they would look after their own interests and when the Chinese acquired power they would look after their interests. This was exactly what the extreme Malays were saying, and accordingly the U.M.N.O.[36] was wrong to allow citizenship rights to the Chinese. It was also what the extreme Chinese were saying, they must have jus soli forthwith, and the M.C.A. was wrong to compromise on this issue. Hence his Note was an attack on the Alliance position from both sides. Their case was that in the course of a few years they could produce a "common nationality" and work a democratic system.

This morning at 9.30 a.m. (2nd Feb) Hamid said that he saw the force of my argument. If anything said by him were to prevent the people of Malaya from living and working together as a band of brothers he would be a very great sinner. He wanted to do everything he could to help, but he feared that it might not work, so he wanted some protection for the Malays, who have been very generous and deserved protection. Would I accept a two-thirds majority and ask Lord Reid to summon an immediate meeting of the Commission. He would then delete everything at [*sic*] Special Position and also – oddly enough – about Provincial Autonomy (This showed, incidentally, that Hamid's theory of federalism was stuff invented to protect the six States in which the Malays were in a majority against a Chinese majority in the Federation). I thought this blatant horse-trading and at first refused, suggesting that Hamid raise the matter when the Commission met on the 4th. Then I decided that perhaps we ought to see Lord Reid about it, + I phoned up.

Hamid put his point, + Lord Reid at once began the advocate's technique of talking at great length in order to think the situation out and see what exactly was in Hamid's mind. He saw no difficulty about Malay reservations or licences. What about scholarships? I said they did not matter much. We both felt very reluctant to tie up Malay quotas in the public services. However, we summoned McKell + Malik to a meeting at 11 a.m. As soon as Malik heard the proposition he appreciated that we were being blackmailed on behalf of the Malays: either give the Malays what Hamid thought they ought to have, or Hamid would publish and be damned. Malik therefore asked exactly

[36] United Malays National Organisation, the dominant political party of Malaya (and later Malaysia).

what we were being offered. Lord Reid took up the point + said he understood that Hamid was offering to remove all objectionable features, which he would define as pages 2–4, 5–8 and 10–22. Malik then said he would prefer to have a discretionary power vested in the Yang because a 2/3 majority would tie up the position for all time. Lord Reid, McKell + I were against this, and eventually Malik agreed so far as Malay Reservations were concerned, because these were determined by law. He did not agree as to Quotas. (He told me afterwards that he would have agreed in the end, since like me he had decided not to dissent). I then asked Hamid if he was prepared to risk a riot by inserting all this political dynamite merely for a few quotas. Lord Reid broke in and said: "Hamid, do you realise that if this goes in the blood of thousands of people may be on your hands? Will you not remove all this and merely express your dissent on Quotas on the simple basis that you do not think the protection goes far enough?" Hamid said he would accept that, whereupon Lord Reid started to try to draft, but Hamid refused this ploy. He said he would go away and produce a draft on Tuesday (5th Feb.). Lord Reid persisted for some time, but Hamid held out, + eventually it was left on that basis.

Rome, Monday 11th February 1957

I left for England early on the 3rd. On the 2nd we dined with the Indian Charge d'Affaires (a Hall[37] man), Hamid not being present. Before I left Hamid asked if he could come along + see the new draft of Article 82.[38] I said I was dressing + going out to dinner, but I told him what I was putting in. He said it was not enough. He wanted an absolute majority + 2/3 present + voting. He asked me to see Lord Reid about it. I said I was going out to dinner + anyhow if he wanted something changed he had better see Lord Reid. He replied that Lord Reid had called him a murderer, and he (Hamid) was going to complain to his Prime Minister, with the request that he pass the complaint to the P.M. of the U.K. I said it was nothing to do with me, + anyhow I was going to England.

The proof of the Final Draft was awaiting me at Trinity Hall. I worked hard at it, finishing at 9.30 a.m. on Monday, 4th Feb. That completed my job, + glad I was to get it finished. 60 copies (20 bound in cloth + 40 bound in paper) were delivered to the Hall on the 9th. I brought them back on the 10th.

Meanwhile Hamid's draft was circulated on the 4th. It still contained a lot of inflammatory material + so the Commission sat down and deleted all the objectionable phrases. Lord Reid was now

[37] Trinity Hall.

[38] The article concerning conditions of preventative detention.

in a strong position, + Hamid's only remedy was to resign + publish in Pakistan, while we would publish the complete story if he did. He therefore gave way, + the dissent as published is pretty innocuous. Hamid still appears as the protector of the Malays and as a superior draughtsman who has been overruled by a lot of amateurs, especially Jennings. I have drafted a reply to some of his points, which I will send to the Tunku. I have not answered his criticisms of my drafting, silence being more dignified.

We signed the Report at 6 p.m. on the 10th (McKell was absent, but he signed it after the Opera) and we had a drink on Lord Reid. Laird left for Kuala Lumpur at 4 a.m. today, taking 10 bound copies + 40 paper-covered copies. Lord + Lady Reid gave us lunch at the Hostaria dell'Oro today. Hamid + Malik are leaving tomorrow (12th). The McKells and Jennings leave on the 13th. The Reids leave for Sicily for 2 weeks holiday on the 14th. So endeth another job.

Hamid's behaviour was, I think, another case of mixed motives:

(1) He did not like the way that he was put into a minority of one, + perhaps the way in which he treated his "Provincial autonomy" as a bit of a joke.

(2) He thought that his principal opponent was Malik, who was against Pakistan politically.

(3) He disliked the way in which I took over the drafting in Rome, though the fact was that he could not keep pace with me and I cared not to go at his pace.

(4) He saw himself as the protector of the Malays, + he feared that he would be found to have been too ready to compromise.

(5) He wanted to disassociate himself from the draft, in case it was criticised.

I still doubt if he realises that he has blackmailed us; + everybody else still feels doubtful about it. Probably he is very stupid, and he has no idea how other people's minds work; but somehow he does not seem to be quite the confidence-trickster that his actions suggest. True it is that, having accepted a compromise on the 21st January, he produced a complete denial of that compromise on the 25th; true it is that he had that denial in draft on the 21st.; true it is that, basing himself on the Alliance proposal, he asked for much more in practice + was ready to accept a proposal which the Alliance did not suggest (in other words, his reliance on the Alliance was eye-wash); true it is that he insisted on keeping inflammatory material in when he knew our strong view that it might cause a riot and would undoubtedly do great harm; true it is that he does not believe in State religions, said so emphatically in October, and yet advised it in January; true it is that he insists upon criticising my drafting although he calls us "brothers"; true it is that he accused us by innuendo of various things that we obviously were not supporting; and so forth. Even so, I do not think he is a crook. I suspect he is merely stupid. There are, too, other factors. He was obviously eating too much, especially of fats, and was unable to sleep; he felt that his hotel accommodation was inadequate to his station (he told McKell that he was an "untouchable").

Even so, we have managed to avoid a row; and so far as I am concerned he is still very friendly. I hope nevertheless that I shall never have to work with him again, for I think him stupid + shall always suspect his motives.

2. 'Constitutional Changes Implicit in the Terms of Reference' of the Reid Commission, 23 August 1956

(1) "A single, independent, self-governing unit within the Commonwealth"

This phrase implies that the Federation of Malaya, must be equated with Canada, Australia, New Zealand, South Africa, India, Pakistan and Ceylon. The Federation differs from these countries in that they were, except for the Indian States[39] which acceded to India and Pakistan, parts of Her Majesty's dominions, whereas in the Federation only the Settlements[40] are parts of those dominions. On the other hand, India and Pakistan were created under provisional constitutions with Governors-General and Constituent Assemblies and have now become republics under permanent Constitutions, so that both countries have ceased to be parts of Her Majesty's dominions.

The Settlements are colonies governed under the authority of Her Majesty in Council, which in effect means under the authority of Her Majesty's Government in the United Kingdom. Persons born therein, and the children of persons born therein, are both British subjects (or Commonwealth citizens) and citizens of the United Kingdom and Colonies. It will be necessary, as a minimum:

[39]The Indian Princely States were formally separate from British India and in the run-up to British withdrawal in August 1947 were given the choice to accede to either the Dominion of India or the Dominion of Pakistan. Malaya also had states not under direct British rule headed by indigenous rulers and, like the Indian Princely States, their powers were subject to British approval in practice.

[40]This refers to the Straits Settlements comprising of Penang and Malacca, which were formally British colonial territories and together with the nine Malay States from 1948 made the Federation of Malaya. They were later joined in 1963 by Singapore (briefly), Sabah, and Sarawak.

(i) to remove the responsibility of Her Majesty's Government in the United Kingdom for the government of the Settlements, as was done by the Indian Independence Act and the Ceylon Independence Act;

(ii) to remove the Settlements from the definition of "Colony" in the Interpretation Act (as was done by the Ceylon Independence Act) and to repeal the Straits Settlements (Repeal) Act, in so far as it applies to Penang and Malacca;

(iii) to repeal the Colonial Laws Validity Act, 1865, in so far as it applies to the Settlements, and to provide that the appropriate legislature in the Federation may repeal or amend any Act of the Parliament of the United Kingdom applying to either Settlement as part of its law (as was done by the Ceylon Independence Act and, in part, by the Indian Independence Act);

(iv) to repeal certain provisions of the legislation of the United Kingdom which at present apply to Penang and Malacca as colonies; and

(v) to remove federal citizens from the category of citizens of the United Kingdom and Colonies and to abolish the power of the Secretary of State to naturalise federal citizens.

The States are not parts of Her Majesty's dominions; and the subjects of Their Highnesses the Rulers are, generally speaking, neither British subjects nor citizens of the United Kingdom and Colonies, but British protected persons. No legislation is needed, except to bring the Federation within the Commonwealth as an independent unit. This would imply the recognition of the Queen either as Queen of Malaya or as Head of the Commonwealth. The latter, which would equate the Federation with India and Pakistan, would probably be preferred, though Her Majesty would remain Queen in Penang and Malacca unless she were willing to surrender her title. Further, it would be necessary to equate the Federation with India, Pakistan and Ceylon by giving federal citizens the status of British subjects or Commonwealth citizens in other Commonwealth countries. So far as the United Kingdom was concerned, this would involve substituting the phrase "Ceylon and the Federation of Malaya" for "Ceylon" in Section 1(3) of the British Nationality Act, 1948. A provision corresponding with that section, or with the appropriate provision in the Constitution of India, would be required in the Federal Constitution.

Other external aspects of independent status, such as membership of the United Nations and of the Conference of Commonwealth

Prime Ministers, would require no constitutional changes. It would be necessary, however, to produce a completely new Federal Constitution. The High Commissioner, as a part of the constitutional machine (the other Commonwealth countries would no doubt wish to exchange High Commissioners with the Federation, but they would have purely diplomatic functions) would disappear.[41] This disappearance would destroy the foundation of the present distribution of powers between the Federation and the States, since it depends on the overriding power of the High Commissioner – which is not the less effective because it has not been used. Also, the relations between the Federation and the Settlements depend upon the High Commissioner representing the Queen in all three. It would seem, too, (though the matter is not free from doubt) that most public officers are servants of the Crown, since they are appointed by the High Commissioner. Above all, the control of defence and external affairs will be transferred from the Queen to the Federation and the obligation of the Queen to defend the States, except by agreement, will disappear.

(2) "Based on Parliamentary democracy with a bicameral legislature"

This phrase implies the substitution for the High Commissioner in Legislative Council of a Parliament consisting of the Yang di-Pertuan Besar[42] and two Houses. It would be convenient, but not essential, for the First House to represent the people and to be called the House of the Raayat,[43] and the second to represent the States and Settlements and to be called the Chamber of States.[44] This Parliament would have the legislative power prescribed by a new Federation Agreement, but provisions would be necessary to settle disputes between the two Houses. Bills would be assented to by the Yang di-Pertuan Besar and not by the Queen and the Rulers.

Though the Parliament would be democratic, the existence in either House or both Houses (as in Ceylon, where it applies to both Houses) of a few nominated members with or without voting rights, would not be objectionable.

Though it is not expressly so provided, it is implicitly accepted that there should be a Prime Minister and other Ministers collectively

[41] Independent Commonwealth states are represented in Commonwealth states by a High Commissioner who heads the High Commission. The post of High Commissioner is purely a diplomatic post and very different from the colonial-era British High Commissioner in Malaya, who held executive and domestic powers within the Federation.

[42] The constitutional head of state of the Federation. The Yang di-Pertuan Besar (later renamed the Yang di-Pertuan Agung) is a constitutional monarch elected every five years by and from the hereditary rulers of the nine Malay States.

[43] Eventually called the Dewan Rakyat.

[44] Eventually called the Dewan Negara.

responsible to the First House of the legislature. They would be appointed by the Yang di-Pertuan Besar according to the state of parties in that House.

(3) "A strong Central Government with the States and Settlements enjoying a measure of autonomy"

This is the present position; but the present system, involving the execution by the States and Settlements of policies laid down by the Federal Government, could not apply in a federal system in which both the Federation and the States (and Settlements) would be fully democratic and might possess Governments from different political parties. It is, therefore, necessary to make a more precise division of powers, especially in respect of finance.

(4) "Machinery for consultation between the Central Government and the States and Settlements on certain financial matters"

This provision is no doubt a recognition that in respect of finance, at least, the present arrangements are unsatisfactory, or at least might become unsatisfactory if different parties were in control in the Federation and in one or more of the States and Settlements. No indication is given of the sort of machinery desired, but there are precedents in certain of the Commonwealth Constitutions which the framers of the terms of reference perhaps had in mind.

(5) "The safeguarding of the position and prestige of Their Highnesses the Rulers as constitutional Rulers of their respective States"

This clause has three aspects. First, it implies that the provisions of the State Constitutions relating to Their Highnesses, the succession to their thrones, and so forth, must be safeguarded, though they must be so amended as to make Their Highnesses and their heirs and successors constitutional Rulers.

Secondly, provision must be made, by means of a Civil List or otherwise, to safeguard the position and prestige of Their Highnesses against encroachment by State legislation.

Thirdly, as mentioned above, provision must be made in the State Constitutions for Their Highnesses to become constitutional Rulers. At present executive power is vested in "His Highness in Council"; and this means "His Highness acting after consultation with the State Executive Council, but not necessarily in accordance with the advice of such Council, nor necessarily in such Council assembled". In certain cases, too, His Highness is empowered to act otherwise than in Council. Further, the State Executive Council includes at least four ex-officio members, is not responsible to the Council of State, and is presided over by His Highness personally. These and other provisions are inconsistent with the position of His Highness as constitutional Ruler. Indeed, the very concept of His Highness in Council, except as a formal body like the Queen in Council in the United Kingdom, or the Governor-General in Council in Canada, is inconsistent with constitutional government. There are other provisions in the State Constitutions which are similarly inconsistent, though of less importance.

It follows that the Commission is required to make recommendations for new State Constitutions. They need not take the form of the present Constitutions, nor need they be similar (as they are now) for all States, large and small. They must, however, provide in each case that His Highness be a constitutional Ruler; and each must safeguard his position and prestige. Since the Queen is in the same position in the United Kingdom, it seems probable that the Ruler was intended to be treated similarly in relation to his State.

(6) "The Position of Her Majesty the Queen in relation to the Settlements of Penang and Malacca"

This provision appears in paragraph 6 of Paper No. 15 of 1956,[45] in which the terms of reference are set out, but not in the terms of reference. It was understood at the London Conference in relation to the terms of reference, that "nothing in the terms of reference proposed for the Constitutional Commission is to be taken as prejudging the position of Her Majesty the Queen in relation to the Settlements of Penang and Malacca".

The provision does not prevent the Commission from making recommendations whose effect would be to remove Her Majesty from any connection with Penang and Malacca, except as Queen of the Federation (if it were so recommended) or as Head of the Commonwealth in which the Federation was an independent country. It does, however, serve notice that Her Majesty's Government in the United Kingdom reserves the right to object to any such proposal if it thinks fit to do so.

The reservation does not imply that Her Majesty's Government in the United Kingdom would, after the enactment of the necessary constitutional instruments, retain any responsibility for the government of Penang and Malacca. Any such interpretation would be inconsistent with the provision of the terms of reference under which the Federation is to become an independent country within the

[45] Not included.

Commonwealth. It implies only that the Commission must consider (but not necessarily recommend) a solution in which Her Majesty was the constitutional Ruler of Penang and Malacca, as Their Highnesses are to be constitutional Rulers of their respective States. Her Majesty could not act except on advice, and the advice could not be that of the Government of the United Kingdom. Accordingly, if the Commission decided that it was desirable to retain the position of Her Majesty in relation to Penang and Malacca, it would be necessary to consider whether advice should be tendered by the Government of the Federation or by the Governments of the respective Settlements.

(7) "A Constitutional Yang di-Pertuan Besar for the Federation to be chosen from among Their Highnesses the Rulers"

"Their Highnesses the Rulers" clearly mean the Rulers of the nine States and do not include the Ruler or Rulers of the Settlements. On the other hand, it is for the Commission to recommend how the Yang di-Pertuan Besar should be chosen and what should be his term of office. As a constitutional authority, he would not exercise the discretionary powers of the High Commissioner, but would act on the advice of the Government of the Federation.

(8) "A common nationality for the whole of the Federation"

With this provision of the terms of reference must be read the statement in paragraph 6 of Paper No. 15 of 1956 that this sub-section "is not to be taken as precluding the Commission from making recommendations which would allow British subjects or subjects of Their Highnesses the Rulers to retain their status as such after they had acquired the proposed common nationality".

The two clauses are not as inconsistent as they appear at first sight. The main implication is that federal citizens shall not, as is at present usually the case, obtain their federal nationality from the fact that they are State subjects or citizens of the United Kingdom and Colonies; indeed, the latter status would be inconsistent with the independence of the Federation. Accordingly, there must be a federal nationality laid down by law and recognised by a federal instrumentality. On the other hand, a federal citizen may be the subject of the Ruler of the State to which he belongs, and indeed this would be desirable in order to qualify him for the franchise in the State. In Penang and Malacca federal citizens would not be subjects of any Ruler, but they could be subjects of the Queen. In fact, however, all federal citizens should be British subjects or Commonwealth citizens on the same terms as Indian or Pakistani citizens, in other words, a common federal nationality is required and must be recommended by the Commission; this need not prevent the Commission from recommending that federal citizens be subjects of their Rulers or citizens of Penang or Malacca; and the inclusion of the Federation of Malaya among the independent countries of the Commonwealth implies that federal citizens will be British subjects or Commonwealth citizens in the same way as Indian or Pakistani citizens.

(9) "The safeguarding of the special position of the Malays and the legitimate interests of other communities"

The "special position of the Malays" under the present law, which has to be "safeguarded", seems to be compounded of the following elements:

(a.) The position of Their Highnesses the Rulers who must by the State Constitutions be Malays.

This matter is regulated by clause (ii) of the terms of reference and is dealt with in paragraph (5) above.

(b.) The provisions of the Federation of Malaya Agreement and the State Constitutions relating to the Muslim Religion and the Customs of the Malays.

These provisions are ambiguous and require clarification; they must, too, be read in conjunction with the need to safeguard "the legitimate interests of other communities", some of which include Muslims. Nevertheless, they help towards that "special position" which has to be "safeguarded".

(c.) Paragraph (d) of Clause 9(1) of the Federation Agreement, which imposes upon the High Commissioner the "special responsibility" of the safeguarding of the special position of the Malays and of the legitimate interests of other communities.

This provision must be revoked, for there cannot be a High Commissioner under the new Constitution. In future the "special position" must be safeguarded in other ways.

(d.) The provisions of Clauses 40 and 40A of the Federation Agreement, which require appointed and elected members of the Legislative Council to be able to read and write the English or the Malay language, the provision of Clause 63 making English and Malay the official languages of the Legislative Council, and the corresponding provisions of the State Constitutions and of the Federation of Malaya Order in Council (in so far as there are such provisions).

(e.) The provisions of the Federation Agreement relating to the Conference of Rulers.

Since Their Highnesses are to become constitutional Rulers, the Conference, if it met at all, would have purely formal or ceremonial functions.

(f.) The omission of any revenue arising from Zakat, Fitrah, Bait-ul-Mal or similar Muslim religious revenue from the provisions of the Federation Agreement relating to finance.

(g.) The provisions of the State Constitutions under which any Malay born in a State is a subject of the Ruler, from which it follows in accordance with the Federation Agreement that he is also a citizen of the Federation, whereas a member of any other community (unless a citizen of the United Kingdom and Colonies) requires more stringent qualifications.

It is not the case, as is commonly assumed, that a person who claims to be a Malay is entitled to registration as an elector. Like a member of any other community, he must prove that he is a citizen, and for this purpose he must prove that –

(i) he habitually speaks the Malay language;
(ii) professes the Muslim religion;
(iii) conforms to Malay custom; and
(iv) was born in a State.

Even so, stricter qualifications, more difficult to prove, are required of Chinese, Indians, etc., other than those who are Malays or citizens of the United Kingdom and Colonies.

(h.) The provisions of the State Constitutions whereby a person who applies for citizenship by registration must satisfy the Rulers that he is able to speak the Malay or English language with reasonable proficiency; and the similar provision of the Federation Agreement relating to citizenship by naturalisation.

(i.) The provisions of the Federation Agreement relating to land, and in particular the provision that Malay reservations are within the federal legislative power only to the extent of ensuring common policy.

(j.) The provision of the State Agreements whereby Their Highnesses desired and His Majesty the King agreed that it should be a particular charge upon the State Governments "to provide for and encourage the education and training of the Malay inhabitants . . . so as to fit them to take a full share in the economic progress, social welfare and government" of the States and of the Federation.

There are, on the other hand, provisions of the constitutional documents which seem designed to safeguard "the legitimate interests of other communities". These are:

(i) The special responsibility of the High Commissioner to which reference is made in paragraph (c) above.

As mentioned in that paragraph, this special responsibility must disappear and be replaced by safeguards in the new Constitution.

(ii) The representation in the Legislative Council provided for "Scheduled Interests" and ""Racial Minorities".

(iii) The inclusion within the reserved power of the High Commissioner of all matters relating to the creation or abolition of any federal public office and to the appointment, salary or other conditions of service of any federal public officer or officers.

This provision must disappear, but in accordance with the London Agreement (Paper No. 6 of 1956) a Public Service Commission, a Judicial Service Commission, and a Police Service Commission are to be set up.

(iv) The power of the High Commissioner to refuse assent to Bills or to reserve Bills for Her Majesty's assent.

In future the Yang di-Pertuan Besar will be a constitutional Ruler and the power of reservation must disappear.

(v) The provision that the Chief Justice and the Judges of the Supreme Court shall be appointed by the High Commissioner for and on behalf of Her Majesty and Their Highnesses.

This provision meant that in practice the Chief Justice and the Judges were appointed by Her Majesty's Government in the United Kingdom. Accordingly, the protection given by the provision will disappear.

(vi) The provision for appeals to Her Majesty in Council.

This provision is not inconsistent with the terms of reference – appeals are still taken to Her Majesty in Council from Australia, New Zealand and Ceylon.

(vii) The provisions of the Federation Agreement and the State Constitutions for the acquisition of citizenship by persons who are not Malays, and in particular the provisions granting privileges to citizens of the United Kingdom and Colonies.

Since Penang and Malacca will cease to be "colonies", it will not be possible to obtain citizenship of the United Kingdom and Colonies by birth in the Federation. In any case, the rules for acquisition of citizenship must be superseded by provisions for "a common nationality for the whole of the Federation".

(viii) Provisions of the general law (in Malaya and elsewhere) granting privileges to citizens of the United Kingdom and Colonies.

As mentioned above, in future citizenship of the United Kingdom and Colonies will not be obtained by birth in Penang and Malacca, or by birth of fathers born in Penang and Malacca.

(ix) The provisions of the State Constitutions to the effect that all religions may be practised in peace and harmony by the persons professing them.

(x) The provisions of the State Constitutions requiring Their Highnesses to govern according to law.

In future the responsibility for executive action will be vested in the State Governments, not in the Rulers.

(xi) The provisions of the Federation Agreement, the Order in Council, and the State Constitutions authorising the use of the English language.

(xii) The provisions of the State Agreements and in particular

(a) The requirement (waived in 1956) that Their Highnesses shall accept the advice of their British Advisers;

(b) The requirement that all persons of whatsoever race in the service of a State shall, subject to the terms and conditions of their employment, be treated impartially.

It is not suggested that the terms of reference require the Commission to safeguard the "special position of the Malays and the legitimate interests of other communities" as they were in 1948 or as they have become by 1956. The lists above give some idea of what was in the minds of those who agreed to the terms of reference at the London Conference. The situation will, however, be altered fundamentally by the new Constitution, for two reasons. First, the guiding hands of Her Majesty's Government in the United Kingdom and its representatives in the Federation will be removed. Secondly, the responsibilities of Their Highnesses will be limited to those of constitutional Rulers. In other words, in the last resort all questions will be decided by majorities in the Federal and State (and Settlement) legislatures. It is the duty of the Commission to frame such provisions as may be needed, in that changed situation, for "the safeguarding of the special position of the Malays and the legitimate interests of other communities".

3. The State Constitutions, 31 August 1956

I. COMPOSITION OF STATE COUNCILS

The present composition of the State and Settlement Councils is given in the Attorney-General's letter of 9th August (C.C. 2111).[46] The size varies from 19 in Perlis to 45 in Perak. There is, however, a large official element in each, and presumably it will be agreed that all official members should disappear. The composition, if it remained unaltered, would then be:

	Population	Nominated	Elected	Total
Perak	1,204,785	7	20	27
Johor	947,755	6	16	22
Selangor	926,205	6	13	19
Kedah	692,329	5	12	17
Penang	550,410	5	14	19
Kelantan	520,640	5	16	21
Negri Sembilan	352,292	5	12	17
Malacca	307,232	5	8	13
Pahang	298,828	5	16	21
Trengganu	265,200	?	15	?
Perlis	86,423	3	9	12

Trengganu has 11 nominated, official and unofficial, but does not prescribe the number of officials. Following the others, we may assume 5 unofficials [*sic*], giving a Council of 20 unofficials.

2. The continuation of nominated members would be criticised as undemocratic, but it might be justified on the following grounds:

(a.) the poor quality of the elected members, especially in the backward States;
(b.) the small size of the electorates if the number of elected members was substantially increased, and the consequent risk of electoral corruption; and
(c.) the need to secure representation of special interests and minorities.

[46] Not found.

3. The dangers are:

(i.) the Mentri Besar[47] might nominate his personal and political friends, and in particular use nomination to keep himself in power;
(ii.) where the Sultan had real influence, he might secure the nomination of impecunious and unsuccessful Tunkus;
(iii.) there would almost certainly be excessive preference for Malays (or, in Penang, for Chinese).

These dangers would be more or less avoided if, instead of nomination being used, additional members were elected by the elected members by proportional representation. This would, however, fail to secure most of the advantages of having non-elected members.

4. An alternative would be to have election for special constituencies defined by regulations: for instance –

Rubber producers,
Tin producers,
Chambers of Commerce, Indians,
Other minorities as appropriate.

The difficulties of this arrangement would be:

(a.) the persons so elected would probably be "communalists" in that they would be more concerned to speak for their interests than to take part in general political work;
(b.) communal representation has been shown by experience to encourage communalism and to discourage the development of genuine nationalist sentiments; and
(c.) one would not necessarily get the best people to strengthen the Council.

5. There need not be uniformity, because the arguments for nonelected members apply differently in different States. In Perak and Penang they would be required mainly to represent otherwise unrepresented interests – rubber, tin and perhaps Indians (if suitable constituencies could not be carved out) in Perak; Indians, Eurasians and the Chambers of Commerce in Penang. In Kelantan, Trengganu and

[47] The Chief Minister in a Malay State.

Perlis the main object would be to secure a better personnel. The following are very tentative suggestions:

Perak:	1 elected by rubber producers; 1 elected by tin producers; 2 nominated to represent Indians and Pakistanis; 2 nominated at large.
Johor:	1 elected by rubber producers; 1 elected by tin producers; 2 nominated to represent Indians and Pakistanis; 2 nominated at large.
Selangor:	1 elected by rubber producers; 1 elected by tin producers; 2 nominated to represent Indians and Pakistanis; 1 nominated to represent other minorities; 1 nominated at large.
Kedah:	1 elected by rubber producers; 1 elected by tin producers; 1 nominated to represent Indians and Pakistanis; 2 nominated at large.
Penang:	1 elected by combined Chambers of Commerce; 1 elected by rubber producers; 1 nominated to represent Indians and Pakistanis; 1 nominated to represent other minorities; 1 nominated at large.
Kelantan:	1 elected by rubber producers; 1 nominated to represent Chinese; 1 nominated to represent other minorities; 2 nominated at large.
Negri Sembilan:	1 elected by rubber producers; 1 elected by tin producers; 1 nominated to represent Indians and Pakistanis; 1 nominated to represent other minorities; 1 nominated at large.
Malacca:	1 elected by combined Chambers of Commerce; 1 elected by rubber producers; 1 nominated to represent minorities; 2 nominated at large.

Pahang:	1 elected by rubber producers; 1 elected by tin producers; 1 nominated to represent minorities; 2 nominated at large.
Trengganu:	1 nominated to represent Chinese; 3 nominated at large.
Perlis:	1 nominated to represent Chinese; 3 nominated at large.

To avoid the danger of a Mentri Besar putting in too many of his friends, and particularly the danger of a State Council being dissolved in order to secure a majority by nomination, and to avoid party politics disrupting the rubber and tin interests, it would seem desirable that nominated members should sit for fixed terms: perhaps, if the normal term of a State Council was 3 years, nominated members should sit for four years, one-half (or thereabouts) retiring every two years.

5. [*sic*] The number of elected members depends in part on the size of the electorate and in part on the nature of the executive authority – anything equivalent to a Cabinet system would, as explained below, require a Council at least four times the size of the "Cabinet". The size of the electorate depends upon the franchise, but if we assume for purposes of study (a) that all adult Malays are enfranchised, and (b) that about half the adult Chinese and Indians are enfranchised, the relation between population, probable electorate, and electorate per present seat would be:

	Population	Electorate	Electorate per seat
Perak	1,204,785	384,000	19,200
Johor	947,755	308,000	19,250
Selangor	926,205	270,000	20,700
Kedah	692,329	280,000	23,300
Penang	550,410	174,000	12,400
Kelantan	520,640	255,000	15,900
Negri Sembilan	352,292	118,000	9,800
Malacca	307,232	107,000	13,400
Pahang	298,828	113,000	7,100
Trengganu	265,200	128,000	8,500
Perlis	86,423	39,000	4,300

The figures for "electorate" are little better than intelligent guesses, but they give a total electorate of 2,176,000, which must be compared with the 1,280,000 registered in 1955; and an estimated increase of 900,000 is quite substantial. On the other hand, any approach to jus soli would gradually raise the figure. Nor must we forget that among the young men and women coming on the register every year will be an increasing proportion of potential electors, because (even under the present law) a high proportion must be qualified as citizens by operation of law.

6. There is, however, another factor which would help to determine the number of State constituencies. It would be administratively more convenient and cheaper to have the State constituencies as subdivisions of Federal constituencies, so that common registers could be used for Federal and State elections and the problem of delineation simplified. Indeed, it would be desirable to have a single Election Commission (as in India) charged with the functions of (a) compiling registers, (b) delineating constituencies, and (c) organising elections, for the States as well as for the Federation. It is usually considered in the West that a reasonably free and uncorrupt [*sic*] election can be hoped for with an electorate of 30,000 – which would require, at present, a population per constituency of about 85,000. (It is necessary to work on population figures because they are ascertainable from the census, whereas electorate figures fluctuate from year to year and may in fact, be inflated by false entries). On this basis the members of the Federal House would be elected as follows:

Perak	18
Johor	11
Selangor	11
Kedah	8
Penang	6
Kelantan	6
Negri Sembilan	4
Malacca	4
Pahang	3
Trengganu	3
Perlis	1
Total	75

The actual distribution might be rather different, since the census figures of 1957 would be used; but, the total being based on estimated population on 31st December, 1955, the increase by 1957 would not be great. It would seem offhand that a Federal House of 75 would be adequate, allowing for State representation in the other House also.

Ceylon has 95 seats for 8,000,000 population, with a larger proportion of citizens.)

7. For State elections it would be impossible to hope for the ideal of 30,000 electorate, but it would be dangerous to come below 15,000. In other words, each Federal constituency could contain two State constituencies. On this basis the number of State constituencies could be:

	Future	Present
Perak	36	20
Johor	22	16
Selangor	22	13
Kedah	16	12
Penang	12	14
Kelantan	12	12
Negri Sembilan	8	12
Malacca	8	8
Pahang	6	16
Trengganu	6	15
Perlis	2	9

This works well for Perak, Johor and Selangor, and is not unreasonable for Kedah, Penang and Kelantan, though in the cases of Penang and Kelantan (if the scheme suggested in para. 4 were accepted) there would be rather a high proportion of nominated seats. For the smaller States there would clearly be too few elected members. The alternatives are:

(i.) to have smaller constituencies, which could very easily become corrupt;
(ii.) to have two-member or three-member Constituencies; and
(iii.) to have annual or biennial elections for the same constituencies, as was formerly the case in the English boroughs.

The third is the least attractive: it is expensive, it encourages apathy through too frequent elections, and above all, it would render impossible the weapon of dissolution, which ought to be usable against a recalcitrant or unworkable State Council. As between the other alternatives, it seems impossible to decide on general principles. It may be convenient to give separate representation to a town inhabited mainly by Chinese and Indians although its electorate would be well below 15,000. On the other hand, it may be convenient to have a three-member constituency, each elector having three ballot papers on each of which he must place one mark, in the hope that the majority community would dissipate its votes and the minority would concentrate them, thus providing a primitive form of proportional representation (the more sophisticated kinds are impossible with an illiterate electorate). Accordingly, the question might be left to the Election Commission to decide on the spot, with a general instruction, rather on the lines of that in Ceylon (which was adopted from South Africa, where it was intended to solve the problem of English and Afrikaner), to secure adequate representation for various interests. On this basis the representation could be:

	Special Interests	Elected	Total	Present Unofficial
Perak	6	36	42	27
Johor	5	22	27	22
Selangor	6	22	28	19
Kedah	5	16	21	17
Penang	5	16	21	19
Kelantan	5	16	21	21
Negri Sembilan	5	12	17	17
Malacca	5	12	17	13
Pahang	5	12	17	21
Trengganu	4	10	14	20
Perlis	4	8	12	12

This is a tentative conclusion, which must be checked against arguments relating to executive government, as suggested in para. 5.

II. EXECUTIVE GOVERNMENT

8. The Rulers will become constitutional monarchs and executive government must be placed under the control, direct or indirect, of the State Councils. It is assumed that the Ruler (or in Penang or Malacca the Governor) would appoint a Mentri Besar (or in Penang or Malacca a Chief Minister) who would have, or hope to obtain, a majority in the State Council. For convenience of exposition, in what follows "Ruler" includes "Governor" and "Mentri Besar" includes "Chief Minister". It is assumed that the Ruler would have power, on the advice of the Mentri Besar, to dissolve the State Council, but that, like the Queen, he need not accept the advice. The Ruler would not be empowered to dissolve without advice, though, of course, he could always appoint a new Mentri Besar who was likely so to advise because he had no majority. Three possible arrangements suggest themselves:

(i.) A Cabinet System.

The Cabinet would be called the Executive Council (to maintain continuity) and would be presided over by the Mentri Besar. It would include four or five Ministers, according to the scope of State functions. There seems to be no case for Assistant Ministers, whose appointments are used, in Singapore, as "jobs for the boys".

The ordinary conventions of Cabinet Government would apply.

This system is well understood throughout the Commonwealth and will be used in the Federation. Singapore experience has shown, however, that the number of members of the legislature must be at least four times the number of Ministers, since, if this is not the case, opposition parties will seek to attract government supporters by the offer of "jobs for the boys". On the basis contemplated in para. 7, the system would work in Perak, Johor and Selangor, and might work in Kedah, Penang and Kelantan. One difficulty is that Ministers must be full-time. They cannot be allowed to continue to run their professions or trades, because conflict arises between private and public interests if they do. In the smaller States it would be difficult to secure suitable personnel, and expensive to pay adequate salaries to enable Ministers to give up their other employments.

(ii.) Local Government System.

Perlis is the size of a small county borough, whose Council has vested in it both legislative and executive powers and exercises those powers on the advice of committees. Something of this kind was obviously contemplated for Penang and Malacca by section 30 of the Order in Council.

It is doubtful if the system would work in the States. It would be new, because even the municipalities have appointed Chairmen. It would not have behind it the vast experience of English local government. Moreover, the legislative powers of the State Councils will be much more than those of English local authorities, which are concerned mostly to carry out in detail the legislation enacted in general (and usually empowering) terms by Parliament. The idea should not be excluded on a priori grounds. If the Commission considers that the States should, in the main, carry out, with such local variations as they think desirable, a general policy laid down by the Federal Parliament, the English local government system would provide a suitable analogy. If on the other hand "a measure of autonomy" means a measure of legislative authority, it would not be desirable to follow this system, even in Perlis: and anyhow the Raja of Perlis has somehow to be fitted into the picture.

(iii.) Cabinet – Committee System.

This system was invented for Ceylon by the Donoughmore Commission[48] and was extended with modifications, to Jamaica. An experiment on these lines is being tried in Penang. It implies (a) that the State Council would have both legislative and executive powers, (b) that executive powers would be delegated to committees of the State Council, which would seek Council decisions on all questions of principle, and (c) that the chairmen of the committees would be members of the Executive Council, which would be responsible to the Council for Finance but otherwise would carry out in the executive field, the decisions of the State Council.

The weaknesses of the system, as exhibited in Ceylon, were (i.) the committees showed less interest in general policy than in detailed administration, particularly as it affected their constituents; (ii.) appointments, promotions and transfers took up a great deal of time, and there was much canvassing by prospective candidates, including (on occasion) public officers already in service; (iii.) there was lack of co-ordination between committees, especially when the chairmen were not particularly friendly; and (iv.) the Board of Ministers (i.e., the Executive Council) were [*sic*] not homogeneous, with the result that Ministers sometimes fought against each other in the State Council. The second of these difficulties would, however, not apply in the States – except as to transfers – if the Public Service Commission had jurisdiction.

9. The conclusion appears to be that none of these methods is suitable for the smaller States and that something new should be devised. It should, if possible, be a development out of the present system because it is familiar. It seems plain that in the smaller States it will be enough to have one full-time Minister, the Mentri Besar, or at most two, the Mentri Besar and the Minister for Finance. The others should be more like the chairmen of committees in English local government; part-time politicians specialising in certain fields of administration. Since they would be part-time, they should be chairmen of committees and not Ministers, except in name, so that any conflict between public and private interests would be overcome by having full committee decisions.

[48] Among other reforms, the 1927 Donoughmore Commission to Ceylon established a system of executive committees based on the London County Council, rather than the Cabinet model that the local politicians wished for.

10. The details would have to be worked out in drafting, but the following would be the main points:

(1.) There would be no elected Speaker, but the Mentri Besar would preside over the State Council. (This is perhaps arguable, and is not essential to the scheme, but it avoids the possibility, which has occurred in Tasmania,[49] of a small body being equally divided and functioning under the Speaker's casting vote.)
(2.) The Ruler should have power to appoint one or more Ministers, in addition to the Mentri Besar, but it would be provided in the Constitution that such Minister would be full-time. One Minister, but not more, might be chosen from outside the State Council, and he would have the right to sit but not to vote.
(3.) All functions not allocated to Ministers would be vested in the Council and stand referred to committees of the State Council, but the chairmen of such committees would be nominated by the Ruler.
(4.) The Mentri Besar, the Ministers, and the chairmen of committees would be members of the Executive Council, over which the Mentri Besar would preside, and which would be collectively responsible for all functions not allocated to committees.

11. This diarchy seems awkward, but it has not the defects of most schemes of diarchy. A committee could be overruled by the whole Council, and accordingly the Executive Council, if it had a majority, could get a committee decision reversed. If the committee proved obdurate, it could be dissolved and reconstituted, though it might be that the Mentri Besar would prefer another Chairman. The committee scheme could not apply to the whole field of government because at least a full-time Minister of Finance would be required. On the other hand, it would be impossible, in a small State, to find enough full-time Minister[s] of the requisite quality. Presumably, it would be necessary to pay small allowances to committee chairmen, but it would be assumed that they had other jobs. Moreover, the system would be flexible: a complete, though small, Cabinet system could be applied if personnel were available. It is suggested that the scheme could be worked with the membership specified in para. 7 above.

[49] In the 1955 and 1956 Tasmanian State elections there had been a hung parliament, with the incumbent Labor government and Liberal Party opposition holding the same number of seats.

III. ADMINISTRATIVE ORGANISATION

12. Even in a large State there would not be more than six or seven Ministries and in Perlis there would probably be only two – the Mentri Besar's Office and the Ministry of Finance. It does not seem either necessary or desirable to departmentalise administration as in the larger Commonwealth countries and (probably) in the Federation. The colonial system, with a State Secretary as the funnel of administration, is at present in use in the States, the Heads of Departments being technical officers. There seems no reason why this arrangement should not continue, with a Secretary to each Minister of fairly low rank (except, perhaps, the Secretary to the Mentri Besar, who might take the place of the Deputy Mentri Besar, where there is one). It may be noted that the constitutional provision for Permanent Secretaries in Ceylon has been, partially at least, a failure, because it has not been followed by a departmental reorganisation (as the original draft provided).

13. The replacement of the Legal Advisers raises questions about the federal legal organisation. Unless that is changed, it would be desirable to continue the present arrangement, except that (i.) he should be summoned to Executive Council only if his presence was required by the Mentri Besar, and (ii.) he should have the right to sit but not to vote in the State Council. A larger State should not be prohibited from having a Minister of Justice, but there would be little for him to do.

SECTION E: MALTA

Jennings was an adviser to the Maltese Government in their constitutional negotiations with Britain. After a Round Table Conference in 1955, in a referendum of February 1956 the Maltese voted overwhelmingly to integrate with the United Kingdom. Integration was taken to mean that Malta would gain powers over almost all domestic policies while Britain kept control over defence and external affairs. Under the proposals Malta would also have representation at Westminster (possibly three MPs), as well as its own parliament. Integration was never realised and instead in 1964 Malta became a fully independent parliamentary state with the Queen as Head of State represented by a Governor-General. The island became a republic ten years later, but within the Commonwealth.

1. 'The Malta Integration Bill', 16 November 1957

If H.M.G. agrees to the incorporation of Malta in the United Kingdom, the Bill to give effect to that decision will inevitably be unique. In some respects, however, it will be a development of precedents set by the union of England and Scotland in 1707 and the union of Great Britain and Ireland in 1801. The Union with Scotland Act did not provide for complete integration, since separate ecclesiastical and legal jurisdictions were maintained and separate administrative machinery has been established in several fields of government. Under the Union with Ireland Act, separate Privy Councils also were retained. The Government of Ireland Act, 1914, intended to give Ireland a substantial measure of autonomy, including a measure of fiscal autonomy; and a slightly different division was made for Northern and Southern Ireland by the Government of Ireland Act, 1920. The measure of autonomy in Northern Ireland has increased since 1920, both by legislation and by the development of constitutional conventions. The arrangement with Malta would therefore not be entirely unprecedented.

2. The unions of 1707 and 1801 were, however, unions of kingdoms, though the kingdom of Ireland was, before 1801, subordinate to that of Great Britain. Malta is not a separate or subordinate kingdom but

a dependency of the United Kingdom. Moreover, it has been agreed that for the time being Malta must have a separate fiscal system with a wider autonomy than that provided for Ireland in 1914. In other respects, too, Malta will have in legal form a wider autonomy than Northern Ireland, though in practice it will be very much limited by the width of the powers in respect of defence and external affairs. Few aspects of life in Malta will not be touched by these powers in the peculiar circumstances of the islands.

3. The normal ambition of a colony is independence within the Commonwealth, and a section of opinion in Malta has that ambition. Though the Maltese Government and the Round Table Conference considered the ambition to be impracticable, it is proper and indeed desirable to take minority opinion into account when framing constitutional proposals. In a dozen years or more, when the advantages of integration have become obvious, it will no doubt be desirable to make the association even closer and to amend the Integration Act accordingly. For the present, however, it is desirable to meet minority opinion by making Maltese autonomy as evident as drafting can make it.

4. The two affirmations proposed for the Bill seek to carry out these objectives. They must, of course, be read together with the other proposals, and in particular with the proposals which maintain the supremacy of the Parliament of the United Kingdom, retain the system of appeals to the Privy Council (in respect of which the Ireland precedent of 1914 has been preferred for purely technical reasons to that of 1920), provide for the reservation of certain classes of Bills which may affect the interests of the whole United Kingdom, and so forth. It is therefore clear that the affirmations are not designed to enable Malta to "have it both ways". They go no further than to provide for Malta the sort of status which Northern Ireland has attained by a combination of law and constitutional convention.

5. The first affirmation is in the same form as the affirmation in section 1(2) of the Ireland Act, 1949. It is intended to be permanent, though it is flexible enough to permit of amendment if need be, and in any case it does not purport legally to bind the Parliament of the United Kingdom. The second affirmation is designed to give Malta a status similar to that of Northern Ireland. It is not intended to be permanent, at least in this form, because closer union is contemplated by both sides. Its inclusion as a substantive provision as not as a [*sic*] preamble is founded partly on the belief that a preamble is the place for a recital of facts and not a statement of parliamentary intention, and partly on the desirability of giving it greater prominence in order to avoid a distinction being drawn between the strength of the two affirmations. It is recognised that no greater legal

force is obtained by reason of its inclusion in the body of the Act.

6. Some apprehension has been expressed lest the future amendment of the second affirmation should call in question the permanence of section 4 of the Statute of Westminster (and corresponding provisions in Independence Acts).[1] It is difficult to see on what such apprehensions are based. Section 4 is in fact not permanent, because it can be amended or repealed unilaterally in any of the countries to which it applies. It has already been repealed in relation to the Irish Free State and the corresponding provision has been repealed in relation to India and Pakistan. Section 4 has been amended in the Union of South Africa. No such power of unilateral amendment is provided for or contemplated in the case of Malta, since there is nothing corresponding to section 2 of the Statute.[2] Moreover, the meaning of section 4 has been canvassed in legal publications for a quarter of a century. It is well known, even to those who hold a different opinion, that in the opinion of the great majority of constitutional lawyers the section merely states a convention and adds a rule of interpretation, and accordingly that it is legally subject to repeal by the Parliament of the United Kingdom. This interpretation does not give rise to political difficulties because, whatever the law may be, the Parliament of the United Kingdom could not in fact repeal or amend the section unilaterally, because any such action would be repudiated, and because any such repeal would be ineffective without a repeal of the whole Statute, which is unthinkable. The proposed affirmation, on the other hand, contemplates that the Parliament of the United Kingdom will in fact legislate for Malta, in some cases by agreement and in others without it; and indeed a consultative machinery is being proposed to minimise conflict in the legislative as well as the executive sphere. The relationship with the United Kingdom is not that of quasi-independence, but of the quasi-federalism which has been read into the Government of Ireland Act by the House of Lords.

7. There are in any event very substantial differences, brought out in a note by Mr S.A. de Smith[3] annexed to this memorandum,[4] between section 4 of the Statute of Westminster and the proposed affirmation.

[1]Section 4 of the Statute of Westminster (1931) stipulated that the Parliament of the United Kingdom would not legislate for any Dominion except by consent.

[2]Section 2 declared that any laws passed by a Dominion parliament could no longer be declared void by the Parliament of the United Kingdom if repugnant to English law, and consequently the Colonial Laws Validity Act (1865) would cease to apply.

[3]Stanley Alexander de Smith, Professor of Public Law at the London School of Economics, later Downing Professor of the Laws of England at Cambridge. De Smith was also a constitutional adviser across the Commonwealth and corresponded with Jennings.

[4]Not included.

They can be put very shortly. Section 4 purports to limit the legislative competence of the Parliament of the United Kingdom and also provides a new rule of interpretation. The proposed affirmation does neither, but merely affirms the intention of Parliament to use its powers as it in fact uses them in relation to Northern Ireland. There might be more room for apprehension if Malta were not incorporated in the United Kingdom; for then it would be necessary to meet Maltese opinion by making Malta a semi-independent country represented in the House of Commons; and the Integration Act would then look like an Independence Act.

SECTION F: NEPAL

Jennings was invited by the King of Nepal, and with the support of the British Foreign Office, to advise on a new constitution for the kingdom in 1958. Though never formally under British rule or in the Commonwealth, Nepal nonetheless had had significant connections with Britain since the early nineteenth century. The Rana family had dominated Nepal from the nineteenth century: the prime ministership and other important posts were hereditary offices held by the family until February 1951, when the family's hegemony over the country ended and King Tribhuvan moved to establish a constitutional monarch and Cabinet government on British lines.

1. Confidential note for the British Foreign Office on the framing of the new Constitution of Nepal, *c.*1958, never sent

My assumption that I was to advise the Constitutional Commission (or Constitutional Drafting Committee) proved to be correct. An alternative draft was circulated with my first draft. It was, technically, a pathetic document, and the claim of Hara Prasad Joshi,[1] the Secretary to the Commission, that it was all his own work, seemed superficially to be justified. It was a collection of bits from other Constitutions, strung together amateurishly. On the other hand Randhir Subba, another member, said that it came from the Palace, but not from the King.[2] This is probably a guess, founded on the suspicion which the Gurkha Parishad[3] has of H.M. My own guess is that Joshi is an ambitious young man who took this opportunity to bring his merits to H.M.'s attention (copies of both were supplied to H.M.). However, the draft was never mentioned in the Commission while I was there.

2. The circumstances made it necessary that the Draft Constitution to "democratic" [*sic*]. Usually this means that it is designed to vest power in a middle-class, and usually English-speaking, oligarchy which

[1]Joshi was also General Secretary of the Nepali Congress.

[2]Mahendra, King of Nepal, 1955–1972.

[3]A key political party in Nepal during the 1950s.

has to pay attention to the needs of hoi polloi because they have the vote, and which will eventually get turned out. What one hopes is that they will stay in office for ten or fifteen years and that meanwhile an Opposition will develop against them and be ready to take over. The difficulty in Nepal was to find the oligarchy. In 1951, I suppose, one would have backed the Nepali Congress, but subsequent events had ruled it out. The Gurkha Parishad thinks that it can get a majority if it is in office (either alone or in an all-party Government) at the election, or if direct rule is maintained over the election period. In any other event it will be the largest party and its support will be necessary for a coalition. On the other hand there is evidently a large "anti-politician" opinion in the country, which considers that most of the members returned will be "independents". Most of this seems to be based on guess-work, and I do not suppose anybody really knows; and certainly it would have been impossible for me to find out.

3. The one stable element is the monarchy, but it was impossible to build too much on that. First, though H.M. is said to be popular in the country at large and is described by his opponents as "obstinate", he does not seem to me to have the character or ability to "go it alone" for long if the constitutional machinery breaks down; and there does not seem to be anything like a Court party capable of carrying on the machinery on his behalf. Secondly, Indian influence (by which I mean unofficial Indian influence) is against the monarchy, too many of the local politicians have lived in India and absorbed Congress ideas, and the ideas of the educated class are, in substance, those of the lesser Congress-wallahs. Thirdly, one must not presume too much on the King's personal popularity and make him too obviously responsible for the efficiency of government. Whatever happens, government is going to be pretty inefficient and (I suspect) corrupt; and a major catastrophe, such as the failure of the monsoon, might cause his popularity to wane.

4. There is in Nepal nothing corresponding to the Congress in India, the Muslim League in Pakistan in 1947, or the A.F.P.F.L.[4] in Burma. Nor is it possible, as it was in Ceylon, to find a personality around which the leading politicians could be collected and which could be given a "build-up". I thought at one time that it would be possible to break all the rules and get a party formed, through H.M.'s influence, out of local (especially feudal) leaders who would respond to a Royal appeal: but I am not sure that such people exist, i.e. people who have a sufficiently broad local appeal to get themselves elected and stay in power for ten years. I therefore came to the conclusion that one must assume the existence of a number of Kathmandu groups, miscalled

[4] Anti-Fascist People's Freedom League – the main political party in Burma from the 1940s to the 1960s.

"parties", rather like the present groups in Pakistan. If some of the more conservative elements came in as "independents", so much the better, for they might help if the conflicts of the groups became acute. On the other hand, I did not want to devise a machine designed for groups, for no such machine would function properly unless there were a strong public service. I have, in drafting, tried to strengthen the ties between the public service and the Crown; but the former seems to me to be excessively weak and indolent. Besides, I had to get the scheme through the Commission, whose members assumed that either the Nepali Congress or the Gurkha Parishad would form a Government under a constitutional monarch, as in the United Kingdom.

5. In the end, therefore, my draft, like most drafts, became a compromise. It provided for Cabinet Government so long as it was practicable, but gave the King ample powers to suspend Cabinet Government; or even the whole Constitution, if it proved unworkable. To give the King a buffer against popular discontent, I invented a Council of State, which he could "pack" if he so desired, or use as an assembly of Kathmandu politicians if he thought that preferable. Besides, his powers of direct rule are temporary; he can always appeal to the people and prove to the politicians whether they have or have not popular support; and, if the electorate does not produce a stable Government, the fault will obviously lie with the politicians. The Commission took this scheme quite well, and I have not had to compromise it much. A Chapter of Fundamental Rights was forced upon me, but it will be easy for the King (but not the politicians) to suspend them if they prove too restrictive.

2. 'Explanatory memorandum on the Constitution of Nepal', *c.*1958

In the Royal Proclamation of the 1st February, 1958, His Majesty the King of Nepal provided that—

"There shall be a Commission to prepare a draft for a new Constitution (answering the needs of the time, country and circumstances) on the basis of the present Interim Constitution, according to necessity, foreign experts will be co-opted to aid and advise the Commission; on the basis of the Constitution thus prepared, general elections shall be held for Parliament; this Parliament shall consist of two Houses and all possible provisions shall be made to safeguard the country's sovereignty, independence and people's rights."

Elsewhere in the Royal Proclamation it was recalled that His Majesty had already proclaimed the 18th February, 1959, as the date for initiating general elections.

2. A Commission consisting of Messrs Bhagabati Prashad Singh (Chairman), Ramraj Panta, S.P. Upadhyaya, Randhir Subba and Hora Prasad Joshi (Secretary) was duly constituted.[5] Arrangements were made through Her Majesty's Government in the United Kingdom for me to reach Nepal on the 28th March, 1958 and to assist the Commission for a period of one month. The time available being so short, the Commission proceeded forthwith to prepare a Draft Constitution; and the result of their labours is attached hereto.[6] The Commission requested me to prepare an Explanatory Memorandum.

General Principles

3. The Royal Proclamation contemplated the setting up of a Parliament consisting of two Houses; and the reference to the Interim Constitution suggested that elections should be based on adult suffrage exercised in general or territorial constituencies. The Interim Constitution also provided for a Council of Ministers, or Cabinet, to aid and advise His Majesty in the exercise of his functions. It was presumed that this Cabinet should be collectively responsible to Parliament, as well as to His Majesty, in accordance with the practice followed in other monarchies operating the parliamentary system of government. There was also in the Royal Proclamation a reference to the safeguarding of the people's rights; and this seemed to require a chapter dealing with the rights of citizens, or civil liberties.

4. On this basis, the Commission has prepared a draft similar in principle to the Constitutions of other countries in Asia operating a parliamentary system of government, but with the modifications which distinguish a constitutional monarchy from a republic and a unitary state from a federal state. The general scheme is as follows:–

(1) Executive authority is vested in His Majesty, but the general direction and control of administration are vested in a Cabinet responsible to Parliament. Because the parliamentary system is new to Nepal, and accordingly guidance cannot be sought from constitutional conventions, care has been taken to define, with such precision as the changing circumstances of government allow, the relations between His Majesty and His Ministers.

(2) Parliament will consist of two Houses, called in the English text the House of Representatives and the Senate. The House of Representatives will consist wholly of members elected by the electors, voting in single member constituencies by secret ballot; and adult

[5] Singh was Chairman of the Public Service Commission, Panta was Principal of the Law College, and Upadhyaya and Subba were leading members of the Nepali Congress and Gurkha Parishad parties respectively.

[6] Not included.

franchise is provided for. There will be a general election every five years, or more often if His Majesty dissolves Parliament on the recommendation of the Cabinet. The Senate, on the other hand, will consist as to one-half of persons elected by the House of Representatives by proportional representation, and as to the other half of persons appointed by His Majesty on the recommendation of the Prime Minister. When Parliament is dissolved the Senators will retain their seats, but one-third of the Senators will retire every two years. Provision is made for the House of Representatives, as the elected House, to override the Senate, except in respect of constitutional amendments; and the Cabinet will be collectively responsible to the House of Representatives. All legislation will require the Royal Assent, but the circumstances in which His Majesty may withhold assent are specified.

(3) The functions of the judiciary will include that of declaring invalid any laws which are inconsistent with the Constitution, and the usual provisos have been inserted for protecting the independence of the Supreme Court.

(4) The financial system contemplated is now customary in countries operating parliamentary government, but has been simplified to suit the conditions of Nepal. The usual provisions for the audit of accounts by an independent Auditor-General have been inserted.

(5) The system of an independent Public Service Commission, already adopted, has been strengthened in view of the transfer of most of the functions of government to Ministers responsible to what may well be a party majority.

A more detailed explanation follows.

Commencement of the Constitution

5. The Draft Constitution has been prepared on the assumption that it will come into full operation on an "appointed day" after general elections have been held, the Senate constituted, and a Prime Minister appointed. Part II, relating to citizenship, will however come into operation on the promulgation of the Constitution because it will be needed for the compilation of electoral rolls. It should be noted that, before elections can be held to provide a House of Representatives as contemplated by this Draft Constitution, it will be necessary (a) to promulgate the Constitution, (b) to enact an electoral law, (c) to appoint Delimitation and Electoral Commissions, and (d) to prepare new electoral rolls. The Constitutional Commission is aware that much preparatory work has already been done, and it should be possible to hold elections beginning in February 1959, but only if expedition is shown in the completion of the formalities involved in

promulgating this Constitution and enacting the electoral law, which is already in draft.

6. Certain other steps will, however, be needed to bring the Constitution into full operation. They include:

(1) The making of Standing Orders for both Houses of Parliament;
(2) The making of Regulations for Government Procedure;
(3) The making of a number of appointments;
(4) The determination of emoluments for the persons who will assume office when Parliament begins to functions [*sic*].

Powers sufficient for this purpose are given to His Majesty by Article 77; and in case difficulties arise in the transition to the new Constitution the usual temporary power to remove them has been conferred on his Majesty by Article 79. It is appreciated that not all the existing laws can be modified before the "appointed day", and accordingly the "Pakistan Formula"[7] has been used in Article 78. It will enable the Courts to apply the laws with necessary adaptations; but this is not an easy task for the Courts, and accordingly as many as possible of the laws should be adapted by Proclamation under that Article before the "appointed day". The Constitutional Commission has already arranged for the preparation of a draft of the Regulations referred to in (2) above.

The Constitution as fundamental law

7. The Constitution will be promulgated by His Majesty in accordance with the powers reserved by His [*sic*] in the Interim Government of Nepal Act, 2007, as amended. When promulgated, however, it becomes fundamental law in accordance with Article 1, and can be amended (subject to the temporary power to remove difficulties in Article 79) only in the manner and form provided by Article 56; that is, any amendment will require the assent of His Majesty, the Senate and the House of Representatives; and, since it is not desirable that a mere temporary majority should have power to amend a written Constitution, the majority in the House of Representatives must be two-thirds of the total number of members. All laws inconsistent with the Constitution, whether made before or after the "appointed day" will become invalid, subject to some minor qualifications (e.g. under Articles 7 and 14) in respect of which flexibility in [*sic*] required.

8. In this way the Draft Constitution carries out the instruction of the Royal Proclamation on the 1st February "to safeguard the Country's sovereignty, independence and people's rights". They cannot lawfully

[7]This probably refers to Jennings' controversial argument used in Pakistan that the Crown's prerogatives filled any constitutional vacuum. See Section H, p. 132, n. 12.

be taken away except by an Act of His Majesty in Parliament in accordance with Article 56; but, as mentioned below, adequate provision is made to enable His Majesty's Government to meet any emergencies that may arise.

The Position of His Majesty

9. The succession of the Crown in accordance with the existing law is saved by clause (2) of Article 1, and clause (3) applied the Constitution to his Majesty's heirs and successors. Machinery for setting up a Regency, if it should prove necessary, is provided by Article 16, referred to below. Executive power is vested in His Majesty by Article 15, which also indicates in general terms (the details are to be found in other Articles) when that power should be exercised on recommendation and when in discretion – thus formulating the conventions operated in other constitutional monarchies. His Majesty will be in supreme command of His Majesty's forces (Article 69), will confer pardons, reprieves, etc., on the recommendation of the responsible Minister (Article 70), and will confer titles and honours (Article 71). Article 72 gives the usual protection from suit, while allowing suits against His Majesty's Government.

Citizenship

10. Citizenship is usually covered by ordinary law. The existing citizenship law has, however, proved difficult to apply in the process of determining what persons were entitled to be enrolled as electors. There was already in draft a citizenship law, amending and consolidating the existing law. The main provisions of that draft have been redrafted as constitutional provisions and inserted as Articles 2, 3, 5, and 6. As in usual [*sic*], Articles 2 and 5 combine the jus soli and the jus sanguinis; that is, a person born in Nepal, or a person born outside Nepal whose father was born in Nepal, is generally a citizen of Nepal, but in subsequent generations Nepalese citizenship is obtained only if the birth is registered with a prescribed Nepalese authority. The principle of Article 4, which confers citizenship on women marrying Nepalese citizen [*sic*], is less commonly accepted than it used to be; but it was felt that the close family relations of Nepal, and difficulties caused by an open frontier, made it desirable that husband and wife should have the same nationality. Article 5 is designed to cover those who had been registered or been naturalised as citizens under the existing law and those who, not being citizens by birth, descent or marriage under Articles 2, 3 and 4, might have claimed citizenship under the existing law; it applies particularly to persons of Nepalese origin whose families had emigrated or who had returned to Nepal. Article 6 contains the usual provisos, and Article

8 is incidental. Article 7 makes plain that citizenship law will remain under parliamentary control, as in most other countries. It will in fact be necessary to enact a new citizenship law in due course, especially to provide for citizenship by naturalization; but there are sufficient provisions in Part II to bring the Constitution into operation without further legislation on the subject.

Civil liberties

11. In formulating the articles of Part III, use has been made of the Nagarik Adhikar Ain, 2012,[8] the Constitution of India and the Constitution of Pakistan. Part II of this Constitution of Pakistan was drafted with the experience of India in mind; and it was thought that the use of comparatively simple general propositions, as in Pakistan, was more suited to the conditions of Nepal. It was thought, however, the process could be carried further and that the qualifying phrases of the several Pakistan Articles might be collected in a single provision in Article 14, which has been given the marginal note "Law and Order". This has enabled the Commission to produce five comparatively simple Articles, most of which could be easily explained even to illiterate citizens, and covering personal liberty, equality, religion, property, and political liberties. That all liberty is subject to the requirements of law and order – and indeed cannot be made effective unless those requirements are satisfied – is made plain by Article 14. Unlike those of the Interim Constitution, those civil liberties are limitations of the power of Parliament, and accordingly Acts of Parliament inconsistent with Part III of the Constitution are rendered invalid by clause (3) of Article 56. A special procedure for dealing with invalid laws in [*sic*] provided by Article 57, but this is additional to the ordinary legal remedies, which include the directions, orders and writs (including habeas corpus, etc.) provided by section 11 of the Supreme Court Ain,[9] 2013.

The Executive Government

12. Most of the provisions of Part IV contain the more or less standard formulae necessary to bring Cabinet Government into operation. The fact that Nepal is a Kingdom, however, and that no opportunity has yet arisen for the development of conventions, has made necessary a closer definition of the position of the Crown in relation to the Cabinet and otherwise. It has been thought wise not to use the English term "advice" because, though familiar enough to those with experience of the British Constitutional system and

[8] Civil Rights Act.
[9] Ain means Act.

its offspring both inside and outside the British Commonwealth, it was felt that, translated into Nepalese, and read by those who had not had that experience, it might convey the idea of a discretion. A distinction has therefore been drawn between acts done by his Majesty "in his discretion" particularly those of appointing a Prime Minister and refusing a dissolution of Parliament, and those done "on the recommendation" of the Cabinet or a responsible Minister. Speaking generally, His Majesty would act on the recommendation of the Cabinet; but in certain cases in which it is customary for a constitutional monarch to act on the "advice" of a particular Minister, the "recommendation" of that Minister has been specified (e.g. the appointment of Cabinet Ministers under the [*sic*] Article 18, the appointment of Senators under 24, and the grant of pardons, etc, under Article 70). The necessary definitions and consequential provisions are contained in Article 15. It would not be easy to go further in the direction of definition without losing flexibility. It is thought, however, that further guidance could be given to Ministers and other servants of the Crown, perhaps by illustration and example, by means of something like a "Manual of Procedure," adding to the Transaction of Business Rules used in most Cabinet systems. Provision has been made for that purpose in clause (2) of Article 21.

13. In accordance with Article 18, the Prime Minister must be a person who, in His Majesty's opinion, can or will be able to command a majority in the House of Representatives. Normally he would be a member of that House; and where a party or a combination of parties has a majority, and also a recognised leader, no difficulty should arise. Where there is difficulty in finding a leader, however, it has in other countries sometimes been found convenient to appoint as Prime Minister a person in the second Chamber, or even outside, and this has been made possible by clause (3) of Article 18. In any event, the other Ministers will be appointed on the recommendation of the Prime Minister. There may also be Assistant Ministers under Article 19, and the same Article also authorises the appointment of temporary deputies from among other Ministers or Assistant Ministers. Only the Prime Minister and the other Ministers will form the Cabinet, which by Article 17 will be charged with the general direction and control of the government of Nepal and will be collectively responsible to the House of Representatives. One aspect of this responsibility is shown by the provisions of Article 18 relating to the vacation of office. Votes of no-confidence will be against the whole Government; and when the Prime Minister ceases to hold office other ministers will, with the delay needed to carry on government, also cease to hold office, though they may of course be reappointed on the recommendation of the new Prime Minister.

14. The laws of Nepal at present make no provision for a Regency or a Council of Regency in the event of the Throne becoming vacant or in the event of the sovereign becoming incapacitated. To meet this need, provision is made in Article 16 for setting up a Council of State. That Council will have no other executive functions. In view of the wide responsibilities which will, however, inevitably vest in the Sovereign as constitutional monarch – and it must be remembered that the Constitution will apply equally to His Majesty's successors, whether male or female, experienced or inexperienced – and the various "crises" which occur with distressing frequency in all countries, it has been thought desirable also to make the Council of State a consultative body if and when such "Crises" and other constitutional difficulties arise. In most mature democracies there are conventions permitting the monarch to consult "elder statesmen", the presiding officers of the legislature, etc. The absence of such conventions in Nepal makes it desirable to provide a formal method of consultation, and the Council of State has been so composed as to meet this need. Apart from the executive functions mentioned above, however, the functions of the Council of State will be purely advisory.

15. This is perhaps a convenient place to mention the problem of "crises". Where there is no written Constitution, as in the United Kingdom, the problem is easily solved. A Parliament with unlimited power, not bound by any formal procedure, and controlled by the Government through its party majority, can within a couple of hours pass all the legislation that may be considered necessary; and there is no doubt that, if Parliament cannot meet, the Queen of the United Kingdom has ample power at common law to do what is necessary to carry on the government. A written Constitution, on the other hand, contains checks and balances, designed for usual times, which become slogs and fetters when the country is in danger. It must, therefore, contain "escape clauses" of sufficient width to enable crises to be met with immediate action even if, were there no crises, it would be unconstitutional so to meet. The ultimate responsibility must inevitably be placed on His Majesty – and that is one reason for establishing a Council of State which he can consult. To provide merely for the suspension of the Constitution would, however, require His Majesty to produce an extreme remedy for what might be a simple case of minor constitutional breakdown. It would, for instance, be undesirable to equip him with power to suspend the Constitution merely because, owing to a conflict of parties, or conflicts about leadership within parties, it was impossible to find a Prime Minister who had the confidence of the House of Representatives. It has therefore been thought desirable to envisage three possibilities:

(1) The simplest case is that just mentioned, when owing to conflict of parties, or conflicts within parties, it is impossible to appoint a responsible Government. This is the case contemplated by Article 22. It provides in effect for a temporary suspension of Cabinet government and enables His Majesty's Government to be carried on for a period of twelve months, or until after a general election, whichever is shorter.

(2) The more difficult case is a breakdown of the parliamentary machinery, due perhaps to a conflict of parties which made it impossible to pass the Budget and thus threatened to overthrow the whole structure of constitutional government. This case is covered by Article 59. If it were possible to continue with one House of Parliament, that would be done; if not, both Houses would be suspended; but again the suspension would be temporary.

(3) The most extreme case would be that of a complete breakdown due to war, internal disturbance, or widespread economic distress. The topography of Nepal is such that the country might be physically split, and any meeting, even of the Council of State, rendered impracticable. This case is covered by Article 59.

The circumstances contemplated are, of course, highly exceptional; it may never be necessary to use the powers thus conferred; but it would be the height of folly not to provide for contingencies, however remote they may now appear.

Parliament

16. The provisions of Part V of the Draft Constitution contain little variation from standard formulae adopted in other democratic Constitutions. Article 27 provides that, in the first instance, there shall be 109 member [*sic*] of the House of Representatives, though this number may be altered by Act of Parliament. The number was chosen because it was ascertained from the Delimitation Commission that it was convenient, given the present administrative boundaries (which are relevant because legal officials have to take charge of elections on behalf of the Election Commission), the difficulties of communication, etc. The average population per constituency will be about 35,000, but there will have to be wide variations owing to the physical features and administrative divisions. The proportion is much the same as in other countries, where communications are much better and elections are more easily conducted. It is estimated that elections will have to be spread over six weeks because of the difficulty of staffing and policing the polling stations.

17. The Senate, whose composition is determined by Articles 24 to 26, is based on that of Ceylon, which in turn was based on that of Burma. It is desirable that the Cabinet should be responsible to one House only; and clearly this must be the House of Representatives; a system of responsibility to both Houses could not work without a series of intricate rules or a series of highly developed constitutional conventions. Neither being practicable in Nepal, the House of Representatives should have clear primacy, and hence the Senate must not be a directly elected body. On the other hand, a Senate elected by the House of Representatives by single transferable vote would be a mere copy of that House, on a smaller scale. To produce a Senate which would be different from the House of Representatives, but not so different as to be in constant conflict with it, the arrangement proposed is that half should be elected by the House of Representatives by single transferable vote and half nominated by His Majesty, on the recommendation of the Prime Minister. After the first elections and nominations, however, there would be elections and nominations every second year, with the result that the uniformity produced at the outset (when the machinery of democracy was getting under way) would not be repeated thereafter. At the first election a group would require only seven votes, thereafter it would require nineteen votes; but the changes in party strength would produce constant variation, both by election and nomination.

18. The relations between the Houses are similarly adapted from those of Burma and Ceylon. Primacy has to be given to the House of Representatives, lest deadlock be produced. The fundamental precaution is that of Article 56, which requires that an amendment to the Constitution be supported by (a) two-thirds of all the members of the House of Representatives, (b) a majority of the Senate, and (c) His Majesty, acting in his discretion. Hence the majority of the House of Representatives, though capable of overriding the Senate, must act within the confines of the Constitution; and the people can turn out the majority of the House of Representatives within five years.

19. The provisions of chapters I to IV of Part V are so much common form in democratic Constitutions that only one point need be mentioned. Section 34 enables the House of Representatives to elect as Speaker a person who is not a member of that House and provides that, if a member of the House is elected, his seat shall become vacant (and another member would be elected in his place). This arrangement has been taken from the Constitution of Ghana,[10] and it has two reasons. First, it may be difficult to find, among 109 members, a member who

[10] This remains the case in the 1992 constitution of Ghana, which states that any Member of Parliament must resign their seat on appointment as Speaker.

has such knowledge of parliamentary procedure that he can easily exercise the responsible functions of Speaker. Secondly, if a member of the House is elected, he cannot effectively and [*sic*] both as an impartial Speaker and as a political representative of his constituents. Various compromises are adopted by convention in the United Kingdom, but they cannot be adopted by Nepal at this stage. Accordingly it seems better, as in Ghana, to modify the traditional formulae and to provide for alternative representation for Mr Speaker's constituency.

20. There is nothing new in Chapters V and VI of Part V of the Constitution. The financial procedure of the Government of India Act, 1935, adopted by India, does not seem to have justified the variations from the traditional system. Pakistan made a partial return to the United Kingdom system, but it is complicated by relics of the Government of India Act. It seemed that a simplified version of the British system would best suit the conditions of Nepal. The essence has been retained without the complications which have resulted from a long constitutional history.

21. Full legislative power is given by Article 55, but it must be qualified by the other provisions of the Draft Constitution, notably the Chapter on Civil Liberties. Under Article 56, an amendment to the Constitution requires:

(1) the support of two-thirds of all the members of the House of Representatives;
(2) the support of a majority of the Senate; and
(3) the Royal Assent, given by His Majesty in his discretion.

The provisions of Articles 57, 58, and 59 have already been mentioned.

The Judiciary

22. There is nothing unusual in Part VI. The usual protection for the Supreme Court is given by Article 60, and reference should also be made to clause (2) of Article 39. Since the Supreme Court may declare Acts of Parliament to be invalid, a rapid procedure is desirable. This is provided partly by Article 57, partly by Article 61 (which is taken from the Constitution of India, Article 226, and is wider than the corresponding provisions in section 225 of the Government of India Act, 1935), and partly from the Supreme Court Ain, 2013.

The Public Service.

23. The normal rule for servants of the Crown is stated in Article 65, but it must be read subject to any Act of Parliament made under Article 64 and to the powers of the Public Service Commission in Article 66. An independent Public Service Commission is to be established by Article 65, and its powers are specified in Article 66.

The latter confers executive power on the Commission, as in Ceylon. The alternative of making a recommendation to His Majesty was rejected because, in that form, His Majesty would be bound by the recommendation (see clause (2) of Article 15), and the provision would merely give His Majesty a good deal of unnecessary labour. If the powers were to make proposals to his Majesty, the exercise of the power would depend on decisions by Ministers; and experience in other democratic countries has shown that political considerations, or even party patronage, might be brought in. To vest the powers of appointment, dismissal, etc., in His Majesty in his discretion would require His Majesty to have a substantial staff, not under ministerial control, for establishment questions. The Ceylon provision therefore seems to be most convenient.

24. Part VIII, dealing with Audit of Accounts, is in the standard form. The Interim Constitution created an official called the "Comptroller and Auditor-General", though he was apparently given no functions as Comptroller and was in fact to be Auditor-General. There are some advantages in having an independent official to control issues of public money, as in the United Kingdom, but it seems an unnecessary complication in Nepal. Accordingly, Article 67 makes the official merely an "Auditor-General", and Article 68 does not confer upon him any control over issue of public money.

Miscellaneous

25. The provisions of Chapter I of Part II relate to His Majesty's powers and have already been referred to. The incorporation of the Nepal Laws (Interpretation) Act, 2010, into Article 75 will explain some apparent omissions in the Draft Constitution, eg. the term "Oath" in Article 74 includes an affirmation or a declaration in the case of a person authorised by law to make it.

Transitional Provisions

26. The transitional provisions are comparatively simple because the necessary powers must clearly be vested in His Majesty, as is done by Article 77. Article 78 has already been referred to, but it must again be mentioned that it would ease the task of the Courts, and make the law more certain if some Proclamations could be issued before the appointed day.

Conclusion

27. In respect of drafting, the Constitutional Commission has had two objectives, to keep the Draft Constitution short and flexible, and to make the language as simple as the exigencies of legal interpretation allowed. The temptation to insert provisions which would be useful in

present conditions, but not necessary, has been resisted because those conditions are likely to change rapidly. On the other hand, an attempt has been made to foresee what difficulties may possibly occur and to provide the powers necessary to meet them.

3. Confidential notes on Nepal, April 1958

The first meeting of the Constitutional Commission at which I was present was held on the 31st March. There was scattered and diffuse general discussion, relating mainly to the Second Chamber, but only Upadhyaya (N.C.[11]) and Randhir Subba (G.P.[12]) took an active part. They seemed to be against a second chamber, but felt that the King was pledged. They therefore supported a second chamber on the Ceylon model. Nothing else of any significance was said, and it was plain that I would have to submit a draft for discussion, as in fact I had assumed (and I had already drafted eight or ten articles, which had to be revised after the discussion). There were no papers before the meeting except the Constitution of 1948 and the Interim Constitution. I asked for copies of the Citizenship Act and the Representation of the People Bill, and they were promised for the 1st April. I also discovered that there was a Civil Liberties Act and asked for a copy. The chairman hardly spoke. The Secretary said practically nothing and took no notes for minutes. Ramraj Panth had been studying the Constitutions of the World (probably some potted edition) and from time to time displayed his knowledge of the composition of legislatures from Denmark to Afghanistan. There was a short meeting on the 2nd April to tell me that there was no Regency Act. I said that I had so assumed and had provided accordingly in my draft. Since I had the rough draft, practically complete, with me, I read such bits as they asked about. They were non-committal about them. This time the chairman was a little more forthcoming, but Panth had exhausted his knowledge.

I completed the draft on the morning of the 3rd April, and it was to be fetched by Joshi at 2.30 p.m. that day. He did not come, but arrived with a typist at 12.15 p.m. on the 4th April. His explanation was that he had been busy. The typescript was brought to me for correction at 11.30 a.m. on the 7th April. I corrected it by noon and asked that a copy be made available to H.M. before lunch, since I was seeing him at 2.30 p.m. He had not received it when I had an audience, but he gave me a lead, and I gave him a lecture, with apologies, on the

[1]Nepali Congress political party.

[12]Gurkha Parishad political party.

constitutional problems of Nepal. Occasionally he made encouraging noises, but said nothing, and at the end of the lecture he indicated, by asking me about Sital Nivas,[13] that the audience was at an end.

No papers arrived, but I saw the chairman of the Election Commission to have a short discussion and to receive the report of the Delimitation Commission, and made an appointment with the Secretary of the Law Ministry to see what I could get from him. The material so obtained consisted of the Citizenship Act, a Citizenship Bill of whose existence I had not been aware, the Civil Liberties Act (a piece of eyewash), the Interpretation Act, and an interesting set of rules on Government Procedure clearly borrowed from India. The Representation of the People Bill was promised from day to day, but eventually I sent for it on the 11th April and got it.

On the 9th April, when no copy of my draft arrived, I had a telephone message sent to Joshi. He said that he would come to see me on the morning of the 11th April. He brought with him not only my own corrected copy of the draft, made on the 7th April, but also another Draft Constitution, of which he claimed authorship. Since it was extremely amateurish, I thought that he was indeed the author, and that he had held up my draft in order to get his own circulated at the same time. I made polite noises and promised to look at it.

Soon afterwards, I received a note from Upadhyaya (N.C.) asking if he could see me on the morning of the 11th April. He came along that morning, and explained that his main purpose had been to find out if Joshi's Draft (as I called it) had been seen by me. He had since learned that a copy had been left with me, but that I had no responsibility for it. I gave my views about Joshi's Draft in no uncertain terms, and tried to get from him what I should do when the Draft was discussed by the Commission. On this he was cagey; and indeed he was cagey about my own draft also.

There was a meeting of the Constitutional Commission on the afternoon of the 10th April, at which I was not present. I was present at a meeting on the afternoon of the 11th April. The lead was taken by Subba, who obviously had some major criticisms of the powers suggested for the King, but did not put them with the force that I had expected. Afterwards I gave a general exposition of the draft, pointing out the controversial provisions (mostly those relating to the powers of the King), and asking for decisions.

It was agreed that we should meet on the afternoon of the 13th.

Subba came to see me on the morning of the 12th April. His final point was the most interesting. He had discovered that "Joshi's Draft" had been prepared by officials closely associated with the

[13] An official government building in Kathmandu.

King, but had not been seen by the King himself. It is plain from internal evidence that the draftsman had seen my draft. Hence the delay between the 7th April, when I corrected the draft, and the morning of the 11th, when the two drafts were delivered to me. He feared that my draft would produce a result very different from what I contemplated. There was a substantial movement against the King, who was surrounded by "reactionary" elements, and if strong powers were given to the King he would probably use them, which would create antagonism to the King which would, in Subba's opinion, be unfortunate. He was very frank about the political position. If direct rule were continued until the elections, the G.P. would obtain a majority of the seats and would be able to form a Government. If the G.P. were to form a Government before the elections, they might obtain 65%. If the N.C. formed a Government, the G.P. would obtain 35–40% of the seats. If K.I. Singh[14] formed a Government, he might obtain 20% of the seats, otherwise he would get very little besides his own. Any Government in power would derive support from that fact, but otherwise the G.P. was bound to win. There was no question of an alliance between the N.C. and the G.P. before the election, unless it was a coalition Government created to run elections: but even that was unlikely. There could be a coalition after the elections if neither party obtained a majority. He was quite certain that there was no need to provide for a possible breakdown of the party system, but he agreed that in time of emergency power must be left with the King. The appeal of the G.P. was rankly religious, because the N.C. had tried to abolish untouchability and so forth. The people in the hills would support them, and they would get a few seats in the Terai.

Subba said that I had probably noticed that only he and Upadhyaya did the talking in the Commission, though he had tried to persuade the others to talk. (As a matter of fact at the third meeting Panth had spoken at length in favour of domicile as the basis of nationality. I tried to explain that it was administratively impracticable, and that India had adopted it because of the refugee problem, but I could not shut him up: the others said little but clearly agreed with me). He gave the impression that the others (including the chairman) were lightweights, but did not say so. On the other hand, he explained that they could not speak frankly in the Commission because of the fear of leakage. Evidently both he and Upadhyaya are in favour of cutting the powers of the King to a minimum, but dare not say so. What he is most anxious to avoid is the formation of a Government either by the N.C. or by K.I. Singh before the elections. Hence (so I interpret the position) he must not say anything against the King at this stage. His

[14]Briefly Prime Minister of Nepal, 1957–1958; leader of the United Democratic Party.

attitude was that of a party manager, and he was astonishingly frank. Never once did he mention the public interest nor – unlike most of those who have spoken to me – did he say anything against India. He did mention the danger from the North. He said the C.P.[15] might get 15 seats, and possibly more later on, but that depended partly on their getting funds from Russia or China and he did not think they would get any from either at this stage, because China had not completely pacified Tibet and must pay more attention to India. Only two parties had any money, his own and the N.C. Theirs came from the A class Ranas (and especially General Magendra): those of the N.C. came from the C class Ranas, and each had a million rupees. K.I. Singh had somehow (there was a hint here) got some money while he was in office, but he had now exhausted most of his funds. I asked if the "local potentates" would not come in as independents. He said they would not, because they were unknown five miles away, and on the average there were 120 villages in each constituency, with perhaps 500 in each. Hence there were 120 "local potentates" and none of them could win a seat. Only his party and the N.C. (with some communist seats) could win seats, if the G.P. got into office they would remain in. Some 20 would be given Ministerial posts, and the others could be satisfied by various means, e.g. Government contracts and licences.

Subba was very interested in the position of the monarchy in the U.K. I explained that the Queen had large private estates which were not under parliamentary control. The Civil List was voted at the beginning of the reign, and most of it was appropriated, though there was a sum of £70,000 or £80,000 (I could not remember the figure) voted for the Privy Purse. Other public revenues were under parliamentary control. He ended with another attack on the King. He was surrounded by reactionary elements[,] his own relatives and the Queen's. If the Constitution provided discretionary powers they would be used, and for the benefit of a small group. The forests had been expropriated, and grants had been made to the Royal entourage. A sum of about Rs. 3,500,000 had been transmitted from the National Bank to Paris.

13th April 1958.

We had a most satisfactory meeting of the Constitutional Commission this afternoon. At the previous meeting, at which objection had been taken to the idea of the Council of State, I had suggested that instead we might put teeth into the Senate, by giving a majority of nominated members and having them nominated at the King's discretion. This idea had seemed attractive to the Commission, but today they went

[15] Communist Party.

back upon it, preferring the Council of State with the innocuous Ceylon Senate, but they wanted the Council of State limited to functions relating to a Regency, etc. I left that point until we had argued about the other powers of the King. They were accepted, after a good deal of argument, especially by Subba and Joshi (who at one stage was quite loquacious). I then turned on Subba the argument which he had put to me privately. I said that the powers of the King were very heavy, and they might have to be borne by a not very experienced King or by a Queen regnant. He (or she) would have to consult somebody, and if no formal consultative body was constituted he would necessarily consult members of his Household. I mentioned that after the death of the Prince Consort Queen Victoria had been accused of consulting "irresponsible advisers", and that it was far better that the King should consult a body which included the Prime Minister and the other Ministers. This argument was accepted, together with an idea suggested by Panth that the Speaker and Deputy Speaker and the President and Deputy President of the Senate should also be members. This of course would do no harm whatever, because the King can add as many of his own nominees as he wishes.

On other points I compromised a little, though not as much as I expected. Subba put to me point-blank the question what would happen if the King's power to dispense with Cabinet Government were removed. I replied that in such a case the King would suspend the whole Constitution, as had been done in Pakistan.[16] That convinced him, since he realised that a power to suspend the Constitution must be included in the difficult conditions of Nepal. (I had at the previous meeting emphasised that Nepal lay between two very powerful neighbours). On the emergency power itself, I agreed to make separate provision for war, etc., on the one hand and breakdown of constitutional machinery on the other, mentioning that this had been done in India. There was also objection to the power to remove difficulties. Since this was not important, I suggested the Indian provision, though I think in drafting it I will give it more teeth. On the question of the King's discretionary power to refuse the Royal Assent, I carried the draft by pointing out that it would be difficult to refuse unless he had the Council of State with him. Kings, like politicians, have to keep their popularity.

I was then authorised to produce the Second Draft, with the amendments suggested by me at the previous meeting. This Second Draft should, I think, be quite satisfactory, since it will provide adequate means for direct rule if democratic government breaks down

[16] In October 1958.

(or becomes corrupt, though I did not mention that), and on the other hand would not enable the King to play fast and loose with democracy.

18th April 1958.

At the meeting of the Constitutional Commission on the 13th April, I said that the second draft would be ready by the 15th April and suggested a meeting on the 18th April, pointing out that I might have to produce a third draft and that my last working day was the 23rd April. The Secretary promised to let me know whether there would be a meeting on the 18th April. The second draft was ready on the morning of the 15th April and was collected later in the morning. The typescript was delivered to me at 1.45 p.m. on the 17th April. I asked Joshi if there was a meeting on the 18th, and he said that he would let me know later in the afternoon whether it was to be on the afternoon of the 18th or on the afternoon of the 19th. Since he did not telephone, I asked Rana to find out. He telephoned this morning (18th) to say that there was no meeting on the 18th, but Joshi would let me knew at about 4.45 p.m. on the 18th whether there was to be a meeting on the 19th. The timing makes it plain that the Commission is meeting without me today. I have therefore arranged to meet the University Commission.

21st April 1958.

I was unfair to Joshi: he had telephoned me on the night of the 17th to let me know that there would be a meeting on the morning of the 19th; but, since I was out, he had not bothered to leave a message or to telephone again. The Commission evidently met on the afternoon of the 18th April and sorted out the points to be raised with me. The meeting on the 19th April went on from 11 a.m. to 3 p.m. with an interval of 20 minutes to enable me to get some lunch. Subba had read the second draft carefully and raised a number of points of detail, often merely of drafting. They were generally quite useful points, which could either be answered satisfactorily, or dealt with by minor amendments. His discussion with me on the 12th April was presumably designed to encourage me to limit the powers of the King; he did not want to propose such limitations himself, perhaps because he did not want his party excluded from office before the general election, or himself excluded if members of his party took office. Joshi had compared "his draft" with my own and raised a number of points of principle. In the main they would have increased the power of the Crown, though on at least one occasion he was against the Crown. He was also anxious to make certain that none of those recently appointed (e.g. to the Supreme Court, Auditor-General, Public Service Commission, etc.) should be confirmed in office by the

Constitution. Generally, however, his ideas were so half-baked that it was not easy to turn them down politely. Upadhyaya sometimes managed to shut up his henchman, but on occasions he decided to let me do it.

The one point on which Joshi was definitely against the Crown was on the question of Crown private revenues. He said, most emphatically, that there were none. I expressed some incredulity, and Subba murmured support. I added that, like Queen Victoria, the King might save money out of his Civil List or receive money by way of legacy. There may, however, have been some sharp practice over this: In the first draft the clause referring to Crown private revenues had been typed twice. I had struck out the second, and somehow the first also had got struck out, with the result that the clause was omitted from the second draft. Subba noticed the error, and I apologised for it, assuming that I was responsible for it. I found, however, that it had been struck out in ink, which I have not used at all. It must therefore have been struck out by Joshi. It may be that on his copy he had struck out the first typing and had therefore done it on mine, not noticing that I had already struck out the second typing. It is, however, odd that it should be the clause to which he took strong objection, and I should not have noticed the omission if Subba had not called attention to it.

The Commission wants me to draft the Manual of Procedure. I said that it could not be done without access to books, and accordingly it must be done in Cambridge, though I explained that work had accumulated during my absence and that there must be some delay. I suggested an Explanatory Memorandum, with which the Commission agreed: and when I asked whether it should be in my own name or theirs, they preferred the former because it would be in the name of an "expert", though I expect they thought it better for me to take responsibility if opposition developed.

The changes required were not numerous, and none were of any great importance. I was therefore able to complete the third draft on the evening of the 20th April and to complete the draft of the Explanatory memorandum on the morning of the 21st April. We are to have a meeting on the afternoon of the 23rd April in order to clean up.

22nd April 1958.

I have been subjected to a curious barrage. Soon after my arrival, Joshi suggested to me (after the first discussion in the Constitutional Commission) that there ought to be some six members of the Lower House appointed by the King. I said merely that the King could exercise no influence through six nominated members; he would want at least twenty-five to do that, since only with so large a number could he prevent the formation of a purely party government. This suggestion duly appeared in "Joshi's Draft", and Joshi raised the point twice in the Commission, where it was turned down in the usual way, i.e. without argument, but with some polite negative. On the evening of the 20th April Rana did not leave as soon as we got back, but said that he had been thinking over the problem of securing political stability, and it had occurred to him that perhaps it could be obtained if the King had power to appoint, say, 30 members of Parliament. I said that, far from producing stability, it might produce exactly the opposite, because the "King's friends" would not have a majority. Next morning, when Joshi appeared to collect the third draft, he said that he would like to put a point to me.

I had seen from the Census Report that there were many tribal groups in Nepal. They were so distributed that quite often they would not secure representation at all in some cases, and in others they would not secure adequate representation. Among the latter he mentioned his own people, the Newaris, who could secure only three representatives, though on a proportionate basis they were entitled to more. This problem could be met by allowing the King to appoint, say, 25 members of Parliament to represent various interests. I gave the obvious answer, that 25 members representing communal groups would prevent the formation of a party Government, and that each of the groups would demand jobs and expenditure for its own people, without reference to national interests.

The same afternoon, Rana came in early. I did not encourage him to talk, but later he came back and asked if I was busy, because he would like to talk for ten minutes. He actually talked for 90 minutes. He said that he had been considering what I had said about political stability the night before, and clearly I was right; but, as it seemed to him, the election of 109 members for territorial constituencies (I had never mentioned this to him) would result in many groups being unrepresented. He then mentioned not only the tribal groups like the Sherpas but also the Ranas themselves, who may have been accused of profiting from their position, but who did give political stability to the country for 108 years, and who had something to contribute. Would not the position be met by the King appointing, say, 30 members to represent the various interests which could not be adequately represented by election? Again I gave the obvious answer, and at greater length.

I had up to that point treated Rana simply as [a] frustrated intellectual who was doubly frustrated as a Rana. He had made no positive suggestions, but had grumbled continually about all the political parties, had said that the only stable influence was the King, and that the "masses" would not support any of them. All this had become a bit of a bore, and I had done my best to limit our talks and to switch him off his one topic. It was now clear that he was the emissary of some group to which Joshi also had access: and I remembered Subba's statement that "Joshi's Draft" had come from the Palace entourage. It is such a feeble document that it must be Joshi's own draft for it could never have been drafted by a lawyer: but probably it does come from some group or other, perhaps in or near the Palace, which is trying to secure influence. I therefore took the offensive, and said that, if the masses would not support the present political parties, it should be easy to get together the various sections which were against the politicians, including the independent members who were being elected to the Advisory Assembly, and form a Government which would last ten years. He said there was little time, and I agreed, but pointed out that the members of the Assembly obviously had influence in their areas and that they would soon be collecting in Kathmandu. I then asked where the political parties got their money. He replied that the Nepali Congress got it from his uncle (he repeated the name twice, but I could not get hold of it). When I asked why, he replied, for the sake of power. Koirala[17] was simply his man, and the uncle had got in as Minister of Finance. The money came from the joint family estate, i.e. from the uncle's share of that estate. (In that case, if Subba is right that the amount is ten lakhs, the Ranas must have done well out of the country). The Gurkha Parishad got its money from General Magendra. (I did not follow that one up). There was much more on the usual lines, but I emphasised that, with adult suffrage, there was no alternative to a party Government based upon a solid party majority. (I did not mention the checks and balances in case he did not know what was in the draft. But there are three copies loose somewhere: top copy goes to H.M., No. 2 to me, and Nos. 3 to 7 to members of the Commission). It would be dangerous for H.M. to take too much personal responsibility, because if something went wrong (e.g. a prolonged drought) the masses might go against him. The only real alternative was direct rule, without a Parliament. Rana said H.M. would not want that: he was a genuine democrat. I made it plain, of course, that I was not accepting Rana's interpretation of the situation: I was merely following out the consequences of his own assumptions.

[17]It is unclear which Koirala Jennings is referring to. The Koirala family were, and continue to be, prominent members and leaders of the Nepali Congress Party.

SECTION G: NEW ZEALAND

The recently arrived Governor-General of New Zealand, Viscount Cobham, wrote to Jennings for advice on what to do in the event of a hung parliament in the December 1957 general election, since a tight contest was expected for the eighty-seat single chamber parliament between the conservative National Party, which had been in office since 1949 led by Keith Holyoake, and the centre-left Labour Party, led by Walter Nash.

1. Letter to the Governor-General of New Zealand, 2 November 1957

Dear Lord Cobham,[1]

I have hidden the previous correspondence so efficiently that I cannot find it myself. In reply to your letter of the 25th October, therefore, I run the risk of repeating and even of repudiating myself.

If the stalemate runs on for six months or so, it would be difficult to refuse a dissolution to the Prime Minister if he was then defeated and advised dissolution, You will remember that MacDonald dissolved after nine months in 1924,[2] in circumstances in which an alternative Government might have been possible. If an alternative Government with a majority cannot be formed, dissolution is the only remedy, and it is reasonable that the Prime Minister who has tried to keep the show going, and not the Leader of the Opposition who has terminated it, should get whatever advantages there are from dissolving while in office. These things are, of course, not quite so simple as they sound in the books. If the Opposition does allow the Government to keep the show going for six months, the real reason, no doubt, is that

[1] Charles Lyttelton, 10th Viscount Cobham; Governor-General of New Zealand, 1957–1962.

[2] Ramsay MacDonald became the first Labour Prime Minister of Britain in January 1924 and headed a minority administration with Liberal Party support against the claims of the Conservative Party, which was the biggest party in the House of Commons. This unstable situation did not last long and MacDonald's administration fell after the October 1924 general election.

they think they have a better chance of winning after an interval: at least it is a reasonable gamble that political or economic conditions will change for the worse and the Government get the blame. If the Opposition plays this game long enough, the Prime Minister may ask for a dissolution without a defeat, and clearly you would have to give it to him if you were satisfied that no stable Government is practicable.

An immediate request for a dissolution is a more difficult matter. If the circumstances are as I imagine them, the result would probably be another stalemate. In Britain in 1910 there was very little difference even after several months.[3] I am inclined to suggest that, without telling anybody why, you should try to persuade both sides to keep the show going until the next register came into operation. The young men and women might then tip the scale. I know nothing about such things as election funds in New Zealand, but not even a trade union wants to pay for two elections in the same financial year. If an appeal to patriotism were also an appeal to bank balances there would be a reasonable chance of success. This does not answer your question; but I think the answer is that neither side should have an immediate dissolution if there is the slightest chance of keeping things going for nine months or so. If there is no such chance, it would be safer for you to allow the Prime Minister to dissolve. It is true that the Opposition might agree to take office without a pledge to dissolve, believing that after a short interval you would be forced to grant a dissolution: but you would be able to see through that one. If the Prime Minister asks for an immediate dissolution, you are satisfied from conversation with him that he would not let help [*sic*] another Government to get through the next Budget, and also satisfied that the Opposition could not get it through without help, you will have no alternative but an immediate dissolution. If necessary you could tell the Prime Minister that you wanted to see the Leader of the Opposition before deciding on a dissolution; but there is no point in doing this if, as is probably the case with a small community like the New Zealanders, all the facts are pretty obvious. Other things being equal, it is safer to take advice than to reject it.

The criticism of Lord Byng is, I think, that he misjudged the situation, and had to grant a dissolution to the new Prime Minister which he had refused to King.[4] This is strictly relevant to my remark that, other things being equal, it is safer to accept advice than to reject

[3]There were two elections held in 1910, first in January and then in December, which instead of breaking the parliamentary deadlock between the Liberal and Conservative Parties actually continued it.

[4]Jennings is referring to Lord Byng, who was Governor-General of Canada during the 1926 constitutional crisis, when he refused Prime Minister William Mackenzie King a dissolution since the Governor-General believed that, as Arthur Meighen's Conservative

it. It is, however, easier to lay down these general propositions than it is to take a decision when the event occurs, and you are doubly unfortunate in having this sort of problem thrust upon you so soon. The more I see of small legislatures (and I am now concerned with Malta) the more sure I become that one must run the risk of corruption with small constituencies rather than run the risk of stalemate with a small legislature.

It is also relevant that the British economy, and therefore the prospects of the sterling bloc, is in a state of suspense. The alternatives seem to be inflation or a row with the trade unions, or possibly both. The stockbrokers are therefore advising the institutions to keep their funds liquid. If something does go wrong, you may have a sufficient change of opinion in New Zealand to justify a second dissolution.

The Maltese problem has proved to be difficult not in its principles but in its details. The conferences should end next week, but there will probably be no final decisions for another month. There is no doubt that there will be agreement, but we are still haggling over minor points. I am looking forward to a visit to West Africa after Christmas, chiefly because I have seen enough of Liverpool Street Station.

Party was the biggest party in parliament, they should be given the opportunity to form a government. King resigned and Meighen assured the Governor-General that he could form a stable administration. However, he was unsuccessful in this task and in turn requested and was granted a dissolution from Byng. The subsequent election returned King's party to power and brought into question the Governor-General's powers and previous decisions. The episode remains one of the most controversial constitutional episodes in the Commonwealth.

SECTION H: PAKISTAN

Jennings had been discussed by the Viceroy of India, Lord Mountbatten, and others as a potential constitutional adviser to the new Dominion of Pakistan as early as 1946, but it was not until July 1954 that he was invited by the Constituent Assembly constitutional drafting committee to help craft a new constitution. Independent Pakistan largely operated under the colonial-era Government of India Act 1935 and the Constituent Assembly had plans to curb the powers of the Governor-General, derived from the Act, over the Prime Minister and Cabinet. Pakistani governors-general had exercised extraordinary executive powers over the country, including ordering the dismissal of Prime Minister Nazimuddin in 1953. On 24 October 1954, in reaction to the political crisis and opposition to the proposed constitution, the Governor-General, Ghulam Muhammad, dissolved the Constituent Assembly and reshuffled the Cabinet. The President of the Assembly, Maulvi Tamizuddin Khan, challenged the legality of the dissolution and filed a petition at the Sindh High Court on 8 November 1954. He won the case. The Governor-General and the Government then took it to the Federal Court to uphold the dissolution and the Governor-General's executive powers. Controversially, Jennings, who had been advising the Assembly, now returned to Pakistan in late November as a paid advocate to advise his new client, the Governor-General, on how best to defeat Tamizuddin Khan's petition before the Federal Court. In March 1956 the Federal Court found in favour of the Governor-General in *Federation of Pakistan and Others v. Maulvi Tamizuddin Khan* [PLD 1955 FC 240] and a new Constituent Assembly was created under Governor-General Order No. 12 of 1955. For greater detail from the perspective of Jennings on his role in this provocative era in Pakistan, see his *Constitutional Problems in Pakistan*, which largely reproduces the memoranda, arguments, and judgements behind his advice to the Governor-General. This chapter focuses instead on his previously unpublished diary and private impressions from this dramatic constitutional period in Pakistan.

1. 'The position in Pakistan', 29 October 1954

The local newspapers have difficulty in understanding what is happening in Pakistan and are therefore giving a wrong interpretation of events. I have had no news from Karachi since I left on the 15th October; but rumours of an impending dissolution of the Constituent Assembly were then in circulation, and accordingly I think my interpretation to be correct.[1]

2. The causa causans[2] of recent events was the dismissal of the Nazimuddin Government by the present Governor-General[3] some 20 months ago. The Muslim League Party[4] which dominates the Constituent Assembly accepted the situation and Nazimuddin[5] himself has taken no part in political agitation. Some of the Ministers then dismissed, however, took things with bad grace, and there has always been a section of the Party looking for a chance to get its own back. Distrust of the Governor-General was responsible for the following decisions, which were incorporated in the draft constitution:

(1) The powers of the President of Pakistan were to be rigidly defined, and in particular he would have no powers to dismiss Ministers.
(2) The powers of the Governor-General were to cease as soon as the new Constitution was enacted. This was expected to be on the 25th December 1954. New elections could not be held until early 1956, but a President would be elected by the Constituent Assembly itself, probably in the last week of December, 1954.
(3) The Constituent Assembly was to remain in being as Provisional Parliament until the new Parliament was duly constituted. Thus, the Constituent Assembly was proposing to get rid of the Governor-General at the end of 1954 or very early in 1955, while keeping itself in power until the spring of 1956. There were rumours that Sardar Abdul Nishtar,[6] formerly Governor of the Punjab and one of the Ministers dismissed by the Governor-General with Nazimuddin, was to be elected President ad interim.

3. The Muslim League Party was not content to wait until the end of the year. Some considerable time ago Gagdar, the Deputy

[1] The Assembly was dissolved by the Governor-General on 24 October. See introductory note to this section and Document H2 in general.

[2] The last link in the chain of causation.

[3] Ghulam Muhammad, first Minister of Finance of Pakistan, 1947–1951; third Governor-General, 1951–1955.

[4] The Muslim League was founded in 1906 to protect certain Muslim interests in British India. It later advocated a separate state of Pakistan, which came to fruition under its then leader, Jinnah. Almost all the leading politicians of Pakistan between 1947 and 1956 came from the Muslim League.

[5] Khwaja Nazimuddin, second Governor-General of Pakistan, 1948–1951; second Prime Minister, 1951–1953.

[6] Sardar Abdur Rab Nishtar, Cabinet minister; Governor of the Punjab, 1949–1951.

President, gave notice of a Bill to amend the Government of India Act by reducing the powers of the Governor-General. This Bill was not proceeded with. Suddenly in the middle of August, while the Governor-General was on the frontiers, a Bill was produced at 5 p.m. one evening, brought up at 9 a.m. next day, passed in ten minutes, was signed forthwith by the President of the Constituent Assembly, and became law. Being a constitutional bill, it did not require the royal assent. In substance it took away all the Governor-General's powers in respect of appointment and dismissal of Ministers and vested them in the Prime Minister. The Governor-General returned to Karachi next day but could do nothing about it.

4. Other matters seem to have had, at most, only an indirect effect, namely:–

(1) The defeat of the Muslim League Party in East Bengal provides an excuse for alleging that the members of the Constituent assembly for East Bengal are unrepresentative. That allegation might equally made [*sic*] about all the members of any legislature which has been in existence for over seven years.

(2) The attempt to make the Constitution "Islamic" has not been very successful, but there are of course people (especially the Hindus and the Muslim left wing) who dislike communal electorates, the requirement that the President be a Muslim, and the primacy given to the Quran and the Sunnah.[7] There is also criticism of the "Muhammad Ali formula"[8] by which a balance between East and West Pakistan was achieved. In particular, it is alleged by some of the Punjab Ministers that it puts power into the hands of the Bengalis. This is mixed up with the problem of fusing West Pakistan into a single Province, which is supported by the Punjab and strongly opposed by Sind. These are the "defects" of the Draft Constitution which can be used as a justification for dissolving the Constituent Assembly. To these allegations can be added the further allegation that the final consideration of the Report of the Basic Principles Committee, on which the Draft Constitution is based, was extremely hurried. In fact, the problem of the financial relations between the Federation and the Provinces was not considered at all.

5. These are at best excuses. The Constituent Assembly was due to meet on the 27th October, when the Draft Constitution (which I

[7]Traditions of the Holy Prophet.

[8]Muhammad Ali Bogra's idea to implement institutional equality between West and East Pakistan. Bogra was a Pakistani diplomat selected by Ghulam Muhammad to become the third Prime Minister, 1953–1955.

finished on the night of the 15th October) was to have been presented. It was anticipated that the discussion in the Muslim League Party and the general discussion (equivalent to second reading) would have been finished about the 15th November, or perhaps a little later. An effort was being made to complete the "consultation stage" and the "third reading" (to use English terminology) by the 25th December, which was Jinnah's[9] birthday. If the enactment of the Constitution was to be prevented, therefore, it was necessary to take action before the 27th October. Hence the necessity for recalling the Prime Minister on the 23rd October.

6. There is no provision in the Government of India Act for the dissolution of the Constituent Assembly. The action taken was therefore both unconstitutional and illegal. This raised certain problems, which seem to have been solved at least temporarily with considerable success.

(1) The Governor-General had no power to dismiss Ministers. He could of course act illegally, as in the case of the dissolution. If, however, the Cabinet stuck together and refused to be dismissed, there would have been two "authorities" giving contradictory orders. The position of the Government servants would have been particularly difficult. The problem was overcome by the Prime Minister's acquiescence or active support (I do not know which it was). The Governor-General acted legally in dismissing Ministers on the "advice" of the Prime Minister.

(2) General Mirza,[10] Governor of East Bengal, has been appointed Minister of the Interior and the Frontiers. This puts him in charge of the Karachi police, the Baluchistan police, and the [North-West] Frontier police. The other police forces are under Provincial control, but presumably subject to federal direction under section 102[11] so long as the emergency proclamation remains in operation.

[9] Muhammad Ali Jinnah, first Governor-General and President of the Constituent Assembly of the Dominion of Pakistan, 1947–1948.

[10] Iskander Mirza, a leading Pakistani political and military figure who after independence held senior positions including Defence Secretary, Governor of East Pakistan, and Minister of the Interior in the Federal Cabinet. In August 1955 he was acting Governor-General in place of the ailing Ghulam Muhammad, whom he formally replaced in October that year, remaining in the post until March 1956, when Pakistan became a republic. He was translated into the first President and served until 1958, when General Ayub Khan took over running the country and Mirza went into exile.

[11] The Governor-General issued a proclamation of emergency under section 102 of the Government of India Act 1935.

(3) There is at present no Provisional Government in East Bengal, where section 92A[12] is in force. Hence East Bengal is controlled by the Federal Government. The possibility of effective opposition from the Punjab, Sind and N.W.F.P.[13] has been met by proclaiming an emergency under section 102. If this proves insufficient, the Provincial Government can be suspended under Section 92A.
(4) The simultaneous proclamation of emergency under section 102 and the dissolution of the Constituent Assembly gives at least the semblance of legality to legislation by Ordinance under section 42.[14] That is, sovereign powers of legislation are vested in the Governor-General acting on the advice of the Cabinet.

There is thus initial dictatorship. It seems very unlikely that either the Governor-General or the Prime Minister would wish to perpetuate this position: but, now that there has been departure from strict legal principles, there is no great practical difficulty about going further. So long as the Army and the police support the Governor-General, anything whatever may happen.

7. The local newspapers say that a general election is to take place and they assume that this will be held on adult franchise. I see no reason for this assumption. There are no constituencies, no electoral rules, no electoral law, and no electoral organisation. It would take at least twelve months to put a complete machine into operation, though possibly something could be improvised in six months. But would a Constituent Assembly so elected have any moral authority? If it produced a Constitution would it have any moral authority? The nearest that this government can get to legality is to put into operation the Rules of the Constituent Assembly applying to casual vacancies. This means in practice, though not legally, that section 92A will have to be taken off East Bengal. Elections would have to be by proportional representation and so there would probably be a Muslim League majority in the Constituent Assembly with a strong United Front minority from East Bengal. Would it be possible to get any sort of Constitution through such a body?

[12] In July 1948 Pakistan restored the Governor-General's Emergency Powers, which had been repealed at independence. Section 92A (corresponding to section 93 of the Government of India Act, 1935, which covered 'Provisions in case of failure of constitutional machinery') was controversially used to justify the Governor-General's executive actions in suspending provincial legislatures after independence, including in the Punjab, Sind, and East Bengal, as well as dismissing ministries.

[13] North West Frontier Province.

[14] The Governor-General issued an Emergency Powers ordinance under section 42 of the Government of India Act 1935.

2. 'The political situation in Pakistan', *c.*1955

Lord Mountbatten[15] "handed over" Pakistan to Muhammad Ali Jinnah, usually known in Pakistan as the Quaid-i-Azam,[16] in a ceremony in Karachi on the 14th August 1947, though the Indian Independence Act did not take effect until next day. The Quaid-i-Azam became Governor-General, with Liaquat Ali Khan[17] as Prime Minister, Ghulam Muhammad as Minister of Finance and Chaudhri Muhammad Ali[18] as Secretary-General. This arrangement was a mistake. The Quaid-i-Azam could not be a constitutional monarch; in whatever post he occupied he would be a disaster because of his overwhelming prestige.[19] He added to the mistake by becoming President of the Constituent Assembly, with Tamizuddin Khan[20] as Deputy President. Possibly the arrangement was justified by the enormous difficulties which faced Pakistan. It had three whole Provinces, but very poor ones, Sind, Baluchistan and the N.W.F.P. It had only part of the Punjab, but it had the capital, Lahore. It also had part of Bengal, but not the capital.[21] A federal capital had to be made in Karachi and a provincial capital in Dacca.[22] They were 1800 miles apart, and there was no communication between them except through India or around Ceylon. There was no army, not even a battalion, for every battalion of the Indian army in Pakistan contained Hindu companies. Rioting, accompanied by assassinations, arson, looting, rape and the abduction of women and girls, broke out on a large scale and on both sides of the border. In consequence a vast movement of population took place, the Muslims trekking to Pakistan and the Hindus to India. Pakistan received eight million refugees and probably

[15] Viscount (later Earl) Mountbatten of Burma, last Viceroy of India, 1947; first Governor-General of the Indian Dominion, 1947–1948.

[16] 'Great leader' in Urdu.

[17] Liaquat Ali Khan, first Prime Minister of Pakistan, 1947–1951.

[18] Chaudhri Muhammad Ali, senior civil servant; Cabinet minister and briefly Prime Minister, 1955–1956.

[19] Jinnah surprised Mountbatten and others by choosing to become Governor-General and not Prime Minister of Pakistan. Despite Commonwealth governors-general being expected to be removed from active politics, Jinnah was conspicuously involved and combined his vice-regal office with the critical political position of President of the Constituent Assembly. He held both offices until his death in September 1948.

[20] Maulvi Tamizuddin Khan succeeded Jinnah as President of the Constituent Assembly in 1948.

[21] The creation of India and Pakistan resulted in a partition of the subcontinent. The Punjab and Bengal provinces were painfully split between the two states. Pakistan was geographically divided into West Pakistan and East Pakistan. East Pakistan would break away and become Bangladesh in 1971.

[22] Now known as Dhaka.

lost five million.[23] A public service had to be built up from Muslims in the public service and such officials as had migrated from India. That some sort of order was produced out of this chaos was due to the skill of Chaudhri Muhammad Ali. Meanwhile the Pathans invaded Kashmir and the Indian Army was sent to defend it. The Quaid-i-Azam ordered the Pakistan Army to the defence of the tribesmen, but it was still in process of organisation and it had no ammunition, with the result that India captured most of Kashmir. India also forcibly annexed Junagadh and M[anavadar][24] whose rulers had acceded to Pakistan.

The Quaid-i-Azam fell ill in July 1948 and died in the following September. Nazimuddin was appointed Governor-General because he was a Bengali, while the Quaid-i-Azam was born in Karachi and Liaquat was a Punjabi. The Muslim League, which dominated the Constituent Assembly, began to split into competing, ambitious and intriguing groups, more or less held together by Liaquat. Even he had his opponents, and when he was assassinated in 1951 Begum Liaquat[25] openly charged that he had been murdered at the instigation of those opponents, though all the investigations (including those of a British police officer) show that the assassin was a fanatic, who believed that the competition which had begin to show itself in high places was due to the failure of Liaquat and his Begum to observe the precepts of Islam. Also, the Rawalpindi Conspiracy[26] had broken out in the army in February 1951. Whether there was a conspiracy is still a matter for argument, but it is clear that there were disaffected persons in the army who would have welcomed a change of government.

On the death of Liaquat, Nazimuddin decided to become Prime Minister and Ghulam Muhammad was appointed Governor-General in his place. With the assistance of his pupil, Chaudhri Muhammad Ali, Ghulam Muhammad had done a good job as Minister of Finance and had, it appears, developed a swelled head in the process. On the other hand, he had not resisted the temptation to allow his son-in-law to make substantial profits. Nazimuddin was weak but

[23]Though exact figures are contested it is estimated that almost 14.5 million and perhaps more were forced to migrate during partition. See, for example, P. Bharadwaj, A. Khwaja, and A. Mian, 'The big march: migratory flows after partition of British India', *Economic and Political Weekly*, 43, no. 35 (2008), pp. 39–49.

[24]The Nawab of Junagadh, a Muslim ruler over a predominantly Hindu state including the vassal territory of Manavadar, acceded to Pakistan in September 1947, to the consternation of India since the state was surrounded by the Dominion of India. India sent troops to the state and occupied it in November 1947. A subsequent plebiscite of the population came out overwhelmingly in support of accession to India in February 1948.

[25]The wife of Liaquat Ali Khan and a political personality in her own right.

[26]This was an attempted coup led by Major-General Akbar Khan with the objective of occupying the disputed territory of Jammu and Kashmir.

victorious. He was very religious and was very much in the hands of the mullahs, who began to claim that an Islamic State should be ruled on Islamic principles. In [1953] religious riots broke out in the Punjab. The Muslims attacked the Ahmadis.[27] Owing to the weakness of Chundrigar,[28] the Governor, and lack of force at the centre through Nazimuddin's sympathy with orthodoxy, the rioters governed Lahore for three days. On top of this, the end of the Korean war, which [*sic*] had boosted the prices of jute and cotton, and the problem was far beyond the capacity of Nazimuddin's Cabinet, especially of the Minister of Commerce, Fazlur Rehman,[29] who is one of the standing jokes of Asia.

In April, 1953, Ghulam Muhammad dismissed Nazimuddin and brought Muhammad Ali back from the United States, where he had secured a reputation as a fly-boy ambassador. On all British precedents, this action was completely unjustifiable, for the Muslim League majority in the Constituent Assembly still supported Nazimuddin. Ghulam Muhammad sought to justify his actions by reference to the provisions of the Government of India Act. In the short run the decision was a good one, for it put Chaudhri Muhammad Ali into effective control.

Nevertheless it split the Muslim League and created the general spirit of distrust which is now so evident in Pakistan. Muhammad Ali was not a good Prime Minister. For all practical purposes Chaudhri Muhammad Ali ran the Cabinet. He could not hold the office, because both he and Ghulam Muhammad were Punjabi, and so there had to be a Prime Minister from Bengal. In fact, though, he dominated the Cabinet and ran it, subject to the direction and control of Ghulam Muhammad. The direction and control were very real, for the relations of the two were still those of pupil and teacher. Ghulam Muhammad's two strokes increased his power, for they could hardly oppose a sick man whose intentions were clearly patriotic. Chaudhri Muhammad Ali was able to persuade him to withdraw his own obviously absurd decisions before they were published, but in effect Ghulam Muhammad exercised power both of initiative and of veto. Muhammad Ali was capable of intrigue at a lower level, but he had no personal or political following at all, and he was treated by Ghulam Muhammad as a subordinate of no particular importance.

[27]The Ahmadis are an Islamic group founded in British India. They are considered heretical by some orthodox Muslims for their beliefs.

[28]I.I. Chundrigar, Pakistani minister and Governor; briefly Prime Minister in late 1957.

[29]Fazlur Rehman, a senior Cabinet minister who held various portfolios, including Interior, Education, and Commerce.

The majority of the Constituent Assembly accepted the dismissal of Nazimuddin somewhat reluctantly, and by April 1954 there was a majority against Muhammad Ali. There should have been elections in East Bengal in 1953, but they were postponed until 1954, the real reason being that the Muslim League there doubted whether they could win. The postponement did not help them. The various Opposition parties came together in a temporary coalition, the United Front,[30] the powerful components of which were the group led by Fazlul Huq[31] and the Awami League[32] led by H.S. Suharwardy,[33] both of whom had been Chief Ministers in pre-partition Bengal. The United Front swamped the Muslim League, which was practically wiped out. Fazlul Huq was asked to form a Government, but some sort of quarrel developed with Suharwardy, and Fazlul Huq never completed his Cabinet. Some indiscreet speeches in India provided an excuse for the suppression of the Provisional Constitution under section 92A of the Government of India Act.

Meanwhile the Muslim League members from East Bengal in the Constituent Assembly had lost their moral authority and began to take a more active part in intrigue against the Governor-General and the Prime Minister. Nazimuddin, though remaining in the Constituent Assembly, sulked in a corner and the lead was taken by Sardar Abdur Rab Nishtar and Fazlur Rehman. Nishtar is not a Sardar,[34] and Nishtar itself is an adopted name, but he has a powerful personality. Fazlur Rehman is an arch-intriguer, the sort of man who takes people into corners in lobbies and puts poison in their ears. They had begun to whittle away the Governor-General's powers and finally, on the 22nd September 1954, took them away altogether by a Bill of which notice was given at 3 p.m. on the 21st and which was passed at 9.10 a.m. on the 22nd, the time having been changed by the President, who also exercised his power to waive notice under the Rules. The President was Tamizuddin Khan, who was in the [*illegible*] of the Nishtar group. It is believed that it was intended to have a vote of no-confidence in Muhammad Ali, by which he would automatically cease to be Prime

[30] A coalition of non-Muslim League parties formed in East Pakistan after independence to contest the 1954 legislative elections.

[31] Maulvi Abul Kasem Fazlul Haq, known as the 'Tiger of Bengal'; founder and leader of the Krishak Praja Party; briefly Chief Minister of the United Front Government in East Pakistan and its Governor, 1956–1958.

[32] A political party founded by Bengali nationalists in 1950.

[33] Husain Shaheed Suharwardy, Bengali politician and Awami League leader; Prime Minister of Pakistan, 1956–1957.

[34] Sardar is an honorific title. Jennings is probably implying that Nishtar was not a Sardar Vallabhbhai Patel, the powerful Deputy Prime Minister and Home Minister of India, 1947–1950, known as the 'Iron Man of India'.

Minister under the new Act. Nishtar would become Prime Minister and would forthwith advise the replacement of Ghulam Muhammad by Tamizuddin Khan. This is brazen talk, but it demonstrates the state of sentiment.

The Constituent Assembly was due to meet on the 27th October to receive the Draft Constitution prepared by the Drafting Committee. The Prime Minister, who was about to return home from the U.S.A., was summoned three days early and arrangements were made for his transport by R.A.F. planes from London. He refused the offer but later in the day chartered a special B.O.A.C. plane and arrived in Karachi on the night of the 23rd. He was at once taken to Government House while Begum Hamida Ali,[35] who wanted to go with him, was sent in another car to the Prime Minister's House. There is no authentic report of what happened at Government House. He was there for several hours, and at 2 a.m. on the 24th it was announced that the Governor-General had dissolved the Assembly and had instructed the Prime Minister to reconstruct his Government.

The Government, which was gradually strengthened between October and December, was a strong one. The real Prime Minister, when the Governor-General did not sit, was Chaudhri Muhammad Ali. The work of the Cabinet was done mainly by him and (after December) H.S. Suharwardy. Iskander Mirza was less powerful than has been thought, but he like Chaudhri had the ear of the Governor-General, while Suharwardy had not. The decisions of primary importance were taken by the Governor-General himself. He regarded Cabinet decisions as advice to him which he was free to reject, and the Cabinet acquiesced in that interpretation. The result was that the Cabinet worked well together. It should be added, too, that the Governor-General was often advised by Gurmani,[36] who had become Governor of the Punjab.

Meanwhile, Tamizuddin Khan, backed up by the Nishtar group, had challenged the validity of the dissolution by writs of mandamus[37] and quo warranto.[38] I was called in to advise the government and came to the conclusion that there was not much chance of success unless we challenged the validity of all the Acts of the Constituent Assembly on the ground that they required, and had not received, the Governor-General's assent. We lost in the Chief Court of Sind but won in appeal at the Federal Court. This decision put the legal system into complete chaos. I had worked out, and drafted, an Ordinance under

[35] First wife of Muhammad Ali Borga.
[36] Mushtaq Ahmed Gurmani, Cabinet minister; Governor of the Punjab, 1954–1957.
[37] A judicial writ from the Crown ordering a public institution to perform a statutory duty.
[38] A legal action challenging the legality of exercise of powers.

which most of the laws would be validated and a new Constituent Assembly summoned, and I ought to mention that the Chief Justice of Pakistan[39] saw it in draft. At the last moment, however, the provision for a Constituent Assembly was deleted and a vague clause inserted under which the Governor-General might have enacted a Constitution by ordinance. The reason was a conflict of opinion in the Cabinet. Some wanted a new Assembly; a minority thought that a Constitution should be enacted forthwith and general elections held as soon as possible. The Governor-General had not made up his mind and so the ordinance was issued with a vague provision which would have allowed either. The Chief Justice almost at once brought up a case from Sind which had been postponed on account of Tamizuddin Khan's case and held the whole ordinance invalid, though we could have produced a very good argument on the validation of laws if we had been given an opportunity. We were not because the Federation was not a party. This decision threw the legal system into chaos again, and there were some who thought that the whole Constitution should be suspended. Chaudhri Muhammad Ali threw his weight against this solution. Provisions for temporary validation and for summoning a new Constituent Assembly were enacted, and this action was upheld by the Federal Court.

Meanwhile there had been, outside the Cabinet, a conflict between Muhammad Ali and Suharwardy over East Bengal, whose Constitution was still suspended. Muhammad Ali tried at first to get the United Front and the Awami League to form a coalition, but Suharwardy and the rest of the Awami League refused. On the other hand, Suharwardy also refused to allow the United Front to form a government. While Suharwardy was in England at the beginning of June, and the Governor-General was out of the country, Muhammad Ali removed the suspension of the Constitution and Sarkar,[40] a member of the United Front, was commissioned to form a Government. It was believed to be part of the bargain that Muhammad Ali should be elected to the new Constituent Assembly by the East Bengal Legislative Assembly. He was, but no other member of the Muslim League was elected. Suharwardy and eleven members of the Awami League, Fazlul Huq and 15 other members of the United Front, 9 Hindus and 2 independents (including Fazlur Rehman who got in with Hindu votes) were elected. The Muslim League and its supporters attained 28 seats in West Pakistan, its members including Chaudhri Muhammad Ali, Iskander Mirza and three other Ministers. Eight seats were left

[39] Muhammad Munir, Chief Justice of the Federal Court of Pakistan, 1954–1960.

[40] Abi Hussain Sarkar, Cabinet minister and Chief Minister of East Pakistan, 1955–1956.

vacant for ten States and tribal areas, and when those were filled the position was:

Muslim League	35
United Front	16
Awami League	13
Hindus	9
Other	7
	80

It will be seen that the Muslim League had lost its majority. Muhammad Ali wanted a coalition of the Muslim League and the United Front under himself; Chaudhri wanted a coalition of all three factions under Suharwardy; Suharwardy agreed with Chaudhri with the growing notion that he did not want the United Front as a party, but believed that he could get the support of five members of the United Front (other than Fazlul Huq) with any real ability; the United Front was prepared to come into either coalition, as a party, but preferred Muhammad Ali or Chaudhri as Prime Minister.

By this time Ghulam Muhammad was so ill that he was out of the picture; and indeed it became necessary either to advise the Queen to dismiss him as peacefully as possible or to ask her to give him leave and appoint an Acting Governor-General. The latter step was chosen, and Iskander Mirza was appointed. A meeting of the Muslim League Parliamentary Party was then held, ostensibly to elect a President. Muhammad Ali had not a single supporter and left the meeting, whereupon Chaudhri was elected and authorised to enter into a coalition with the Awami League. Matters went so far that Suharwardy believed that he had been formally appointed; at any rate the announcement by Reuters and the foreign press seemed to have come from him. Then something went awry. Suharwardy says that the Muslim League feared that the Awami League would sweep West Pakistan and wipe out the Muslim League altogether at the next election. Chaudhri merely says that Suharwardy's price was too high. Possibly Fazlul Huq had been canvassing the Muslim League until the alternative suggestion that Chaudhri should become Prime Minister. This was attractive because then the Muslim League might win West Pakistan, losing East Bengal to the United Front. At any rate, another meeting of the League Parliamentary party was held and Chaudhri was authorised to negotiate a coalition with the United Front. Chaudhri tried to get Suharwardy in as Deputy Prime Minister, but in vain, and so a coalition was formed between the Muslim League and the United Front.

Since the Hindus support the government and one of them, K.K. Datta,[41] is in the Cabinet, the Government has 60 seats in an Assembly of 80. It is, however, a very weak Government. The only person of Cabinet [*illegible*] is Chaudhri, and he is no politician. He can handle a Cabinet or a party meeting, but he cannot handle the Assembly. Suharwardy, who is leader of the Opposition of 20, is a first-class tactician, and he is clearly doing his best to break up the government by obstruction. My own impression is that he will succeed.

I must, however, go back to the Ministry of All the Talents which followed upon the dissolution of October 24th. There have been some argument in favour of a unification of West Pakistan, which included three Governors' Provinces, two Chief Commissioners' provinces, States, four of which were incorporated in the Baluchistan States terrain, and the tribal areas. Chaudhri Muhammad Ali as well as Iskander Mirza were in favour of it. The Governor-General suddenly decided in favour on the 22nd March 1955.[42] The decision was so sudden that I had to draft the necessary Order in the middle of a Cabinet meeting. The main reasons are political and economic: i.e. it is believed that a better and more efficient government will be possible when provincial rivalries are removed. On the other hand, the political loss of West Bengal by the Muslim League is also a factor, for it is believed that the League will win West Pakistan more easily when it is a must, and that a strong West Pakistan will be a counterpoise to a unified East Bengal. This might not be so if Suharwardy had become Prime Minister, for the Awami League has branches in West Pakistan as well as in East Bengal.

3. Kashmir Plan, 3 August 1955

Dear Prime Minister,[43]

A couple of weeks ago, when I had a few hours to spare, I drafted a hypothetical agreement between India and Pakistan over Kashmir. I have not seen any official papers on the subject, and accordingly I do not know to what extent the ideas in the draft have been considered and rejected. I am, however, encouraged by your broadcast of the 1st August to send you a copy, in case there is anything in it which has not yet been considered. Apart from other considerations, if a draft

[41] A member of the Constituent Assembly.

[42] This was supposedly an attempt to reduce the differences in Pakistan.

[43] Muhammad Ali Bogra. Just over a week later he would be replaced by Chaudhri Muhammad Ali.

of this kind were proposed to India and rejected the effect on world opinion, after publication, would be profound.

Yours sincerely,

W. Ivor Jennings, 3.8.55

1. There shall be a Jammu and Kashmir Commission (hereafter referred to as the "Commission" consisting of:
   (1.) a chairman appointed in accordance with the provisions of Article 2;
   (2.) two persons appointed by the Government of India, one of whom shall be neither a citizen of India nor of Indian origin; and
   (3.) two persons appointed by the Government of Pakistan, one of whom shall be neither a citizen of Pakistan nor a Muslim.
2. The four persons appointed under clauses (2) and (3) of Article 1 shall at a meeting at which all four are present elect by majority vote a person not being one of themselves nor a citizen of India nor a citizen of Pakistan, to be chairman of the Commission:

   Provided that, if a majority cannot be obtained within 72 hours from the commencement of the first meeting for this purpose, the question shall be referred to the President of the International Court of Justice, who shall appoint the chairman.
3. (1.) There shall be two Joint Secretaries to the Commission, nominated respectively by the Government of India and the Government of Pakistan and appointed by the Commission.
   (2.) The Governments of India and Pakistan shall, at the request of the Commission, second to the service such civilian staff (including police) as the Commission may require:

   Provided that such staff in each grade shall consist equally of citizens of India and citizens of Pakistan.
4. (1.) The Commission shall appoint a person, who shall be citizen of Burma or citizen of Ceylon and shall not be a Hindu or a Muslim, to be Commander-in-Chief of all armed forces in Jammu and Kashmir until the termination of this Agreement.
   (2.) The Government of India shall transfer to the services of the Commission an armed force of *y* officers and men, fully armed and equipped, being *x* officers and men for every thousand persons in the portion of Jammu and Kashmir under the control of the Government of India at the date of this Agreement.
   (3.) The Government of Pakistan shall transfer to the services of the Commission an armed force of *z* officers and men, fully armed and equipped, being *x* officers and men for every

thousand persons in the portion of Jammu and Kashmir under the control of the Government of Pakistan at the date of this Agreement.

(4.) The Commission may require the Governments of India and Pakistan jointly to make agreements with the Governments of Burma and Ceylon to place at the disposal of the Commission such armed forces and equipment as the Commission may deem necessary, in addition to the forces under clause (2) and (3) of this Article, to maintain law and order in Jammu and Kashmir until the termination of this Agreement.

(5.) All armed forces provided under this Article shall be under the command of the Commander-in-Chief appointed under clause (1) of this Article and subject to the general direction and control of the Commission.

5. (1.) The Governments of India and Pakistan agree to make arrangements with the United Nations whereby the members of the Commission shall be deemed to be temporary employees of the United Nations, and entitled to privileges and immunities as such, until the termination of this Agreement.

(2.) The members of the Commission shall be entitled to remuneration at the rate of 12,000 Swiss francs per mensem[44] from the date of their appointment until the termination of this Agreement.

(3.) The members of the civilian staff and armed forces employed by the Commission under the Agreement shall be entitled to the same remuneration as they are entitled to in Burma, Ceylon, India or Pakistan, as the case may be, together with such additional allowances as may be agreed between the Commission on the one hand and the Governments of India and Pakistan on the other hand.

6. It shall be the duty of the Commission:

(1.) to assume responsibility from the Government of Jammu and Kashmir from a date to be fixed by the Commission until the termination of this Agreement;

(2.) to organise a plebiscite of the people of Jammu and Kashmir in accordance with Article 8; and

(3.) to transfer Jammu and Kashmir, or portion thereof, to the control of the Government of India or the Government of Pakistan in accordance with Articles 9 and 10.

[44] Per month.

7. (1.) For the purpose of clause (1) of Article 6, the Commission shall have and may exercise all the powers and functions of all public authorities having powers or exercising functions in Jammu and Kashmir and the Governments of India and Pakistan agree that all persons and authorities in Jammu and Kashmir shall obey the orders of the Commission.

(2.) For the purposes of this Article "public authority" shall include the Parliament of the Union of India, the Constituent Assembly of Pakistan, the Government of Pakistan, the Constituent Assembly of Jammu and Kashmir and the Government of Jammu and Kashmir, and all public authorities shall cease functioning on the date fixed in accordance with clause (1) of Article 6.

(3.) The Commission may dissolve any public authority not specified in clause (2.) of this Article and assume its powers and functions or it may give such directions to any such public authority as it may think fit.

(4.) All armed forces of the Union of India and of the Dominion of Pakistan other than those transferred to the service of the Commission under Article 4, shall be withdrawn from Jammu and Kashmir in accordance with a scheme framed by the Commission in consultation with the local commanders of those forces.

8. (1.) For the purposes of the plebiscite arranged in accordance with clause (2) of Article 6, every town and every village in Jammu and Kashmir shall be a separate plebiscite area, and the Commission shall make such arrangements as to ensure that every person entitled to vote under this Article is enabled to cast that vote if he so desires.

(2.) A person shall be entitled to vote in respect of a plebiscite area if he prove to the satisfaction of the Commission that:

(a.) He was a subject of the Maharajah of Jammu and Kashmir[45] on the 14th August 1947; and

(b.) He had attained the age of 21 years on or before the date of this Agreement; and

(c.) Either:

(i.) he had been resident in the plebiscite area for a period of twelve months before the date of this Agreement; or

(ii.) he had been resident in the plebiscite area for a continuous period of two years after the 14th August 1947 but had, less than twelve months before the date of

[45] Hari Singh, last Maharajah of Jammu and Kashmir.

this Agreement, become resident in another plebiscite area; or

(iii.) he had been continuously resident in the plebiscite area for a period of five years immediately before the 18th July 1947 but had subsequently resided in India or Pakistan in some other plebiscite area in Jammu and Kashmir:

Provided that no person vote in more than one plebiscite area.

(3.) Where a person claims a right to vote under sub-paragraph (iii) of paragraph (c) of clause 2 of this Article, the Commission shall make arrangements for the investigation of the claim and, if the claim is sustained, for the exercise of his right to vote in the place in which he resides, or as near as possible thereto, and the Governments of India and Pakistan agree to provide the facilities necessary for this purpose.

(4.) This article shall apply to a female person as it applies to a male person.

9. (1.) The voting under Article 6 shall be by secret ballot, each person voting being issued one ballot paper containing in Hindi, Urdu and English and in any other language spoken in the plebiscite area, the following

"1. For accession to India"
"2. For accession to Pakistan"

In the first case there shall be shown, in black and white, a representation of the flag of the Union of India; and in the second case there shall be shown, in black and white, a representation of the flag of Pakistan.

(2.) In every polling station and at every place set apart for the counting of votes there shall be an equal number of Indian and Pakistani officers; any such officer may have a protest recorded against a decision of the presiding officer, and every such protest shall be reported to the Commission.

(3.) Subject to this Article, Rules may be made by the Commission for the conduct of the plebiscite.

(4.) The Governments of India and Pakistan agree to give the force of law in their respective territories to any orders issued by the Commission to control propaganda relating to the plebiscite in Jammu and Kashmir, provided that any such orders shall apply equally to India and to Pakistan.

10. (1.) The votes recorded for accession to India and for accession to Pakistan, respectively, shall be published by the Commission in respect of every plebiscite area, and copies of the record

shall be sent to the Government of India, the Government of Pakistan, and the Secretary-General of the United Nations.

(2.) The Commission shall have the power to declare that the plebiscite has decided for:

(a.) the accession of Jammu and Kashmir to the Union of India; or

(b.) the accession of Jammu and Kashmir to the Federation of Pakistan; or

(c.) the division of Jammu and Kashmir between the Union of India and the Federation of Pakistan.

(3.) If the Commission declares that the plebiscite has decided for the accession of Jammu and Kashmir to the Union of India, the Commission shall make arrangements with the Government of India for:

(a.) the repatriation of the staff of the armed forces employed by the Commission and their replacement by staff and armed forces of the Government of India;

(b.) the transfer of the powers of the Commission to the Government of India; and shall make arrangements with the Government of Pakistan for the transfer to Pakistan of any persons who wish to leave the territory of Jammu and Kashmir and enter the territory of Pakistan;

and when these arrangements have been carried into effect this agreement shall terminate.

(4.) If the Commission declares that the plebiscite has decided for the accession of Jammu and Kashmir to the Federation of Pakistan, the Commission shall make arrangements with the Government of Pakistan for:

(a.) the repatriation of the staff of the armed forces employed by the Commission and their replacement by staff and armed forces of the Government of Pakistan;

(b.) the transfer of the powers of the Commission to the Government of Pakistan; and shall make arrangements with the Government of India for the transfer to India of any persons who wish to leave the territory of Jammu and Kashmir and enter the territory of India;

and when these arrangements have been carried into effect this agreement shall terminate.

(5.) The Commission shall not declare that the plebiscite has decided for the division of Jammu and Kashmir between the Union of India and the Federation of Pakistan unless:

(a.) The majority in favour of the accession of Jammu and Kashmir to the Union of India or the Federation of Pakistan does not exceed sixty-six per cent of the valid votes cast; and (b.) Notwithstanding that there is a majority in favour of the accession of Jammu and Kashmir to the Union of India or the Federation of Pakistan there is an area contiguous to Pakistan or to India, as the case may be, in which the majority in favour of the accession to the Federation of Pakistan or the Union of India, as the case may be, exceeds sixty per cent of the valid votes cast and that area is in the opinion of the Commission capable of being governed as part of the Federation of Pakistan or the Union of India, as the case may be.

(6.) If the Commission declares that the plebiscite has decided for the division of Jammu and Kashmir between the Union of India and the Federation of Pakistan, the Commission shall:

(a.) demarcate the boundary between the portion allocated to the Union of India (hereinafter referred to as the "Indian sector") and the portion allocated to the Federation of Pakistan (hereinafter referred to as the "Pakistan sector"); and

(b.) make arrangements with the Governments of India and Pakistan for the repatriation of the staff and armed forces employed by the Commission and their replacement in the Indian sector by the staff and armed forces of the Government of India and in the Pakistan sector by the staff and armed forces of the Government of Pakistan;

(c.) make arrangements with the Government of India for the transfer of the powers of the Commission in the Indian sector to the Government of India and with the Government of Pakistan for the transfer of the powers of the Commission in the Pakistan sector to the Government of Pakistan; and

(d.) make arrangements with the Government of India for the transfer to India or to the Indian sector of persons who wish to leave the Pakistan sector and enter the territory of India or the Indian sector and with the Government of Pakistan for the transfer to Pakistan or to the Pakistan sector of persons who wish to leave the Indian sector and enter the territory of Pakistan or the Pakistan sector;

and when these arrangements have been carried into effect this Agreement shall terminate.

(7.) In demarcating the boundary between the Indian sector and the Pakistan sector, the Commission shall so arrange that:

(a.) the whole of the Indian sector shall be accessible from the territory of India without passing through the Pakistan sector;

(b.) the whole of the Pakistan sector shall be accessible from the territory of Pakistan without passing through the Indian sector; and

(c.) the Indian sector and the Pakistan sector are convenient areas for the government of those sectors as parts of the Union of India and the Federation of Pakistan respectively;

(d.) and accordingly the majority for the accession of Jammu and Kashmir to the Union of India or Federation of Pakistan in plebiscite area shall not be conclusive.

11. The expenditure of the Commission in excess of the income received by the Commission on behalf of the Government of Jammu and Kashmir shall be met in equal amounts by the Governments of India and Pakistan; the sums so required shall, on the requisition of the Commission, be placed to the account of the Commission at the Federal Reserve Bank of India, New Delhi, and the State Bank of Pakistan, Karachi, and the said Banks shall have the authority from their respective Governments to convert such sums at the official rate of exchange into any currency as may be required by the Commission.

12. Notwithstanding the provisions of the Agreement relating to its termination, the Governments of India and Pakistan agree that any person who remains in such territory of Jammu and Kashmir as becomes part of the Union of India shall have all the rights, privileges and immunities of a citizen of India under the laws of India and any person who remains in such territory of Jammu and Kashmir as becomes part of the Federation of Pakistan shall have all the rights, privileges and immunities of a citizen of Pakistan under the laws of Pakistan.

13. (1.) If any dispute arises over the interpretation of this Agreement between the Government of India and the Government of Pakistan or between either Government or both Governments and the Commission, it shall be referred to for decision to the International Court of Justice.

(2.) For the purposes of the Statute of the Court the Governments of India and Pakistan and the Commission shall be parties to the dispute and the decision of the Court shall be binding upon all the parties.

14. This Agreement shall come into operation when the Governments of India and Pakistan have exchanged instruments of ratification thereof.

SECTION I: FEDERATION OF RHODESIA AND NYASALAND

The Federation, formed in 1953, consisted of Southern Rhodesia, which had had internal self-government since 1923 (though London retained powers of veto over laws concerning the black African population), and the British Protectorates of Northern Rhodesia and Nyasaland. These territories correspond to modern-day Zimbabwe, Zambia, and Malawi respectively. In London between December 1960 and February 1961 there was a conference to review the Federation of Rhodesia and Nyasaland. In February 1960 the British Prime Minister Harold Macmillan famously spoke in Pretoria of the 'wind of change'. For the Federation, and elsewhere in the continent, the speech was delivered in the context, on the one hand, of the rise of black African nationalism and sense of self-determination, and, on the other, the strong will of most of the leaders, who represented the minority white settlers who wanted to preserve their disproportionate power vis-à-vis the black majority. The Federation was therefore a complex political arena and Jennings was asked to comment on the issues that were discussed at the conference in London.

1. Opinion given to the Office of the High Commissioner for Rhodesia and Nyasaland working on behalf of the Monckton Commission,[1] Rhodesia House, London, 23 July 1960

Re: The Federal Constitution of Rhodesia and Nyasaland

1. Does the Constitution give the right of secession to any Territory?[2] The phrase "right of secession" is ambiguous. It could mean a right to secede from the Commonwealth, and it is generally used in that sense because both Burma and the Republic of Ireland exercised that right. It is presumed, however, that what is meant is the right to secede

[1] In March 1960 the British Cabinet established the Monckton Commission to investigate the future of the Federation.

[2] The African leaders had proposed the right to secede from the Federation.

from the Federation of Rhodesia and Nyasaland, without necessarily breaking the link with the Crown. The answer is "No".

What is usually called the Constitution of the Federation is the annex to the Federation of Rhodesia and Nyasaland (Constitution) Order in Council, 1953, though strictly speaking the Constitution includes the first twelve sections of that Order. The Order has the force of law in each of the Territories by reason of the Rhodesia and Nyasaland Federation Act, 1953, passed by the Parliament of the United Kingdom. The Order provides in section 1 for the federation of the Territories, and that section cannot be revoked except by (a) the Parliament of the United Kingdom, or (b) the Federal Legislature under sections 97 and 98 of the annexed Constitution, read with section 12(10) of the Order in Council. Even after 1963, however, the Federal Legislature will not have power to revoke or amend sections 13 and 14 of the Order in Council.[3] These refer to the Federation and the Federal Legislature and to the Territories. It follows that the Federation cannot be broken up, by the secession of one or more of the Territories, except under the authority of an Act of the Parliament of the United Kingdom: see section 1(2) of the Rhodesia and Nyasaland Federation Act, 1953.

The Constitution does not confer upon any of the Territorial legislatures any power to revoke or amend any provision of the Order in Council or the annexed Constitution. On the contrary, section 14(2) of the Order in Council – which cannot be amended by anybody except the Parliament of the United Kingdom – expressly forbids it. Any amendment to the Constitution of any of the Territories made after the 1st August 1953 which is inconsistent with the provisions of the Order in Council shall to the extent of that inconsistency be void. Each of the Territories will therefore be part of the Federation until the Parliament of the United Kingdom otherwise provides.

2. If there is no such specific right in the Constitution, has any Territory any such inherent right?

It is not clear what is meant by "inherent right". The Colony of Southern Rhodesia is part of Her Majesty's dominions and is therefore subject to the legislative authority of the Parliament of the United Kingdom. The legislative powers of the legislature

[3] The Federation, sometimes called the Central African Federation, when designed in 1953 was hoped by the white settler leaders to bring the territories closer in status to Australia, New Zealand, and South Africa, meaning the removal of the United Kingdom's controls on the Federation's internal and external policies. The sections of the Order in Council annex stipulated the United Kingdom's continued position in the Federation and also that the Constitution should be reviewed, which happened in late 1960. The Federation lasted until 1963.

of Southern Rhodesia are limited by (a) the Southern Rhodesia Constitution Letters Patent, 1923, and (b) the Federation of Rhodesia and Nyasaland (Constitution) Order in Council, 1953. Its power to amend the former is limited, and it has no power to amend the latter. What is more, any amendment to the Constitution of Southern Rhodesia which is inconsistent with the Order in Council is void to the extent of the inconsistency. So far as the law is concerned there is no right to secede from the Federation, inherent or otherwise.

In the other territories Her Majesty has jurisdiction by treaty, capitulation, grant, usage, sufferance or other lawful means. Though the point has recently been questioned by learned counsel (in relation to the extension of the Habeas Corpus Act to one of the Territories), there is no reason to doubt that Her Majesty in Parliament has power to legislate for either of the protectorates in as ample a manner as it [*sic*] has power to legislate for the Colony of Southern Rhodesia. The Rhodesia and Nyasaland Federation Act, 1953, and the Federation of Rhodesia and Nyasaland (Constitution) Order in Council, 1953, are therefore part of the law of each of the Territories. The legislature of neither has no [*sic*] power to amend either the Act or the Order in Council, and therefore there is no right to secede, inherent or otherwise, so far as the law is concerned.

It may be, however, that "inherent right" means not a right conferred by law, but such a right as was claimed by the thirteen American colonies whose representatives signed the Declaration of Independence in 1776, i.e. a natural or moral right to rebel because of actions or decisions of the Government or Parliament of the United Kingdom. This seems to be a matter of conscience on which I have no qualification to advise.

3. What will be the legal position when any one of the Territories becomes fully independent? Will such Territory then have a legal right to secede?

The phrase "fully independent" seems to be a misnomer. A State or Territory is fully independent only when it is recognised as an international person. A State within a Federation, e.g. New York or New South Wales, is not fully independent, though it may have full self-government within the ambit of the Federal Constitution, and presumably this is what is meant.

The limitations on the full-self government of Southern Rhodesia are contained in the Letters Patent of 1923 and could be removed by a further grant of Letters Patent by the Queen. Northern Rhodesia and Nyasaland could be given responsible government or full self-government by Orders in Council under the Foreign Jurisdiction Act, 1890. This does not necessarily mean that they would cease to be

British protectorates. Indeed, they would for international purposes have to remain British protectorates until the Federation became fully responsible for its own external affairs, though it would be possible for them to be annexed to the Crown as Southern Rhodesia was in 1923.

The Queen has, however, no power to repeal or amend the Rhodesia and Nyasaland Federation Act, 1953, or to revoke or amend the Federation of Rhodesia and Nyasaland (Constitution) Order in Council, 1953. In other words, any grant of full self-government to any of the Territories, unless it was done by Act of the Parliament of the United Kingdom, must be within the ambit of the present Federal Constitution. An Act of Parliament would be needed for Southern Rhodesia if it were intended to give to its legislature power to repeal or amend Acts of the Parliament of the United Kingdom extending to the Colony as part of its law. The Colonial Laws Validity Act, 1865, applies to the Colony in relation to Territorial legislation, though by section 13(1) of the Order in Council it applies to the whole Federation in relation to Federal legislation. A precedent can be found in section 7(2) of the Statute of Westminster, 1931, whereby the Provincial legislatures of Canada were empowered to repeal or amend Acts of the Parliament of the United Kingdom within the ambit of Provincial powers. The Constitution of Canada, i.e. the British North America Acts,[4] was saved. That is to say, the federal structure of Canada was retained unaltered. The Parliament of the United Kingdom need not follow its own precedent. It could confer a right to secede on Southern Rhodesia, but in view of the provisions of the Rhodesia and Nyasaland Federation Act, 1953, it would have to be done by express words. A mere grant of full self-government to Southern Rhodesia under the royal prerogative, or a grant of full self-government to either of the protectorates under the Foreign Jurisdiction Act, would confer no right to secede from the Federation. The law stated in answer to the preceding questions would continue to apply.

Notes on Constitutional Proposals for the Federation of Rhodesia and Nyasaland

I. Fifty–Fifty

So far as I know, "fifty–fifty", or equal communal representation, has been tried for any length of time only in United Canada before 1867. The English Canadians in Canada West (now Ontario) were at first fewer in number than the French Canadians in Canada East (now Quebec), but the two divisions of the colony had equal representation.

[4]Major constitutional Acts for Canada dating from 1867, after the 1839 Durham Report recommended responsible government and closer union of British North America.

The system worked, when it worked at all, only when there was an Anglo-French coalition. Effectively there were two Prime Ministers, and the Government had to have a majority among the members of both divisions. When that situation could not be obtained, there were frequent and unstable Governments. In fact, the growth of population in Canada West made the system unworkable, for the majority in Canada West demanded "representation by population", and this was fiercely resisted by the French Canadians, since they believed that their religion, their laws and their language were in danger. Within ten years there were ten Governments; and in three years there were four Governments and two general elections. It was this experience which led MacDonald[5] and Cartier[6] to suggest to the Maritime Provinces a federation in which Ontario and Quebec would be separate Provinces.

2. Something like "fifty–fifty" was in operation in the Punjab and in Bengal[7] under the Government of India Act, 1919; but the examples do not help because there was an official bloc holding the balance of power and there were few Indian Ministers (though in both Provinces Ministers were drawn both from the Hindus and from the Muslims). Under the Government of India Act, 1935, the balance of power was held by members for "special constituencies" like landowners, university graduates, Chambers of Commerce; but too little experience was obtained before the outbreak of war in 1939.

3. A scheme for "fifty–fifty" (i.e. half Sinhalese and half minorities) was put before the Soulbury Commission on Ceylon in 1945.[8] When the Tamils (the largest minority) worked it out they realised that equality of representation was not enough to protect them against what they called "Sinhalese domination". By offering portfolios to well-disposed (or impecunious) Tamils or allying themselves with one of the smaller minorities, the Sinhalese could in fact secure a majority. It was therefore thought necessary to provide that the Sinhalese should have less than half the Ministries, and that the Governor should preside over the Council of Ministers. The scheme was quite unrealistic, because in fact neither the Sinhalese nor the Tamils were united – they were split into parties or groups. The scheme was rejected by the Soulbury Commission in favour of a scheme of balanced representation produced by me for the Ministers: but events showed that the Tamils had some justification for their fears. Political parties were able to capitalise the prejudices of the Sinhalese-speaking voters

[5] Sir John A. MacDonald, first Prime Minister of Canada, 1867–1873 and 1878–1891.

[6] Sir George-Étienne Cartier, French Canadian politician and minister.

[7] Both the Punjab and Bengal had significant populations of Hindus and Muslims, as well as other communities, such as the Sikhs in the Punjab.

[8] By the Tamil Congress Leader G.G. Ponnambalam.

and to win seats for a "Sinhalese-only" policy which seriously threatens the Tamils.

4. In Pakistan after the partition of India the main problem, which held up Constitution-making for nine years, was that, while the Bengalis of Eastern Pakistan had the numerical preponderance, the people of West Pakistan, and especially the Punjabis, had a larger part of the wealth, education and experience. It was agreed in 1954 that there should be "representation by population" in the Lower House – thus giving the Bengalis a majority – but that the members from West Pakistan should predominate in the Upper House, and that the Government should be responsible to both Houses. This required some difficult drafting, and I had no great expectation that the experiment would be successful. The Draft Constitution had other defects which induced the Governor-General to dissolve the constituent assembly before the Draft was formally reported. In the second constituent assembly it was agreed that East Pakistan and West Pakistan should have equal representation in a single Chamber, and that the Punjabis should have only forty per cent of the representation in West Pakistan. How this would have worked we do not know, for General Ayub Khan[9] suspended the Constitution before elections were held.[10]

5. Fifty–fifty could be applied in the Federation of Rhodesia and Nyasaland in one of three ways, which may be exemplified as follows:

(1) 50% Europeans; 48% Africans; 2% others.
(2) 48% Europeans; 50% Africans; 2% others.
(3) 49% Europeans; 49% Africans; 2% others.

What would happen is highly speculative. It would depend in part on other proposals, e.g. whether the balance was obtained by communal representation with separate rolls, reserved seats with common rolls, or the "gerrymandering" of constituencies. Equality of representation could also be brought about, at least in part, by nomination.

6. In a matter of this kind it is impossible for anybody to speak with assurance even if he knows exactly what the proposal is. The consequences of any constitutional change depend very largely on the accidents of personality and on extraneous events. To a considerable extent what happens in the Federation depends upon what happens elsewhere, especially in Africa. The idea of the unity of interest of Africans, meaning by that term all those who are not descended from recent migrants from Europe or Asia, is widely prevalent and is being

[9] Field-Marshal Ayub Khan, President of Pakistan, 1958–1969.

[10] In 1958 martial law was declared in Pakistan, and the 1956 constitution (upon which Jennings had advised) was abrogated. See Section H.

reinforced by propaganda from several centres. On the other hand, it seems to be true in Africa as in Asia that nationalist movements easily split through competing personalities and ambitions if not through competing policies. The experience of Asia suggests that this involves a "ganging up" against the common "enemy", in this case the Europeans, followed by a series of splits as soon as offices have to be distributed and policies which apply differently to different groups have to be devised. Even when a party is being led by persons of the highest integrity, as in India, there is a good deal of corruption at the lower levels – jumping on the bandwagon, jobs for the boys, nepotism, appeals to communal sentiment, and, though less often, bribery. Perhaps Pakistan is in this respect more typical than India, for there "politics" became such a dirty word that it was easy for an army officer to sweep all the politicians out of office. The lesson from Ceylon is that if politicians think that they can win votes by appealing to communal prejudice – race, religion, caste or colour – they will so appeal; and Ceylon would now be as anarchic as the Congo if the army had not accepted instructions from the Governor-General given in his personal capacity.[11]

7. Fifty–fifty clearly will not work if the Europeans "gang up" against the Africans and vice versa. Actually the latter is more likely to happen than the former. The Europeans share the traditions of the United Kingdom and would continue to divide into parties, even if the parties had much in common. The Africans, on the other hand, would probably "gang up" against the Europeans until they had power in their hands, when they might split into fragments around personalities. Fifty–fifty is itself a recognition of communal conflict and therefore encourages it – as everybody pointed out in India from 1909[12] to 1947 in relation to communal representation generally. I hesitate to draw conclusions from a wide experience without knowing much of the particular background in the Federation, but I should have thought that a series of constitutional devices which gave the Europeans a majority for the time being but allowed the Africans to acquire a developing share of power would be better for the Federation in the long term. It could be done by appropriate manipulation of the franchise and the constituencies. I appreciate, however, that the Federal members must make suggestions which are politically possible. Invariably in these cases there is a choice between bad alternatives.

[11] During the 1958 communal riots.

[12] The India Councils Act 1909 (commonly referred to as the Morely–Minto Reforms) established elections for selected seats in provincial legislatures, including a separate electorate for Muslims.

8. To the specific questions about Ministers it can be answered that when Fifty–fifty worked in United Canada (and usually it did not) there was a combined Government which really consisted of two separate Ministries, one English and one French, in coalition. In effect there were two Prime Ministers, Baldwin and Lafontaine[13] or MacDonald and Cartier. Each needed a majority in his own division. This was necessary because neither the English nor the French were unanimous. The moderates, who were prepared to work with the moderates in the other division, were attacked by the extremists in both divisions: and if the extremists in either division could not get a majority among their own people there was no solution, because extremists could not cooperate with extremists or extremists with moderates. Only a brilliant and sensible pair like MacDonald and Cartier could hope to keep the moderates together and in a majority; and it was they who decided that the job was too difficult and that the only solution was to break up the Union so that the English and the French could regulate their own way of life within a broader Federation. The conditions in the Federation of Rhodesia and Nyasaland are utterly different, but there is something in the idea that if the moderate Europeans combine with the moderate Africans they will be attacked by the racial extremists on both sides, and that at some stage the extremists would be sufficiently numerous to make responsible government impracticable.

9. The essential difference between the Federation and United Canada is, of course, that the two sides, though equal in number under Fifty–fifty, would be unequal in everything else – experience, education, economic condition and perhaps (since the Africans would be drawn from a very small educated class) native ability. If one party had a sufficient majority among the Europeans it might be able to attract a minority of the Africans by the offer of Ministerial posts. Would those Africans not be regarded as "stooges" of the whites, be violently attacked by other Africans, and perhaps be thrown out at the next election? One must also contemplate the other possibility, that the Africans would stick together in order to get into office with the aid of liberally-minded Europeans and then split.

10. We have little experience of other possible consequences. In United Canada it became necessary to give English and French languages equal status; and in Pakistan it became necessary to give equal status to Urdu and Bengali. In India babel is on its way, though

[13] Referring to the partnership between Robert Baldwin from West Canada and Sir Louis Hippolyte-LaFontaine from East Canada to form a political partnership and establish responsible government for United Canada in the wake of the Durham Report.

it is being kept back by common sense in the centre.[14] Every language group insists upon education and administration (at the local level) through its own language. It is useless to point out that the unity of India has been brought about by the common use of the English language, not only because of communal sentiment, but also because every elector thinks that there will be jobs for the boys when his own language is used. The village boy cannot get an English education, except with great difficulty; he might get a Government job, however, if his own language was the medium of administration. What is more, a constitutional device like a Public Service Commission cannot prevent discrimination between members of language groups if the legislature decides that one of the languages must be used in administration.

II. The Kenya Proposals

11. The Kenya proposals provide for a legislature of 65, of whom 53 would be directly elected for territorial constituencies, while 12 would be indirectly elected by the elected members sitting as an electoral college. Of the 53 directly elected members, 20 would be elected for reserved seats for minorities. The principle qualifications for the franchise will be literacy (or age of 40+) and an income of £75 per annum. It is not very easy to comment on these proposals, because they depend on a detailed knowledge of the country; and still less easy to comment on their application to the Federation, because that would depend on a detailed knowledge of the Federation also. The following comments should therefore be read with some reserve.

(1.) Franchise

Three of the four methods of enfranchisement are notoriously difficult to administer. The fourth is of no importance.

(a) Literacy.

This replaces a qualification based upon school attendance. No definition of literacy has been offered, save that it may be in English or Swahili, or the home language. Apparently potential electors have to call on district officers to demonstrate that they can read and write, presumably because so difficult a job cannot be entrusted to clerks. In most Asian countries literacy has never been accepted as a qualification because judgments about literacy, when honest, are necessarily arbitrary and because there is often a good deal of political pressure, especially when candidates of different caste or tribe are standing. Any literacy qualification benefits the younger at the expense of the elder and the townsman at the expense of the villager.

[14] After considerable debate, English was kept as an official language after Independence.

(b) Age 40+
This is a necessary alternative to a literacy qualification, which benefits the young. In most places whether a person is below or above 40 is anybody's guess.

(c) Income of £75
The Working Party has added a property qualification because many African landowners could not produce figures of income. In fact, income figures can rarely be produced except by persons in regular employment at a weekly or monthly wage.

(2.) Reserved Seats

In a reserved seat the electors are all qualified persons on a common roll, but the candidates must be Europeans or Asians, as the case may [be]. Judging from the maps, the reserved seats are in the settled areas, which are fairly concentrated in Kenya. I have no evidence of the proportions that the African electors are likely to bear to the European or Asian electors. If the proportion is large, the African electors in effect decide which European or Asian candidate is to be elected.

The case for reserved seats as against communal electorates is argued in several Asian reports; but in Asia it was always assumed that the minority in the constituency would be substantial. Also, a reserved seat was usually combined with an open seat in a single constituency, so that the first Hindu and the first Muslim past the post were both elected. This meant, of course, that the Hindu electors usually voted for the open (i.e. Hindu) candidates, while the Muslim electors generally voted for the Muslim candidates. This is not proposed in Kenya because this kind of racial voting was thought to defeat the purpose of the common roll. I should have thought that there was something to be said for it as a compromise between the purely communal electorate and the selection of European or Asian candidates by African electors. In fact, the Kenya proposal really means that African electors will choose among European candidates according to their racial policies: and racial attitudes is [*sic*] not the only problem of government. To some extent, however, this difficulty is met by the proposal for communal primaries.

(3.) Primary Elections

The idea of the communal primary was first worked out by the Simon Commission in India (Report, Vol. II, pp. 86–7).[15] The Report sets out the advantages and the disadvantages, which therefore need not be repeated. In a Muslim reserved constituency, only the Muslim electors would vote in the primary, and each would have as many

[15]The Simon Commission was sent to India in 1928 to investigate potential constitutional reforms. It recommended the retention of communal electorates.

votes as there were candidates. A candidate could not stand in the secondary unless he obtained a fixed proportion, say 60%, of votes in the primary. Since this scheme was never put into operation, we do not know if it would have worked.

The Kenya scheme is slightly different, though the essential difference is that the proportion is reduced to 25%. It is difficult to believe that a European elector would vote for two or three candidates in a primary and let the African electors choose between them in the secondary. He will surely vote for his own candidate in the hope that none of the others will get the quota. There is also a risk that there will be what used to be called dummy candidates, i.e. candidates who do not hope to get the quota but hope to attract enough votes to prevent others getting the quota. (Before the Kaiser's war there were cases of Conservative candidates surreptitiously subsidising Labour candidates in order to split the Liberal vote). In any case, since the African vote in the secondary would be, at least initially, unpredictable, there might be candidacies prepared to gamble on getting a quota in the primary and a majority in the secondary. The system might break down if racial antagonism became fierce, since all the "liberal" candidacies would be rejected in the primaries and the elections would in fact be communal. On the other hand, if the system worked it would encourage "liberal" candidates.

A fixed percentage is very arbitrary. Assuming that in a primary most electors would cast only one vote the percentage would be very low where there were two candidates and very high when there were five. A more logical arrangement would be to give each elector only one vote and to have as quota the total vote divided by the number of candidates plus one. Thus, if 6000 people voted, a candidate would be required to get:

2000 if there were two candidates

1500 if there were three candidates

1200 if there were four candidates

1000 if there were five candidates.

Incidentally, this would make it easier to run a primary for an Asian reserved seat. On the other hand, it would encourage people to put up candidates.

I should like to see the experiment of the primary, in some form or other, tried; but I should want to know a good deal more about the Federation and about the connected proposals (franchise and constituencies) before I could recommend it to the Federal members.

(4.) National Seats

I do not know what is meant by proportional representation with a single non-transferable vote, and I suspect that the phrase is Colonial Office eyewash. I have not been able to find a copy of the Regulations, but it seems to mean that the 53 elected members are given one vote in each group. If all 33 Africans are stupid enough (and they would not be) to vote for Blogg, then Mogg, Fogg and Dogg would get in on the European and Asian votes.

I have no experience of this form of indirect election. For the Senate of Ceylon, however, the members of the House of Representatives form an electoral college to elect fifteen Senators by single transferable vote. The effect at the first election was that seven votes were needed for a seat, and there was some remarkable canvassing (though, as far as I know, no bribery) before the election. The quality of the Senators so elected was not high, and most of the better Senators got in by the other door, nomination by the Governor General (i.e. the Prime Minister).

In fact, election to the Senate tended to be a consolation prize for candidates defeated in the constituencies, whereas most of those appointed by the Governor-General were former public servants and others who were prepared to serve but not to stand for election. Some of the Ministers obtained office by this latter route and undoubtedly strengthened the Government.

Indirect election as a means of getting in sound people who are not good demagogues is not to be despised: but with a small electoral college it opens the way to canvassing, jobs for the boys, seats for contributors to party funds, and other forms of corruption.

2. Diary from the London Conference reviewing the Federation's Constitution, 1960–1961

Tuesday, 6th December 1960

The request from the Federal Government of Rhodesia and Nyasaland that I should act as their legal adviser in relation to the Constitutional Review was unexpected. My first task was to advise the officials, who were conducting a preliminary review (which I have not seen). My second was to answer in writing certain questions from the Federal members of the Monckton Commission. Unfortunately they did not ask enough, with the result that in Chapter XVI they assented to doctrines of constitutional law which cannot be sustained, and which seem to me to be tendentious. It appears (as I suspected) that these doctrines were laid down by Lord Shawcross[16] before he left the Commission and were assented to by the Federal (and Southern Rhodesia) members without adequate consideration. Actually, they never saw the Report as a whole before it was published. They saw drafts of chapters and paragraphs, but the compilation was done in England. How important this was I do not know. It may be that this is an excuse; and I do not know whether they ever saw Chapter 16 as a whole.

I was asked to comment on this Chapter, and did so in a lengthy opinion which was published as a Federal White Paper. The Attorney-General of Northern Nigeria commented on it in a speech, in which he partly accepted my thesis but deemed that the convention of legislative non-interference applied to the Federation. I was asked to reply to that, and did so – I think effectively – by quoting the Report of the Joint Select Committee of 1934 on the petition from Western Australia.[17] Apparently the Federal members knew about this Report but did not appreciate its significance.

It is now plain that the appointment of the Monckton Commission was a complete mistake. It was pressed by H.M.G. + accepted by Welensky[18] most reluctantly. It had already been agreed in 1957 that secession was not an issue; but H.M.G. said that if there was no Commission on the Federation there would have to be one on the Protectorates. This question of secession would have been raised even if there had been no Commission; but the Report, and the discussion preceding it, has put the Africans into a good negotiating position. I think H.M.G. hoped for a solution produced by the magic of Moncktonian diplomacy.[19] That has not emerged: for Africans and Europeans both reject the solutions.

The conference met for the first time yesterday. The proceedings very formal. I did not attend. H.M.G. has made up its mind to begin with a long series of speeches. There are 73 delegates, and so there will presumably be 73 speeches. Today there were only six, partly because there was some jockeying for position. We are, however, to adjourn for Christmas not later than the evening of the 20th. This gives us eleven days of speech-making. It is plain that all delegates, except possibly those of the U.K., have already taken up positions. On the other

[16] Hartley Shawcross, Baron Shawcross; Attorney-General in the Labour Government, 1945–1951. Shawcross had to leave the Commission owing to illness.

[17] This petition from the State of Western Australia related to its request to the Westminster parliament for legislation to secede from the Commonwealth of Australia.

[18] Sir Roy Welensky, leader of the United Federal Party; Prime Minister of the Federation of Rhodesia and Nyasaland, 1956–1963.

[19] Walter Monckton (later Viscount Monckton of Brenchley), British Conservative minister and legal adviser; Minister of Labour, 1951–1955.

hand, I suspected today that most are willing to compromise. It is true that we heard more of the principal African leaders, though Sir John Moffatt[20] (N. Rhod.), who purported to speak for African opinion as a whole, did speak. He was sufficiently confused as to suggest that he was hedging. The two Africans, Chiefs Mwase[21] (Nyas.) and Mpanda (N. Rhod.) – who are not extremists – seemed to suggest that they objected less to Federation than to having Federation forced on them. They were also more interested in the Territorial Constitution than in the Federation; but this arises because of their vested interests as Chiefs – they are concerned with land and local govt. They are, of course, quite right. After the nationalists achieve power the Chiefs will be probably suppressed, as in Ghana.

Sir Roy Welensky and Mr W. Field,[22] Leader of the Opposition, both spoke. Both were quite moderate. Field raised objections to the interference of the U.K. in the internal affairs of S. Rhodesia. He also suggested that Federation be replaced by a Central African Alliance (I thought of "Associated States of Central Africa") because, as Chief Mpanda said later, "Federation is a striking word". He also laid down five propositions:–

1. A solution must be found now, i.e. no right of secession in five years
2. No arbitrary lowering of standards, i.e. not one man, one vote, at this stage
3. No constitutional changes in Nyas. + N. Rhod. without consideration of Federation's point of view
4. No parity
5. No interference in S. Rhod.

The P.M. (U.K.)[23] had originally decided to preside; but the decision to have a speech-making marathon apparently induced him to hand over to Duncan Sandys[24] (C.R.O.[25]). The Federation delegation believe that the marathon is punishment for the refusal of the Federation to postpone until after Christmas, as U.K. had proposed. I doubt this, for the U.K. delegation today was so strong as to suggest that a good deal

[20] Sir John Moffatt, member of the Northern Rhodesia Legislative Council and leader of the liberal Central African Party.

[21] Chief Mwase of Kasungu from Nyasaland.

[22] Winston Field, Rhodesian MP; later Rhodesian Front Prime Minister of Southern Rhodesia, 1962–1964.

[23] Harold Macmillan (later Earl of Stockton), British Conservative Prime Minister, 1957–1963.

[24] Duncan Sandys (later Baron Duncan-Sandys), British Conservative minister; Secretary of State for Commonwealth Relations, 1960–1962.

[25] Commonwealth Relations Office.

of work was being delayed in Whitehall – the Ministers, two Ministers of State, two Deputy Under-Secs. of State, two legal advisers, etc.

Monday, 12th December 1960

I ought [to] have said last Tuesday that one of the reasons given to Macmillan + Welensky for appointing the Monckton Commission was that the Conservatives did not expect to win the General election + therefore wanted a Report which would more or less tie the Labour Government's hands.

The marathon has continued its weary way. On the first three days we had 6+5+4 speeches. I left early on Friday, but a chief made a short speech, so perhaps the average was maintained. There has been little sign of willingness to compromise. The African speeches have been variations of the theme "Secession NOW". Dr Banda[26] made a very fluent speech. He is a natural orator who has learned the tricks of the trade. He says very little in substance because he makes few points. In fact, his substance is of poor quality. He obviously has no conception of the future of Nyasaland. Federation should not have existed because we did not want it. H.M.G. must lead us until we are ready to govern ourselves. It is true that we are not rich: but is Somalia better off than we are? They haven't even got water. Kaunda,[27] of N. Rhodesia, is less of an orator but able. His position is stronger because N. Rhod. could govern itself. Indeed, he said that N. Rhod. had been milked. Nkomo,[28] of S. Rhod., made much the best impression of the three nationalist leaders. His line was not really different: indeed it had been concocted at a meeting of the three on the 4th December: but he put the case in a more conciliatory manner and with greater thought for the effects of his arguments on the Europeans present. British subjects – worthy subjects of the Queen – Union Jack – and so forth. He was, however, too long. He spoke for 75 minutes, and almost exclusively on S. Rhodesia.

The only African to speak against the nationalist line was Phiri of Nyasaland. His attack on intimidation was particularly impressive because it was so courageous. (We have always thought of nationalist leaders as exhibiting courage; but they are in fact conforming + they know that if arrested, they will be well treated and yet become

[26]Dr Hastings Banda, Nyasaland political leader; imprisoned in 1959 for his criticisms of and political activities against the Federation's leadership; released 1960; first President of the Republic of Malawi, 1966–1993.

[27]Kenneth Kaunda, Zambian African National Congress leader; also imprisoned in 1959 and released in 1960; first President of Zambia, 1964–1991.

[28]Joshua Nkomo, Zimbabwean political leader. He went on to found the Zimbabwe African People's Union in 1961, which was committed to liberating Rhodesia from white settler rule.

martyrs). On the other hand it would not have impressed the Africans: he is one of "Welensky's stooges". The extreme white case was put by Harper[29] of S. Rhod. He is against Federation + against partnership. Either rule the country or get out, until Africans reach the same level as ourselves. Africans have been given the vote to provide a majority for the present Govt. (Welensky or Whitehead?[30]).

Duncan Sandys and Iain Macleod[31] entertained the leaders – Welensky, Field, Whitehead, Banda, Kaunda and Nkomo at Chequers over the week-end. They all went to church + Banda read the lesson. I have written notes on "Government by Consent", the suspension of the Malta Constitution, + Article 99 of the Constitution.[32] I have also drafted some paragraphs of a speech for Welensky.

Same day, evening

In my note this morning I ought to have explained Dr Banda's walk-out on Friday afternoon (9th December). Sir Edgar Whitehead was explaining, coolly and dispassionately, the economic effects on Nyasaland of the dissolution of the Federation. Dr Banda cannot refrain from a running commentary on any speech with which he does not agree – he has no parliamentary experience whatsoever – and he was becoming quite a nuisance during Sir Edgar's speech. The official report does not mention most of his interruptions. He kept saying, for instance, "It's no business of yours". He also said, "This is a question of politics, not economics". Like a true demagogue (or a revivalist preacher) he gradually worked up his indignation, and then decided to walk out. The newspapers say that he had already called a press conference; but my own impression was that his walk-out was unpremeditated. On the other hand, he is quite a skilled orator, and he went out shouting, making the most of the occasion. The other members of the Malawi party followed him. Two chiefs, of Malawi sympathy, hesitated for a few moments and then went out to consult Dr Banda – there were amused comments about "stooges" from some of the pro-Federation Africans as they went. They came back to collect their papers, and then left as unobtrusively as possible.

This afternoon Dr Banda + the Malawi party were back. I was not present at the beginning of the conference, but I was told that a

[29] William Harper, right-wing Southern Rhodesian MP; later a minister under Ian Smith.

[30] Sir Edgar Whitehead, United Federal Party Prime Minister of Southern Rhodesia, 1958–1962.

[31] Ian Macleod, British Conservative minister; Secretary of State for the Colonies, 1959–1961.

[32] This refers to the riots and political deadlock in Malta in 1958–1959 over the issue of integration with the United Kingdom. The Maltese Constitution was suspended and Britain assumed direct rule in March 1959.

series of notes was passing from Dr Banda to Kaunda and Nkomo. The session was due to end at 5.30 p.m. At 5.25 p.m. Kaunda rose to make a point of order while a Dr Hersch of S. Rhod. was speaking. What he said was, in effect, that the chiefs and people of N. Rhod. had sent him with reluctance, and that they now proposed to withdraw. Dr Banda then got up to speak, + said that they had put their point to H.M.G. and would now withdraw. Duncan Sandys was not very quick on the uptake, but when Welensky began to protest he said that this was not a point of order + speeches were not allowed. Thereupon Kaunda, Banda, Nkomo and their henchmen straggled out. It was not a well-organized demonstration, but I suppose it will look effective in Central Africa.

Wednesday, 14th December 1960

The "walk-out" has proven to be more effective than I thought. In the absence of other news, the U.K. newspapers have played it up as if it were not a mere stunt but a demonstration of the irreconcilable differences between black + white. In Rhodesia it looks even more sinister. Whitehead is receiving cables asking why he is letting the black extremists get away with it. The meeting of the S. Rhod. Conference fixed for yesterday was postponed, presumably at Whitehead's insistence. He has insisted on a meeting tomorrow – in Nkomo's absence if he did not attend the federal meeting today. Actually Nkomo did not attend, so I presume that Whitehead will insist. Whitehead's small majority in S. Rhod. puts him in a difficult position. The Rhodesians say that, if there were a plebiscite or a general election, the Dominion party[33] would get a majority for secession and no African representation.

The U.K. Ministers are behaving abominably. There was a period yesterday when Duncan Sandys, who was presiding, was asleep. He woke up to find a note from Welensky saying that, even if everybody else went to sleep, the chairman should stay awake. The Earl of Perth,[34] too, was asleep, while Macleod and Alport[35] were reading Cabinet papers. Welensky's note was retribution for an earlier note from Sandys asking why so many federal Ministers were absent – as a matter of fact, they were outside having tea. This afternoon Sandys was absent, though I think he was negotiating with Welensky and Whitehead, who did not return after tea. The other U.K. Ministers

[33]A right-wing party committed to preserving white minority rule. It later became the Rhodesian Front.

[34]John Drummond, 17th Earl of Perth; Minister of State for Colonial Affairs, 1957–1962.

[35]Cuthbert Alport (later Baron Alport), Minister of State for Commonwealth Relations, 1959–1961; British High Commissioner to the Federation of Rhodesia and Nyasaland, 1961–1963.

were reading official papers, even Macleod, who was presiding. Alport, who was one of them, was the only representative of the C.R.O., for neither Sir Hugh [*sic*] Lintott[36] nor Sir Ralph Hone[37] was present. Sir John Martin[38] was the only U.K. delegate paying any attention to the proceedings. This was a pity, for after Dr Banda had pretty well been stopped from making an incoherent + largely irrelevant marathon speech, there were four relevant and cogent speeches, nearly all of them too long, as usual, but containing useful arguments from four quite different points of view. So far as arguments go, the federalists have won hands down; but only Martin, who has been both assiduous and attentive, will realise it. I do not suppose anybody will weep if Nyasaland secedes: it would simply cease to be a liability of the Fed.n + become a liability of the U.K. instead: but from the point of view of the people of Nyasaland it would be quite stupid.

It is plain that the U.K. has not the slightest idea what to do next. They have allowed discussion on the dissolution of the Fed.n, + they have to give their views on that subject at some time or other. I have, however, drafted some specific proposals in case Welensky wants to incorporate them in his speech.

Saturday, 17th December 1960

When Whitehead found that Nkomo did not attend on the 15th, he removed him and his stooge from the list of S.R.[39] delegates. The S.R. Conference then met on the 16th and again today. I should like to have been present, and indeed I would have been more useful there than in the federal conference, since one of the essential questions is transition to full self-government. I am to advise the N.R.[40] delegation, whose conference opens on the 19th, but I have meetings in Cambridge that day, + anyhow I do not think I shall be needed until they get down to business in January. I have also undertaken to advise the paramount Chief of Basutoland if the S. of S.,[41] at his request, asks me. I do not know if the two jobs are compatible, but I can ask the S. of S. that if he writes to me.

Kaunda, his stooge, and the two sympathetic chiefs returned to the federal conference on the 16th – Kaunda putting in a token appearance five minutes before we adjourned. This was apparently

[36] Sir Henry Lintott, Deputy Under-Secretary, Commonwealth Relations Office, 1956–1963.

[37] Sir Ralph Hone, Head of the Legal Division, Commonwealth Relations Office, 1954–1961.

[38] Sir John Martin, Deputy Under-Secretary of State at the Colonial Office, 1956–1965.

[39] Southern Rhodesia.

[40] Northern Rhodesia.

[41] Secretary of State.

under pressure from Macleod. One of the N.R. Ministers asked today why they were not given an explanation of his return, but Macmillan ruled him out of order. The fact is that the Ministers had refused to attend the N.R. conference until he returned to the federal conference. The N.R. conference will now open on the 19th, though there is no time to do anything because the delegates are leaving on the 20th.

Welensky read a fighting speech today, written by Evans but containing some material from me. He was followed by Duncan Sandys, who read a typical Whitehall woollie. It did become clear, however, (1) that there was no question of secession, and (2) that partnership was fundamental. The conference will adjourn until some time in the new year + I will then take up franchise, membership, powers, protective clauses, etc. Macmillan followed with some "come to Jesus" paragraphs. They had both seized on Dr Banda's "We are not against federalism; we are against this federation".

Sandys' proposals had clearly been cleared with Welensky + Whitehead. The next step is to settle, at least tentatively, the S.R. + N.R. Constitutions. Roberts (N.R.) had already pointed out that they cannot settle the N.R. Constn. until they know the conclusions on the Fed. Constn. This means, I suppose, that they will accept an African majority provided that (a) the Federat.n retains a European majority (or 50–50 or possible 33–33–33) and wide powers, and (b) there are ample protective clauses.

One great snag is that there must be a general election in S.R. before May. What Whitehead hopes, in fact, is to have a successful S.R. conference – from his point of view – and then to dissolve in March. He cannot give much away, for the Dominion Party – which supports white supremacy and no damned nonsense about it – has considerable support. He could give way somewhat on the franchise if he could be sure that (a) he would not lose too many European votes, and (b) he could be sure that he, and not Nkomo, gained the African votes. This of course is what Welensky did in 1956.

31st January 1961.

The N.R. Constn. Review Conference began yesterday, but without representatives of the United Federal Party[42] or the Dominion Party. I was to have advised the former; but my instructions have been cancelled. Exactly what has happened is not clear. It seems from the newspapers that there was some sort of Colonial Office document which went to Welensky. Since it did not go to the Africans, it

[42]The centre-right party of Sir Godfrey Huggins (later Viscount Malvern; Prime Minister of Southern Rhodesia, 1933–1953; first Prime Minister of the Federation of Rhodesia and Nyasaland, 1953–1956) and Sir Roy Welensky.

was probably not an intense plan but a reply to representations by Welensky. Possibly the U.F.P. decided that they could not discuss an African majority for N.R. until the question of the Federation had been settled. Greenfield[43] and Rodgers are in England on behalf of the U.F.P., but they are not taking part in the Conference, and anyhow Greenfield comes from S.R.

Friday, 3rd Feb. 1961

I went to London today to see Greenfield + Rodgers. The speech which Macleod made on the 19th Dec. had been sent in draft to Rodgers, who criticised it and suggested amendments. No change whatever had been made. I am not sure how this connects with what follows, except in so far as it made the U.F.P. suspicious of him.

A couple of weeks ago, Macleod sent to Welensky the outline of a scheme which he proposed to put to the N.R. Conference after the usual general chatter. It provided for an African majority among the elected members, the balance being held by ten official and nominated members. This was to be achieved by a double roll. Roll A would emphasise the Europeans and the wealthier Africans, the latter being 25% of the electors on the roll. There would be 14 Europeans and 4 Africans elected on this roll. Roll B would include all the electors on Roll A, but other Africans would be enfranchised on a much lower franchise, so that the Europeans would be 25% of the electors. On Roll B 14 Africans and 2 Europeans would be elected. Hence there would be 18 Africans and 16 Europeans elected. In the Ex. Co.[44] the Africans would have three Ministers and the Europeans two.

The U.F.P. decided not only to boycott the Conference, but also to prevent Macleod, if at all possible, from presenting this scheme officially. Rodgers explained that, in this view, an African majority, such as had been conceded in Nyasaland, would inevitably lead to a demand for responsible government. (In reply to a subsequent question from me, he said the fact that Kaunda's party was favouring some sort of compromise which would ensure a European minority was inducing Nkumbula[45] to ask for more).

Welensky discussed the whole matter with Sandys when the latter arrived in Salisbury for the S.R. Conference. Rodgers understood that Sandys had suggested that Greenfield and Rodgers should go to London to see Macleod. The C.R.O., however, denies this.

[43] Julian Greenfield, Federation Minister under Huggins and Welensky.

[44] Executive Council.

[45] Harry Nkumbula, African political leader in Northern Rhodesia.

Greenfield has seen Alport – who is now to become High Commissioner in Salisbury – several times; by this he is only a "Post Office" and has no authority to decide anything. More important was the fact that Alport took Greenfield to dinner with Macleod. Greenfield was to have had 30 minutes with McL. before dinner; but McL. was late + they had only 15 minutes. The scheme is now revised. On Roll A 14 Europeans and 2 Africans would be elected. On Roll B – on which there would be no Europeans – 16 Africans would be elected. McL. was willing to do a deal. If the U.F.P. accepted an African majority the composition of the Leg. Co.,[46] with the two Rolls operating might be such that the U.F.P. would have a majority and would then get all the seats in the Ex. Co. The deal could be kept secret + the U.F.P. could go on opposing the scheme, so that it could be imposed on N.R. by H.M.G. G[reenfield] said that this scheme astonished him; but he replied that he had the most positive instructions not to accept an African majority in any circumstances whatsoever. He pointed out, too, that what the U.F.P. hoped to have was not a single multi-racial party but two multi-racial parties.

The discussion was continued over dinner, in spite of the presence of Mrs Macleod. At one point Greenfield changed the conversation in order to bring Mrs McL. into it, but she brought it back to politics by saying that she was sure Iain wanted to talk about them. There were, however, times when McL. was simply sulking, neither eating nor talking. He is extremely angry at being thwarted (I had sensed something of this from his semi-private reputation. I had used the phrase that he was "on the make").

Greenfield has seen Lord Kilmuir,[47] who said very little but listened carefully. More important, G. has seen Macmillan, who turned on the charm and repeated many of the phrases which he had used when Welensky was at Chequers (I did not ask what these were – I heard all this in a report which G. made to Welensky over the phone. I heard a joke, however, about Greenfield looking to see if there was a Presbyterian Church nearby). Macmillan had asked what was to be done. Greenfield said that Macleod had better see Welensky either in Salisbury or in London. Asked which he preferred, Greenfield said London. Macmillan said he thought so too, but he also thought a special visit by Welensky might be embarrassing. The Commonwealth Prime Ministers were meeting in March,[48] and perhaps Welensky could

[46] Legislative Council.

[47] David Maxwell-Fyfe, Viscount (later Earl of) Kilmuir, British Conservative minister; Lord Chancellor, 1954–1962.

[48] Where they discussed, among other matters, South Africa's place in the Commonwealth.

come a few days early. (Welensky himself agreed with this). Macmillan said that the difficulty was to find a formula which would enable Macleod to close down the present Conference. This led Greenfield + Rodgers to believe that they had succeeded in breaking it up. They are going to Chequers tomorrow, + they are trying to push Evans (who arrived in London today) in, too.

I got very little information about the S.R. conference. Evidently the liaison between Welensky and Whitehead is poss. It seems, however, that Nkomo is being "moderate". He wants "one man, one vote", but so arranged (presumably by determination) that the Europeans get 14 seats out of 60. Sir Ralph Hone had produced a lengthy document, containing both a Bill of Rights and a series of protective clauses, which was designed for the Federal Constn., though it would apply to Territorial Legislation. (I brought the document away with me). Greenfield pointed out that there was all sorts of discriminatory legislation in operation, e.g. old age pensions and other social security measures. (I mentioned that according to one newspaper, Whitehead had accepted the idea of a Bill of Rights provided that it was not applied to existing legislation). Sandys had some ingenious ideas about representation, e.g. each constituency electing four members on two Rolls – though I did not follow the technical details.

12th February 1961.

I know nothing more except what has appears [*sic*] in newspapers. Neither Greenfield nor Taffy Evans has got into touch [*sic*] with me, though they are still in London; and so is Rodgers. What follows comes from newspapers.

Agreement was reached at the S.R. Conference, except by the Dominion Party. Sandys is back in London and has been involved in discussions with Macmillan, Macleod and Greenfield. Apparently Nkomo has accepted 15 seats in a house of 65, with a double roll. Whitehead has accepted a Bill of Rights in principle, but discussion about details has been adjourned. Evidently the Bill of Rights is not to be retrospective. These proposals would go to a referendum in S.R. in May. This suggests that Whitehead wants to postpone the referendum until the Federal talks have concluded.

The N.R. Conference has been continuing haltingly, discussing incidentals. In between sessions there have been "private talks". In short Macleod has been stalling. The Africans have been getting angry, + a protest was signed by all members of the Conference, including Sir John Moffatt + his other members of the Central African Party (who has an article in the current *Spectator*, including an attack on the unnamed constitutional lawyer) They went in a body to see Macmillan in the middle of the week. Kaunda, who is supposed to be a disciple of

Ghandi [*sic*], has talked about troubles "worse than Mau Mau".[49] The Conference is supposed to end on Tuesday (14th Feb.). 75 Conservative members have signed a motion asking the Government to support the principles of 1958 (apparently paras. 16 + 17 of the proposals of March 1958). This is, of course, Welensky's line. Speaking generally, however, the U.F.P. has had a bad press. I am not sure that Greenfield + Rodgers have been right to be so inaccessible. They have been anxious not to say anything which would make Macleod's withdrawal more difficult. It was, of course, a serious blunder to let his original draft "leak".

Sunday 26th February 1961

I have included some cuttings in this file + need not summarise. I have no private information whatever. Evans left on the night of the 18th February, evidently taking a copy of the Macleod plan with him. Greenfield and Rodgers left during the week. None of them communicated with me. This is a pity, for I would like to have heard more of the politics behind the plan. It seems evident that the essence of the plan came from Sandys, though there are elements of Macleod in it. What Macleod has been fighting for is an African majority, because that was the proposal which "leaked". He seems to have got it, as the attached paper shows.[50] To get a 7% or 10% quota on the upper roll (Roll A) an African will have to be a "moderate", except perhaps in constituencies where there are few Europeans. It seems unlikely that any European could get a 7% or 10% quota on the lower roll (Roll B). Hence there will be 30 Africans and 15 Europeans, but between 7 and 10 would be "moderates".

[49] A violent 1950s uprising in Kenya by mainly Kikuyu people against British rule. The British inflicted torture and severe punishment on suspected rebels.

[50] Not included.

SECTION J: SINGAPORE

The main political parties in the Crown Colony of Singapore had joined together to form an all-party delegation to argue for further self-government in London in April–May 1956. Jennings was tasked with advising the delegation on how best to frame their independence claims to the British. Singapore briefly joined the Malayan Federation in 1963, before becoming an independent republic in 1965.

1. 'Singapore Chronicle' diary, 1956

En route out of Beirut, 25 March 1956

My connection with Singapore is evident from the correspondence. I was apparently recommended from Ceylon and Pakistan, and David Marshall[1] phoned me from Arosa in Switzerland. I have not yet met him or any of the Singapore Ministers. My connection with the Federation of Malaya (on this occasion) began with Tunku Abdul Rahman's[2] visit to London in Feb. 1956. He also had heard about me in Colombo and Karachi, but had not associated the name with his fellow undergraduate of 1922–25. He attended a dinner at Chatham House, + then learned (not from me) that the two Jennings were one and the same. He came to tea at St. Cath[arine's] one evening + asked if I would serve on the Constl. Commission. The correspondence in the Malaya file follows.[3]

In view of the decision that I should fly to Singapore for consultations, I stayed with Raeburn[4] on the night of the 23rd, and de Smith[5] came to dinner. They seemed to agree with my line, namely, that we should ask for independence subject to emergency powers (i.e.

[1] David Marshall, first Chief Minister of Singapore, 1955–1956; founder of the Labour Front and Workers' Party in Singapore.

[2] See p. 58, n. 9.

[3] See Section D.

[4] Walter Raeburn QC. Raeburn had been pupil master to Marshall at the University of London. Raeburn would assist Marshall, Jennings, and the Singapore delegation during the London conference.

[5] See p. 99, n. 3.

the old Pakistan section 92A[6]), to be exercised by the Commissioner-General or a C-in-C.[7] under the control of H.M.G. This would make a Singapore Independence Act with an Emergency Powers section inserted. If we failed to get this, we could fall back upon the original plan, i.e. independence with a cession of foreign affairs + defence: but this would be the end of the negotiation not the beginning.

Before going to London I had received a phone call from the Colonial Office asking if I would like to see the S. of S.[8] I said I would, and that I would be available on Saturday morning (24th March). The reply was that the S. of S. would not be available on that day, but would I see Sir John Martin[9] instead? I said I would – hence his letter in the Singapore file. I saw Sir John at the C.O. from 11 a.m. to 12.15 p.m. He explained the situation in Singapore, most of which I knew already. His main points, or strictly speaking those which impressed me, were:–

[*following two points struck through*]

(1) H.M.G. are as anxious for a friendly settlement as they were in the case of the Federation

(2) There is however, a fundamental difference between the Federation and the Colony, namely, that Rahman has a solid majority which he seems likely to retain for at least 5 years, whereas Marshall's position is precarious.

<u>Singapore, 28th March 1956.</u> I arrived at 1.30 p.m. on the 26th and was met at the airport by David Marshall, by whom I was at once subjected to a press conference. Considering that I had had no notice whatsoever, it passed off quite well. At least there were no heavy breaks. The C.M.[10] got down to business on the way to Raffles, an embarrassing method, for I like to start from scratch + not to have to talk in front of a driver. A meeting of the All-Party delegation had been summoned for 4.30 p.m., and I was apparently to be thrust on without any real conversation with the C.M. Fortunately he phoned at 3.30 p.m., and I then said that I would like to see him at that point. I read my summary of Sir John Martin's points, which pleased him mightily. He said the tone was quite different from that of the last conversation with Lennox-Boyd.[11] He also mentioned L.B's refusal

[6] See p. 132, n. 12.

[7] Commander-in-Chief.

[8] Secretary of State for the Colonies.

[9] See p. 166, n. 39.

[10] Chief Minister.

[11] Alan Lennox-Boyd (later Viscount Boyd of Merton), British Conservative minister; Secretary of State for the Colonies, 1954–1959. Jennings sometimes abbreviates his name to L.B. in this chapter.

to see him in February when he phoned from Arosa. I was able to explain that – L.B. was just going off to Cyprus + could not say so over the phone. The explanation was not quite convincing, for L.B. when pressed has said that he did not want to see Marshall before April. I explained that L.B. had probably become more accommodating through his failure in Cyprus.[12] He was an up and coming member of the Conservative Party (as Lord Reid[13] had emphasised last week when I dined with him) + he did not want a second failure, which would destroy the good impression he had made over the agreement with the Tunku.

At the meeting there were present all the party leaders – all Chinese except Marshall and one Malay – and we got on quite well. From the draft resolution I was able to get the obnoxious word "cede" removed and replaced by "offer an agreement whereby . . . " This was something like my third attempt, but it was good to get unanimity on so difficult a subject, + Marshall was evidently pleased.

It was agreed that I should prepare the draft of the agreement + that it would be considered by party leaders. There was difference of opinion over the question whether it should be disclosed at the outset of the negotiations, but eventually I solved that one by saying that they could decide that point when they had seen the draft. This unanimity was achieved of course by postponing a decision, which is always popular, but in fact I did get the impression that the left-wing (P.A.P.[14]) would play. One possibly disruptive feature did appear. Lim Song Sie (?),[15] the P.A.P. leader, did seem to suggest by implication that Lennox-Boyd would be persuaded if he listened to a leftist diatribe by Lim S.S. The fact that L.B. is a Conservative politician and the consequences which flow from it, are not completely understood. I must write a note for Marshall on this subject.

Singapore 29th March. I have now completed (a) the draft agreement (b) the draft memorandum, and (c) a note on tactics. There is nothing more I can do until Marshall goes through this material. He seems to spend much of his time making speeches and talking to pressmen. Since he has to say something new about "merdeka"[16] each time,

[12]On 9 March 1956 Makarios, Archbishop and Primate of the Greek Orthodox Church in Cyprus, was controversially arrested and exiled to the Seychelles owing to his links with the EOKA terrorist organization that was fighting to end British rule on the island and unite with Greece.

[13]See p. 57, n. 1.

[14]People's Action Party, founded in 1954. It has held power continuously since 1959.

[15]Jennings is probably referring to either Lim Chin Siong or Fong Swee Suan, both leftist leaders in the PAP at that point.

[16]'Self-government' or 'freedom' in Malay.

we have a series of pronouncements which are not always consistent with each other and will in any case prove embarrassing when we get to London. In particular, he disclosed to *The Times* correspondent something about the "escape clause" which I call section 92A, + thereby set the P.A.P. on the scent, whereas I would rather explain this personally to Lee Kuan Yew[17] and try to get him to agree. If the P.A.P. would accept this clause, I am sure H.M.G. would agree.

I met Marshall at a cocktail party at [*illegible*] last night – the first time I had seen him since the night of the 26th. He said that Geoffrey Lloyd[18] was in Raffles for the night + would I see him. As it happened, Marshall became ill at that moment – it looked like the heart – but eventually [*illegible*] phoned Lloyd, and I dined with the Caths. He seemed to be in complete agreement in that H.M.G. must take the risk of "merdeka" provided that it has the "escape clause" in section 92A to provide a judicial backing for intervention if it ever becomes necessary. To refuse "merdeka" at this stage would be to ask for trouble; to grant it merely uncertain risk of trouble after the general election; such trouble may never develop, but if it does the U.K. will have forces ready at hand to take over.

Marshall came in while the above was being written and saw the draft agreement. He made a few modifications in it + then took it away to be duplicated for circulation.

Singapore, Easter Sunday, 1st April. Marshall came in to see me on the morning of the 29th and approved the draft agreement with some amendments. Later that morning the draft memo was typed + I took it in. He was rather more critical of it, as I expected, because the memo was carefully drafted to "make it easy for H.M.G." (Herbert Morrison's[19] phrase). Still, with some amendments it went through.

Hamid Jumat,[20] the Malay member, came to see me in the afternoon of the 29th, with Marshall's consent. We got on [good] terms at once by talking about the Tunku – Marshall had told him that I knew the Tunku as an undergraduate. Jumat said that the Malays had begun the demand for Merdeka, but if Singapore alone was to get Merdeka with the Malays only 17% they wanted to know what they were going to get out of it. They could hardly obstruct Merdeka; but would it be possible to write in some provision for raising the standard of the Malay minority? I pointed out that it was easy enough

[17] Lee Kuan Yew, PAP Secretary General; Prime Minister of Singapore, 1959–1990.

[18] Geoffrey Lloyd (later Baron Geoffrey-Lloyd), British Conservative politician.

[19] Herbert Morrison (later Baron Morrison of Lambeth), British Labour minister; Deputy Prime Minister, 1945–1951.

[20] Abdul Hamid bin Haji Jumat, Minister of Local Government, Lands, and Housing in the Marshall ministry.

to put in negative provisions against discrimination, etc., but that positive provisions could not be more than directive principles of sound policy – and I quoted some of the provisions of the Pakistan Constitution (the fact that I was so familiar with Islam went down well). He said that he would like something of the sort inserted, so I said that he had better get an appropriate directive inserted in to the draft agreement, and I drafted a clause accordingly.

In the evening I dined with the Trinity Hall men (Lamb, Lloyd, Chua and Atcherley).

Good Friday was an easy day and I read Perry Robinson's Transformation in Malaya[21] in order to get some knowledge of Communist background. I saw Goode[22] at his home on Saturday, 31st March, at 11 a.m., by appointment made by Marshall. He was a little cagy at first, assuming me to act merely as Marshall's advocate. I soon cleared this out of the way. I had reached the conclusion that we could persuade the C.O.[23] only if I let them know, indirectly, exactly what was being proposed. I had put the "escape clause" to Martin hesitatingly; I explained the scheme to Geoffrey Lloyd in general terms; and I went into some detail with Goode (Chief Secretary). Goode on his part explained that though he was C.S. to the Ministers generally, he could not divest himself of his responsibility to H.M.G. + so he tended to think and speak as an agent of H.M.G. rather than a member of the Singapore govt.

The position was that Singapore contained about 3000 active M.C.P.[24] members, in spite of the fact that it was an illegal body. It had members and sympathisers on the P.A.P. Lee Kuan Yew was not a past member, but he (Goode) was convinced that Lim Chin Siong was, though since he had come back (late) to Assembly he had acted overtly as a P.A.P. politician and not covertly as a M.C.P. man. The strength of the M.C.P. really lay in the fact that they had permeated three large unions, particularly those engaged in transport and could pretty well paralyse Singapore when they wanted to. The rest of the unions were behind Marshall's Labour Front; but the M.C.P. followed the usual tactic of exploiting every grievance. Also, whenever the M.C.P. wanted to start a row they could. They had a lot of emotional schoolboys and schoolgirls, not genuine communists, but always eager to demonstrate for Merdeka. Also, there was the general emotional appeal to the overseas Chinese of the homeland: and since

[21] J.B.P. Robinson, *Transformation in Malaya* (London, 1956).

[22] See p. 62, n. 19.

[23] Colonial Office.

[24] Malayan Communist Party. An illegal organization and critical player in the insurgency known as the Malayan Emergency.

the defeat of the Kuomintang a large part of this emotion had been transferred to Communist China.[25] Hence the security situation was not good. It rested on the police, a body of 6000 men with about 300 (?) [*sic*] officers of whom 60 were European and the remainder mostly Indians, Eurasians and Chinese. The men were, generally speaking, Malays, and so the handling of riots might take on a racial tinge, the rioters being Chinese and the police being Malay. Also the police, though a fine body of men, could not be trusted if the Malays happened to be the people who started the row, as in the riots of 1952 (?).[26] Behind the police were the British Army, consisting mainly of Malay O.R.[27] with British officers; but there was usually one battalion with British O.R., + they worked on the basis that a British O.R. was, in the circumstances, worth three Malays. On the other hand, if trouble developed and a few B[ritish].O.R. got killed there would be the usual reaction in Britain against the use of "Mum's boy" to maintain order in these remote areas, and one of the major difficulties in the Merdeka plan was that the local politicians having got the local situation in a mess, would expect to be able to call on "Mum's boy" to get him out of it. They had, however, decided to establish a battalion of the Federation Regiment in Singapore; it would be mainly Chinese and Malay in composition. Even so, the situation did depend upon the British Army. Hence the fundamental difficulty in the Merdeka demand was the issue of internal security.

Marshall had mentioned the proposed Defence Council to him, but Marshall seemed to think of it as a means for associating the local people with external defence; what was needed was some device for associating the forces with internal security. I explained that I saw it as exercising both functions, + that it had been made an executive body accordingly. Goode thought that there was some hope in the scheme, but it was important that the Army should know how the situation was developing + therefore have regular intelligence reports. I said that, if the Council worked successfully, the practice of weekly intelligence reports ought to develop. If the C.O. wanted that in writing they had better raise it in London. Goode was also struck by my suggestion of having a U.K. Representative other than the Gov. Gen. + with section 92A. On the other hand, he thought that having the C.Os.[28] on the Council might do more harm than good, because of the constant

[25] By 1949 the Chinese civil war was largely over, with the Communist Party controlling the mainland and Chiang Kai-chek's Kuomintang movement confined to Taiwan.

[26] This probably refers to riots in 1950, mainly involving Malays angered over a perceived legal bias against Muslims. The lower ranks of the police were often staffed by Malays.

[27] Other ranks (i.e. non-officers).

[28] Colonial officials.

nagging which would go on, as in the Council of Ministers. "What you fellows want is discipline. Can't govern without discipline." I said this was a question of personality and instanced [*illegible*] in Ceylon. Also, I said that the antagonism to the ex officio members in the Council of ministers was due to the fact that they were the representatives of "colonialism", through the policemen. In Ceylon the War Council rested on the C. in C.'s directive + so had "teeth", but it never used them + genuine collaboration was obtained because Ministers were asked to help, not advised on behalf of H.M.G.

Goode ended by saying that he was much more cheerful as a result of our conversation. If I could persuade the delegation on the one score + the C.O. on the other, the scheme might work. Incidentally, one must not think of the delegation as "government" and "opposition". Hamid Jumat was not wholly with Marshall (as I knew). On the other side Lim [*illegible*], William Tan, Lim [*illegible*], and [*illegible*] Lim[29] were further to the right than Marshall + very concerned with the safety of their property.

Thursday, 5th April 1956. The debate on the Merdeka motion opened yesterday, the motion being moved by Marshall and seconded by Lee Kuan Yew (P.A.P.). It was continued this morning but I was unable to listen, since I had to see H.E.[30] Marshall made quite a sensible speech, possibly a little too dramatic, but not unreasonably so. At any rate from my point of view it did no harm. Lee Kuan Yew is much more intellectual, though he had a difficult time in expressing preference for the Commonwealth over Communist China. Still he did; and made plain that the P.A.P. is anti-Communist. Whether Lim Chin Siong agrees I do not know.

I saw the Governor (Sir Robert Black[31]) for 1½ hours this morning. He is clearly against Merdeka, though I think I shook him a bit when I said that I thought the C.O. was for it, as the better of two hard alternatives. He emphasises – overemphasises – that Singapore is not "viable"; he has not seen my memo in which this point is dealt with at some length. He also emphasised, at some length, internal security, and he clearly has no solution to the problem, but he was apparently not ill-disposed toward mine. Listening to him, I thought that Singapore was perpetually on the verge of insurrection. When I suggested the need for troops was an exceptional need he said, rather haughtily, that of course that was theory, but he was concerned with practicalities. It is, unfortunately, difficult to tell the Queen's

[29]Probably members of the Liberal Socialist Party (as William Tan certainly was).

[30]His Excellency the Governor.

[31]Sir Robert Black, British colonial administrator; Governor of Singapore, 1955–1957.

representative that he and not I was being theoretical. He was perhaps not quite as dogmatic as on Tuesday night, when he was posing for the benefit of the ladies, but he clearly has not as good a brain as the C.S. (Goode). He was very insistent on the need for agreement with the Federation, and seemed to think that a local nationality would render fusion difficult. I pointed out that there would have to be double nationality in the Federation, + that the franchise for federal purposes need not be the same as the franchise for State purposes. The problem is difficult, but it need not be rendered more difficult by what I would call theoretical and he practical considerations. In short, he really put to me the difficulties which Sir John Martin put at the C.O., but without Martin's anxiety to find a solution. That is of course understandable, since H.E. does not want to lose his job; but I do not think he is capable of exercising imagination. Possibly his going early (he is leaving tomorrow) will enable him to sort things out with the C.O. I wish, however, that Goode were going with him.

Cambridge, Saturday 21st April 1956. My neat s. 92A, which I thought solved the problem of internal security, was debated on the insistence of Lee Kuan Yew at a meeting of party leaders at the Chief Minister's Office on the 6th April. Also, the Defence Council was made to represent both sides equally, with no casting vote. I was turned out of the meeting when this was discussed, but I told Marshall afterwards that this scheme would not go through. He said he did not want it to go through because there was a serious risk of a communist govt., + he did not want to take that risk. I asked whether I could tell that to the C.O. He said that I could, provided that I made plain that the scheme as originally drafted was the maximum offer that could be made.

Some other amendments, of no great importance, were made at a meeting of the whole delegation (less two) on the 2nd April or thereabouts. I left Singapore on the 7th for Madras, changed planes for New Delhi, left New Delhi for Bombay on the night of the 8th, and reached England by the night of the 9th.

On my return I replied to a letter from the S. of S., sent to me before I left England, taking the opportunity of offering to explain matters to the S. of S. or Sir John Martin. I had no reply until the evening of the 17th, when a private secretary phoned to ask if I could see the S. of S. on the 18th. It was difficult to fit in, but eventually we fixed on 5 p.m. to 6 p.m. At 4.30 p.m. I saw Sir John Martin with Wilde and Manklelow of the M/A+F.,[32] but this was to arrange about the Royal

[32] Ministry of Agriculture, Fisheries, and Food.

Commission during my absence in Malaya. Lord Reid will arrive in Penang on the 26th May, but I said that I would prefer to leave England after the May Races on the 9th June. Our Australian colleague is Sir William McKell, sometime Governor-General – clearly a passenger; the Canadian, Indian and Pakistani have not yet been nominated, but urgent cables have been sent to the capitals.[33]

Lennox Boyd is a flashy and emotional politician, whose mind fluctuates between extremes as he talks. He has clearly been prejudiced against merdeka by Black, + he was much less encouraging than Sir John Martin had been. He twice said in relation to particular suggestions (I forget what) that he would "rather have another Cyprus". With him were John Hare (Minister of State),[34] Sir John Martin, his P.S., and Lord Reid (who had had a discussion before I arrived). Practically the whole conversation, however, was a battle between Lennox Boyd and me. When he bit hard, I bit back. I did not persuade him, but I did get under his guard occasionally, and I am inclined to think that he will be a little more flexible when he comes to the conference, especially as he is seeing Marshall on Saturday and is taking him to Brighton to stay with Herbert Morrison.

Lennox Boyd's main points were:

(1) It is impossible to conceive of Singapore as an independent State: the whole of it can be seen from the top of Government House.
(2) Marshall had presumably asked again for internal self-government; now he wanted external affairs also; he could not possibly consent to the possibility of having a Chinese ambassador in Singapore.
(3) The suggestion to have as Governor a constitutional monarch was ridiculous. He would appoint an assistant principal from the Office. The governor must have reserve powers.
(4) Internal security was vital. He could not have "Mum's boys" shot down by Chinese communists because the Singapore Ministers had neglected to maintain order.
(5) He could do a deal with Marshall, but he had no majority, and what he had to assume was that Lee Kuan Yew would obtain power.

Much of this was bluster. He clearly does not want another Cyprus but he is afraid of the Conservative right wing. He is willing to enlarge the Leg. Assembly + to remove the ex officio Ministers. I told him at one point that he was foolish to do this if he thought Singapore

[33] See Section D.
[34] John Hare (later Viscount Blakenham), British Conservative minister; Minister of State for Colonial Affairs, 1955–1956.

was going Communist. My main point, however, was that my section 92A – which I read – offered an escape if difficulties did arrive. At the end he offered me a drink, but I had to decline because of a meeting at Marshall's. As I went out, Martin asked if I could let him have a copy of section 92A – i.e. paragraph 12(3) in the original draft. I sent it to him the next day from the office of the Royal Commission, with a covering letter stressing that our scheme involved the least risk. I mentioned, too, Lee Kuan Yew's reply to a question by [*illegible*] as to what would happen if "merdeka" was refused – "There would be a row".

Marshall had a meeting of party leaders at St James Court, Buckingham Gate, at 6 p.m. – Hamid Jumat (who left early), Lim [*illegible*] + Lee Kuan Yew. I learned that the emasculated draft agreement had already been sent to the C.O. I had intended to suggest that it was unwise to send a draft which would be rejected. Marshall said that the S. of S. would want to divide with committees. It was agreed to resist this proposal and to get the main lines settled before there was any committee work. Asked to comment on the draft, I said that two questions would be objected to. (1) external relations, and (2) internal security. Nothing was said about the former. On the latter Marshall + Jumat favoured section 92A, while Lim wanted something stronger. Lee was prepared for intervention by H.M.G. if the Govt. of Singapore failed to observe the Constn., i.e. if a communist minority seized power, but not if a communist majority was elected. I put the case of communist-engineered strike threats but received no reply.

On the 19th Raeburn, S.A. de Smith + I had a meeting at Raeburn's Chambers. We did not get very far, but had a general discussion about the situation.

Lee Kuan Yew came to Cambridge on the 20th + we dined him in Hall. [*Illegible*] dined in, and they came back to the Lodge for drinks afterwards. Lee repeated his point about a communist majority, and would not accept my argument that one could never let a Communist Govt. take office because it could not be turned out. I tried to make it plain, too, that Singapore would get merdeka if he, Lee, was prepared to play, because H.M.G. believed that he, Lee, would obtain a majority. He suggested, rather vaguely, that he did not at present contemplate a majority. He also said that his own views were roughly those of Nye Bevan,[35] with whom he has been in consultation. I wonder if we can somehow get across to the S. of S. that a refusal of merdeka will produce [*illegible*] opposition?

[35] Aneurin Bevan, British Labour politician; Minister of Health, 1945–1951.

Cambridge, 6th May 1956. The conference has been at work for two weeks. I have had no time to make a personal record, but the official record in File II will indicate progress. A verbatim note was taken of the first meeting + so I need not attempt to summarise from my notes. I noted that the S. of S. "made a blustering speech, barely professional, and not in much of an order." I cannot now remember whether the Singapore delegation met on the 24th April. I think there was a meeting of party leaders in Raeburn's Chambers at which we held an inquest, but anyhow the lawyers met. On Wednesday 25th April the S. of S. made his specific proposals. We had a lawyers' meeting the same evening + came to the conclusion that we should (a) draft a Singapore independence Bill with a transitional clause, and (b) submit an explanatory memo. This was discussed by the party leaders on Thursday 26th + the programme was agreed. This [*illegible*] the meeting on Friday 27th. Since the press had been informed of the meeting, however, and cancellation would have led to speculation, it was agreed to have a formal meeting; the legal advisers were not at the meeting; but we spent the time in drafting and considering drafts. The Bill was drafted by Raeburn and de Smith, while I drafted the memo. In consequence of discussions on Friday 27th we considerably amended our respective versions and they were circulated to the delegation the same night.

I should mention that there was a cocktail party on the night of the 26th, + we then discussed with Sir John Martin the question of producing the documents for him and Sir [Kenneth] Roberts-Wray[36] on the afternoon of the 30th.

On the morning of Saturday, 28th, we had a meeting of party leaders and deputies to consider the Draft Bill and memo. The Draft Bill was further amended, but the memo was completely rejected. It was of course drafted in order to persuade H.M.G. The delegation feared that the conference would break down + that the memo would have to be published in Singapore. Hence it had to be a political manifesto, which Marshall agreed to draft. We had another meeting on Monday 30th, when further amendments were made to the Bill. There was a fierce argument between Marshall and Lee Kuan Yew over the memo. Lee said that Marshall had put in his own political views, which differed fundamentally from those of the P.A.P. Hence Lee wanted large chunks cut out. Eventually, Marshall agreed to another meeting in the afternoon, while we were at the C.O.

Raeburn, de Smith + I had lunch at my club to discuss our tactics. Raeburn, as usual, got his way, though I argued with some reluctance.

[36] Sir Kenneth Roberts-Wray, Legal Adviser to the Colonial Office and the Commonwealth Relations Office.

My method is to lay all our cards on the table, because I know H.M.G. wants a decision. Raeburn thinks in terms of advocacy leading to a settlement. The effect was, of course, that Martin and Roberts-Wray were "cagey", + the discussion was really not valuable. We could not in any case produce the memo. + all Raeburn's advocacy was upset by a telephone message from Marshall to me saying that the Singapore delegation was prepared to accept that H.M.G. control external defence and external affairs until merger with the Federation. Our whole scheme for independence was of course based on the assumption of a transitional period of ten years (it was six in the Bill, but [*illegible*]), ending in Statute of Westminster status. The message therefore completely destroyed our case.

The Bill was circulated on Tuesday 1st May + Marshall read his memo. The S. of S. asked for an adjournment until Thursday or Friday so that he could consider the matter. We therefore had a break of two days, filled for me by the work of the Royal Commission on Common Land, and we met again on Friday 4th May. I have as yet no summary of his statement, but I presume there will be one. We lawyers had an inquest afterwards and agreed –

(1) to try to find a formula to express the "common interests" of the U.K. and Singapore in internal security – a point on which the S. of S. seemed to be insistent;
(2) to revert to the idea of a "containment area" to deal with such matters as the acquisition of land;
(3) to provide for a "declaration of abnormality", after which the High Commission may issue what are in effect defence regulations.

I should mention that I had lunch with Martin at the club – we met by accident – on Friday + I tried to sell him the containment idea. As a matter of fact, the discussions are coming round to my original scheme, which is to be found in File I, i.e. containment areas for normal times and section 92A in abnormal times, the powers being exercised by a Defence Council with executive powers. Both the *Sunday Times* and the *Observer* today (Sunday, 6th May) say that the S. of S. wants a Council with executive powers, while Marshall wants a council with advisory powers. In point of fact, we started out with a council with executive powers, then the S. of S. made it advisory only, and now he is coming back to an executive body. The S. of S. will continue his statement tomorrow (Monday, 7th May). He is handling the situation much better now than at the beginning, and he was quite impressive on Friday. Marshall, too, is proving surprisingly flexible, though I am not sure that it will be possible to agree on Tuesday. The gap between H.M.G. and the Singapore delegation is quite wide.

The delegation is becoming, for all practical purposes, Marshall and Lee Kuan Yew, with Lim Chin Siong in the background being fed by the C.P. of G.B.,[37] whom he is said to visit every night. The Lib. Socs.[38] occasionally put Marshall on the straight path, though it is done more often by Lim Koon Teck[39] than by Lim Choon Mong,[40] who is as woolly as ever. Lim Yew Hock[41] rarely says anything; Jumat is often ill; Braga[42] is helpful from time to time. Lee Kuan Yew is something of an opportunist, but I suspect that he contemplates (a) a P.A.P. Government after the election (the Labour Front has agreed to a general election for 50 members), and (b) a breakdown of constitutional machinery, out of which conflict independence will somehow be obtained. On the other hand, he is (I am sure) really honest in his belief in a United Malaya. His loyalty, as he once said, is to Malaya, and he is a Malayan. He wants a Malaya which follows Nehru's[43] policy; a neutralist quasi-socialist policy. His British affiliations are with the left wing of the Labour Party, but he is quite willing to use the Communists to help him to get into power, fully aware that the tail will wag the dog if he is not careful, and yet willing to run the risk. He has the great advantage that he can speak to the electorate in Mandarin, and that he is learning Cantonese and (I believe) Hokkien, whereas Marshall can speak English only "under the old apple tree"[44] (a joke, incidentally, which must be unintelligible to the Chinese-educated). I doubt if we have, as yet, "sold" the Commonwealth to him, though of course I have not yet ascertained the effect on him of the past two weeks. He is out every night, enjoying the fleshpots, though I am not sure with whom – probably not the Fabians.

Cambridge, 7th May 1956. The S. of S. continued his "questions" this morning, and it became plain that his scheme was quite unacceptable. Perhaps he was being persuaded of Marshall's queerness that he could go further. He made it plain (a) that there could not be a Governor-General, (b) that the Colonial Office and not the C.R.O. would retain control, (c) that the Constn. might be suspended twice a year, (d)

[37] Communist Party of Great Britain.

[38] The centre-left Liberal Socialist Party of Singapore.

[39] Lim Koon Teck, a leading lawyer in Singapore.

[40] Leader of the Liberal Socialists.

[41] Lim Yew Hock, Minister of Labour; successor to David Marshall as Chief Minister, 1956–1959.

[42] A.J. Braga, Minister of Health, 1956–1959.

[43] Jawaharlal Nehru, Prime Minister of India, 1947–1964.

[44] When Marshall had been made Chief Minister he was told that there would be no office space for him, in response to which he threatened that he would work 'under the old apple tree' in central Singapore.

that a power of legislation by O. in C.[45] would be retained. While all this was going on, Lee Kuan Yew passed a note to Marshall asking for an adjournment for a private discussion. Marshall rather cleverly asked the S. of S. to put his proposals in writing and so secured an adjournment without asking for it. We then had a dog-fight at a private meeting. Lee's tactics have become clearer. He wanted to accept the C.O. scheme + then to go back to Singapore to say that Singapore had not got "merdeka" and that the electorate should vote P.A.P. in order to get it. It [has] now developed, and Lee Kuan Yew said he would cable his party forthwith explaining the situation. Marshall, shouting, dared Lee to do it, and adjourned the meeting.

Cambridge, 9th May 1956. All seemed quiet in the Singapore delegation yesterday, and I doubt if Lee Kuan Yew carried out his threat. The S. of S. produced his scheme and, in effect, explained that wide powers were needed because the U.K. Government could not trust the S'pore Govt., but the S'pore Government could trust the U.K. Govt. not to use the powers except in extremis. The wide powers allowed, of course, for interference in all kinds of petty details. Marshall put the case of the S'pore Govt. refusing to provide 6 telephones for one of the bases, and Roberts-Wray agreed that the High Commissioner could issue a Defence Regulation which would, if necessary, be followed by an Order in Council.

The S. of S. could spare only ¾ hour because he had to read a statement in the H of C.[46] as usual he did nearly all the talking, + then insisted on reading the draft, which we had all read. Then he left John Hare in charge. The Minister was much less capable than the S. of S., but in the circumstances it made no difference. It was agreed to meet today at 4 p.m. and Marshall, with a gesture, asked the Governor whether he could have a meeting of Ministers at 3.15 p.m. H.E. said he could, apparently forgetting (a) that his functions are being exercised by an Acting Governor and (b) only 7 Ministers and the A.G.[47] are in London. Anyhow, Marshall can resign without having a meeting of Ministers.

We had a meeting of the delegation afterwards, when we were asked a number of questions about the effect of the document. The Lib. Socs were apparently inclined for acceptance but did not want to give a lead, + Marshall was clearly against. We produced our scheme of the 4th May in a last attempt to reach a compromise, + it

[45] Order in Council.
[46] House of Commons.
[47] Attorney-General.

is being considered by the delegation tomorrow morning. Meanwhile the parties are to produce memoranda on their attitudes.

Cambridge, 12th May 1956

On the afternoon of Wed 9th May there was a meeting of the Singapore delegation from which we were excluded. It seemed that Marshall was in a minority of one, the others pressing him to carry on the discussions. The meeting at 4 p.m. was therefore for the purpose not of terminating the conference but for ascertaining the views of the S. of S. on (a) nationality and (b) Malayanisation. The S. of S. was both tactful and conciliatory, while Marshall was calm. It was agreed that H.M.G. should produce papers on these subjects + that they should be discussed on Thursday or Friday. This was, from the point of view of H.M.G., excellent tactics. Clearly the delegation had agreed to break up the conference and to go into united opposition for "merdeka" if agreement could not be reached on these points. The S. of S. showed that there would not be obstacles to agreement and that, if the delegation was ready to agree on internal security and compensation, they could have citizenship and Malayanisation. Thus, if the conference broke down it would be because of Singapore's refusal to accept the precautions necessary to prevent communism.

On nationality on Thursday 10th May the S. of S. was particularly accommodating and pretty well accepted everything. The meeting was short and was little more than a conversation between Roberts-Wray and myself. He was not quite so helpful on Malayanisation on Friday 11th May, but there was nothing that the Singapore Government could not accept. Two working parties were set up, though the nomination of Singapore representatives was postponed until May.

Today everything went wrong. H.M.G. had issued a new paper, bringing together all its views on the constitutional issue. Nearly the whole of it was acceptable, though it became clear that clause (16)[48] was the crux. It had been tempered as a result of the discussion on the 8th and 9th but it was still a hard unit for Marshall. Unfortunately he did not see it until midnight last night, I saw a copy only 10 minutes before the meeting; and Raeburn got his copy after we had gone into the meeting. Marshall was obviously bad-tempered and started off with a provocative statement. The S. of S. was equally bad-tempered – there is to be a debate on Cyprus on Monday + he is obviously not looking forward to it - and he was equally provocative. One word "impossible" – which did not seem to me to be particularly

[48]This refers to the contentious issue of the UK's powers over defence in Singapore.

provocative in its context – was seized upon by Marshall, who asked for an adjournment until Tuesday in order to prepare a reply which was evidently a rejection. The S. of S. flatly refused to adjourn + enable the Singapore delegation to prepare a counter-document. If the delegation was not able to accept para. (16) or something like it they would say so here and now. Lee Kuan Yew then butted in and asked for an adjournment of 30 minutes. The S. of S. agreed and we adjourned to the committee room. There the rest of the delegation, and Raeburn + I, did attempt to talk Marshall over. Raeburn's suggestion that Marshall go to see the S. of S. to ask for an adjournment to Tuesday was eventually accepted. Marshall apparently put the case on the grounds that (a) the delegation did not get the papers until midnight + had had no time to consult advisers, and (b) tomorrow was the anniversary of the Singapore riots, if the end of the merdeka commission was called tonight there might be bloodshed. He came back saying that the S. of S. was prepared for an adjournment for the purpose of discussing clause (16) only. If that was agreed, he would be prepared to discuss that. When Jumat asked if they could not present this case as a whole, the S. of S. said he could not prevent them from submitting any memo. they pleased, but he would not discuss anything until clause (16) was out of the way.

On that basis we adjourned until Tuesday, 15th May. At a short meeting of the delegation it was agreed that de Smith should draft a Bill on the lines of the last para. (a para. which could, we thought, be exploited), + the delegation would meet tonight, without advisers, to consider Raeburn's compromise draft on para. (16). I suggested that Raeburn might try to draft more closely in line with that para., + I will myself have a shot at it tomorrow morning. Anyway, the merdeka commission still survives!

Cambridge, Friday 18th May 1956. On Sunday, 13th May, Jumabhoy, Minister of Commerce and Industry, and his wife came up to dinner. He brought with him a document which I took to be an agreed statement of the delegation which was clearly unacceptable, + I spent several hours in trying to get it into an acceptable form. It turned out to be a draft of Lee Kuan Yew which had not been accepted by anybody. There had in fact been no agreement about anything.

When I arrived at 10 Carlton House Terrace at 10.30 a.m. on Monday 14th, Raeburn was closeted with Marshall, trying to persuade him to accept a compromise form of (16), i.e. of the Roberts-Wray draft produced on the 9th May. We had a meeting (Marshall, Lee Kuan Yew + advisers) about 11 a.m., but it was interrupted by telephone calls from Singapore + by a call paid on Marshall by Malcolm

MacDonald.[49] Malcolm was directed to take back to Lennox-Boyd another of Marshall's last words – the powers of paragraph (16) for 2 years and no more.

At 12 noon we had a meeting of the delegation, when Lee Kuan Yew tried to put over his scheme and failed. Then Marshall tried to put over the Raeburn modification of the Roberts-Wray draft with a time limit of 2 years, and was clearly failing. At that point he was called out for a telephone call from Singapore. He came back with the suggestion, thrown out by his party executive, that the Roberts-Wray draft would be acceptable if the Chairman of the D[efence] + S[ecurity] Council was appointed by the Government of the Federation. Lee Kuan Yew was enthusiastic, but the Lib. Socs. did not like it and voted against, though they said they would not oppose in the meeting with the S. of S. They were willing to accept a Singaporean appointed by the S. of S., or anybody appointed by collaboration between the Govts. of U.K. + Singapore. They did not say so until afterwards, and then only privately, but they did not want a Malay.

It was eventually agreed, by a majority, to accept the Raeburn draft with a chairman appointed by the Federation, being a Malayan, + we were authorised to sell the idea to the S. of S. Raeburn undertook that job. He saw Martin and Roberts-Wray, who were sympathetic but (of course) non-committal. He got to the S. of S. at 10.30 p.m., after the House of Commons rose. Lennox-Boyd (who had been engaged up to 8 p.m. in the debate on Cyprus) had been drinking + was very abusive of Marshall, calling him a prima donna + so forth, + swearing heavily. He did not, however, totally reject the Raeburn draft with the Labour Front addendum, though Raeburn thought the chances of acceptance were not considerable.

The conference again met at 9.30 a.m. on the 15th May. The S. of S. was quite conciliatory and Marshall read a memorandum which had presumably been argued by the delegation and which put the case quite moderately. The S. of S. asked some questions and then asked for an adjournment until 4 p.m. Meanwhile Marshall had an appointment with the P.M.[50] I had to leave, however, in order to go to Cornwall for a meeting of the Royal Commission on Common Land, + so the rest of my information comes from the newspapers. It appears that the S. of S. rejected the proposal to have a Malayan chairman, which would put the U.K. in a minority on the D. + S. Council. Marshall offered to accept the Raeburn draft, with a U.K.

[49] Malcolm MacDonald, British politician and diplomat; Governor-General of British Territories in South-East Asia, 1946–1948; Commissioner-General in South-East Asia, 1948–1955.

[50] Sir Anthony Eden (later Earl of Avon), British Conservative Prime Minister, 1955–1957.

chairman, for a period of three years, but the S. of S. said that he had a pathological objection to fixed periods. The conference then broke up + Marshall gave an ill-tempered statement off the cuff to the press. He saw the Labour leaders on the 16th May + developed the idea of a Proclamation which had to be laid before and apparently approved by the H. of C. This was not a new idea, for it was in one of my early drafts. He put it to Lennox-Boyd on the 17th, but only two other delegates went with him and Lee Kuan Yew gave a press conference in which he talked about the political importance of Marshall's proposal. The S. of S. was therefore able to say that he was prepared to negotiate with the Singapore delegation or with the Govt. of Singapore but not with a minority.

Marshall has discovered that the Governor could not accept his resignation in London, + accordingly he will go back on Monday (20th May) in order to resign there. He says he intends to go out of politics. It is not clear, however, that the Labour Front as a whole will resign, + it seems probable that Black (Governor) will try to form a Lib. Soc. and Labour Front coalition, in which case no immediate dissolution will be needed.

2. 'Singapore Constitutional Conference post-mortem', *c.*1956

Though H.M.G. and the Singapore delegation got so near agreement that a post-mortem is required to explain why the conference failed, their approaches were quite different:

(1.) True to the traditions of the Conservative party, the SOS[51] could not agree that colonialism was an evil to be eradicated as soon as possible. His approach was that self-government was the logical development from colonial trusteeship. Hence, while the delegation was willing to take risks for the sake of merdeka, the SOS thought it would be better for the people of Singapore, and not merely advantageous to British interests, if H.M.G. retained control. The delegation wanted independence subject to such limitations as it was necessary to concede; the SOS was prepared to grant such concessions as it was necessary to concede, provided that ultimate control was retained. In formal sessions, at least, the delegation failed to give sufficient emphasis to their almost pathological dislike of colonialism, while the SOS never succeeded in convincing the delegation that British rule was needed for

[51] Secretary of State.

anything more than the protection of British interests, including those of Australia and New Zealand.[52]

(2.) In respect of communism, too, the approach was different. The SOS thought of it as an unmixed evil from which Singapore must be protected at all costs. Most of the delegation thought of it merely as a worse evil than colonialism. The SOS seems not to have appreciated that communism means government by Malayan Chinese, in association with the mother-country, in the interest of the Malayan Chinese proletariat. It would be strongly objectionable to the Lib. Socs. because it would interfere with "business" and profits. It would be objectionable to most of the others because it would be undemocratic and would compel transfer from one "power bloc" to another, possibly more but possible [*sic*] less objectionable. But all were conscious that Chinese communism had a very powerful appeal among the electorate, and that their hope of political survival depended on their persuading the electorate that democratic merdeka offered more than Chinese communism. The more they had to concede to H.M.G., the smaller were their chances.

(3.) The SOS kept insisting that external defence meant, or at least included, the external defence of Singapore and not merely the defence of British interests, whereas the[y] thought of it merely as a concession to British requirements. In this they were not wholly logical, for they did want protection against a communist coup d'état, at least until local forces had been provided, and aggression by communist China would have the same effect; but for reasons given in the next paragraph the Singapore politicians agree with Nehru that aggression from China during the foreseeable future is unlikely.

2. The view that direct communist aggression is unlikely is widespread in Asia. It is believed that at the Calcutta conference of 1948[53] the decision was taken to start resistance movements against all "imperialist" powers in Asia, in the belief that the nationalist forces would join in and that assistance could be given by means of "volunteers" from the communist countries. Partly owing to the action of what the SOS calls the "free world" and Asia calls the Anglo-American bloc, the policy was not a success. What is more, the communists have lost ground in all the countries in which

[52] Singapore had long been a pivotal base for the defence strategies of Australia and New Zealand.

[53] A youth conference in Calcutta attended by delegations from many Asian countries. The British believed that the conference, with Soviet backing, encouraged local communist parties to start armed insurrection again colonial rule.

democratic Asian Governments were established. The present party line, it is argued, is to form a common front with the left wings of nationalist movements, in the hope that (as in Czechoslovakia) the communists can get into positions from which they can seize power by coup d'état. Hence what the communists fear most in Singapore is a democratic merdeka from which they are excluded. What Singapore fears is not attack from communist China or anybody else, but communist subversion which they control or a conflict between the two "power blocs" in which an atom bomb gets dropped on Singapore because it is an Anglo-American base. The insistence of the SOS on the common interest of Britain and Singapore, and especially his repeated jibe that Singapore was asking to be defended but refusing the necessary powers, was irritating because it was regarded as a wilful perversion of Singapore's case. Singapore was not asking H.M.G. to undertake external defence: it was agreeing to the use of Singapore bases because it did not expect that H.M.G. would be willing to give them up and the complete extrusion of H.M.G. would have been unrealistic.

3. Even so, the conference ought not to have broken down, because the whole delegation had accepted the political necessity of the bases and because the whole delegation except Lim Chin Siong did not want to give H.M.G. a temporary power of intervention to prevent unlawful action. The problem was, therefore, to find a boundary between the powers of the Government of Singapore and those of H.M.G., a problem which ought not to have been beyond the capacity of the respective legal advisers. Possible causes of failure were:

(1.) Initially, the case for Singapore was formulated on the basis of a slightly qualified Dominion status. As the Chief Minister saw it (after discussion with Nehru), Singapore would be accorded independent status and would then cede powers to H.M.G. [As] mentioned below, the legal advisers did not think this a practicable policy, and therefore they built up a case for a Singapore Independence Act with a six-year transitional clause. This case was promptly destroyed by the sudden acceptance by the delegation of a permanent cession of external defence and external relations. The delegation then had to accept a definitely inferior status which was getting very near colonial status. The SOS did not seem to appreciate that status was fundamental, because the fundamental objective of the delegation was to separate nationalists and anti-colonialists from communists, to offer liberty and equality as an alternative to communism. Every concession by Singapore therefore strengthened the communists and it was evident that Lim Chin Siong wanted either complete breakdown, in which case they could point to the failure of constitutional methods to achieve merdeka against the imperialists, or an agreement which was admitted to confer nothing more than a dressed-up colonialism. The enormous concessions made on status made it very difficult for the delegation to admit concessions on powers.

(2.) The SOS failed to recognise the value of the offer of "defence areas" or "cantonments". The original draft of the Heads of Agreement was more specific, but in the final draft the paragraph was left vague in case Singapore was offering to concede more than H.M.G. needed. Within limits this power could have been expanded; and it is probable that under it H.M.G. could have obtained most of the powers that it sought to obtain by Orders in Council. The delegation obviously could not place on record the advantages of the "cantonment" offer, but might not the legal advisers have done so? In point of fact a list of powers, based on a memorandum of what Lee Kuan Yew was willing to concede, was prepared, but it was then too late to use it. The difficulty was that H.M.G. never said what powers it wanted in respect of the bases, but simply claimed a blanket power by Order in Council which went (as the SOS really admitted) far beyond its needs.

(3.) The crux of the problem was internal security. The idea of a specific definition of "defence", perhaps on Indian lines, was discarded at the outset. A list of defence powers looks formidable because it has to be elastic enough to cover everything from communist permeation to total war; but possibly something on these lines might have been attempted by H.M.G., and this would have accorded with Lee Kuan Yew's memorandum. To the Singapore legal advisers the Defence Council seemed a more fruitful idea. There is no doubt that the delegation would have accepted a UK majority, at least by casting vote, if H.M.G. had not introduced a legislative power so wide as to allow interference with any aspect of internal self-government. The argument that H.M.G. could be trusted not to abuse the power was useless, for it was no answer to what would clearly be the communist assertion that this power demonstrated the survival of colonialism. The SOS did issue an invitation to the delegation to cut down the power to reasonable proportions, and something on those lines would have been attempted if the Labour Front in Singapore had not cabled the suggestion of a Malayan chairman appointed by the Federation. This so appealed to the nationalist sentiments of the majority of the delegation that it was impossible to go back to the original idea of a Defence Council with a UK chairman with limited powers.

(4.) It is not clear that the SOS appreciated the reason for insistence on a power of total suspension, while refusing a power of partial interference. The original suggestion would have allowed interference by H.M.G., through the Defence Council, to such extent as was necessary to maintain internal security. This was objected to by the P.A.P. but could probably have been carried by a majority if suitably drafted. What the delegation as a whole wanted was a clear-cut division between government by Singapore and government by the UK. The delegation did not want a diarchy under which the Ministers could be accused of being Imperialist stooges. They wanted complete responsibility within a specific boundary, with complete responsibility for the UK beyond that boundary. It was of course realised that the Ministers could always turn diarchy into suspension by resigning, but this would have transferred responsibility for a breakdown from the UK to Singapore. Efforts were made to develop the idea of a state of emergency or, though the word was inelegant, abnormality, but they were frustrated by the demand for almost unlimited legislative powers.

(5.) Though the idea of parliamentary approval of Orders in Council came from the Labour party at the last moment, it was not new. It was originally suggested that a declaration of emergency should last for a limited period unless renewed by resolution of the House of Commons. The idea disappeared with the substitution of a power of suspension for a power to issue proclamations of emergency, and it reappeared too late to be of use, for the delegation would have lost face if they had accepted, after the breach, the same proposal with a slight procedural amendment.

4. The first drafts of the Memorandum and the Heads of Agreement were produced in Singapore and were designed to provide a scheme which H.M.G. could accept. They were subsequently modified for reasons which were not explained to the legal advisers, but they were probably due to:

(1.) The intention to publish the Memorandum as soon as it was circulated; it then had to be dressed up for local publication instead of being so drafted as to enable the SOS to convince his colleagues.

(2.) Refusal to face the fact from the outset that, if the delegation did not produce a scheme for internal security which H.M.G. could accept, the SOS would probably produce a scheme which the delegation could not accept.

(3.) A reluctance to concede too much at the outset in case H.M.G. was willing to accept less.

In the result, the Memorandum was less persuasive in London than it could have been, and yet not a perfect instrument for local propaganda: it was half-and-half. Further, H.M.G. was faced with Heads of Agreement which, taken as a whole, it could not accept. Accordingly, they should not have been circulated, but kept in reserve for suitable modification after H.M.G. had made its position plain. Indeed, it is now plain that the original draft, with its double concept of cantonment powers in normal times and proclamations of emergency in abnormal conditions would have formed a better basis for working out an agreed scheme than the circulated document, and would probably have prevented the circulation of the Roberts-Wray draft which, in effect, caused the breakdown.

5. This does not answer the question whether the idea of producing an acceptable scheme at the outset was a good one. The tendency of the delegation, especially those who were accustomed to the settlement of litigation out of court, was to put forward large demands, on which they were willing to compromise, in the hope of "horse trading". This is of course a desirable practice if both sides are going to do it. Given the sense of subordination which "colonialism" creates, and which some Governors are never able to overcome even in the stage of representative government, it may be inevitable. Also, the delegation containing four parties and having no officials of the standing of the C.O. officials (a result of the failure to start Malayanisation at a much earlier stage), it was impossible to ask H.M.G. to state the limits of its concession and to remit the matter to officials and legal advisers to work out an acceptable scheme. It would seem that in the circumstances the right procedure was to submit a scheme which, after consideration of details, might be acceptable; and this, of course implied laying all the cards on the table whenever the delegation, its individual members, or its advisers, saw members of the UK delegation whether in public or in private. On the other hand, the SOS did give way on points which he had at first said to be essential, and the UK officials were compelled to be rather cagey about ideas which were put before them with a view to ascertaining whether they were likely to be acceptable. In the result, there never was an examination of all the devices which might have been used to enable the two sides to reach agreement, and the conference broke down although both sides, probably, considered that some compromise might prove acceptable. If we could have dropped the idea of overriding legislation and gone back to the original scheme of proclamations of emergency – and there might have been other methods of meeting both points of view – agreement could probably have been reached.

6. Lee Kuan Yew may be right in his public pronouncement that he will be back after a few months and that he will be willing then

to concede less than he would have conceded now. Much depends, however, on the events of the next few weeks. If Singapore gets through the next few weeks without an outbreak or a dissolution (which Kuan Yew is now almost certain to win, with communist support) it may be worth while for H.M.G. to make a generous offer perhaps on the lines of our original proposals. The Labour Front will have been destroyed and the leftist Opposition strengthened, but if the citizenship proposals are accepted before a general election there is a reasonable chance of a reasonable Government being elected by the older electors, especially if the Lib. Socs., can find some supporters among the non-English-speaking people.

SECTION K: SOUTH AFRICA

In May 1960 the South African Government informed the Commonwealth Prime Ministers meeting in London that there would be a referendum in October on whether South Africa should remain a monarchy in the Commonwealth. The South African Prime Minister, H.F. Verwoerd, and his Nationalist Party wanted republican status, and the referendum resulted in a majority in favour of a republic. It is not clear who sought Jennings' opinion on the consequences of South Africa becoming a republic, but it may have been the South African businessman Harry Oppenheimer, who had corresponded with Jennings on constitutional issues. The change to republican status and the objective to remain within the Commonwealth required endorsement from the other members. South Africa's request was not supported and its membership lapsed when it formally became a republic in May 1961.

1. 'The Union of South Africa as a Republic', *c.*1960

Presumably the legal advisers of the Union Government have satisfied themselves that the Union Parliament has power, under the South Africa Act[1] and the Statute of Westminster to convert the Union into a republic. This would accord with the view taken by the legal advisers to the Hertzog Government in 1929.[2] Some English lawyers have expressed doubts about it because, unlike the Irish Free State, the Union was before 1931 a colony to which certain parts (or perhaps one should say uncertain parts) of English constitutional law applied, and the Statute of Westminster must be interpreted in the light of those parts of the common law. However, this is an abstruse subject which need only be mentioned by way of precaution and put aside. For present purposes it will be assumed that no question of validity arises.

[1]The South Africa Act 1909 of the British parliament created the Union of South Africa.

[2]J.B.M. Hertzog, Boer general; Prime Minister of South Africa, 1924–1939. As Prime Minister he had always argued that South Africa had political independence and that the 1926 Balfour Declaration confirmed this. The 1929 general election increased his majority against the South Africa Party under the more empire-minded Jan Smuts.

If the Union does become a republic, some legislation will be required in the United Kingdom, and possibly in other countries of the Commonwealth. This is because the present law of the United Kingdom assumes that South Africa is part of Her Majesty's dominions, so that general provisions distinguishing Her Majesty's dominions from foreign countries, would have to be adapted. If the Union remained within the Commonwealth as a republic, it would be comparatively simple in form. It would presumably take the same form as the India (Consequential Provision) Act, 1949, or the Ghana (Consequential Provision) Bill which is at present going through the United Kingdom Parliament without opposition.[3] The Queen would be empowered to adapt the laws of the United Kingdom and of other territories under the control of the United Kingdom Government by Order in Council. The important point politically is, however, that legislation would be needed.

If, on the other hand, the Union ceased to be part of the Commonwealth the nature of the legislation would be very controversial. When Burma became a republic outside the Commonwealth in 1947[4] a clean cut was made. Burma became for all legal purposes a foreign country and Burman citizens, unless they were domiciled in the United Kingdom and opted for British nationality, became aliens. This was, however, before the British Nationality Act 1948, and comparable legislation in most other Commonwealth countries, created the status of Commonwealth citizen. The only case since 1948 is that of the Republic of Ireland: and that is a special case not only because of the proximity of the Republic to the United Kingdom, but also because of the confusion of status which had arisen between 1922 and 1948.[5] Irish citizens as such did not become Commonwealth citizens under the Act of 1948, but most of them became such citizens because they were British subjects before 1948. The arguments which applied to Ireland in 1949 would not apply to South Africa, but the compromises adopted in the Ireland Act, 1949, might form precedents. Most of the other countries of the Commonwealth would have to face similar problems, for only in Pakistan and Ceylon are South Africans aliens under the local nationality laws. In the Federation of Malaya a constitutional amendment would be needed to transfer the Union from the definition

[3] It received the royal assent in 1960.

[4] Burma actually became independent of the United Kingdom on 4 January 1948.

[5] Between the 1922 Anglo-Irish Treaty and the Republic of Ireland Act 1948 (which took effect on 18 April 1949), Ireland functioned as a quasi-Dominion within the Commonwealth. Republican status, unlike the case of India in 1950, ended membership of the Commonwealth.

of "Commonwealth country" to that of "foreign country", though in the present temper of the Malayans it would not be difficult to secure the necessary majorities.

This is the legal background to the now accepted rule that a Commonwealth country which becomes a republic can remain within the Commonwealth only if the other Commonwealth countries consent. Until 1950, all countries of the Commonwealth were dominions of the Crown.[6] Until 1949, indeed, the Crown was regarded as the indispensable link. The Balfour Declaration of 1926, for instance, spoke not only of "autonomous communities" but also of "common allegiance to the Crown"; and these phrases were repeated in the preamble to the Statute of Westminster. Both Burma and Ireland went out of the Commonwealth when they became republics. So strong was the feeling that the Crown was the essential link that in 1949, when the Government of India gave notice that, though the Constituent Assembly had decided upon a republican form of government India wished to remain within the Commonwealth, a substantial section of opinion thought that the two things were incompatible. The enactment of the British Nationality Act in 1948 had, however, brought a change which now appeared significant. Until 1948 British nationality was based on allegiance to the Crown. Under the Canadian Citizenship Act of 1946, however, some persons would become Canadian citizens who were not born within His Majesty's allegiance and therefore would not be British subjects. At a conference attended by representatives of India, Pakistan and Ceylon as well as those of the older Commonwealth countries, it was agreed that the "common status" which had been agreed upon by the Imperial Conference of 1930 should be based not on allegiance but on local nationality law. In other words, a Canadian citizen would be ipso facto a Commonwealth citizen. Since Canada was one of the dominions of the Crown, Canadian citizens would be in allegiance with the Crown; but the Act of 1948 said nothing about allegiance and therefore a person could be a Commonwealth citizen without being in allegiance. In other words, a citizen of an Indian republic could be a Commonwealth citizen.

It was therefore easy to get agreement from the United Kingdom, Canada, Australia, New Zealand and South Africa that there was no objection in principle to India's remaining within the Commonwealth as a republic. The doubts came from Pakistan and Ceylon. This may seem odd; but both countries had Prime Ministers of sturdy common sense, who realised that the monarchical form, as it had been worked out in Canada, Australia and South Africa, had very great advantages,

[6] India became a republic on 26 January 1950.

but that if India became a republic there would probably be political pressure, of a purely emotional kind, for Pakistan and Ceylon to follow suit. However, when they found that the other Commonwealth countries were prepared to agree, they acquiesced in the view of the majority.

It was less easy to devise a formula than it was to decide the principle. This was because Australia insisted on a formula which reasserted the monarchical principle in relation to the other Commonwealth countries, while allowing a republic in the case of India. The problem was to draft in such a way that India did not appear as a sort of second-class member of the Commonwealth. Sir Stafford Cripps[7] took the problem home for the week-end and produced a perfect solution. It was used for Pakistan in 1955, but it was not repeated in 1956 when the Ceylon Government announced that the two Houses of the newly elected Parliament had set up a Joint Select Committee to draft a republican Constitution. The Prime Ministers simply took note of the announcement and agreed that Ceylon could remain in the Commonwealth as a republic. The same procedure was used in 1960 in relation to Ghana.

Meanwhile, however, the Indian formula had included one phrase which is relevant to South Africa. It was stated to be the intention of the "people of India" that India should become a sovereign independent republic – a phrase taken from the preamble to what was then the Draft Constitution.[8] It was justified by the fact that a fully representative Constituent Assembly had been set up. Similarly in Pakistan there was a Constituent Assembly. In Ceylon there had been a general election, with the republican proposal as one of the proposals of the successful majority, followed by resolutions in both Houses. In Ghana there was both a referendum and a general election. In respect of South Africa it might be argued that the white electorate, or strictly speaking a majority of it, cannot decide the matter for Her Majesty's subjects in South Africa seventy per cent of whom have not the vote. On the other hand, it may also be argued that a decision by the other Commonwealth countries which would have the effect of depriving four-fifths or more of Her Majesty's subjects in South Africa of their British nationality or Commonwealth citizenship would be unfortunate.

[7] Sir Stafford Cripps, British Labour minister; Chancellor of the Exchequer, 1947–1950. He also led the 'Cripps Mission' to India in 1942 to secure Indian co-operation in the war with the promise of self-government.

[8] 'We, the people of India, having solemnly resolved to constitute India into a sovereign ["socialist secular" added in 1976] democratic republic . . . '.

The latter argument would, in fact, be convincing against any proposal to eject South Africa on the ground of its Government's racial policy, so long as it retained the monarchy. It is possible to imagine such a proposal being made by one of the Asian or West African Prime Ministers, for it would give him much kudos in his own country and elsewhere. This would especially be so if, as some who have recently been in South Africa recently fear may be the case, race relations deteriorate between now and the next meeting of Prime Ministers. The fact that ejection has never yet been proposed is not convincing, for the Commonwealth is as good at creating precedents as at following them. No part of Her Majesty's dominions can, however, be disposed of without legislation, and in any case much controversial legislation would have to be passed, not only in respect of citizenship, but also in respect of other matters in which an independent country of the Commonwealth is differentiated from a foreign country. It is, however, impossible to believe that any Government or Parliament in the United Kingdom would consent to a proposal which deprived fourteen million South Africans of their Commonwealth citizenship, without their consent. In this attitude the United Kingdom would be supported by most if not all, of the other Commonwealth countries. It is, of course, as well known in the rest of the Commonwealth as it is in South Africa that the present policy, euphemistically called separate development, is merely the policy of a minority of the white minority. What is more, in the recent troubles some of the Commonwealth Governments have discovered unexpected merits in the concept of Commonwealth citizenship. The United Kingdom Government has given active assistance only to citizens of the United Kingdom and Colonies and British protected persons, who got swept into the gaol after Sharpeville.[9] It seems, however, that the High Commission territories and the East African territories have been open to refugees, and of course the ports of the United Kingdom have been open to all South African citizens, without distinction of race or colour, who could reach them. More significant, perhaps, is that two other Commonwealth Governments are alleged to have given assistance to political refugees from the Union who had no passports. Indeed, the fertile mind of the Attorney-General of Ghana[10] has been directed to the problem of inventing papers for Commonwealth citizens who would normally travel on South African passports.

[9]In March 1960, the South African Police killed an estimated sixty-seven people among a large crowd in the township of Sharpeville who were protesting against restrictions on the movement of African people.

[10]Geoffrey Bing QC, British Labour MP; Attorney-General of independent Ghana, 1957–1961.

Though it would be almost, if not quite, impossible to eject the Union from the Commonwealth if it remained a monarchy it would be politically difficult for most of the Prime Ministers to assent to a resolution authorising it to remain within the Commonwealth as a republic. Hitherto resolutions of that kind have been carried unanimously. It does not necessarily follow that this practice would be followed, and some of the Prime Ministers, at least, would find great force in the argument [that] a mere minority decision should [not] deprive all South Africans of their Commonwealth citizenship. Nevertheless, it ought to be appreciated that every Prime Minister would find himself embarrassed by the necessity of a decision which appeared to give some support to a racialist policy. This is not, as the Nationalist leaders seem to think, because the Union Government has a bad press. No doubt political emotions are strengthened, as all political emotions are, by picturesque reporting: but not all the reporting has been picturesque, and some ten million people in the United Kingdom alone have seen Sharpeville on television. In fact, the more the Nationalist leaders defend themselves the more they arouse antagonism, for their premises are regarded as fundamentally immoral. The clearer this becomes, the more public opinion outside becomes convinced that such events as those in Sharpeville and Langa[11] are the consequences of Government policies. Mr Louw's[12] arguments that shooting has occurred in territories under United Kingdom rule falls completely flat because, though the dead of Uganda are just as dead as those of Sharpeville, they are not the consequences of a policy which opinion regards as immoral.

A decision by a majority of white South Africans to establish a republic, followed by a request from the Union Government that the republic remain within the Commonwealth, would therefore put every other Commonwealth Government on the horns of a dilemma. If the Prime Ministers agreed, each of them would have to justify himself in his own Parliament, except in Pakistan, where there is no Parliament. Even in the United Kingdom, where emotions are less strong than in India, Pakistan, Ceylon, Ghana, Malaya and Nigeria, it is reasonably certain that a South Africa (Consequential Provision) Bill would be opposed, whereas the corresponding Bills for India, Pakistan and Ghana went through without opposition. The Conservative Government's African policy was criticised by its opponents at the general election of 1959. Its support of the Union at the United Nations, though it can be defended on legalistic grounds,

[11] Three protestors were killed and several injured in protests in the Langa Township echoing those in Sharpeville (see p. 201, n. 9) at the same time in March 1960.

[12] Eric Louw, South African diplomat and minister; Minister of Foreign Affairs, 1955–1964.

has been severely criticised on other grounds. The weakness of the present Opposition makes such criticism less effective than usual; but it is still true that a small shift of opinion could turn out the Government. From the point of view of the Conservative party, indeed, there is an even greater danger, that if the United Kingdom supported South Africa's continued membership, some of the other Commonwealth countries might wish to secede. The imperialist emotions which developed late in the nineteenth century have been transmuted by the Anglo-Boer war[13] and the development of nationalism in the other parts of the Commonwealth into full acceptance of the concept of the Commonwealth as a concert of independent nations. It is considered by Conservatives as well as by others that the process whereby six dependent peoples of the British Empire have been converted within the space of thirteen years, into independent nations of the Commonwealth will be regarded by history as a tribute to British statesmanship. The mysticism which formerly surrounded the Empire now surrounds the Commonwealth. Suppose the six Commonwealth nations of Asia and West Africa insist that the choice lies between them and the Union of South Africa? I do not know the answer, but it is relevant that there are other African peoples on their way to independence and that it is almost certainly in their interest that they should remain in the Commonwealth, at least for a time: for they will still need the assistance which the United Kingdom Government and other British institutions (such as the universities) can properly give to independent countries within the Commonwealth which still need such assistance for social and economic development. Would it be worth while to break up the Commonwealth merely because a minority Government in South Africa insisted upon a racial policy which hardly anybody outside the Union is prepared to defend?

There is, however, the other horn of the dilemma. If the Prime Ministers refused to allow the Union to remain within the Commonwealth as a republic, the logical step would be to pass legislation in all other countries of the Commonwealth declaring the Union to be a foreign country and depriving all South Africans of their Commonwealth citizenship. It might be possible to compromise, perhaps on the lines adopted when Eire became a republic. Those who were Commonwealth citizens when the republic was created might be regarded as Commonwealth citizens for all time, so that if they migrated to Commonwealth territory they might acquire the local citizenship on the very easy terms allowed in most of the Commonwealth to Commonwealth citizens. Incidentally, this is probably the point to emphasise that the distinction drawn by

[13] 1899–1902.

Nationalists between English-speaking South Africans and Afrikaans-speaking South Africans is quite incorrect. Both have no other home but South Africa, and both have the same right to move to other parts of the Commonwealth if they so desire. Neither, probably wants to do so: but the distinction has no warrant in fact.

The desire for a republic derives from one of two sources. The first is to have a system of government in which the Head of State takes an active part in political life. The Queen's representative, like the Queen herself, is an impartial arbiter, a supporter of good causes, and an adviser behind the scenes. It would be difficult for him, and perhaps embarrassing to the Queen, if he were given substantive powers other than those very useful reserve powers which the Queen possesses by common law but which nobody ever hears about so long as the parliamentary system functions efficiently. To bring a British type of Constitution somewhere nearer the American it is necessary to have a republic. That, I take it, is the main purpose in Ghana. It is not quite unprecedented in the Commonwealth, for under the Maldivian Constitution of 1951 the President of the Republic[14] had power to appoint, and did appoint, himself to be Prime Minister also.

That, I take it, is not the purpose in South Africa. The other purpose is nationalistic or sentimental. In Ireland there was a tradition of conflict between Irish politicians and Dublin Castle,[15] and they never found it possible to develop loyalty to Buckingham Palace. In India, by what most of us would now consider to be a misinterpretation of Indian psychology, successive Viceroys thought it necessary to imitate what they thought to be "oriental" splendour. There was, too, a history of conflict which had by no means disappeared in 1949. After the death of Muhammad Ali Jinnah (who night indeed have been an active Head of the State), Liaquat Ali Khan thought that Pakistan needed a Dominion-type Constitution and very sensibly advised the appointment of Sir Khwaja Nazimuddin as Governor-General. When Liaquat was assassinated, however, Nazimuddin stepped down to become Prime Minister and advised the appointment of Ghulam Muhammad, who in due course claimed that he was bound not by the British precedents but by the express provisions of the Government of India Act and dismissed Nazimuddin.[16] These events and the example of India made it necessary that Pakistan should have a republican form of government.

In South Africa, I take it, the demand for a republic is a consequence of the Anglo-Boer War: and the argument being pressed is that, since

[14] Muhammad Amin Didi.
[15] Seat of British rule in Ireland.
[16] For more detail, see documents H1 and H2.

some at least of the Afrikaans-speaking South Africans can have no sense of loyalty to the Queen it is necessary to break the link. On this I can, of course, express no opinion. Some observations on the practical difficulties to be overcome may, however, be permitted from one who has produced as many republican drafts as monarchical drafts.

The first difficulty is to make certain that a suitable Head of the State will be produced by the constitutional machinery provided. Any form of election, for instance, is almost certain to produce, at some stage, a political conflict for office. Nor does it necessarily follow that the personality and the politics of the successful candidate will not necessarily be attuned to those of the Government for the time being in power. Even a President who is a "constitutional monarch" has powers which may give rise to conflict. What is more, he will have to be given a fixed term subject to impeachment. Where conflict arises between Government and Governor-General, the latter can usually be induced quietly to resign: republicans have to put up with their President until his term of office expires.

The second difficulty arises over the President's powers. The royal prerogative includes emergency powers which are hardly ever needed because emergency legislation can generally be enacted. They could be used, and have been used, where legislation was impracticable. They would not be, and indeed could not be, used by a hereditary monarch or his personal representative. If they are made express in a Constitution, however, attention is drawn to them and they are given unique emphasis. There is consequently a danger that they will be misused, especially if a conflict develops between the President and the Prime Minister.

The third difficulty is to create a focus of loyalty in substitution for the Crown. The Americans have exalted their Constitution; the French have converted France into Marianne.[17] These things can be done over time, and no doubt the intention of the Nationalist politicians is to create a focus of loyalty which will, because of the memories of the Anglo-Boer War, be more effective than the Crown. On the other hand, experience elsewhere shows the transition can be difficult. It is easy for a politician, a general or a colonel to assume that he has been chosen by destiny to "protect the country" against anarchy, or corruption, or even misgovernment, by vesting all governmental powers in himself. Indeed, the more numerous the emergency powers vested in the armed forces, the police, or the politicians in power by legislation, the greater the risk that they will seize more. In the system of government which the countries of the Commonwealth have inherited, ministers, military officers and policeman are servants of the

[17] The idealized female symbol of republican France.

Crown; and, though the protection so provided is not very great they are in fact somewhat inhibited by their duty to the Crown. It is possible to devise suitable formulae in a republican Constitution: and indeed in one republic now under military rule[18] I actually suggested one. Even so, a draftsman's formula has not the force of an inherited tradition. It is so easy for those in power to suspend the Constitution and defend themselves by explaining that they do it only temporarily and from the highest patriotic motives. It is less easy where the highest formal authority is a monarch who has no political ambition, is incorruptible, and to whom loyalty and service are due.

[18]That is, Pakistan.

SECTION L: SUDAN

Sudan had been administered by Britain and Egypt as a joint-authority condominium since the 1899 Anglo-Egypt Treaty, until the British as the effective rulers left in December 1955 and an independent republic was proclaimed on 1 January 1956. The civilian administration would be overthrown by military coup in November 1958, just a few months after Jennings visited.

1. Diary: 'Sudan Visit, 1958'

18th July 1958, Khartoum. We arrived from Malta via Benghazi in the early hours of the 12th July, + were met by the Deputy Att[orney]. Gen[eral]. The Minister of Justice + the Acting Att. Gen. saw me the same day, + I was supplied with copies of the Constitutional Committee's Draft (C Draft) and the Government Draft (G Draft).[1] The latter is based on the former, but omits some of the fundamental liberties and waters down the rest virtually to nothing. I made a series of notes on the technical and drafting defects of these Drafts, that avoided going into political issues. It was finished on the 14th July but the typing was not completed until the 16th July. A copy went to M/J,[2] but I asked for others to be returned to me for correction, which I have done today (Muslim New Year's Day).

The Secretaries had asked for a meeting with me today to discuss their project for a federal Constitution. It was postponed until tomorrow; but six members, who had not been informed, did turn up, and we had some informal discussion about federalism. They were all Negroes, from 6 ft to 6 ft 6 ins. tall. Their case is that they are quite a different people, mostly pagan but some Christian. They know no Arabic except pidgin Arabic. They do not want Islam as the State religion. On being pressed, they admitted that they could not operate a Federal State forthwith, but wanted it inscribed in the Constn. and introduced gradually. They did not want one State, but two, North and South Sudan. One man wanted federalism in ten years, but on being

[1] Not included.
[2] Minister of Justice.

pressed said "approximately", i.e. 10 or 15. I suggested 25 as more reasonable because, especially, of shortage of personnel. Possibly one might put federal provisions in, and have them brought in, at any time after 1964, by resolution of ¾ of all Southern members in the legislature. We are to have a meeting tomorrow, but at present I see no possibility whatever of getting the job completed by the end of July.

19th July. About 40 Southerners turned up this morning. They were to have come at 10 a.m. but they began coming at 9.10 a.m. + began cross-examining me forthwith. I did my best to explain that it was not my business to decide political issues, or even to advise on political issues, except the technical aspects. They seemed to have been given the impression that I was a sort of one-man Commission, and at about 11.15 a.m. the question was put to me: would I help them to produce a federal Constn.? I replied that I could not do that. I was employed to advise the Sudan Government, and those questions would be settled politically. I was willing to answer their questions, but my function was to help the Constitutional Committee. Therefore one of them stood up, made a short and quite gracious speech and said that they would not take up more of my time. Several of them, as they went out, expressed the hope that I should enjoy advising the Northerners! Two remained behind to ask what I meant by the remark that between a unitary Constn. and a Federal Constn. there were many gradations. I mentioned Scotland, Northern Ireland and the S. African provinces.[3]

20th July. Last night the Speaker of the H. of R.[4] gave a dinner party. I sat between him and the M/J. I suggested to the latter that I should draft a Federal Constn. for the Southerners, so as to show what it was exactly they wanted. M/J. seemed to agree, though I think he wanted to meet the Southerners, with me, first. In any case, however, I propose to do some experimental drafting.

24th July. What I did was to sketch out some possible compromises in a short document which has now been typed. I have also received, and read, a series of amendments to C Draft by M/J. They improve the Draft a little, but they were prepared before my memo. was seen. In fact, everybody has been too busy to bother about me, and for the past 12 days I have done an average of one hour a day at most. Parliament is still sitting, + it is not yet clear that it will adjourn today, as it was supposed to. There are also suggestions of a change

[3]Examples of regions within unitary systems that hold asymmetric powers compared to other regions within the state.

[4]House of Representatives.

of government. If this goes on much longer I shall have to suggest a change of environment, for I am getting very bored.

6th August 1958. Parlt. did adjourn on the 24th July + M/J saw me on the 25th. Both the Govt.+ the Parlt. had been too busy, because of the Middle East crisis (American troops in the Lebanon + Br. Troops in Jordan[5]) to do anything about the Draft Constn. I gathered – though he did not exactly say so – that there was no longer any question of a meeting of the Constn. Committee, because the members had either left or were leaving to do their cultivation now that the rains had come. M/J therefore asked me (a) to redraft the Draft Constn., and (b) to prepare a memo. on procedure.

The M/J. gave a dinner party for us on the 30th July. By that time I had completed the redraft and had started on the Explanatory Memorandum. Since I should finish on the 31st July + typing will take several days, I suggested that we spend the week-end in Juba. He agreed, + the Min.y/J made the necessary arrangements.

Before we left, however, we had tea with the Italian and French Ministers, who had invited three Catholic Southerners (making a point) to meet us. We had a long discussion about federation, + I think I saved some doubt whether it was really federation or administrative devolution that they required. They really want control of (a) education, (b) police, and (c) agricultural development, mainly because they want Southerners to replace Northerners. This, as I pointed out, is what Scotland has. At any rate, they went so far as to say that they ought to formulate their requirements in detail, not to limit themselves to general advocacy of federation.

They object, however, to certain matters, namely (a) Arabic as national language, (b) Islam as national religion, (c) the fact that most provisions of the Draft cannot be amended in any way whatsoever, and (d) membership of the Arab League. I pointed out that (d) would not be removed by federation, because foreign affairs must be a federal subject.

The Draft is certainly very bad, full of gaps, inconsistencies and ambiguities. I have tried to make it watertight + at the same time more elastic. It has apparently been produced by very amateurish amateurs, who have lifted precedents without attempting to see the draft as a whole. Since most of the Constn. could not be amended,

[5]The month before was an especially tense month in the Middle East, with the coup d'état that dramatically brought down the monarchy in Iraq causing crises across the region, including American and British military intervention in Lebanon and Jordan respectively to prevent the incumbent regimes from suffering a similar fate to that of Iraq.

the result probably would be little relationship between the Constn. on paper + the Constn. in practice.

In Juba we had tea with the Deputy Governor who had arranged for me to circulate among the ladies + thus speak to everyone. The D.C.'s[6] in Torrit and Yei, on the other hand, had arranged for formal meetings, at which (somewhat embarrassed) I had to speak. It was not so bad in Torrit, where there were only three politicians: but at Yei there was a crowd of 300–400, many of them active politicians. I did my best to be non-controversial, but since every question raised federation I had to say something about it. My remarks, translated into the local language (which probably meant that my 3000 words were reduced to 600) did not always please the active politicians among my audience, though I did my best to emphasize that federation was a matter for Parlt., not for me. One local M.P. said flatly that what they wanted was federation of the U.S.A. type. My point that funds would have to be provided by the Fed. Govt. did not seem to get home.

The plain fact is that the Southerners do not want to be governed by the Northerners, but that the more educated of them realise that they cannot govern themselves because they have neither the money nor the personnel. They say, however, that they could get foreign aid – and do not take kindly to the answer that foreign aid would go to the Sudan, not to the South – and that the absence of [*illegible*] federation did not prevent Sudan independence. The latter is quite a point. One cannot reply that there has probably been (and educated Sudanese say privately that there has been) a great deterioration of efficiency since independence; and that independent or federal government or even administrative devolution in the South would produce even greater inefficiency. The line between stability and anarchy is fine: but the descent from efficiency to marginal stability is slow, and one can always go a little lower without obviously approaching anarchy. The rebellion in the South in 1955 was a warning (though of exactly what is not quite clear to me – I have not dared to ask for a copy of the report of the inquiry). The Northerners, of course, argue that the Southerners cannot govern themselves, but they probably exaggerate. They talk about the naked Southerners as if clothes were the answer: but I see no reason to suppose that the illiterate and unclothed Southerners are any less capable of self-government than the illiterate Northerners. The weakness in both parts of the country is as usual in the middle-class. The Northern middle-class is small and not very efficient: but the Southern middle-class is very small indeed. Even so, the Southern politicians assume that they can govern themselves as easily as the

[6] District commissioners.

Northern politicians; and they and their English-educated friends are being refused "jobs for the boys".

Some of the Southerners say that under the British they were governed fairly, and there is some racial sympathy with Luganda;[7] but I have not heard it seriously suggested that Luganda and the Southern Provinces of the Sudan should form a single self-governing territory. On the other hand several Northerners (including the M/J) have said that they would rather give the South independence than agree to a federation. They evidently think – though they have not so put it – that they have undertaken the white man's burden. The Government of Sudan by the British was "imperialism"; the Government of the South by the North is philanthropy. In fact, of course, there is the same mixture of motives as in British imperialism.

9th August 1958. My redraft + explanatory memorandum, corrected, went back to the Ministry this morning. My letter on procedure went to the M/J on the 6th. With it went a letter saying that I presumed my work was finishing and that I could leave on the 11th. I have had no reply to either: but M/J phoned while I was lecturing at the university on the 7th and again while I was at the Club last night. He phoned again this morning, but made no reference to my letter. He has given me a minor job to do – though the documents have not yet arrived – but I cannot make out whether (a) he has not received my letter or (b) he is deliberately stalling. The latter is possible because there are stories about a change in government, possibly a national government, and possibly a reinforcement of the present government. These may be due to an anxiety on the part of the N.U.P.[8] to get jobs; but Al Mahdi[9] (titular leader of the Umma[10]) has recovered + is apparently having talks with Al Mirghani[11] (leader of the N.D.P.[12]). I will try the Attorney-General on Monday if I do not see him before.

17th August 1958. Hearing nothing from M/J, I decided to phone him this morning. Not being able to get through, I phoned the A.G., explaining what I wanted, + later the Minister phoned. Al Mahdi is giving a dinner party on the 20th, + thereafter we can go. M/J says he will see me tomorrow.

[7] A language group proximate to South Sudan in neighbouring British East Africa.

[8] National Unionist Party, which won the first parliamentary elections in 1953 under Ismail Al Azhari, who became the first Prime Minister.

[9] Sayyid Abd al-Rahman al-Mahdi, Sudanese religious and political leader.

[10] The Umma party won the February 1958 elections.

[11] Sayyid Ali al-Mirghani, leader of the People's Democratic Party (see n. 12 below).

[12] Jennings is probably referring to the People's Democratic Party, which was a breakaway party from the N.U.P.

Meanwhile I have done nothing except (a) to write a short memo on the question of the National Committee on the Constitution, which was, I discovered, set up by the Council of Ministers, and (b) see three Southern members on the 11th August. They made it plain (1) that they proposed to keep the transitional Constn. going until they were ready for a federal Constn. and (2) they would oppose any Draft Constn. which –

(i) insisted that the Constn. should be unitary;
(ii) provided that Islam should be the State religion; and
(iii) provided that Arabic should be the national language.

I tried to convince them that –

(a) A federal Constn. could not, in the conditions of Sudan, free them from Northern control because the main sources of revenue, i.e. import + export duties, would be federal.
(b) Islam, as State religion would not matter if there were ample provisions for other religions.
(c) Arabic could be the national language if there were ample provisions for other languages.

I did not persuade them, and I fear that they will boycott the National Committee if Chapter I of the Draft Constn. remains in. The National Ctee is, however, foolish to keep Chapter I as it stands. I should like to see the Chapter dissolved and my Part I substituted via Government Draft sent straight to Parlt. I have heard nothing of my suggestion to this effect. Nor has my invitation been accepted that a case should be put to the Government to decide whether Parlt. has to amend by Bill, with a ¾ majority in a joint meeting, or whether there is a Const. Assembly which can decide by majority.

2. 'The problem of the Southern provinces – some possible solutions', undated

A. Solutions within existing framework

1. Separation of the Judiciary

The Southerners feel strongly about the maintenance of their laws and customs; and in any case it must be difficult for Arabic speaking judges to administer justice in areas in which Arabic is little understood and rarely spoken. Though it would take time to produce judges of good quality, speaking the local languages, the first step to that end would be a distinction within a unified judiciary arranged as follows:

Court of Appeal for Sudan, sitting in Khartoum or Juba as might be necessary.

High Court sitting in Khartoum.

High Court sitting in Juba.
Courts of Provinces.
District Courts.

The above Courts would have jurisdiction in all civil matters, except matters relating to Muslim personal law, which would apply only to Muslims, and to Muslim charitable trusts. These excepted matters would be dealt with by the Sharia Division of the Judiciary.

The criminal Courts and the Local Courts would function as at present, but supervision would be vested in the respective High Courts.

2. Separate Public Service Commissions

Another grievance is that local officials in the Southern Provinces are nearly all Northerners. This is unavoidable in present conditions, but the grievance would be felt less strongly if the Southerners had influence on Southern appointments. This could be done if:

(a) all appointments and promotions were made (as in Australia, Ceylon, etc) by a Public Service Commission consisting of a chairman and two members, one of whom should if possible be a Southerner; and
(b) all appointments and promotions in specified categories in the South (which could be gradually expanded) were made, subject to general direction (about qualifications, etc) laid down by the Public Service Commission by a Sub-Commission consisting of the Chairman of the Public Service Commission and two members, both being Southerners.

3. Separation of Administration

The following matters, relating to the Southern Provinces, are those of specific local concern and could be handled by one or more Ministers, who would be members of the Council of Ministers, but who would have offices in Juba as well as in Khartoum. The Juba offices would deal with all purely administrative matters which did not require reference to the Council of Ministers. The matters referred to are:

(a.) Local Government, i.e. district administrations and urban and rural councils;
(b.) Primary intermediate and secondary education;
(c.) Public health, other than major epidemics and quarantine;
(d.) Agriculture, other than major schemes of development deemed to be such by resolution of the Council of Ministers;
(e.) Animal production;
(f.) Irrigation, other than major works deemed to be such by resolution of the Council of Ministers;

(g.) Social Affairs, except in so far as affected by legislation applying to the whole of Sudan;
(h.) Works, in so far as applying to the above; and
(i.) Legislation applying only to the Southern Provinces.

4. Special Legislative Procedure

The above arrangements would imply that some legislation would only apply to the Southern Provinces i.e. the laws applying to the Southern Provinces would in some respects differ from the laws applying to the Northern Provinces. It is suggested that all Bills applying only to the Southern Provinces should, after second reading (or its equivalent) stand referred to a Southern Provinces Grand Committee, consisting of all members for constituencies in the Southern Provinces, plus such other members as the House might appoint for a particular Bill. The Bill as reported by the Grand Committee would then go to the House for third reading (or its equivalent) and, on being passed, go to the Senate.

B. Devolution without taxing powers

The advantages of the above schemes are (a) they maintain the national unity while recognising the special interests of the South; (b) they avoid all budgetary questions, which must be difficult because, for many years to come, most of the sources of revenue are likely to be in the North, and (c) in the most important fields of administration Southerners, speaking one or more of the local languages, would gradually be appointed to local posts. These might, however, be difficult [*sic*] in securing one or more Southern Ministers who would be willing to accept collective responsibility in the Council of Ministers. The schemes below, which would replace Schemes 3 and 4 above, would overcome this difficulty, but might in other respects be more difficult to work; and, while either would give the Southern Members and Ministers more power over local affairs, it would give them less power over national affairs.

5. Division of House of Representatives into two Chambers

For this purpose, the Northern and Southern members of the House of Representatives would be members respectively of a Southern and a Northern Chamber, each of which would be empowered to initiate legislation relating only to matters set out in the list under Scheme 3 above. The legislation would be passed or rejected, without amendment, by the House of Representatives and the Senate (in the same way as Church of England measures in the Parliament of the United Kingdom). This would not prevent the House of Representatives and the Senate from passing such legislation in the usual way, and in the event of inconsistency the legislation passed in the usual way would prevail.

The Ministers charged with the subjects set out in Scheme 3 above would be elected by and be responsible to the Chamber concerned, but would not be members of the Council of Ministers unless appointed thereto by the President on the advice of the Prime Minister. They would, however, be consulted by the Council of Ministers in the framing of the Budget (which would be submitted to the House of Representatives and not these separate Chambers).

The Southern Chamber could sit in Khartoum or in Juba, as its choice; though while Parliament was in session it would normally sit in Khartoum.

6. A separately elected Southern Chamber

It would be possible to work Scheme 5 even if it were not thought necessary to constitute a Northern Chamber. It might, however, be preferable to have a separately elected Southern Chamber meeting in Juba. This is not recommended because (a) it would be more expensive, (b) there might be a shortage of personnel, (c) there might be conflict between the Southern members in the House of Representatives and the Southern Chamber, and (d) the Southern Chamber as such would have no influence on the Budget. Nevertheless, if the Southern Provinces have their own "legislature" in Juba, Southern susceptibilities might be met.

C. Devolution with taxing powers

Devolution with taxing powers is difficult because (a) the greater part of the revenue of Sudan comes from import and export duties, which must be levied nationally, (b) it is impracticable to devolve income taxes and death duties (except perhaps on agricultural land) without leading to evasion and raising problems of double taxation of the utmost complexity, and (c) the expenditure on the Southern Provinces must be vastly in excess of their taxable resources, and accordingly large grants from national funds would be required. It would be impracticable to determine the amounts of these grants for a long period, and there would have to be lengthy and complex negotiations at least once every five years.

The taxing powers which apparently could be devolved are:

(a) Date Tax;
(b) Animal Tax;
(c) Land Tax;
(d) Poll Tax;

(e) Ushur;[13]
(f) Tribute;
(g) House Tax;
(h) Business Profits Tax;
(i) Income Tax on agricultural land;
(j) Death duties on agricultural land.

These sources would not bring in much total revenue in the Southern Provinces, but would enable either scheme 7 or 8 to be operated.

7. Devolution without division of powers
There would be an elected Southern Chamber, as in Scheme 6, but it would be desirable to have a Chief Minister and a Minister of Finance as well as the Ministers required under Scheme 6. This would give a full government to the Southern Provinces, which would negotiate with the Government of Sudan about the grant from national funds. There would be a separate Southern Province Budget, providing expenditure on the items mentioned in scheme 3. It would also be desirable to have a separate Public Service Commission for the Southern Provinces, though for some considerable time to come most of the senior employees would have to be Northerners.

8. Devolution with division of powers
This is apparently what the Southern members mean by a "federal Constitution". The essential difference between scheme 7 and scheme 8 is that the federal (or central) legislature would have no power to legislate on the matters set out in scheme 3, and so it would be unnecessary to devolve powers on a Northern Province Chamber (with a similar Northern Province Government). Also legislation enacted by Parliament could then be declared ultra vires, if it trenched upon the powers of either Chambers [*sic*]. This arrangement would have disadvantages as well as advantages; in particular, where there is a division of powers there is usually a field which cannot effectively be covered by legislation because it trenches on both federal and State matters. One could try to meet this, however, by a drafting formula.

It would be impracticable to put Scheme 7 and Scheme 8 into operation until (a) agreement had been reached about central subsidies, which would have to be substantial, and (b) the Southern Provinces were able to recruit suitable administrative and technical personnel. This might require a delay of fifteen to twenty-five years.

[13]Ushr is an Islamic tithe.

SECTION M: CONSTITUTION-MAKING AND POLITICAL OBSERVATIONS

1. 'Republicanism in Asia', 1952–1953

I.

Though it appears only occasionally in the books, there was a republican strain in British politics throughout the 19th century and even into the 20th century. The Radicals regarded the monarchy with cool detachment. "The utmost that can be said against it", said the Radical Programme of 1885, "is that it occasionally operates in a manner favourable to the opponents of political reforms, and that, as it promotes a good deal of sycophancy and snobbery, its social influence is of questionable value ... It can scarcely fail to happen that a Sovereign concerned in perpetuating the pomp and circumstance of his or her office should, from time to time, make suggestions to Ministers which it is not practicable to follow, and should indulge in a tendency to control the affairs of State which is inconsistent with the free play of our popular institutions. But of these things no serious account need be taken ... One thing indeed, in the interests of the Throne is earnestly to be deprecated – an imperial and especially a military policy undertaken at the royal instance and wish ... Short of this, however, and so long as the functions of royalty are recognised as being ornamental and consultative, the Throne has nothing to fear from Radicalism. Radicals have something else to do than to break butterflies on wheels".[1]

This was not even fairest praise. Something of that attitude passed into the Labour Movement. For the most part the Crown was ignored. Nothing even so positive as the comments of the Radical Programme ever appeared in the Labour manifestoes. It was in fact a dangerous topic because the Crown was too popular. Queen Victoria, in spite of her political prejudices and the seclusion of her widowhood, died

[1] The *Radical Programme* (London, 1885) was a series of articles first published in the *Fortnightly Review* and overseen by the Liberal party politician Joseph Chamberlain which advocated radical reform in Britain, including land redistribution, disestablishment of the Church of England, free public education, and universal male suffrage. This quotation is taken from 'Measures', pp. 38–41.

as "the little old lady".[2] Edward VII in his own person represented the relief from Victorian Nonconformity which was characteristic of the early years of the present century. It was, however, George V who set the tune. It was perhaps a little odd that the typical country squire should acquire popularity in making class constituencies, and yet there is not the slightest doubt of it. He and his Queen – and somebody ought to write a book about the influence of Queen Mary – represented the common man and the common [wo]man far better than any of the politicians. He was not clever but he was honest. Queen Mary was the sort of woman that most female electors would like to be. The combination of Stanley Baldwin[3] and George V was quite irresistible if Labour "intellectuals" like Harold Laski[4] and Sir Stafford Cripps gave the impression that the Labour Party was against the monarchy.

Laski, probably, was the last of the republicans, but even he knew that the cause was lost. Somewhere about 1934 or 1935 he purchased, as President of the Rationalist Press Association, the last copy of Bradlaugh's *House of Brunswick*[5] and presented it to me with the remark that it would never be reprinted because republicanism was dead. The Labour Party itself would not be republican, for it would lose too many votes. In January 1934 Sir Stafford Cripps, in answer to a question from the floor after a speech, made a criticism of "Buckingham Palace". At once there was a wave of protests, which compelled him to explain away his remarks. Mr Dalton,[6] with equal indiscretion, explained why the Labour Party could not tolerate this sort of speech. "Every time he opens his mouth", he said of Sir Stafford, "he loses 20,000 votes". The monarchy has forced its way back into the British Constitution. Now we have a Queen and her name is Elizabeth; any political party which dared to touch the monarchy would lose, not 20,000 votes, but 300 seats. The spread of democracy has cemented the monarchy.

The American commentator said in 1938 that "the Crown is an undemocratic institution".[7] What he meant he did not explain. If he meant only that George V had never stood for election his facts were correct but his inferences incorrect, for the King was the one

[2] A phrase used by Lytton Strachey in his biography of Queen Victoria, first published in 1921.

[3] Stanley Baldwin (later Earl Baldwin of Bewdley), British Conservative Prime Minister, 1923–1924, 1924–1929, 1935–1937.

[4] Harold Laski, British Labour politician; Professor at the London School of Economics, 1926–1950.

[5] Charles Bradlaugh, *The Impeachment of the House of Brunswick* (London, 1874).

[6] Hugh Dalton (later Baron Dalton), British Labour minister; Chancellor of the Exchequer, 1945–1947.

[7] Dean E. McHenry, *The Labour Party in Transition, 1931–1938* (London, 1938), p. 270.

man in any of the English-speaking countries who could have got a 98 per cent vote. If popular support is the test of democracy, the Crown is as democratic as the Presidency of the United States. If the test be whether the holder of the office has popular support, the answer is that King George V had more popular support than President Roosevelt.[8] If it be alleged that George V used his authority to obstruct the operation of public opinion the answer is a denial that he did anything of the kind. Even in 1931, when his initiative led to the formation of the National Government and thereby led to criticism of the monarchy,[9] the event showed that he had correctly interpreted public opinion. If it be said that the monarchy helps to maintain an undemocratic class system, the argument is more plausible. The assumption that what the monarchy helps to sustain is a decayed autocracy is, however, a persistent fallacy. Political influence is no more hereditary in the United Kingdom than it is in the United States. Wealth has less influence in the United Kingdom than it has in the United States. Merit can carve a career as early in the United Kingdom as in the United States. Titles, hereditary and otherwise, hide class origins, but nobody has political influence merely because he has a title. Nobody suggests that there is complete equality of opportunity in the United Kingdom; but it would not be easy to claim that there is complete equality of opportunity in the United States. Those whose ideas have been founded on that tendentious document, the American Declaration of Independence, should not assume that the monarchical system of Britain is less democratic than the presidential system of the United States. The monarchy is one of the pillars of a democracy which is at least as responsive to public opinion as the democracy of the United States.

II.

These counts have been necessary in order to destroy the illusion that monarchy and democracy are incompatible. It is not suggested that the monarchy has been equally successful in Asia. On the contrary, it is evident that there has been a failure to touch the imagination. This is a field in which the monarchs, especially Victoria and George V, have been more forward than the Governments. The task was, however, difficult if not insuperable and it is very much easier to say what should have been achieved than to work out a practicable policy for achieving it.

[8]Franklin D. Roosevelt, Democrat President of the United States of America, 1933–1945.

[9]Jennings is referring to criticism of George V made by his former LSE colleague Laski in *The Crisis and the Constitution* (London, 1931).

The peoples of the United Kingdom, in spite of their diversity of origin, are remarkably homogenous; with few exceptions they have a common language and they are all educated at least to the level of the popular newspaper. They can be reached by the newspaper and the radio. Most of them live in or near towns which can be visited from time to time. Since both George V and George VI – and Elizabeth II is following the same tradition – made frequent visits to provincial cities and the East End it is probable that two-thirds of the adults of the United Kingdom have seen the monarch in person. From time to time, too, there are great ceremonies in London and Edinburgh which attract millions to the capitals. Those who have seen the Queen, as well as those who have not, read about her almost daily in the popular press. The organisation known as "Buckingham Palace", in charge by [*sic*] the Principal Private Secretary, takes immense care over the attitude to public opinion. Its failure under Edward VIII proves the rule. The Queen belongs to us and we belong to the Queen.

No such attitude could be created in Asia. There was, of course, a long monarchical tradition, longer than in Britain. At the Conference of Prime Ministers in October 1949[10] the then Prime Minster of Ceylon[11] pointed out that he represented the oldest continuous monarchy in the Commonwealth. Through the Kandyan Convention of 1815,[12] which vested the Crown in George III, his heirs and successors, the Sinhalese monarchy had been in existence for nearly 2500 years. Sometimes the monarchs had been Sinhalese, sometimes Tamils, and, since 1815, British; but there had always been a monarch. It was, however, not easy to establish a direct, personal relationship between Sovereign and people, even in Ceylon, where communications were good and literacy was high. In British India it was even more difficult. The mass of the population was illiterate and lived in remote villages. It was divided by language and religion and its social hierarchy was based on caste. Occasionally a subordinate officer of Government would appear, though a more frequent visitor was the Congress politician. In Ceylon the villager had a vote from 1931;[13] in India adult franchise was established under the Republic.

It is possible to argue that more might have been done. The Sovereign was represented by the Viceroy, at first in Calcutta and later in New Delhi, and by the Governor of Provinces. They kept

[10]A meeting of Commonwealth prime ministers where the key item on the agenda was India's decision to become a republic and the country's wish to remain in the Commonwealth.

[11]D.S. Senanayake.

[12]The agreement between the Kandyan Chiefs and the British to replace the Kandyan monarchy in the interior of Sri Lanka with the British one.

[13]The year when universal suffrage had been introduced to the island.

a state of oriental – or possibly pseudo-oriental – splendour copied from that exhibited by the Maharajahs and inspired by that of the Moghul Emperors. From time to time they went on tour, visiting Maharajahs and Rajahs, performing ceremonies in the towns, and generally showing the flag. Unlike the Sovereign in Britain, however, they could not concentrate on social and ceremonial functions because they were also administrators. Probably as Kipling[14] suggests, the Indian Army carried the Sovereign's name into the villages more readily than any other instrumentality: but this applied more to Rajputana and the North-west than to the East and the South. Even in Ceylon the Governor was remote. Besides, he was a promoted civil servant, spending in Queen's House the last five years of an official career, most if not all of which had been spent in debilitating tropical climate.

The section of opinion which mattered most, the Congress politicians and the "intelligentsia" of the towns, was not attracted by the devices designed to secure the loyalty of the Indian Army, the Indian Princes, and the general populace. In the Army a distinction was drawn between the imported officer who carried the King's commission and the Indian officer who carried the Viceroy's commission. What is more, the Army was regarded not merely as a means of external defence but also as a means for maintaining internal order or, as the Congress politicians would put it (not wholly correctly) suppressing popular movements. The Sovereign's Indian title, Emperor of India or King-Emperor, was itself an offence because it bore witness to that "imperialism" which denied self-government and – again in the opinion of the Congress politicians – enriched the United Kingdom. The Indian Princes were autocrats whose rule was sustained against popular movements by the British Raj. The appeal to the people was an appeal by the "imperialists" against patriotic nationalists like the Congress politicians. Finally, there was a persistent belief among the Hindus that since the Mutiny British policy had favoured the Muslims. Most of the active politicians were Hindu, who took to western education more quickly than the Muslims. It was thought that a deliberate policy of "divide and rule" was being followed. Communal tension was, it was thought, fostered if not fomented by the British. Communal representation was invented by the British in order to keep the nationalist movement divided.

The ideas of the Congress politicians were English to a surprising degree, though it is not so surprising when the causes are examined. Though appeals to "our cultural heritage" were so frequent that

[14] Rudyard Kipling wrote many poems and stories of British India in the late nineteenth and early twentieth centuries.

they have become a source of cynicism, every idea expounded by the Congress politicians was derived from their study of political literature in the English language. The universities of Bombay, Calcutta and Madras had been established in 1857 in the likeness of the University of London as it was then. To this day student language is essentially English; "Matric.", "Inter.", "Honours", Pass" are incomprehensible to those who do not understand the English university system. The courses in political science, constitutional history and constitutional law were based on English materials – Burke,[15] Bagehot,[16] Dicey,[17] Hallam,[18] Stubbs,[19] Erskine May,[20] Anson[21] and even the hated Macaulay.[22] In the present century were added Laski and G.D.H. Cole.[23] The studies in "comparative government" brought in some American ideas but in a very superficial form, and stock answers were given, mostly favourable to the British Constitution.

The intelligentsia which filled the Congress party was for the most part educated in Indian universities from the age of 14 or 15 to the age of 20 or 21. There were, however, some like M.K. Gandhi[24] and Jawaharlal Nehru who studied in England. In the neighbouring Island of Ceylon at the present time the Prime Minister, the Leader of the House of Representatives and one of the two Tamil Ministers were educated in Cambridge; the leaders of the three Opposition parties were educated in Oxford, London and Cambridge respectively. Several other leaders on both sides were educated at the Ceylon University College which taught for London examinations from 1926 to 1942. Ceylon is more anglicised than India and Pakistan, but the principle is the same. Directly and indirectly Indian ideas were British ideas.

The notion that the more one learns about another country the more sympathetic one becomes, is by no means true in Asia. The jingo was a rare bird in Britain but not uncommon in Asia. I remember a Ceylonese remarking, before 1948, that he was a slave in Ceylon and became freer as he got nearer the Straits of Dover. This was no doubt

[15] Edmund Burke, sixteenth-century Irish-born political philosopher and English MP.
[16] Walter Bagehot, nineteenth-century English political journalist.
[17] A.V. Dicey, Venerian Professor of English Law at the University of Oxford, 1882–1909.
[18] Henry Hallam, English constitutional historian.
[19] William Stubbs, English constitutional historian.
[20] Thomas Erskine May (later Baron Farnborough), Clerk of the House of Commons, 1871–1886; constitutional expert.
[21] Sir William Anson, Liberal Unionist politician and constitutional expert.
[22] Thomas Babington Macaulay (later Baron Macaulay), English historian and politician.
[23] G.D.H. Cole, English political theorist.
[24] Mohandas Karmarchand Gandhi, Indian political leader.

post-prandial exaggeration, but there was something in the idea that racial discrimination was less noticeable in England than in Ceylon. Conversely the Ceylonese in Ceylon was often more sympathetic to Britain than the Ceylonese in Britain. There is undoubtedly a latent understanding and appreciation which often contrasts rather strangely with patent dislike and distrust. An attack on "British Imperialism" will be followed by a division which is fundamentally British in its texture. Emotionally the Congress politician was, until 1948, an opponent of Britain, but the assumptions on which he based his opposition rationally were British. A century of "English education", defective though that education often was, had had a more profound influence than even the Indians were aware.

The sections of English opinion among which the Indian student in England found sympathy were on the left in politics. The Communist Party of Great Britain has been charged with the responsibility of indoctrinating Indian and colonial students. In the depression of the 'thirties it was hardly respectable for an Indian student to be anything but a communist. On the other hand, Stalinist regimentation was not only repellent to Indian individualism but also in fundamental conflict with the English ideas in which the educated class had been held. The success of the Communist Party has therefore been small. Far more influential was the Labour Movement from the conservative Fabianism of Sidney Webb[25] to the non-Stalinist Marxism (or perhaps pseudo-Marxism for he was never a convincing Marxist) of Laski's later (post 1931) period.[26] It is odd to reflect that, though he never passed Suez, Laski had greater influence in India than Lord Curzon.[27]

III.

The Indians, like the Irish, studied all the Constitutions of the world and then enacted the British Constitution. Even their Bill of Rights, which obviously started with that of the United States, finished as a summary of several chapters of Dicey's Law of the Constitution.[28] This form of government, it is true, is republican; but it is what may be called a republican form of constitutional monarchy. The Queen's functions are vested in a President elected for five years by an electoral college. In the neighbouring Island of Ceylon, which has retained the

[25] Sidney Webb (later Baron Passfield), British Labour minister; Secretary of State for the Colonies, 1929–1931.

[26] This refers to the split in the Labour Party when Ramsay MacDonald and other Labour ministers were expelled from the party for ending the Labour Government and agreeing to form a National Government with the Conservative and Liberal parties.

[27] George Nathanial Curzon (later Marquess Curzon of Kedleston), Viceroy of India, 1899–1905.

[28] First published in 1885.

monarchical form, most (but not quite all) of the Queen's functions are vested in a Governor-General appointed for five years on the recommendation of the Prime Minister of Ceylon. Plus ça change plus c'est la même chose.[29]

India, like Ceylon, decided to remain within the Commonwealth, and accordingly to recognize the Sovereign as "Head of the Commonwealth". This is purely a nominal title, but India's membership of the Commonwealth does carry certain implications:

(1.) The system of communication and consultation developed in relation to Canada, Australia, New Zealand and South Africa extends to India, Pakistan and Ceylon. There is regular contact between the Commonwealth Relations Office and the Ministries of External Affairs, which are kept informed of British policy and, in fact, derive much of their knowledge of international affairs from London. Theoretically the traffic is two-way; but it is not clear whether there is much traffic into London.

(2.) The other Commonwealth countries assume that their defence arrangements by sea and air may have to be extended to India, Pakistan and Ceylon in collaboration with the armed forces of those countries. Officers and men are trained in the United Kingdom and all the equipment is of British origin. Common signals are used and the fleets can manoeuvre as a combined fleet. When, for instance, the Queen (as Princess Elizabeth) was due to visit Ceylon in 1952, it was arranged that she be escorted to Colombo by the Royal Navy, the Indian Navy, the Royal Pakistani Navy and the Royal Ceylon Navy.

(3.) The Commonwealth countries, including India, are represented in each other's countries not by ambassadors but by High Commissioners. In London, at least, these High Commissioners meet in conclave with a representative of the Government of the United Kingdom at least once a week.

(4.) Citizens of all Commonwealth countries, including India, are British subjects or Commonwealth citizens; and in most of the countries have privileges which are not shared by aliens. In the United Kingdom, in particular, they have the same privileges (including the franchise and the right to be elected to Parliament) as citizens of the United Kingdom and Colonies.

What, then, is the difference between India, which has become a republic, and Ceylon, which has not? There are superficial differences. "O.H.M.S." appears on official envelopes in Ceylon, but not in India.

[29] The more things change, the more they stay the same.

In India the royal arms have been replaced by Asoka's column.[30] In Ceylon, nobody has yet tried to alter the legend "G.R." which appears on the scarlet post-boxes. In Ceylon the flags are flown on the Queen's birthday: on special occasions the Union Jack flies by the side of the Lion of Lanka; "God Save the Queen" and "Namo, Namo, Matha"[31] are played in succession. There are, too, constitutional differences, though they are formal. The Queen appears in the Constitution, though generally she acts through a Governor-General whose appointment is advised by the Prime Minister of Ceylon. The declaration of war, the making of peace, and the signature, and ratification of treaties would be done in the name of the Queen but the Government of Ceylon. Clearly the differences are psychological, and even then they are not great. An Englishman is as much at home in India as he is in Ceylon; but he is also as much an alien in Ceylon as he is in India. In short, the differences are so small that they are difficult to describe.

2. 'Constitutional issues in South Asia', undated

For constitutional purposes, South Asia cannot be regarded as a unit. Of the constitutional issues in Afghanistan I know nothing. In the Khyber Pass I put one foot over the border, but the sentry looked so menacing that I hastily withdrew it. On constitutional issues in Nepal in the north east and the Maldive Islands in the south west I could make some remarks, but they would be irrelevant to the main theme. Burma I shall mention only in passing. The core of my remarks will relate to India, Pakistan and Ceylon.

Ceylon's background was different from that of British India. The maritime provinces retained some relics of the Portuguese and Dutch occupations. Though it was placed under the East India Company in 1796, it became a crown Colony in 1802. It is, I think, true to say that ever since it has tended to look towards London and not towards Madras, Calcutta or New Delhi. This was only partly a matter of government. The economic development of Ceylon was due to our coffee, tea and rubber plantations, owned by Europeans in a [*illegible*] the United Kingdom, whose produce was exported to the United Kingdom and sold there. Colombo was more of a European city even than Bombay or Calcutta. The constitutional system was

[30] More commonly spelled 'Ashoka', this refers to the Indian emblem of four lions back to back on a circular object, which is a modern adaptation of the Mauryan Emperor Ashoka's emblem and is used as an official symbol of the Republic of India.

[31] The national anthem of Sri Lanka.

essentially British, not British-Indian. English education, as it was called, was more highly developed in Ceylon than in British India, so that at independence 10% of the male adults spoke English, and many middle-class families used English as the language of the home. Many of the politicians and senior civil servants were educated in England, whereas none of the leading politicians or senior civil servants had been educated in India. Though there was a sort of theory that Ceylon showed in the culture of India, the number of Ceylonese who knew anything about the culture of India was small; and few of them were Sinhalese.

I have heard it said in India that the Indian National Congress fought the battle of independence for Ceylon. That may be true in the sense that pressure from British India, from 1917 onwards, caused British opinion gradually to accept the notion that the non-European territories of the British Empire, as it was then called, could achieve self-government: but this was as true of Ghana as it was of Ceylon. On the other hand, the conflict between the Indian National Congress and the Muslim League in the forties seems actually to have delayed self-government for Ceylon. The records will probably show that Ceylon did not get self-government in 1946 because the Indian problem had not been resolved. It is said that Sir Stafford Cripps advised the Cabinet to postpone self-government for Ceylon in order not to prejudice the negotiations in India.

The conflict of Hindu and Muslim, the wariness in which the taciturn and truculent Jinnah forced the Congress to give way, the massacres of 1947, and the problem of Kashmir, divided British India psychologically even more emphatically than geographically. In Karachi in the early fifties, India appeared to be an alien and unfriendly entity. West Pakistan was looking eastwards, over Kashmir, towards East Pakistan. On the other hand, independent India seemed to be looking inwards and to be unaware of the impression which its actions in Junagadh, Kashmir and Hyderabad,[32] and at a later stage Goa,[33] were creating.

The decision of the communist parties of Asia at Lucknow at the end of 1948 to change the attack on imperialism to an attack on what was, for the first time, called colonialism, was strategically sound. It put the communist parties behind the nationalist parties and hid the fact that, at that time, the imperialist powers were the Soviet Union and India. On the other hand, the Indian nationalists received criticism with a

[32] The princely state of Hyderabad was annexed to the Indian Union by the Indian army in September 1948.

[33] Goa was a Portuguese territory until it was annexed to the Indian Union by the Indian army in December 1961.

pained surprise. There had always been an India, a political entity from the Himalayas to the Palk Strait, and some extended it to the most southerly tip of South Asia, Dondra Head. It is a curious tendency of nationalism to appropriate geography. If Ruritania includes Arcadia geographically, it must include Arcadia politically; the Arcadians are really Ruritanians, though for some reason they do not realise it; and they must be forced to accept this geo-political destiny. It could reasonably be said that the accession of Junagadh to Pakistan and the refusal of the Nizam of Hyderabad[34] to accede to India were politically absurd; but the accession of Kashmir to India was equally absurd, and there is no evidence that the Goanese wanted to be forced to be free of Portuguese control.

Nevertheless, there were common elements in the constitutional evolution of Burma, India, Pakistan and Ceylon. The evolution began in Ceylon because drafting began in 1943, though it was the last of the four countries to become independent. The release of Burma from Japanese control caused it to lead the way. The young men of Rangoon took over and produced a sort of proto-type of the Constitution of India.

The draftsman was the late Sir Benegal Rau,[35] who used his Burmese experience when he came to draft his Constitution of India. In India the Congress Party took over in August 1947 under an expurgated version of the Government of India Act of 1935. It might also be described as an expurgated version of the British Constitution. The Governor-General, at first Lord Mountbatten, represented the Queen; there was a Cabinet responsible to the Constituent Assembly; and the Constituent Assembly had both constitutional and legislative powers. The view was taken that the Constitutional Assembly as such was a sovereign legislative body, while the Constituent Assembly as federal legislature was subject to the restrictions of the federal system established by the Government of India Act. India had a large number of experienced politicians and lawyers, the Constituent Assembly operated efficiently, and the Constitution of India was produced in November 1949 to come into operation in 1950.

Pakistan had a much more difficult problem. When Chaudhri Muhammad Ali went to Karachi as Secretary-General in 1947 he had neither a typewriter nor a typist. He had to build up the Government of Pakistan from the basement. Pakistan, like India, had a system of responsible government based on an amended version of the Government of India Act. Muhammad Ali Jinnah confused

[34] Osman Ali Khan, ruler and Nizam of Hyderabad, 1911–1948.

[35] Sir Benegal N. Rau, Indian civil servant; constitutional adviser to the Constituent Assembly of India and Burma.

the matter by becoming both Governor-General and president of the Constituent Assembly. Though Liaquat Ali Khan was prime minister, the Cabinet was effectively controlled by Jinnah. We can appreciate the revenue to which Jinnah was entitled without approving the process of establishing a Caesar. Caesar is unfortunately mortal. In 1948 Jinnah died, and Liaquat decided to establish ordinary Cabinet Government with Nazimuddin as a constitutional Governor-General. Liaquat was assassinated in 1951, and Nazimuddin became Prime Minister with Ghulam Muhammad as Governor-General.

Who suggested this arrangement I do not know, but it was all wrong. Nazimuddin was an admirable Governor-General and Liaquat an admirable Prime Minister. Nazimuddin was a weak Prime Minister and Ghulam Muhammad wanted to be a Jinnah. Can you imagine the British Constitution with Winston Churchill[36] as King and George VI as Prime Minister?

The dismissal of Nazimuddin in 1953 was perhaps justified by the weakness of his Government, but it split the Muslim League and gave the Governor-General some implacable enemies. The new Prime Minister was another Bengali, Muhammad Ali Bogra, who had been a good ambassador but was not a good Prime Minister. The real Prime Minister was the Minister of Finance, Chaudhri Muhammad Ali, a Punjabi who worked closely with the Punjabi Governor-General. He was an able administrator to whom Pakistan owed its machinery of government, but he was no politician, and he could not control the Constituent Assembly.

The story of the crisis of October 1954 is long and complicated, and some of it is still unknown.[37] I shall not try to retell it. It does, however, illustrate the degree to which the work of preparation for partition was [*illegible*]. Nobody could have foreseen that after seven years Pakistan would be without a Constitution; but one reason for that situation was that the Assembly was such an unsuitable body to produce a Constitution. When the litigation was over, in 1955 and the second Assembly was in being, it was easy for the draftsmen, working in the Ministry of Law under the direction of Chaudhri Muhammad Ali, to produce a draft Constitution as a Government Bill, which was approved by the Assembly in a few weeks. Its failure to function was not due to its defects, for I doubt if, technically, it had any. And here I ought to say that I dropped out in September 1955, and it was Mr Justice Abdul Hamid who saw the draft through its final stages. No doubt the coup d'état of 1958, which was brought about by Generals Iskander Mirza and Ayub Khan, was due in part to their personal

[36] Sir Winston Churchill, British Prime Minister, 1940–1945 and 1951–1955.

[37] For the 'story', see section H.

opinions about democracy in general. But the system as it worked in Pakistan was not democracy. It was an oligarchy of politicians whose bad habits had been acquired in the first Constituent assembly. I do not think that this justifies a military coup d'état, but it helps to explain it.

This brings us back to the general issue in all three countries. When Ceylon became independent in 1948 the communists scrawled all over the country the slogan "Fake Independence". What they meant was that the white capitalists had handed political power to the brown capitalists so that all the capitalists, without distinction of race, creed or colour, could continue to make profits out of the workers and peasants. There is always just enough truth in communist propaganda to make it unpleasant. In 1947 and 1948 the British Government transferred power to the English-educated middle class of India, Pakistan and Ceylon.

The prospects were favourable, at least in India and Ceylon – Pakistan's prospects were more of a speculation. In India and Ceylon there was an efficient administration to which the rapid retirement of a relatively few European officers would not make much difference. The Indian National Congress had not much experience of government, but it had wide support in the middle classes and an organisation in depth. In Ceylon the leading politicians had had experience of government, but a governing party, the United National Party, had to be created, and it had no organisation in depth.

Ceylon had had adult suffrage since 1931, but the peculiarities of the 1931 Constitution had discouraged party politics, and in most parts of the country candidates fought on their reputations. It was, for instance, a qualification to have played cricket for the premier Buddhist college. The Westminster model changed all that, but the consequences were not apparent until Mr S.W.R.D. Bandaranaike was thrown out, or to be technically correct resigned, in 1952.[38] Mr Bandaranaike was the exact opposite of Chaudhri Muhammad Ali. He was the worst administrator since John Bright,[39] he was an inconvenient colleague, to put it mildly, but he was a first-rate politician. Even before 1947 he had a party of his own, the Sri Lanka Freedom Party. It was wholly Sinhalese and it appealed especially to the Buddhist villages. As Minister for Local Government Mr Bandaranaike was able to use his control of patronage to put sympathisers into positions of authority. Also, he assiduously cultivated the Buddhist monks, though he himself

[38] Actually 1951.

[39] John Bright, British orator and Liberal minister; President of the Board of Trade, 1868–1871.

was what Ceylon calls a political Buddhist, a Christian who became a Buddhist when he contemplated entering politics.

As an entity, the S.L.F.P. was absorbed into the U.N.P. in 1947. But it had never had much of an organisation, and it was easy enough to reconstitute it in 1952. Its task was now to put up candidates against the U.N.P. in the rural areas in which most of the electors were Sinhalese and Buddhists. It could leave the urban areas to the communists. Its appeal was frankly religious and racial. It would give Buddhism and the Sinhalese language their rightful place. This appeal was particularly attractive because nationalism is an imported concept shared in the main by the English-educated middle class. It made Mr Bandaranaike Prime Minister. Since he was not a good one, he would probably have been ejected long ago. His assassination made him a hero and his widow his political successor.[40] She has much more common sense than her late husband and has the advantage of being a Kandyan.

The Ceylon Tamils of the middle class have always been more communally-minded than the English-educated Sinhalese. They are a closely-knit community with a good deal of inter-marriage within the dominant caste. The Tamils of my generation took easily to English education, but many of them spoke Tamil at home. They are for the most part Hindus. On the other hand, those who were politically minded were also nationalists. They were, if I may so put it, communists within the nationalist framework: and it was this odd combination, I think, which led them into the singular folly of supporting the Sinhalese demand for making the mother tongue, as it was called, the national language. It was a singular folly because, though the Tamils spoke of national languages, many Sinhalese used the singular. As far back as 1945 it was obvious that the communal interest of the Tamils lay in the pre-war slogan, "English, more English and better English". It is a good slogan for the Dravidian-speaking people of South India who have at last realised the consequences of having Hindi as the national language, even though the use of English is authorised indefinitely. I am not arguing for English, either in Ceylon or in India; I am simply saying that, after independence, the English language becomes politically neutral.

Bandaranaike's use of the language issue and the religious appeal was so successful that the U.N.P. had to adopt it. It thus lost Tamil support. Also, the communists are strong, particularly the Lanka Sama Samaja Party, which calls itself Trotskyist. The Ceylon communists show, however, a remarkable tendency to fragmentation. Indeed,

[40]Sirimavo Bandaranaike, SLFP Prime Minister, 1960–1965, 1970–1972, and then again under the Republic of Sri Lanka, 1972–1977 and 1994–2000.

the development of Ceylon politics since 1956 is one of necessary fragmentation. This is a familiar weakness of the Westminster model which Westminster itself does not exhibit. It produces unstable coalitions.

If one could think only in communal terms this might not be a bad thing. Ceylon could get through its period of communalism because of the divisions among the Sinhalese. On the other hand, Ceylon's essential problem is economic, and what it needs most is a strong and stable government. It may get it in time, though the changes will have to be political, not constitutional. A substantial increase in the number of members might help. There are at present 157, which is not unreasonable in relation to the population. The effect of increasing the size is to diminish the influence of the back-benchers, to make them more amenable to the whip, and to discourage potential would-be leaders from using intrigue to get supporters.

On the whole, however, Ceylon's politicians have played the Constitution according to its rules. They have been helped by a strong judiciary. I would not guarantee that all elections are fought according to the rule-book.

India's record has been quite different. The explanation is clearly to be found in the Indian National Congress, which has held together longer than many of us had anticipated. This was, I think, not due entirely to the predominance of Jawaharlal Nehru, though that obviously helped. It was largely due to the fact that the Congress was organised in depth and became, after it ceased to be the instrument for outing British rule, the political bandwagon at all levels of power and influence. Indeed, in the fifties it was recognised that a man who wore a Gandhi cap was on the wagon. If this ceases to be the case there may be fragmentation in India as in Ceylon, though in India it may be worse because it can now be based on linguistic States. Nehru's insistence that politics should not be based on religion or language was wise, and the fact that he had to agree to a reorganisation of the States on linguistic lines was unfortunate.[41]

The weaknesses of the Government of India are largely administrative, and they were inherited from British rule. The rise in educational standards may help, though there is no easy means of instilling a sense of responsibility into the lower ranks of the administration.

The strength of the Congress has helped to diminish the powers of the States, for when State politics became either too exciting or too corrupt it has been possible to choose weapons. The Congress

[41] In the States Reorganisation Act, 1956, which majorly altered the state boundaries in an attempt to accommodate Indian plurality.

machine could be used with the implied threat of a take-over of the Government of India. The effective power of the States has, however, been much weakened by their increasing dependence on the financial resources of the Government of India and their reluctance to increase taxes within their power. It has been said that India is no longer a federation, but this is a question of definition and, according to my definition, it still is.

Finally, the strength of the Congress has enabled the Constitution to be amended. In particular, the Bill of Rights has been made more flexible. In some lectures which I delivered in the University of Madras in March, 1952, I was critical of that Bill.[42] To a small extent my criticisms have been met by the amendments. Generally, however, I now think the criticisms to have been exaggerated. Almost any Constitution can be worked successfully if it is worked by reasonable men. The justices of the Supreme Court have been reasonable. They realised, I think, that the Bill of Rights introduced very little that was new into Indian law because it was founded essentially on the common law. What was new, and also important, was the judicial review of central and State legislation. I have not used all the judgements, but the Supreme Court seems to have done the job well.

Things are very different over the border in Pakistan. The fundamental problem was, and still is, balance between East and West Pakistan and the balance within West Pakistan. A reasonable compromise was reached in the first Constituent Assembly, but the constitutional problem was complicated by the common action of the Bengalis and the dissident members of the Muslim League in the West. This led to the litigation of 1954–55 and the summary of the second Constitutional Assembly, which enacted the Constitution.

Meanwhile, as I said earlier, the first Constituent Assembly had developed bad habits but we particularize. Because the Pakistan Assembly was historically an offshoot of the Indian Assembly, it was a small body whose membership never exceeded 80. It met in Karachi for short sessions, usually two or three times a year for three weeks or a month at a time. Some members had official jobs outside Karachi; some were members of provincial legislatures; some could not be bothered to leave their families for not very important business. The average attendance was less than 50 and not more than 53 voted on any decision. The amount of work done was small, and members, many of whom lived together in a hostel[,] had much time on their hands. This is the kind of situation which no experienced constitutional lawyer

[42] Sir Ivor Jennings, *Some Characteristics of the Indian Constitution – Being Lectures given in the University of Madras during March 1952 under the Sir Alladi Krishnaswami Aiyer Shashitaahdapoothi Endowment* (Madras, 1953).

would contemplate, because it invites political intrigue within the party structure.

What is more, the Assembly adopted the Indian view that the Assembly acting as constituent assembly and not as federal legislature was a sovereign body. This meant not only that it had all the powers of the Parliament of the United Kingdom but also that in it there was no Government and no Opposition. It was just a body of 40 or 50 individuals authorised not merely to produce a Constitution but also to tinker with the Interim Constitution. The draftsmen were officers of the Assembly who had no consultation with or instructions from the Ministers or from civil servants. Their instructions came from the drafting committee presided over by the President of the Assembly.

This was, I think, not in accordance with the Indian Independence Act, but that Act was in many places ambiguous. I do not know its background, but I would suspect that Parliamentary Counsel had inadequate instructions from the India Office, who in turn had inadequate advice from the Government of India, which for this purpose consisted of Lord Mountbatten, Nehru and Jinnah. Presumably the only way to get agreement was to leave everything as vague as possible. One must not complain, for in the end the vagueness enabled the Federal Const. to find a way out of the impasse of 1955.[43]

There were no serious problems in India, because there was no leadership from the Congress and everybody was anxious to get on with the job. Even so, there was the story of the Bengali member who had 500 amendments to the Draft Constitution but who had the good fortune to lose his papers in the train. In Pakistan it was most unfortunate. The phrase which is commonly used is that it was a shambles. That is not accurate. It was much more like C.P. Snow's mythical college electing a Master.[44]

The second Constituent Assembly had leadership from the Government. It is not true, as Professor Callard[45] suggests, that the distinction between the constituent assembly as such and the federal legislature was maintained. Separate sittings were arranged so as to separate constitutional business from legislative business: but constitutional Bills were drafted in the Ministry of Law and were introduced by the Minister. There was no drafting committee, and the Draft Constitution was a Government Bill, carried through by the Government's majority and the use of the closure. Nevertheless, the second Assembly were a body of eighty persons with at least four groups and a considerable number of independents. Two of the groups

[43] See documents H1 and H2.
[44] C.P. Snow's novel *The Masters*, published in his *Strangers and Brothers* series in 1951.
[45] Keith B. Callard, author of scholarly books on Pakistan.

were Bengali, the Awami League led by Suharwardy and a United Front led by Fazlul Huq. In effect there was an unstable group system, which was even more apparent after the Constitution took effect. The Constituent Assembly became the National Assembly pending the enactment of an election law. It never was enacted, and the Assembly was dismissed by the coup d'état of 1958.

Ayub Khan, as President of Pakistan, enacted the present Constitution in March, 1962. It is based on what is called "basic democracy". Each of the two Provinces is divided into 40,000 units. In each unit an election, under adult suffrage, is held for an Elector, and the 80,000 Electors form an Electoral College which elects the President and also, when organized into constituencies, elects the National Assembly and the Provincial Assemblies.

The system of government is presidential, with a Council of Ministers not in the National Assembly and Parliamentary Secretaries in the Assembly. The Assembly has legislative powers, a limited financial power, and constituent powers by a two-thirds majority of all the members. The president has, however, power to appeal to the Electoral College by referendum. The President also has power to dissolve the National Assembly, but if he does he has to stand for re-election or cease to be President. The President is now a party politician, for he is president of the Muslim League which, evidently, controls a majority of the Electoral College and of the National Assembly.

Perhaps this is what Iskander Mirza meant when he spoke of "controlled democracy". There is a Government party and five Opposition parties. There is little likelihood of this coalescing. The Assembly has only 156 members, initially the same as the House of Representatives in Ceylon.

3. 'Some Asian prime ministers', 1955

Since they became independent in 1947, India, Pakistan and Ceylon have had eight Prime Ministers. I have known seven of them and have advised five. It will therefore be convenient for me, before my memory begins to mix fiction into fact, to set down what I know of them, even though the material cannot be published. I must, however, first explain how much, or how little, I know of them.

India has had the same Prime Minister for eight years. I have met Jawaharlal Nehru twice in Ceylon and once in India, but only at social functions, though on two occasions I had quite long talks with him. Such acquaintance helps enormously in the reading of newspapers, but my knowledge of his work came [*illegible*] from those newspapers.

Also, I have read Pakistani as well as Indian newspapers for nearly a year and have thus acquired a somewhat detached approach to his work.

Liaquat Ali Khan was Prime Minister of Pakistan from partition until his assassination in 1951. I can say all I know of him offhand, because it is very little. He has left a good reputation behind, though it is not clear how much of it is reflected glory from the Quaid-i-Azam, Muhammad Ali Jinnah, whose lieutenant Liaquat was until Jinnah died in September 1948. Certainly he had not the commanding personality of Jinnah, and by 1951 the Muslim League was beginning to split. At least there was enough opposition to induce Begum Liaquat to believe that his assassination was due to a conspiracy among his political opponents. This is, however, almost certainly an invention, which the Begum wants to believe because the other allegation is that her behaviour led, indirectly, to the assassination. Though she had been a Christian, she became Liaquat's second wife. She did not, however, accept the dependent status which the tradition of Islam imposes upon wives, but on the contrary led the agitation for the emancipation of women. This necessarily created antagonism to Liaquat among the conservative elements in the population, and particularly among the mullahs, whose political influence in an Islamic State is necessarily considerable. His assassin was, in fact, a person who believed that the corruption which he thought to be prevalent in Pakistan was a punishment for the sins of the leaders, and especially Liaquat, whose unveiled wife publicly took part in his political activities and encouraged the millat,[46] the people, to have his ways.

This story is relevant to the next part of the story. After the death of Liaquat, Khwaja Nazimuddin, who had been Governor-General since Jinnah's death, demanded that it was his duty to become Prime Minister. He formed a Government and recommended that the Minister of Finance in Liaquat's government, Ghulam Muhammad, should be Governor-General. Nazimuddin was a devout Muslim from East Bengal. Ghulam Muhammad was an almost equally devout Muslim from the Punjab. There was no dearth of suspicion about the private life of either. There was, however, the difference that Ghulam Muhammad had no considerable contact with the mullahs, whereas Nazimuddin was profoundly influenced by them. That influence arose from his devotion to Islam; but it was assisted by persons whose support of the mullahs may be alleged to be inspired by the part that the mullahs can play in elections, notably by two of his ministers, Sardar Abdul Ras Nishtar, whose name is not Nishtar and who is not a sardar,

[46] The Muslim religious community.

and Fazlur Rehman. I have met all these persons and have worked with all except Nazimuddin himself. Nazimuddin I know only because he is a member, and indeed an Honorary fellow, of Trinity Hall. He had ceased to be Prime Minister before I reached Pakistan and, though he remained a member of the first Constituent Assembly, he took no active part in politics. He was the titular leader of what was usually called the Nishtar group, which has now been dissolved as a political force and is represented in the second Constituent Assembly only by Fazlur Rehman. He secured Hindu votes in East Bengal and slipped in. Accordingly, though I had close contacts with the Nishtar group because it dominated the Drafting Committee of the first Constituent Assembly, my contacts with Nazimuddin have been purely social.

The Nishtar group wanted what was called an Islamic Constitution, and it put up a proposal which would in effect have enabled the mullahs to declare legislation ultra vires on the ground that it was repugnant to the Quran and the Sunnah. The proposal was strongly opposed in the Constituent Assembly, but it might have gone through had there not been other causes of complaint against the Nazimuddin Government. One was the rioting in the Punjab in 1953. It was a series of attacks by the orthodox Muslims, led by the mullahs, on the Ahmadiyyas, who are regarded as heretics because Ahmad in effect is claimed as a prophet, though according to orthodox Islam Muhammad was the last of the prophets. It was extremely weakly handled, both by the Central Government, of which Nazimuddin was Prime Minister, and by the local Governor, Chundrigar, who was one of the Nishtar group; and Lahore was in the hands of the rioters for several days. The causa causans,[47] however, was the fall in the prices of jute and cotton early in 1953. The government was too weak to handle such a problem, and Fazlur Rehman as Minister of Commerce, is alleged to have frittered away the foreign balances. Ghulam Muhammad, who had been not only Minister of Finance but also Professor of Economics, took the bit between his teeth, dismissed the government, and sent for Muhammad Ali, who put the problem into the hands of the present Prime Minister, Chaudhri Muhammad Ali.

It would perhaps be hazardous to say that too much religion is bad for a politician. Nazimuddin is, as I have said, a devout Muslim, Nishtar and Fazlur Rehman and less intelligent lawyers – or like Chundrigar, may be or not – I have no means for judging: but there is grave danger in the use of religion for political ends among a population whose low standard of life and lack of education make

[47] The last link in the chain of causation.

religion the only solace. It was said of George Lansbury[48] that his bleeding heart went to his bloody head. Religion can very easily become a danger. It can, as we saw in Lahore, lead to bloody heads in a different sense. It can be used by intelligent politicians to feather their own nests and secure their own power. Nazimuddin, I believe, was in no way corrupt; he was just impotent.

Muhammad Ali and Chaudhri Muhammad Ali I have been called upon to advise. I was, however, unable to establish personal relations with Muhammad Ali, for reasons which will appear; and accordingly I know less of him than I know of his successor.

Ceylon has had three Prime Ministers. D.S. Senanayake was Leader of the State Council – a near approach to being Prime Minister – from 1942 and was Prime Minister from 1948 until he fell from his horse and died in 1952. During the whole of that period I knew him very well, both officially and personally. His son Dudley, who was Prime Minister for eighteen months, I know mainly as his son, though I also advised him occasionally after he became Prime Minister. Sir John Kotelawala I knew both personally and as Minister from 1941 until he became Prime Minister at the end of 1953. I was out of the country so much in the last years of my service in Ceylon that most of my contacts with him during that year were social.

It may be significant that four of the eight Prime Ministers are Cambridge men – Nehru of Trinity, Nazimuddin of Trinity Hall, Dudley Senanayake of Corpus, and Kotelawala of Christ's. They are as diverse as a Cambridge man expects, and hopes, that Cambridge men will be. I should have regarded Chaudhri Muhammad Ali as a typical Cambridge man, if there were such a person: but in fact he was educated in the degree factory that used to be called the University of the Punjab. Even the worst type of Indian education, apparently, cannot spoil a good man. As it happens, I know quite well this Oxford man who just failed to become Prime Minister, S.W.R.D. Bandaranaike of Christ Church, and H.S. Suharwardy of Balliol.[49]

Banda, as he is usually called, has all the hallmarks of the Oxford Union Society. He speaks very fluently and very well though (like Nehru, at times) he never knows what he is going to say and probably does not remember what he did say. He comes from a family, or rather two families, which owe their power and prestige to British rule. The Bandaranaikes and the Obeysekeres[50] are both Christian families, and indeed the Obeysekeres are Cambridge men whose

[48] George Lansbury, British Labour Party leader, 1932–1935.

[49] Suharwardy had affiliations with St Catherine's College, University of Oxford.

[50] Prominent Sinhalese families in Colombo.

names are included in the annals of the C.U. Boxing Club, for several of them have been blues. These families, of whom the Bandaranaikes and Obeysekeres are two, have completely monopolised the office of Maha Mudaliyar[51] for 150 years. Old Sir Solomon,[52] father of S.W.R.D., was a "brown sahib", a Victorian gentleman who prided himself on his friendship with Queen Mary. His only son, the present Banda, was educated by English governesses until he reached the age of 16. This was clearly a mistake, for he would have much more common sense and knowledge of humanity if he had been knocked about at school – Christ Church did its best by dunking him in the pond soon after he arrived, a process which stimulated his antagonism of British rule. Later, Banda was sent to St. Thomas' College, the best Christian school, but he is not known as one of its most loyal alumni. At Oxford he became Junior Treasurer of the Union. On his return to Ceylon he became a Buddhist, but it should be said in his favour that he has never paraded his alleged Buddhism as Sir John Kotelawala does frequently. He also became a democrat, but this was a necessary reaction to his aristocratic upbringing, and in fact he has never been able to explain what he means by democracy.

I do not think I exaggerate when I say that as a Cabinet Minister Banda was the worst in the world. At Cabinet meetings he always arrived late, without having read his papers. He looked though the agenda and reopened all the questions already decided.

He spoke on every subject at great length, even though he knew nothing about it. On one occasion which I know about because the Cabinet was discussing a draft made by me, he kept the subject going for eight hours, and the only change made was the addition of four lines in the middle of a long draft. As Minister he had long conferences which apparently reached conclusions, but which never, or hardly ever, led to action. Perhaps this was because he had an indifferent staff, but he had an indifferent staff because he was Banda. They were nice fellows who could get on with anybody except an efficient Minister. Yet Banda almost became Prime Minister. He was much the best speaker in the House of Representatives, and probably still is. His reputation for oratory and cleverness was so great that he became Leader of the House, though the job was easy because D.S. Senanayake was always there and really did the management. Eventually D.S. Senanayake forced him to resign and then, to his astonishment, accepted his resignation. He went straight into Opposition; and so, when D.S.

[51] The highest native title and an office given by the British to selected elite Sri Lankan families.

[52] Sir Solomon Dias Bandaranaike.

died a few months later, the Governor-General sent not for Banda but for the dark horse, Dudley.

I am sorry to be so critical of an Oxford man. I can be kinder to the other Oxford man, H.S. Suharwardy. He was born in Bengal and educated at Calcutta before he went to Oxford, where he took both Jurisprudence Schools and the B.C.L. He was called to the Bar of Gray's Inn and went back to practise at the Calcutta Bar. At that time the Calcutta High Court enjoyed a high reputation, and success at the Bar was a high qualification. Suharwardy is not much of a lawyer, but he is a persuasive advocate. He was also successful in politics, eventually becoming Chief Minister. He had been active in the Muslim League and went to Pakistan after partition. He kept his feet in India, however, and when he went into Opposition to the Muslim League he was disqualified for membership of the Constituent Assembly. He then formed a party known as the Awami League but had a long illness from which he was recalled, after the dissolution of the first Constituent Assembly, to be Law Minister. He was, next to Chaudhri Muhammad Ali, the ablest Minister in Muhammad Ali's reformed Cabinet, which was, comparatively speaking, a Cabinet of high quality. What is more, in the second Constituent Assembly he was the only member of the Cabinet who could handle the legislature. Though really the weight of the Government rested upon Chaudhri Sahib, in public Suharwardy was the leader: and had it been possible for him to wait a little longer behind the façade which Muhammad Ali presented, he would almost certainly have become Prime Minister.

In one sense he was not a good administrator, because the constant succession of files bored him. His main job was to organise his party, and he had a constant succession of political callers and of persons asking for favours. He was a prominent social figure, frankly enjoying the numerous parties, public and private, to which he was invited. Hence he did most of his work in the small hours of the morning. Nevertheless, he took a point very quickly – far too quickly for the average administrator – and he put it persuasively.

Hence for matters of high importance – and my own work came mostly within that category – he was almost the perfect Minister. One told him what was wanted; he modified the proposal to make it politically acceptable; and then he got it through Cabinet and the legislature. For the ordinary matters of administration, which went no higher, he was not so good. He was impatient of explanation, disliked details of all kinds, was always late for an appointment, and never accessible in his office. It was not this, however, which lost him the office of Prime Minister. He had no political friends, though he had plenty of toadies and followers. He could not bear to have equals and, though he joined hands with Fazlul Huq to defeat the Muslim League in East Bengal, he quarrelled with him almost immediately. He spent too much of his time organising his own party in West Pakistan to please the Muslim League, but he could never attract any prominent Leaguers into his own party because it had to have only one leader. When it came to the point that he had not a single follower of Cabinet rank, he insisted on being Prime Minister because he was Suharwardy; with the proposed coalition between the Muslim League and the Awami League he would have brought Suharwardy and twelve dumb followers. The Muslim League badly wanted Suharwardy, but not at that price. So Oxford missed its first Prime Minister in this part of the world.

Let me turn to the Prime Ministers of whom I know something.

Nehru

Jawaharlal Nehru came from a distinguished Brahmin family settled in Kashmir. Brahmins are not popular among the English-educated in India, but they still have great prestige among the masses, whose lives are still dominated by religion and caste. On the other hand, Nehru's Brahminism does not annoy the bright young men from lower castes because he has long since suppressed his caste in his egalitarian nationalism. What is more, he proved his sincerity in the most difficult way, by allowing his daughter to marry a Sudra.[53] He then gains both ways; and I regret to have to say that I suspect he is not unaware of the fact. He was given the courtesy title of pandit because the males of his family always have been pandits; but I have seen no evidence that he is learned in the Vedas;[54] indeed his education at Harrow and Trinity, which was, oddly enough, the product of his father's nationalism, must have prevented him from acquiring any real background of Sanskrit learning. Nor has he acquired anything more than a superficial western culture. He is in fact a good example, perhaps the best example, of the nationalists of his generation. He is extremely fluent in English, so fluent that he rarely troubles to prepare his speeches and therefore does not always know what he is going to say until he has spoken for 10 or 20 minutes. He has a wide general knowledge, which he was able to increase during his periods of imprisonment under British rule. What is more, those friends enable him to work out a consistent philosophy of nationalism. It is not a profound philosophy; it is based on a superficial knowledge of English

[53] A caste group in India that is not within the Brahmin group to which the Nehrus belonged.

[54] Ancient Hindu scriptures in Sanskrit.

and Indian history; and it is highly coloured by the nationalism which he inherited from his father, Motilal Nehru.[55] Nevertheless he is able from time to time to read good professional lectures to the Indian National Congress. They carry little weight among the hard-boiled politicians who lead that organisation; they are invariably distorted when reported in Pakistan; and they are never read elsewhere. They may have some effect on the young men; but this is doubtful, for the third nationalist generation is apt to be cynical, particularly when it sees how many Congress politicians jumped on the bandwagon from 1940 onwards.

Nehru's strength, as well as his fundamental weakness, derives from the adulation which he receives from the masses. Let me mention the weakness first, because the strength has more complex elements. It is still difficult to believe that the great mass of the population of India had any objection to British rule. No Englishman can enjoy the prestige of the Brahmin, and in any case neither the Englishman who held high office in India nor the members of the Indian Civil Service could have much contact with the ordinary Indian villages or townsmen. The great tradition of that Service, which the Indians as well as the English members inherited, could not percolate into the lower ranks of the administration, which were probably not much less corrupt under British rule than they had been under Moghul rule or than they were in the Indian States. In any case the ordinary man knows no history. The village headman is the Vicar of Bray;[56] he continues like Tennyson's brook, and he is the man who matters. The man who did touch the masses was Mahatma Gandhi, not because he was a politician or a nationalist, but because he was a saint. Nehru was not only a Brahmin; he was also a devoted follower of Gandhiji, the father-in-law of Gandhi's son.[57] Wherever he goes he is met by adoring crowds, who are willing to break all police barriers in order to see, hear and if possible touch him. Sometimes he finds it a bore, as a film star must; but he is also a politician and he approves of it; he even likes it. His publicity managers do not need to arrange demonstrations, as the Hollywood press agent has to do; but his movements are carefully devised to obtain the maximum publicity for Jawaharlal Nehru. No human being can remain insensible to this adulation, and some of Nehru's characteristics are due to an exaggerated sense of his own merits, to which 350 million people are prepared to certify.

[55] Motilal Nehru, Indian lawyer and leading member of the Indian National Congress.

[56] The protagonist of a satirical eighteenth-century song, who changes his beliefs to match the monarch of the day.

[57] This is an astonishing error from Jennings as an expert on South Asia. Mahatma Gandhi was not related in any way to Nehru's son in-law Feroze Gandhi.

There is no doubt, I think, of the sincerity of Nehru's opinions, both political and social. He has, as I have said, an immensely consistent political philosophy for a politician because British rule compelled him to stop talking for lengthy periods and enabled him to do some thinking, in the highly emotional context of imprisonment in the most comfortable quarters that His Majesty could find. His problems derive from the fact that the Indian National Congress is not composed of philosophers. Most of the leaders of his own generation were sincere if misguided. Dr Rajendra Prasad, for instance, seems to be a nice old man rather of the George Lansbury type, though his bleeding heart led him without abilities on his part, to what used to be called Government House. Many of the slightly younger men, on the other hand, are just ambitious politicians. The anxiety of people for prestige is one of the political factors which has never been adequately studied. We in Britain seem to have solved it, as usual, by institutions. We have converted the peerage and the orders of knighthood into means for rewarding merit, or at least obvious merit. Anybody who does anything worth while gets letters after his name, and perhaps a rank before his name. Tom, Dick and Harry can become Lord Thomas, Sir Richard, and Mr Harry O.B.E. India, rather stupidly, has scrapped those insignias which are intrinsically valueless but in terms of prestige valuable. In India one has to be either a millionaire or a Minister. The prestige attached to Ministers is far higher than that attached to a K.C.I.E.,[58] or even a K.C.S.I.[59] One has a furnished home with a police sentry, a car with a flag on it, an armed guard, a [*illegible*] and a P.S.,[60] uniformed peons, and a claque of ordinary public servants and ambitious political followers. One can, too, render service to one's friends at the public's expense. The Minister who falls, falls into outer darkness. He even ceases to be Honourable. The prizes of office must be glittering because otherwise nobody would want them; but in India, and in Pakistan also – though as it happens much less so in Ceylon – they are perhaps too attractive.

What is more, the Congress lost its raison d'être with the attainment of independence. It is becoming gradually a party of the right caste, supported financially by the merchant princes of Calcutta and Bombay, but at present its main characteristic is that it provides a career for the ambitious. Since there are more ambitious people than seats to fill, and more seats than jobs, and since the average politician is by definition no better than the average, the Congress is dominated by petty intrigue and personal squabble which from time to time

[58] British honour of Knight Commander of the Most Eminent Order of the Indian Empire.
[59] British honour of Knight Commander of the Most Exalted Order of the State of India.
[60] Private secretary.

erupt into political crises. At the [*illegible*] level this is rarely important because Nehru makes his own selection, and few are powerful enough to defy him. At the state level he has constantly to be called in to settle disputes and to keep the Congress Ministries in power. He tried to pass on this job by resigning the office of President of Congress and having a full-time President appointed: but this has not much diminished his work because, if the dispute is fierce enough, he alone can settle it.

Nor can he avoid the intrusion of politics into his chosen field, that of international affairs. Here he lectures everybody else as he lectures his own people, though attention is often drawn to the fact that his government does not practise what it preaches. An armed invasion of Hyderabad, an independent State, is a "police action"; Kashmir is legally Indian because it acceded to India, though it has a Muslim majority; Junagadh and Manavadar acceded to Pakistan, but are Indian because they have Hindu majorities; Goa is Indian because it is part of the sub-continent. It is not easy to defend these actions in terms of Nehru's own principles. It should be remembered, however, that he is not quite a dictator, and anyhow that dictators have to be able to dictate. The aggressive nationalism which sought to force independence is still aggressive nationalism, even when it is exhibited in satyagraha.[61] If Nehru is aware of his inconsistency he has nevertheless to be inconsistent because he is surrounded by politicians who do not share his philosophy. I am not sure, however, that he is wholly aware of his inconsistency. His actions in Kashmir seem to show that he is aware of it, for it must have gone hard with him emotionally to accept the idea of a plebiscite, though he did accept it; and now his emotions as a Kashmiri Brahmin compel him to find excuses to not carrying out his undertaking. In respect of Goa he probably does not realise the inconsistency. Goa is not merely part of India; it is, in his terminology, a colony, and colonialism is the deadliest of the sins; nor does it matter that Portugal denies that it is a colony, for any person with a white face who claims a foothold in Asia is an imperialist. Hence there is no comparison at all between the Sudetenland[62] and Goa. The Sudetenland was a conflict between two independent States; Goa is a conflict between virtue, represented by India, and colonialism, represented by Portugal.[63] Nor is there a parallel in the conflict between communism and capitalism: they

[61] Gandhi's non-violent resistance philosophy.

[62] Referring to the German annexation of the Sudetenland region from Czechoslovakia in 1938.

[63] Portugal ruled the Indian enclave of Goa from 1510 until 1961, when the Indian Army annexed it after Portugal had refused offers to negotiate the territory's status peacefully.

are simply different forms of government, neither of them vicious or virtuous in itself.

Muhammad Ali [Bogra] and Chaudhri Muhammad Ali

There is no relationship between Muhammad Ali and Chaudhri Muhammad Ali, whom I propose to call Chaudhri. Muhammad Ali is a Bengali from a well-known family. Chaudhri is a Punjabi of quite lowly origin, who has worked his way up by merit and integrity.

Muhammad Ali was born in East Bengal in 1909. His grandfather, Nawab Ali Chowdhury, was the first Muslim to be appointed a Minister in undivided Bengal, and later he became a member of the Executive Council of the Government of India. Muhammad Ali graduated from Calcutta University in 1930 and entered politics almost at once, working his way up until in 1946 he became Minister of Finance in undivided Bengal. He opted for Pakistan and was elected to the Constituent Assembly from East Bengal. He was Ambassador to Burma in 1948, High Commissioner to Canada in 1949, and Ambassador to the United States in 1952. He was recalled in 1953 to become Prime Minister on the dismissal of Nazimuddin by Ghulam Muhammad. Within six months a vacancy occurred in the Constituent Assembly through the death of a member, and the Muslim League majority of the East Bengal Legislative Assembly elected him to fill the vacancy. That majority disappeared at the general election in April 1954, but Muhammad Ali was re-elected in 1955 by means of United Front votes. He is therefore the only Muslim League member from East Bengal, and there are only five members of the League in the East Bengal Legislative Assembly, which contains 309 members.

It will be seen that Muhammad Ali has no political backing worth mentioning. He became Prime Minister because Ghulam Muhammad who is a Punjabi, wanted a Bengali as Prime Minister, and one not associated with the Nazimuddin faction. He returned to the Assembly in 1953 only because the Muslim League, as a body, decided to support Ghulam Muhammad. He was elected in 1955 only because he had done a deal with Fazlul Huq whereby Sarkar, who was Huq's deputy, became Chief Minister in East Bengal, in return for which the United Front supported his re-election. It could not have been a coincidence that Suharwardy had been sent to London to contact me. The dissolution of the Constituent Assembly in October 1954 was effected by Ghulam Muhammad, without the knowledge or comment of the Prime Minister, while Muhammad Ali was in the United States. Arrangements were made for his return by R.A.F. plane; but Muhammad Ali refused to accept these arrangements and chartered a special B.O.A.C.[64] plane. On his arrival in Karachi he was met with a Government House car with a military escort and taken straight to Government House, while Begum Muhammad Ali, who wished to accompany him, was escorted to the Prime Minister's house. Five hours later, at 2 a.m., it was notified that Muhammad Ali had agreed to reconstruct his government. So far as is known, he had consulted no-one in the interval, and it may be that he was not allowed to meet anybody.

From November 1954, when I returned to Karachi on instructions from the Governor-General, to April 1955 all major decisions were given effect to by documents drafted by me. On no occasion did I receive instructions from Muhammad Ali. Sometimes they came direct from the Governor-General, sometimes from the Cabinet – over which the Governor-General himself presided when matters of importance were under discussion – sometimes from Chaudhri, who was Minister of Finance, and sometimes from Suharwardy as Law Minister. On one important occasion they came from Gurmani, Governor of the Punjab, who was then staying at Government House. Chaudhri was in frequent consultation with the Governor-General, and on two or three occasions he told me to ignore instructions from the Governor-General because he would get them changed – and he did. There was no lack of contact between the Governor-General and the Prime Minister; but I do not think he had the slightest influence on the course of events. The Governor-General took advice from Chaudhri, General Iskander Mirza (Minister of the Interior), Gurmani, and occasionally others. The Prime Minister was "consulted" regularly, but that word has to be placed in quotation marks because, so far as I could see, he was told what to do and not asked for advice as to what should be done. Effectively the Governor-General was the Prime Minister, and Muhammad Ali was a convenient Bengali façade.

It may seem surprising that the Prime Minister should accept so ignominious a position. One reason, and perhaps the most important, was that he was intellectually out of his depth. He did not know what to do in the different positions in which his Government found itself. Chaudhri and Suharwardy did know what to do; or, if they did not, they soon found out. The Governor-General exercised an overriding power of decision, and sometimes he made serious mistakes; but Chaudhri then persuaded him to change his mind. When I returned to Karachi in June, the Governor-General was hors de combat. He had had a serious relapse in May, soon after I left, and had gone to Europe for treatment. When he returned in July he was such a sick man that

[64] British Overseas Airways Corporation.

he was incapable of taking decisions. Ordinary Cabinet government was thus restored. It happened that I was summoned to Cabinet meetings frequently at this stage: I was not present for the discussions of purely political issues, but my Bills had high political importance and there were other issues on which professional advice was needed. The Prime Minister did not speak very much, but when he did speak he had nothing to say. I do not remember a single significant remark. He was listened to politely and then politely ignored. The effective decisions were taken by Chaudhri, in the course of cross-talk with Suharwardy, interspersed by suitable comments by me. In short, the Prime Minister was a nonentity.

The fact that he was a nonentity, however, made him stick to office more firmly. Chaudhri was not trying to push him out; he was simply doing his job for him because somebody had to do it. When Muhammad Ali did at last resign, Chaudhri suggested that Suharwardy should become Prime Minister. As I shall explain presently, Chaudhri has certain defects, and he was obviously aware of them; and he had no wish for the semi-regal trappings with which Asia supplies its Prime Ministers. On the other hand Muhammad Ali, being fundamentally third-rate, enjoyed them. He liked his large house, his armed escort, his State visits to other countries, the sense of power. Moreover he had an ambitious social secretary, Aliya, who became his second wife; but I must mention her presently.

Pakistan is an odd country, and it is even odder to one who has lived in Ceylon. In Ceylon there are no secrets: everything appears in the newspapers, sometimes before it has happened. Gossip is the greatest industry, and the newspapers thrive on gossip. In Pakistan, as a Pakistani once put it to me, something must be happening if there is nothing in the newspapers. So far as I am aware, not a word of comment or criticism about Muhammad Ali's weakness or incapacity appeared in the press until several days after his resignation, and then only incidentally in a couple of leading articles in praise of Chaudhri. Nevertheless, the fact was known in political circles. Muhammad Ali was known to be a mere façade for personal government by Ghulam Muhammad.

No doubt a Prime Minister who cannot measure up to his job can continue for a long time if he has popular support. I have already explained that, after April 1954, Muhammad Ali had no support at all in his own Province; nor had he acquired any in West Pakistan. Had he produced something spectacular, such as a decision on Kashmir, things might have been different: but everybody suspected that he was a child in negotiation with Nehru, who is regarded in Pakistan as the devil incarnate. Muhammad Ali was a poor speaker and in fact made few speeches. He was known to drink whiskey and his relations with

Aliya were suspect. Then he was foolish enough to marry Aliya as his second wife.

Begum Ali, his first wife, was not in purdah, but she did not make herself into a public figure like the second Begum Liaquat, or even Begum Chaudhri. She is a quiet, domesticated and charming middle-aged woman who could hold her own at a dinner-table – though she entertained rarely – or at big receptions. Everybody who knew her liked her, and most knew, or at least suspected, that she had done a great deal to forward her husband's causes, especially as a diplomat. Begum Aliya, the second wife, is a Canadian citizen of Lebanese origin, and presumably a Muslim. I have never said more than "good morning" to her, but she seems to be a pert and moderately attractive young woman. The circumstances in which Islam permits second marriages are not well defined, though it is agreed that a second marriage is permissible where the first produces no children. This could not apply to Muhammad Ali, for he has two sons at Marlborough.[65] Anyhow, the Prime Minister decided to brave public opinion. He arranged a meeting of ambassadors at Geneva, without anybody being able to explain this unusual conference. He flew in via Beirut, and married Aliya there. There was an immediate storm in Karachi, which increased when the first Begum Ali went into purdah and Begum Aliya appeared in public as the Prime Minister's wife. Whatever Islam says about polygamy, it does not say that the second wife may replace the first, but only that both wives must be treated equally. Others had done the same, including General Iskander Mirza, who had married a Persian: but this was flaunting their inferior status and insecure position in the faces of all the women of Islam; and in Pakistan, unlike many Muslim countries, women have the vote.

A reconstruction of the Government was inevitable in August 1955 because eight of the fourteen Ministers had failed to get seats in the second Constituent Assembly and because the Muslim League could not command a majority unless it had the support of one of the Bengali factions, either the United Front or the Awami League. Moreover, Ghulam Muhammad was too ill to say anything; in fact he could neither speak nor write. The Cabinet therefore agreed that Iskander Mirza should become Acting Governor-General. Iskander had been reasonably discreet about Muhammad Ali, but he had been in the Cabinet for ten months and knew that he did not count. Muhammad Ali already had his own scheme. He was to be Prime Minister in a coalition between the Muslim League and the United Front. Chaudhri had a more sensible scheme; Suharwardy was to be Prime Minister in a coalition between the Muslim League and

[65] A leading public school in England.

the Awami League. Both miscalculated. At the party meeting before the reassembly of the Constituent Assembly, Muhammad Ali found that he had no support at all. He left the meeting after an hour, and the meeting elected Chaudhri as leader, on the understanding that he would negotiate a coalition with the Awami League under Suharwardy as Prime Minister. Suharwardy insisted that half the Cabinet be Bengali, and he thought he could bring at least five of the 16 members of the United Front. Fazlul Huq was, however, too clever for him. He suggested that Chaudhri become Prime Minister with United Front support. For the Muslim League this was a much more attractive proposition. If Suharwardy became Prime Minister, the Awami League would split the vote in West Pakistan, and perhaps destroy the Muslim League there as it had already been destroyed in East Pakistan. If Fazlul Huq came in, the Muslim League would win West Pakistan, while the United Front and the Awami league would split East Pakistan. Chaudhri wanted a tripartite coalition to get the Draft Constitution through; but Suharwardy insisted on being Prime Minister and Fazlul Huq insisted on Chaudhri being Prime Minister. The Muslim League preferred the lesser evil, and so Chaudhri took office with Suharwardy in the Opposition.

Chaudhri was born in 1905 in East Punjab, and so technically he is a refugee from India. He had a brilliant academic career in the University of the Punjab coming first in the first class in every examination up to the M.Sc. He was for some time Lecturer in Chemistry at the Islamia College, Lahore, but Government service was too attractive for him and he entered the Indian Audit and Accounts Service by competitive examination in 1928. After only four years he was despatched to Bahawalpur State, the largest State now in Pakistan, as Accountant-General. He cleared up the finances of the State and was recalled to the Government of India in 1936. Two years later he was Under-Secretary, Finance Department, and by 1945 he was Financial Adviser, Military Finance and Supply. At partition, he was a member of the steering committee of the Partition Council, which made the complicated financial arrangements, and he had thus became Secretary-General to the Government of Pakistan, or in other words head of the public service. On the assassination of Liaquat Ali Khan in 1951, Nazimuddin became Prime Minister, Ghulam Muhammad replaced Nazimuddin as Governor-General, and Chaudhri replaced Ghulam Muhammad as Minister of Finance.

It will be seen that Chaudhri is essentially an administrator, and a very successful one. He reads his papers very thoroughly and he masters them: that is, he finds the weak spots immediately. He is, however, extraordinarily popular with the abler members of his staff, because he makes suggestions so modestly: "Would it be better if we could . . . ", "Do you think we might . . . ", "Would it be possible . . . ", and so forth, are his phrases. Nor are his interests limited to finance. In the litigation which followed the dissolution of October 1954[66] there was a conflict of opinions among counsel which could be settled only at political level: and Chaudhri settled it. In the subsequent legislation, his view was often better than Suharwardy's, because he saw the political implications. Moreover, it was Chaudhri who gave me instructions about the Draft Constitution. At this stage, indeed, I could not make out the constitutional position at all. Suharwardy was my Minister, but often I was dealing most with the Minister of Finance. I assumed, correctly, that Chaudhri was speaking for the Governor-General; but the position was not very different after Ghulam Muhammad fell ill. The expectations then became clear. Chaudhri was in fact Prime Minister and Muhammad Ali was a mere figurehead.

This may give the impression of a dominating and even domineering person. If so, this impression is false. Chaudhri was quiet and modest, never putting himself forward, but he was the man to whom everybody turned for a decision. On the other hand, he did not take decisions until he had heard the argument. Suharwardy jumped to a conclusion, and sometimes we had to argue him out of it. If Chaudhri saw that I was hesitating, he stopped the discussion and asked for my opinion. He never came to Cabinet with his mind made up: if he thought something was wrong, or could be improved, he never said, "I think": what he did say was "H.M. Law"[67] or "Sir Ivor", or whoever was most concerned with the question, "does this mean that . . . ?" Having heard the explanation, he would ask if it would not be better to modify the proposal along certain lines. Sometimes he had pitched on a weakness which we had ourselves noticed; sometimes he brought out a weakness for the first time. Quite often, if the proposal came from me, and I was sitting behind Suharwardy, we simply worked it out across the table at a pace which, so far as I could see, only Suharwardy could follow; and sometimes we even left him behind. In short, Chaudhri had a first-class intellect without the arrogance which often goes with it. He could sometimes remain silent for ten minutes while discussion went on. He would then say "it seems to me that . . . "; and that was the Cabinet's decision.

Much of his strength lay in the fact that he had no ambition and no axe to grind. He was simply doing his job, and the Prime Minister's as well because Muhammad Ali was incapable of doing it. All this

[66] See documents H1 and H2.

[67] Honourable Minister of Law.

was quite unknown outside the Cabinet, except to a very small circle. He never made public speeches and he gave no interviews to the press, except when some new financial policy had to be explained, and then he had a formal press conference. In fact, he hated making speeches of any kind. On the other hand, he could give masterly lectures. One day at the end of a long Cabinet he said that he would like to make a few observations before the Cabinet adjourned. In twenty minutes, without a note, he gave a complete and convincing explanation of Pakistan's financial position, with particular reference to a proposal then before the Cabinet. At the end there was a pause: then Suharwardy broke in: "What you mean," he said, "is that we shall be bankrupt". "That", replied Chaudhri, "is exactly what I do mean."

The Ceylonese Prime Ministers

It will be plain that I regard Chaudhri Muhammad Ali as a very remarkable man. D.S. Senanayake was even more remarkable because he was unique. He had more of Chaudhri's intellectual capacity. In the academic sense he had no brains at all; but he had a fund of common sense and a remarkable intuition.

The United National Party, which D.S. founded, is of course referred to as U.N.P., and this name is guyed in Ceylon as the "Uncles' and Nephews' Party". D.S. Senanayake, Dudley Senanayake and Richard Senanayake[68] were members of the same Cabinet. Kotelawala and J.R. Jayewardene, Kotelawala's rival, are cousins of Senanayake. The Speaker, Sir Francis Molamure,[69] and the owner of the powerful newspaper, D.R. Wijewardene,[70] were relatives. Lady Molamure[71] and another Kotelawala were in the Senate, and there was a third Kotelawala in the House of Representatives. They are all of the highest caste govigama,[72] but they are regarded by the other families, the de Sarams, the Bandaranaikes and the Obeysekeres, as upstarts. They seem to have got their wealth from plumbago mining; the profit they invested in cocoanut estates, though the Molamures and the Kotelawalas also bought tea and rubber.

The older Senanayake, who made the money, had three sons of whom D.S. was the youngest. They all went to the best Christian

[68] Richard G. Senanayake, nephew of D.S. Senanayake and UNP minister; Minister of Trade and Commerce, 1952–1956.

[69] Sir Francis Molamure, Speaker of the Ceylon House of Representatives, 1947–1951.

[70] Don Richard Wijewardene, press baron and ally of the UNP.

[71] Adeline, Lady Molamure, wife of Sir Francis Molamure; first female member of the pre-independence legislature; member of the Senate afterwards.

[72] The highest Sinhalese caste group.

school, St. Thomas' College[73] and, by some schoolboy freak, they were all known as "John", with an adjective. D.S. was known as "Kaley John" or "Jungle John", apparently because he was hairy, as strong as a horse, and as tough as a mule. The plumbago miners were the toughest, wildest, and most obstreperous labourers in Ceylon. Once, when they had taken the fiery local liquor, arrack, they started rioting, using pick handles. D.S. seized a pick handle himself and went in among them. "Come on", he said in Sinhalese, "let's fight this out". They threw down their weapons and went down the mine. When James Griffiths[74] was Colonial Secretary, D.S. told him that he too was a miner, but he did not explain that his methods were very different from those of the Mineworkers' Federation.

D.S. played cricket quite well, but never passed Matriculation, almost a sin in Ceylon. He became a clerk in the Survey Department, over which ultimately he became Minister, but his father decided that he had not the brains for Government service and accordingly he was sent to look after the family's mines and estates. He became a progressive farmer, introducing new breeds of stock and new methods of cultivation. He also got on very well with the villagers because he had none of the arrogance of the English-educated, knew and talked to anybody, helped them out of difficulties, and so forth. He had no interest in politics until 1915, but he did take part in the temperance movement; that was not politics but Buddhism. He was no philosopher, but he accepted the simple tenets of Buddhist philosophers and did his best to observe them.

In 1915 riots broke out in Kandy because of the playing of Buddhist drums before a mosque during Ramadan. The Muslims attacked the procession and the Buddhists retaliated by sacking Muslim shops. The riots spread over a large part of the Island. No doubt they were not purely religious, for rice was scarce and expensive and the Muslims were the middlemen. The situation was however extremely badly handled by the Governor, who proclaimed martial law and armed the planters, some of whom, as a Royal Commission found afterwards, exercised their powers in a most military manner. The Sinhalese leaders involved in the temperance movement did their best at once to stop the rioting and to protect the villagers against the planters. In return many of them, including D.S., were arrested. He always took his imprisonment as a great joke, for he soon made friends with his gaolers. The imprisonment did, however, turn his mind to politics, and he was elected to the Legislative Council on the Congress ticket in 1921. In 1931 he became Minister of Agriculture and retained that

[73] A leading school for boys in Colombo.

[74] James Griffiths, British Labour minister; Secretary of State for the Colonies, 1950–1951.

office until he became Prime Minister in 1947, when his son Dudley kept the office in the family.

His success as Minister is possibly a matter for argument. There is something to be said for the view that a farmer ought not to be Minister of Agriculture. He had one dominant passion, to restore the irrigation systems of ancient Ceylon, a most expensive process which became more and more expensive when the initial scheme seemed to be a failure. He was therefore in constant conflict with the Governor and the three officials, whom he called the three policemen, who formed part of the Board of Ministers under the 1931 Constitution. Nor did he get on well with most of his experts, many of whom resigned and found jobs elsewhere. He did not, however, mind obstacles, human or otherwise: he simply removed them. On the other hand, when once he found somebody whom he thought he could trust, he did so without reservation. I was one such, and so I have a very high opinion of him; but there are others, including at least two Governors, who regarded him as a menace.

One of his difficulties was that he was very inarticulate, especially in English. He made very poor speeches, and he could not even read a speech in such a way as to make it sound intelligent. I wrote some of his more important speeches, and once I spent a whole evening making him rehearse. I was in the gallery next day and the speech was a complete flop; but it read very well in the newspapers the next day. In private he was equally inarticulate, and his instructions often took the form of quotes or clichés like "'S matter of fact" or "I meant to say". At this his familiar, Sir Oliver Goonetilleke, had to translate: but I personally soon got to be able to read his mind. He was, too, very impulsive. As I have already mentioned, he had a remarkable intuition, but sometimes it led him astray. Nor could he be persuaded to revoke decisions very easily. Once when he was clearly wrong Sir Oliver had to work on him for a whole week; and this decision was important because it would undoubtedly have led to controversy with the United Kingdom. On the other hand, he was usually right. With I think one exception, I drafted every formal document sent by the Ceylon Ministers to the Secretary of State between 1943 and 1948. He let me put things in my own way until he came to a phrase which might be misinterpreted or which might have pledged the Ministers too far. Then he broke in with a grunt and a cliché: almost immediately I could see what was wrong and yet I had carefully thought over that memorandum, whereas he had merely heard it read once. I am told that even in matters of finance he was equally quick.

After D.S. became Prime Minister he dominated the Government and the legislature as Nehru does in India, and yet he had nothing of Nehru's slick facility with words and ideas. He was just a kind-hearted old farmer who could distinguish between a thoroughbred and a hawk, whether human or otherwise. He was a diabetic who kept himself alive with insulin until his heart gave out, and he died as he would have wished, riding a spirited horse which he had been advised by his doctors not to ride.

On his death, two of the uncles and nephews were candidates for the succession, Sir John Kotelawala and Mr J.R. Jayewardene. Actually, D.S. had already demanded that his son Dudley should be his successor. Knowing that D.S. might die at any moment, Lord Soulbury had taken the precaution of asking him. It seemed a good appointment. Dudley was as honest as his father, and intellectually a good deal abler. He had passed from St. Thomas' College to Corpus,[75] where he had done nothing astonishing; but, unlike his father, he could write a memorandum or make a speech.[76]

4. 'Constitution-making in Arcady', undated

The development of the British dependencies towards independence led to the rise of the Constitution-makers. The legal advisers at the Colonial Office did most of the work; but not all the countries concerned were under the control of the Colonial Secretary and not all colonial politicians wanted to rely exclusively on the Colonial Office. Quite often several persons were involved as legal advisers to different groups or as members of a commission. Sometimes they acted in succession, building on (though often modifying) each other's work. Rarely could a Constitution-maker produce a Constitution with the label which the pavement-artists of London used to use, "All my own work". Indeed, no draftsman likes to work alone. There are often fierce battles which nobody ever hears about – two draftsmen facing each other across a table picking holes in a draft which one of them has made – and they may go on for weeks.

One must not tell the secrets of the conference, the Cabinet, or the party. It is easier to try to imagine the production of the Constitution of a mythical country called Arcady by a mythical draftsman called Wilkins. Arcady will be unrecognizable because the story will be pure fiction.

Wilkins was not entirely ignorant about Arcady before he went there. His field of study and practice included it. As soon as the Chief Minister's letter reached him he took down the reference books

[75] Corpus Christi College, University of Cambridge.

[76] Unfortunately the manuscript ends here and does not continue to cover, as Jennings promises, Dudley Senanayake and Sir John Kotelawala.

and looked them through; then he went round to the library to see what else he could find. Actually, he found little except travellers' tales, sportsmen's recollections, and anthropologists' exercises. How the people of Arcady lived, worked and thought had never attracted the authors: and that was what Wilkins wanted to know. Any lawyer can draft a Constitution for anywhere: the difficulty is to persuade people to make it work.

Early in his career Wilkins had tried to plan for fifty years. Later, he lowered his sights. If a Constitution could be made to work for fifteen or twenty years it would probably go on working, in some fashion or other, for a long time. Wilkins would not be able to foresee the political, social and economic changes in Arcady for fifty years even if he knew Arcady well. Knowing little of Arcady, but having studied patterns elsewhere, he could foresee some of the early difficulties.

By what Wilkins would call professionally the transitional clauses, political power would be transferred, to put it in legal terms, from Her Majesty's Government in the United Kingdom to Her Majesty's Government in Arcady (it makes no difference, except to the draftsman, whether it is to be Her Majesty's Government in Arcady or the Government of the Republic of Arcady – becoming a republic is a gesture, like wearing a dinner jacket). What the formula means is that British officials would transfer power to local politicians. Those politicians would be those who had led the struggle for independence. They would be drawn from the English-educated middle classes; they would be combined with the highest nationalist ideals. On the other hand, Wilkins could assume that a good many people had jumped on the band-waggon and would be disappointed if they did not get good jobs, that political leaders were at least as likely to quarrel in Arcady as anywhere else, that nobody had worked out a post-independence policy for social and economic development, and that the nationalism of the political leaders was shared by only a thin layer of the people. All these characteristics raised problems which would be in Wilkins' mind while he was advising committees and drafting documents. The more he knew about their local application the better.

Among those who met Wilkins at the Arcady airport was a lawyer whom we will call Henrico. He had been assigned to help Wilkins as "junior". Wilkins welcomed him with open arms. Henrico was a barrister of Lincoln's Inn; and in the English tradition all lawyers are brothers – they could not fight each other so fiercely and dine together afterwards if they were not. Henrico's job was not merely to help Wilkins but also to give him local colour. He knew a good deal about his own people; he knew the local laws; he had worked with the politicians and knew their foibles. What is more, he would be able to criticise Wilkins' drafts. When two lawyers work together their job is to disagree until they agree. That is to say, they argue with each other until they convince themselves. What they then decide is probably right, for the decision has been examined from all angles.

Henrico's first task was to give Wilkins a set of papers showing what had already been done. He told him that there was a committee of the Cabinet to which Wilkins would be the principal adviser. Henrico explained who they were and what hobby-horses they rode. They had fixed a meeting for the next morning, though at this stage they wanted to do no more than give him their general ideas. As Henrico prepared to leave Wilkins asked him to get the latest Census Report. This request surprised Henrico, but the Census Report was the fundamental document, though Wilkins confessed that he had been to countries where even this was not available.

Arcady is a unit of government only because of British rule. Like the people of England, the people of Arcady derive from centuries of migration. The migrations of the Europeans to most parts of the world, the migration of the Chinese to other parts of Asia and far beyond, and the migration of Asians, Africans and West Indians to Europe, are merely the latest events in a long historical process. Where a mixed population has had firm government for centuries, as in England, a homogeneous people is formed by inter-marriage. Where firm government is very recent, as in Arcady, the population will be divided by race, religion, language, caste, or tribe. In some countries the euphemism "community" is employed, and sectionalism of any kind is called "communalism". For instance, everybody in Arcady knows that a Bigender has not the slightest chance of getting elected for a particular constituency because he does not belong to the right community or, to put it more bluntly, the constituency contains a substantial majority of Littlenders and few of them would vote for a Bigender.

The Census Report is not always very explicit about these communal differences, but it is usually the best source available. Nor would Wilkins hear much about communalism from the people whom he was advising. They were by definition strong nationalists, who were in principle opposed to communalism, and they thought that the whole population had the same nationalist ideas as they had. This was a fallacy, because nationalism was imported from Europe; it was therefore strongly entrenched only in the English-educated middle-class; but it was an amiable fallacy. Wilkins had also to remember that the politicians had come together to get power from the British. As a cynical Constitution-maker (not Wilkins) once put it: they knew that they must not start dividing up the swag before they got it.

Such communal differences as there were among the political leaders would therefore not appear prominently. If, however, one politician proved to be particularly obstinate in argument over a particular point, Henrico might be able to supply the explanation in a whisper, "He's a Littlender".

It was obvious that the way in which the Constitution of Arcady would work after independence depended on the fact that the population was divided communally into Bigenders and Littlenders. This was, however, only one of the facts of life that Wilkins had to know. Not all of them would be in the Census Report and he would have to pick up a good deal of information as he went along.

It became plain at the first meeting of the Cabinet committee that the Arcadians had already agreed on the outlines of a scheme. The Littlenders had at first wanted their own show in a section of Arcady in which they would have a majority. They had suggested a federal Constitution with two States, or alternatively a unitary Constitution like that of the United Kingdom, with a separate Parliament for the Littlenders like that of Northern Ireland. The Chief Minister, who had had ample opportunity of studying constitutional law while he had been in prison for political offences, had suggested that perhaps a separate system of local government and a separate judiciary would do. He appealed to the patriotism of the Littlenders and the well-known tendency (though it is extraordinary [*sic*] difficult to prove) of the British to "divide and rule". He pointed out that the Scots ruled Scotland as Scots and England as Britons, though the English were in a majority. The Littlenders were not certain that the Bigenders would be as complacent as the English, especially when the question of jobs for the boys came up. However, they were willing to consider a Scottish solution if Wilkins would produce a draft. Wilkins, who had never produced a Scotland before, was glad to oblige.

On the other hand, the Bigenders insisted on "one man, one vote". They laid no emphasis on the fact that this would undoubtedly give the Bigenders a majority in Parliament. They spoke rather of the advantages of democracy, which the Chief Minister defined as "government of the people, by the people, for the people". He stressed "by the people" and made his customary speech about the "poor villager". Wilkins was more dubious about this. He knew that if the poor villager got the vote he would probably get what he really wanted, which was more land: but the breaking-up of large estates was not an unmixed blessing, for it usually resulted in a fall of agricultural production, a lowering of the standard of living, and a reduction in the reverence of Arcady. He thought, too, that if the urban labourer had the vote he would almost certainly demand higher wages. Wilkins was, however, not an economist, and he found it difficult to persuade the Ministers to talk about the close relations of economics and politics. ("We are not interested in economics", said the Chief Minister, "We are interested in power".) He therefore pointed out that Britain had taken years to achieve "one man, one vote". ("We have to move faster in Arcady", said the Chief Minister.) He suggested that a very wide franchise led to demagoguery and corruption. He even wondered if the sort of people who were then Ministers would be elected in ten years' time. He was a democrat, and he hoped to see "one man, one vote" in Arcady, but he thought they ought to reach it by stages. The Ministers were, however, obdurate. The Chief Minister closed the discussion by saying, "We can trust our people".

Next day, Wilkins and Henrico set to work. In two weeks they had a draft, but it took them three months to get it through the Cabinet Committee, the Cabinet, and the Legislative Assembly. It was acclaimed by the people of Arcady. The Secretary of State, when informing the House of Commons that the Constitution had the approval of Her Majesty's Government, spoke with appreciation of the single-minded patriotism of the Arcadian Ministers and their anxiety to follow the best British traditions, including (he added to resounding cheers) the creation of a second Scotland. He fixed the 5th November as Independence Day, partly because it enabled him to make a joke about Guy Fawkes, but mainly because it was the Chief Minister's birthday.

There were great rejoicings on the 5th November, and Wilkins was there to receive the Independence Medal. He accepted it with pleasure, for he had enjoyed working with the Arcadians, though he did mention in his speech that making a Constitution was easy and that what was difficult was to make it work efficiently. Privately he wondered whether the poor villager and the urban labourer expected rather more than a march-past of schoolboys and schoolgirls, a firework display, and a vote: and what would happen if they did. The Chief Minister (who had now become Prime Minister) was well aware of the problem. He was a little worried by the development of an Opposition, which suggested that the Bigenders had had a raw deal, that no provision had been made for the Arcadianisation of the public service, that the wages of all labourers ought to be doubled, and that estates of more than 500 acres should be divided up so as to give the villagers more land. However, he thought that he could win the next election on his prestige as the Father of Independence, and also the one after that, provided that London and Washington (and if necessary Moscow) made generous grants to Arcady as one of the under-developed countries. He agreed with Wilkins that, if his party could get through the third general election, the future of Arcady as a democratic country would be reasonably assured. That, after all, was his patriotic object: and, whatever happens, he himself will go down to history as one of the world's greater statesmen.

Let it be emphasised that this story is pure fiction. Truth is always much more complex: but it is the kind of thing that might happen.

5. 'Constitution-making', undated

To the question, when is a people fit for self-government, the answer is, never. You have only to watch the behaviour of British politicians during a general election to raise doubts whether the British people are not fit for self-government. They are fitter than most peoples, but it is always a question of degree. Self-government cannot be refused to the British dependency, Arcadia, on the grounds that the Arcadians are not fit for self-government. You can say only that they are not fit enough.

To the question, when can power be transferred to the people of Arcadia – that is, when can British rule and jurisdiction be withdrawn – the answer is, as soon as an acceptable substitute to British rule has been provided. The process of government, whether in a democracy or in a dictatorship, depends upon confidence. By that I mean the confidence of a citizen in the behaviour of his fellow-citizens. We slept in our own beds last night because we were confident that the vast majority of the people of Britain would obey the law. We have gone about our business today on the assumption that our fellow-citizens would behave not only lawfully but normally, that the buses would be running, traffic would keep to the left, the shops would be open and shopkeepers would exchange goods for currency notes, and so forth. We are here tonight because we assume that the life of England seems normal and that our own families are safe at home. A slight deviation from the normal, such as a bus strike or a hold-up in Piccadilly, will not break down confidence. Law and order, in the broad sense, continue to prevail. On the other hand, since law and order depend on confidence, anarchy is only just round the corner. It was touch-and-go during the General Strike of 1926, though efficient government and the common sense of the British people saw us through. Before Hitler's War an organisation had to be set up in case intensive bombing put essential services out of action and destroyed public morale. In April 1942 public morale broke down in Colombo but imaginative government under Defence Regulations prevented the break-down from being complete – for instance, Sir Oliver Goonetilleke called out the Audit Department to reopen the cook-shops. In Singapore in 1956, when the Chinese schoolboys rioted, a sort of law and order was maintained under martial law and morale was quickly restored. In Ceylon in

1958 inefficient government led to a breakdown, and there would have been complete chaos if Sir Oliver Goonetilleke had not taken over.

The best, and from our present point of view, the most relevant example in the Commonwealth occurred in India in 1947. The transfer of power was insufficiently prepared, with the result that many millions of people lost confidence in the maintenance of law and order, and it was restored only after several weeks. Palestine provided another example whose consequences are still with us. The lessons seem to have been learned; and nowadays the British Government tries to slow up the process of transfer of power so as to get the people concerned used to the idea of a change of government. Nigeria supplies an admirable example. The Belgian Government, on the other hand, had not sufficiently studied British colonial history; and the example of the Congo is not to be followed.

The process of Constitution-making is part of the process of transferring power. It has, however, a long-term objective as well as a short-term one. Strictly speaking, "long-term" means forever. The Constitution sets Arcadia on the road of constitutional government which leads to eternity. In fact, lawyers, nobody knows what Arcadia will be like even in fifteen years' time, i.e. after the third general election. This is the important election, because by that time the Arcadian Democratic Party, whose success in attaining independence we all celebrate, will probably have broken up. The prestige of the Arcadian equivalent of Nehru, Nkrumah[77] or the Tunku[78] may still keep the party together for that election, but it is unlikely that he will last twenty years.

Even so, the draftsman has not the gift of prophecy. I cannot now be sure, but probably it did occur to me in 1943 that S.W.R.D. Bandaranaike might become Prime Minister of Ceylon, and I know that he was, officially at least, a communalist. I am, however, quite sure that I did not foresee the communal tensions to which politicised agitation would give rise. In fact, I took my views of the Sinhalese villages from D.S. Senanayake and other English-speaking Sinhalese, and events have proved them to be wrong. Nor did I foresee the coup d'état engineered by Generals Iskander Mirza and Ayub Khan in Pakistan, though in the Sudan I did suggest that the formulation of the President of the Republic as Commander-in-Chief of the armed forces ought to be labour saving. I do not give that as an example of prescience, for I know very little about the Sudan and I was simply

[77]Kwame Nkrumah, first Prime Minister of the independent realm of Ghana, 1957–1960; President of the Republic of Ghana, 1960–1966.

[78]The Malayan leader Tunku Abdul Rahman.

working on general principles. Nor could I have foreseen the coup d'état in the Maldive Islands in 1952, nor its fundamental cause, the attempt by the Burmese Government to force up the world price of rice.

In any case, the draftsman's imagination has very little scope, for he is merely an adviser. Colonial politicians, like other politicians, are apt to think in terms of the next general election and the four years of office which they expect to follow it. It is not easy to persuade them to think on what will happen when they lose a general election and thus political opponents take office. In fact, everybody is excessively concerned with the immediate aftermath of independence, even the Secretary of State for the Colonies, though his advisers can take a more detached point of view than the local or imported draftsman.

Let us consider what really happened in Arcadia before it became an independent member of the Commonwealth. The Arcadian Democratic Party was founded by Mr Joseph Bamba, of Balliol College. His fierce attacks on imperialism and colonialism at the Oxford Union Society anticipated a successful political career in Arcadia. He is in fact a person of considerable ability – probably not the sort of ability which would make a good professor or a good civil servant or even a good lawyer – but he has the personal qualities which enable him not only to secure a following among the educated men of his own country but also to appeal successfully to the mass of the people. His reading for P.P.E.[79] was desultory but during his periods of internment as an undesirable agitator he was able to study the British Constitution and to decide what his country needs. He has considerable personal ambition but also a broad social sympathy. In Ceylon we used to joke about the "poor villager" who used to figure in almost every political speech; and, of course, much that was said about him was political clap-trap; but there was also plenty of sympathy for the under-dog. It must also be remembered that colonial nationalism is an exotic plant with which only the educated Arcadians are familiar. Mr Bamba therefore has two speeches. The one appeals to his educated friends and its promise of exciting jobs to come. The other appeals to the villagers by promising economic improvement as soon as the imperialists have been ejected.

Mr Bamba was of course unpopular with the European administrators of Arcadia, and he spent some months in internment as an undesirable agitator. This internment was quite valuable to him, for it enabled him to study the British Constitution with closer attention than he was able to give it at Oxford: and he decided that what Arcadia needed was responsible government with adult franchise. It

[79] The Oxford degree of Philosophy, Politics, and Economics.

also strengthened his support in the country. What is more, as soon as a politician gets to the stage of being gaoled he becomes a matter of concern to Whitehall. Mr Bamba was fortunate that the Secretary of State liked him. This was fortunate because, as I would suspect that some recent examples have shown, personal antipathy can hold up constitutional development. This is, indeed, not wholly a personal matter. The fundamental question in the mind of the Secretary of State was whether Mr Bamba and his friends were capable of running Arcadia after independence. The Governor is not always a good judge because he has borne the brunt of the attacks on colonialism. Sir Andrew Caldecott,[80] for instance, misjudged D.S. Senanayake, whereas the Labour Ministers[81] appreciated him. On the other hand, the rapid progress of Malaya was due to the Tunku's remarkable capacity for handling people. Mr Bamba had the advantage of being an Oxford man, and this started him off on the right foot at the Colonial Office.

During the five years which followed his first contact with the Colonial Office, the constitutional future of Arcadia was mapped out. Mr Bamba started with the assumption that Arcadia needed responsible government with adult suffrage. If Arcadia had had a strong European minority, like Kenya or Rhodesia, the demand for "one man, one vote" would have caused difficulty; but the only difficulty in Arcadia was that the highly respectable tribal authorities had no great sympathy with radical young men like Mr Bamba and feared that their prestige would be undermined. The Secretary of State used his well-known skill as a negotiator to obtain a compromise which Mr Bamba proposed to ignore as soon as he had powers in his hands. Neither the Secretary of State nor the Members of Parliament who approved the Independence Bill knew this, and the Secretary of State received the congratulations of the House for solving a difficult problem – on paper. There were great celebrations in Arcadia, where Royal Princes and Mr Bamba, now Prime Minister, received the homage of a grateful people.

Every case is of course peculiar. There have been, however, some common elements. In the first place, if we except European politicians in Rhodesia and Kenya, all local politicians have asked for adult franchise and responsible government. In the second place, power had been transferred from a European bureaucracy to a small Asian or African oligarchy. Indeed, except in Nigeria, where there were competing personalities based on tribal loyalties, and in Singapore, where Lee Kuan Yew thought it better to let David Marshall and Lim

[80] Sir Andrew Caldecott, Governor of Ceylon, 1937–1944.
[81] In the United Kingdom.

Yew Hock to do most of the negotiating, the transfer has in effect been to a single political leader – Nehru in India, Jinnah in Pakistan, Senanayake in Ceylon, Nkrumah in Ghana, the Tunku in Malaya, Nyerere[82] in Tanganyika. In the third place, in every case except Rhodesia the administration has been weakened by the premature retirement of European officials.

In the initial stages the franchise is not very important. Mr Bamba and his bright young men of the Arcadian Democratic Party have no difficulty in winning a large majority at the first two general elections. Trouble begins when personal rivalries produce a party split. Even in India, where Nehru has maintained his personal prestige, government at State level is tending to be a chaos of competing personalities. Pakistan from 1953 to 1959 was governed by intrigue. Ceylon politics began to degenerate in 1951 when Bandaranaike was virtually dismissed. The relevance of the franchise is that the competing politicians discover that high-souled nationalism does not win elections. There will probably be a good deal of corruption, especially in the form of intimidation and personality. Almost all politicians have to dig deep into the pork-barrel. Local prejudices, especially religious, racial, tribal or linguistic, have to be played upon. We have enough experience to enable the Constitution-maker to foresee this development, but he cannot do much about it. Mr Bamba and his friends would consider it an insult to his people if the development were even mentioned. It is of course not a racial characteristic: we can supply plenty of examples from the European peoples of the Commonwealth. In any case the Arcadian Democratic Party believes that its high ideals and generous sentiments will be perpetuated. Above all, it is quite impossible to enfranchise only the educated class. That was theoretically practicable in Asia but it is not practicable in Africa because the educated class is far too small.

Responsible government, too, is not an easy system to operate. It will work quite reasonably well so long as Mr Bamba is alive and maintains his prestige. But lesser politicians are as ambitious as lesser politicians in Britain, and they do not all share the polite public-school conventions. An efficient and high-principled administrator like Chaudhri Muhammad Ali simply gets pushed aside. Collective responsibility may become, as it did in Ceylon and tends to become in Britain, a mere fiction. The ministers have to speak for themselves because they are competing for powers and popularity. Moreover, nobody can guarantee a stable party system when the Arcadian Democratic Party breaks up, as it is certain to do.

[82]Julius Nyerere, first President of Tanzania, 1964–1985.

Why have responsible government at all? One answer is that Mr Bamba insists on it because he wants to be Prime Minister. Another is that the American system is unworkable, outside its home, because it depends on conventions that we cannot reproduce – e.g. the willingness of the legislature to vote funds for a President whose brand of politics may be disliked by the majority. A compromise is possible. In the Maldives, Amin Didi[83] was both President and Prime Minister; but that experiment disappeared through a coup d'état eight months later. In Pakistan one of my drafts provided for an active President with a Vice-President as leader of the legislature, but it was necessary to provide that the Budget might be certified once. The Ghana device of linking the presidential and the parliamentary elections is ingenious, but I doubt if it will work when the government party breaks up. Obviously more experiments on such lines are possible. Experimentation is, however, limited by two restrictions: first is the restriction imposed by the present situation in Arcadia and by the personnel available: is your President going to be a Mahdi or a Mirghani? Secondly, if our Mr Bamba becomes President and Prime Minister is it not likely that one of his successors will quietly order Mr Speaker to take away that bauble?

If, however, responsible government is established, the Constitution-maker must face the possibility of a breakdown. It can easily happen in a small legislature, as we know from experience in Canada and Australia in the nineteenth century. There is no difficulty in this country. A stalemate is not very likely with 630 members, and if it did happen the Queen would swiftly install a Caretaker government and dissolve Parliament. Also, if a Cabinet refused to accept a dismissal of parliament there is still a remedy left, dismissal by the Queen. Similarly in Nepal there was no difficulty with a popular monarch who had all power to himself to take over if ever the machinery broke down. There would be no difficulty in Arcadia if Mr Bamba could be persuaded not to hanker after a republic and were wise enough to advise the Queen to appoint a good Governor-General from some other Commonwealth country – he need not have a white face. One hesitates, however, to leave much power in the hands of a promoted politician, whether as President or as Governor-General. I fully understand why Ghulam Muhammad dismissed Nazimuddin in 1953, though I think that Oliver Goonetilleke chose a wise course when he decided not to dismiss Bandaranaike in 1958. Ghulam Muhammad in fact reverted to the status of partisan politician, as the legislation of 1954 showed. Only an ambiguity in the Indian Independence Act and some judicious law-making by the Federal Court enabled us to keep

[83] See p. 204, n. 14.

Pakistan on the constitutional path. Even so, there was an interval of three days during which we had to advise magistrates to pretend that invalid laws were in place; and by way of precaution I drafted a Proclamation suspending the Constitution – I have it still among my papers. The heat which his actions generated, among men who had been his Cabinet colleagues, was probably one of the causes of the deterioration in Pakistan politics, which produced, or helped to produce, Ayub Khan's coup d'état.

I have mentioned that a small legislature helps towards political instability. Let me elaborate a little. One does not build up a great political party like the Conservative Party or even the Indian National Congress in a year or two. Usually a political party starts as a group of active politicians with a fringe of hangers-on looking for jobs. It is possible to organise in depth, as the Tunku has shown in Malaya and Lee Kuan Yew in Singapore, but what one really wants is a huge pyramid with a not too conspicuous star on top. MacDonald and Henderson[84] could dislike each other intensely and yet sit in the same Cabinet because they had the solidarity of the Labour Party behind them: but try to imagine MacDonald, Henderson and Snowden[85] in a Parliament of 25, which the misguided enthusiasm of the Rendel Commission[86] provided for Singapore.

I have so far barely mentioned the problem which causes the Constitution-maker the most trouble. The population of Arcadia is not homogenous. It may be divided according to religion, race, tribe, caste or language. What is worse, the Arcadian politicians are quite likely to play these differences down. Being fervent nationalists themselves, they believe that nationalism is a national phenomenon. In Arcadia it is not only unnatural; it is imported from England, one of the consequences of colonialism that do not get attacked in Turtle Bay. The only nationalist in an Arcadian village is the headman; and even he is not so nationalist as to allow his daughter to marry a Christian, a fisherman or an Englishman, or even to vote for one. Even the Communist Party chooses its candidates according to race, tribe or caste, if not religion; Sir John Kotelawala's main objection to communists was that they were anti-national.

[84]Arthur Henderson, British Labour minister; Secretary of State for Foreign Affairs, 1929–1931.

[85]Philip Snowden (later Viscount Snowden), British Labour minister; Chancellor of the Exchequer, 1924 and 1929–1931.

[86]In 1953 the British Government established a constitutional commission under Sir George Rendel that reviewed Singapore's constitutional position and recommended a legislative assembly with an elected majority and a ministerial form of government modelled on Westminster.

There are so many devices for dealing with communalism that I can do no more than barely to mention them. They are:

(1) Federalism or some other form of devolution;
(2) Weighted representation in one or both Houses of the legislature;
(3) Communal electorates, reserved seats, communal primaries, multi-member constituencies, and other electoral devices;
(4) Bills of rights and non-discrimination clauses, with or without judicial review;
(5) Councils of State with or without refusal of assent, or special magistrates;
(6) Public service commissions and other devices for taking fields of governmental action out of politics.

(The rest is mostly routine.)

Constitution-makers are forced to be modest, for they know that they cannot foresee the future. They are trying to regulate that future knowing that everything depends on the behaviour of human beings, and especially that peculiar genus of species [*sic*] homo, the politician. Much depends, too, on economic conditions and even on natural phenomena. The failure of a monsoon could destroy several Constitutions. What I myself try to do, within the limits of my instructions, which are sometimes tightly drawn, is to provide such machinery as might last fifteen or twenty years. If it does, the political life of Arcadia will adapt itself to the Constitution and that Constitution may last forever, though moulded by each generation to suit its own ideas and conditions.

6. 'Magna Carta and constitutionalism in the Commonwealth', 1964–1965[87]

The Great Charter which was extended to the greater part of the Commonwealth as part of the Common Law was that sealed by King Henry III in 1225. Indeed, it was that Charter which received the name Magna Carta. So far as I know, the name was first used in King Henry's Confirmatory Charter of 1236. It first appeared on the statute book in cap. 5 of the Statute of Marlborough, 1267. The full title, Magna Carta de libertatibus Angliae, was used in the inspeximus[88]

[87]In order to remain consistent, all legal and legislative references are made in the historic way that Jennings wrote them and have not been modified to conform with modern usage and referencing. At the invitation of the UK Government's Central Office of Information, Jennings published a slim volume for public consumption entitled *Magna Carta and its Influence in the World Today* (London, 1965). The following is very different from that volume.

[88]A historical term meaning a charter in which a grantor confirmed inspecting and examining an earlier charter.

of 1297. This inspeximus is the authoritative text, for it was enrolled on the Statute Roll. It was the text used by the printers of the 16th century and by Coke[89] in his Second Institute.[90] Since the text was that of 1225, Magna Carta usually appeared in the printed collections of statutes as the statute of Henry III. It was in this form that the territories overseas knew it, either from Coke or from the Statutes at Large.[91] In the Statutes of the Realm,[92] however, the Record Commissioners printed the whole inspeximus and so Magna Carta appeared as the statute 25 Edward I. The example was followed by the Statute Law Revision Commissioners. What is left as Magna Carta in the law of England, Wales and Northern Ireland – so far as I know it was never extended to Scotland – appears as the statute 25 Edward I on page 31 of the first volume of the third edition of Statutes Revised, published in 1960.[93]

Even in the 17th century there was confusion between King John's Charter of 1215 and King Henry's Charter of 1225. The text then in use, and indeed the only text known to exist, was that of 1225. The lawyers of the 17th century thought, however, that the text used by them was that of 1215. John Selden[94] pointed out that the text in Matthew Paris[95] contained two chapters which were not in the printed version, and we now know that they were taken from King John's Charter of 1215. They were the provisions relating to scutages[96] and aids, in the modern connotation Chapters 12 and 14. Generally speaking, however, in the great constitutional disputes of the 17th century the lawyers quoted from the Magna Carta of 1225 as if it were King John's Charter of 1215, to which the name Magna Carta thus became attached. Blackstone[97] in 1759 sorted out the various charters and published the texts.[98] Following the long historical tradition and

[89] Sir Edward Coke, English jurist; Chief Justice, 1613–1616.

[90] The *Institutes* were a set of legal treatises by Coke published from 1628. The second was formally titled *The Second Part of the Institutes of the Laws of England; Containing the Exposition of Many Ancient and Other Statutes.*

[91] A collection of statutes issued since Magna Carta and published in various editions from the early nineteenth century onwards.

[92] A record of all statutes from Magna Carta onwards, compiled between 1810 and 1828.

[93] An abridged collection of statutes. It was actually published in 1950: Robert Drayton (ed.), *The Statutes*, third revised edition (London, 1950).

[94] John Selden, seventeenth-century English jurist and scholar.

[95] Matthew Paris, thirteenth-century English Benedictine monk and chronicler.

[96] A form of taxation related to military service to the Crown.

[97] Sir William Blackstone, eighteenth-century English jurist; first Venerian Professor of English Law at the University of Oxford.

[98] William Blackstone, *The Great Charter and Charter of the Forest, with the Other Authentic Instruments: to Which is Prefixed an Introductory Discourse, Containing the History of the Charters* (Oxford, 1759).

not the statute book, he printed the Charter of 1215 as Magna Carta regis Johannis, and following the statute book he printed the Charter of 1225 as Magna Carta Regis Henrici III. 9 Hen.3. The Record Commissioners, in their volume of Charters of Liberties, followed this example, though in the Statutes of the Realm they printed Magna Carta de libertatibus Angliae as 25 Edward I. Even though he knows that it derives from a mistake by the chroniclers of St. Albans, no lawyer can object to the long historical tradition which gives the name Magna Carta to King John's Charter; but he must insist that the Magna Carta available for export was that of 1225. My references will be to the latter.

The reception of English law in territories which are or have been under English or British rule and jurisdiction came about in three ways. When Englishmen settled in territories in which there was no settled system of law they carried with them the laws and liberties of England so far as they were compatible with the conditions in their new country. They did not, for instance, have a church established by law, nor did they take the feudal land law of England, though the land was deemed to be vested in the Crown. In conquered or ceded territories with a settled law, however, that law was presumed to continue until it was changed by or under the authority of the Crown. To this rule there were exceptions, though I need not mention them all.

First the ceded or conquered colony came under the rule and jurisdiction of the Crown. The whole of English constitutional law therefore applied, and in particular the Crown established courts on the English model.

Secondly, there is authority for saying that where the existing law was contradictory to the fundamental principles of the common law it was void. This was actually applied only to torture, which Coke regarded as inconsistent with cap. 29 of Magna Carta, but which was authorised by the Spanish law taken over by the British after the French wars.[99] This doctrine would probably have extended to imprisonment without trial, and perhaps to the whole concept of due process of law read into cap. 29.[100]

Thirdly, there were existing laws which, by reason of their nature, could not be extended to English settlers or to the transactions, such as those covered by the whole body of commercial law, which they engendered. The tribal laws of West Africa continued to apply to members of the tribes and to the lands which they occupied. Such laws could not apply to the European settlers or to the freed slaves

[99] *Fabrigas v. Mostyn* (1774), 20 St. Tr. 81, 187; *R. v. Picton* (1812), 30 St. Tr. 225.
[100] *Fabrigas v. Mostyn*, loc. cit.

of Sierra Leone – though the problem of Sierra Leone was met by regarding it as a settled colony to which English law applied. Again, the Hindu law and the Muhammadan law of the Indian sub-continent could not apply to Christians, whether English or Indian. These laws in fact became personal laws governing family relationships and the ownership and devolution of property.

I ought to add that many territories which were subject to British rule and jurisdiction were not, initially, classed as colonies. They were protected States, protectorates or mandated territories of the League of Nations. They included most of the territories in Africa except the four West African colonies, each of which had a protectorate in the hinterland; the South African colonies and Basutoland; and Mauritius and the Seychelles, which were regulated by the Napoleonic Codes. They also included the whole of Malaysia and Brunei, except the Straits Settlements of Malacca, Penang and Singapore. The Straits Settlements were regarded as settled colonies to which English law applied, though the settlers were mostly Chinese.

I need not enter upon the enormous complications which these rules produced. It would be necessary to study each territory in turn in order to show the evolution of its present legal system. Perhaps I may take one example, that of Ceylon. The maritime provinces were ceded by the Dutch and so the old law of the province of Holland, the Roman-Dutch law, applied. But the Dutch had retained the Tamil personal laws, the Thesavalamai,[101] the Muhammadan personal law, which they had attempted to codify, and the Sinhalese system of tenure of land. These laws still apply, but the British, by legislation, introduced the English system of courts and civil procedure and, via India, the whole of English criminal law and procedure. In 1815 the Kandyan provinces were ceded by the Kandyan chiefs subject to the maintenance of Kandyan law and the authority of the chiefs. After a rebellion in 1817, however, the authority of the chiefs was much diminished and in 1830 the Kandyan provinces were absorbed into the legal system of the maritime provinces, subject to the maintenance of Kandyan law, which in fact operated as a personal law and as a law relating to the tenure of land. Since 1830, too, there has been a considerable application of English law by legislation, notably commercial law. Consequently, when I lectured on the legal systems of Ceylon – note the plural – I had to say something about English law, Roman-Dutch law, the Thesavalamai (in a background of Hindu law), Muhammadan law, Kandyan law, and Sinhalese tenures generally.

I have, however, mentioned only incidentally ways of extending English law otherwise than by inheritance.

[101] Personal laws applying to Sri Lankan Tamils in the Northern Province of Sri Lanka.

It will be seen that, in a conquered or ceded colony which had a legal system not applicable to settlers or to such matters as commercial transactions, there was a hiatus to be filled. Usually, it was filled by legislation. If it was not, courts administered according to "justice, equity and good conscience", and in a few countries of the Commonwealth this may still be done. In effect, the courts are recognized to have a legislative function. They were and are staffed by English lawyers or by lawyers of local origin trained in English law. It was inevitable that they should regard English law, shorn of its technicalities, as exhibiting "justice, equity and good conscience". This is, accordingly, the second method of receiving English law. It was not, however, as important as legislation.

In some places the whole of the local law was superseded by English law. In others particular parts of English law, or particular statutes, might be applied. I need not go into details because everywhere in what was formerly British Asia, except in Ceylon, English law applied subject of course to the exceptions of Hindu and Muhammadan law, where applicable, and to Malay custom. In what was formerly British Africa, too, English law applied except in the Republic of South Africa, Rhodesia, Mauritius and the Seychelles, but subject to the exception of African tribal law.

When I say that English law applies I usually mean the common law of England. This is not true in India and Pakistan, where the courts may have to fall back on "justice, equity and good conscience". Generally speaking, however, the common law is English law as at the date of settlement or of the extension of English law by legislation. Sometimes the extension consists of the extension of an existing local law to a wider one.

For instance, Ghana consists of the former Gold Coast colony and the former Gold Coast Protectorate. What was extended to the Protectorate was not the law of England but the law of the colony.

What I am emphasising, however, is that not only the English common law but also the English statute law was extended, subject in each case to compatibility with local conditions. Magna Carta is regarded as a statute, and it was applied and extended by other statutes. It is of course true that these statutes have been incorporated into English common law by reason of the development of common law remedies. The historians have demonstrated that many of the concepts which have been read into Magna Carta are not there. One cannot, for instance, find in Magna Carta the concepts of trial in open court, the independence of the judges, trial by jury, or habeas corpus. For that matter, due process of law is not there, though it is in one of the confirmations of Magna Carta, cap.3 of 28 Edward III (1354):

> "No man of what estate or condition that he be, shall be put out of land or tenement, nor taken, nor imprisoned, nor disinherited, nor put to death, without being brought in answer by due process of law".

What is important, however, is not what is in Magna Carta, but what is in the common law of a territory because of Magna Carta. The reaction against the Whig concept of history has gone too far. It is creating the episodic concept of history which tells us that the Governor quarrelled with the Chief Justice because of incompatibility of temperament. I do not deny the importance of temperament; but if the Chief Justice objected to the Governor's use of imprisonment without trial I am enough of a Whig to think of due process of law and cap. 29 of Magna Carta.[102] There has been a progressive development of the liberties of England, and the liberties of England have been freely exported.

This does not mean that the whole of Magna Carta has been exported. All the provisions relating to tenure, its services and incidents, were obsolete after 1645, and in any case the law laid down in Littleton's Tenures[103] was not exported. Again, most of the provisions relating to the administration of justice were rendered obsolete by the reforms of King Edward I. Some of the miscellaneous provisions related peculiarly to English conditions. What remained were a few provisions forbidding distraint[104] except on the orders of a court, cap. 29, a provision giving priority to debts due to the Crown, and above all the general principle of government according to law. This general principle, I take it, is expressed in the American term "constitutionalism". Since that term assumes a written constitution, it is not appropriate for England, Scotland, or Great Britain. Nor was it appropriate to colonies, at least in the early stages of their development.

The term "constitution" was used of the charter or other instrument of government in an American colony at least as early as 1739. Even the Crown colonies had constitutions, for they were governed under commissions issued to the governors setting out in some detail how the governors were to exercise their powers. The term has been used ex post facto. It was not used contemporaneously because it was inappropriate. In most Crown colonies the Governor in Council had both legislative and executive powers. Moreover, until the 1870s each

[102] It is unclear what episode Jennings is referring to here. It is possible that he is pointing to a case from the British colonies.

[103] A text by the fifteenth-century English judge Sir Thomas Littleton on property law.

[104] Seizure of property.

governor received a new commission. Even in the 20th century the legislation setting up constitutions was not described as such. We had Government of Ireland Acts, Government of India Acts, Ceylon (Legislative Council) Orders in Council, and so on. We have British North America Acts, but a Commonwealth of Australia (Constitution) Act. Even in 1909 we had a South Africa Act. In short, the idea of a constitution was really established when responsible government was conferred, though even then the use of the term was unusual. English lawyers have generally preferred "government according to law" or "the rule of law".

It might be thought that one could hardly say that government according to law existed where both legislative and executive powers were vested in a Governor or a Governor-General acting with, or even without, the advice of a council nominated by him. Moreover, at the lower levels of administration the same officers – the collectors, the district commissioners, or the government agents – exercised both executive and judicial powers. This is, however, to confuse the doctrine of the separation of powers with the doctrine of the separation of authorities exercising powers. The governors-in-council could alter the law; but until they altered it they had to observe it. The distinction between legislative and executive action was clear, because legislative enactments had to be sent to London and might be disallowed. The administrative officers exercising both executive and judicial powers themselves separated the functions by having formal sittings in court for judicial business, and their decisions were subject to appeal to courts staffed by professional judges.

The impression of many English lawyers, however, is that American lawyers tend to lay excessive stress on constitutional limitations. It seems to some of us that the great success of the Constitution of the United States rests in large part on the fact that most of it derived from the common law and that, in the main, it remains attuned to the common laws of the several States. I shall say more about this when I speak of bills of rights. For the moment I wish to assert only that the influence of Magna Carta in England does not depend on the acceptance of broad general propositions: it depends on the degree to which those general propositions have been worked out in detail by the courts of common law and accepted not only by the courts, but also by professional opinion and by public opinion. The liberties of England are the liberties of the man on the Clapham omnibus.

It is not my function to explain the intricacies of government according to law in the United Kingdom; but I have to explain what was exported to the territories under British rule and jurisdiction overseas, and especially those in Asia and Africa.

First, we have the apparatus of the law itself, what one might call the essential concepts of the judicial administration of the civil and criminal law. These concepts have been exported to all parts of the Commonwealth and to most of the countries formerly under British rule and jurisdiction. This is so even where the common law of the country concerned is by origin French or Spanish or Dutch. Some qualifications have to be made in places like Malta and Cyprus, where other European influences have been at work: but go where you will in the Commonwealth in Asia or Africa and you will find that the courts are the heirs of the courts in Westminster Hall, acting "fairly and freely, without favour and without fear", applying common law remedies even when the wrongs are not common law wrongs. One result of not having a written constitution in the United Kingdom is that, until very recently, the governments of the United Kingdom have not thought that the establishment of legislative, executive or judicial institutions in a colony or protectorate was a single operation. The Crown appointed a governor and, usually, gave him legislative powers in council: but they did not empower him to establish courts or appoint judges. Those things were done by the Crown; and even in the last stages of colonial rule the colonial legal service was distinct from the civil services of the respective territories. All were appointed by the Secretary of State in the name of the Crown; but the civil servants were subordinate to the Governor, while the judges were not.

Secondly, we have the apparatus ancillary to the administration of the law, and above all the legal profession. In no other legal system is there an equivalent of the English bar. The medieval concept of the gild resulted in the establishment of common law corporations of lawyers within walking distance of Westminster Hall. The Inns of Court and Chancery, including Sergeants' Inn which housed the Judges, have coalesced into the four Inns, Lincoln's Inn, the Inner and the Middle Temple, and my own Inn, Gray's. Judges, Queen's counsel and junior barristers sit cheek by jowl on the bench, and in hall is a collection of members from the junior student to the Master Treasurer, who presides over hall until the bench leaves and Mr Senior takes over. These are the four pillars of the independence of bench and bar. The members of these four Inns have all the prejudices of the common law, not merely as principles of law and legal administration, but as eternal principles which ought to be maintained even if the law says otherwise. Because of a state of emergency it may be necessary for Parliament to authorise detention without trial: but it will not be forgotten in the Inns that this breach of cap. 29 of Magna Carta can be justified, if at all, only by the state of emergency. Some judges will not be ready to acquiesce unless the intention of Parliament is made abundantly plain, and so one gets famous dissenting judgments like those in Rex v. Halliday[105] and Liversidge v. Anderson,[106] which themselves become texts on the liberties of England. Nor must it be forgotten that the lawyers in the service of the Crown, the Attorney-General and the Solicitor-General, the Treasury Solicitor, the Director of Public Prosecutions, the Parliamentary Counsel to the Treasury, the legal advisers to the Government Departments, are all members of their Inns of Court, imbued with the same common law prejudices or traditions as their brethren sitting on the bench or practising within or at the bar.

I particularly draw your attention to the fact that, in the system of responsible government, legislation is drafted by Parliamentary Counsel or legal draftsmen who are professional lawyers in the service of the Crown. They receive instructions from civil servants acting on behalf of Ministers, but they have a profound influence on the form of legislation and on much of its content. They are particularly valuable in protecting the liberties of the subject. The Minister's object may perhaps be attained most simply by ignoring those liberties. The greatest happiness of the greatest number, or at least votes at the next election, may be attained by doing injustice to the smallest number. Those who are accustomed to defending John Smith against the Queen, or the owner of a small tenement against the Minister of Housing and Local Government, or a person of hostile origin against the Secretary of State, do not take kindly to injustice wheresoever, by whomsoever and under whatsoever authority it be committed. Parliamentary Counsel and legal draftsmen are members of the bar, as vigilant as defending counsel to protect the liberties of England.

What is more, their efforts are supported in Parliament. This brings us to the third point, that the liberties of England arising out of Magna Carta have become part of the common stock of ideas. Nullus liber homo . . . is translated not like home . . . ; and mal libre homo . . . is translated no free man . . . . Cap 29 can be translated with the language of Hoxton or Limehouse, and is so translated by people who have never read Magna Carta even in translation. Many people quote the authorised version of the Bible, or Shakespeare, without knowing it because much of the imagery has passed into ordinary speech. For nearly seven hundred years Magna Carta has been part of the law of England. It was confirmed at least 55 times. It was one of the earliest documents to be printed. It was argued over in the Stuart reigns. It has been quoted to many generations of schoolboys. The assumptions of the man in the street are not very different from those of the judge on the bench or the advocate at the bar. The assumptions

[105] *R. v. Halliday* [1917] A.C. 260.
[106] *Liversidge v. Anderson* [1942] A.C. 206.

are made articulate in Parliament; and I think that everybody agrees that the House of Commons is at its best when it uncovers a case of injustice. The Minister, if he is wise, will ask for time to investigate. If he defends his Department, the hounds will be after him as if he were a fox on the run. What is more, if legislative proposals are so framed as to be likely to lead to injustice, he has to defend his draft against a House which is traditionally the protector of liberty. There are lawyers in Parliament who may find themselves unwittingly supporting Parliamentary Counsel against the civil servants: but most members can take a point as quickly as members of the bar.

How far has all this been exported? The answer is, I think, nearly all of it. There are, of course, no Inns of Court. There are, however, a bench and a bar which look and behave much as if they were in Westminster Hall. Many of them have in fact been called to the English bar. In most parts of the Commonwealth there are councils of legal education or law schools teaching the essential principles of Magna Carta. If an English lawyer goes into a court in Accra, or Lagos, or Dar-es-Salaam, or Lahore, or Delhi, or Colombo or Kuala Lumpur he finds himself very much at home. The technique of parliamentary drafting by government draftsmen is everywhere the same. Sir [Thomas] Erskine May's Parliamentary Practice[107] is on the table of every legislature from Victoria, B.C., to Nairobi, and from Dar-es-Salaam to Hong Kong or Wellington, New Zealand. In every legislature there are lawyers who speak the language of Magna Carta.

There are, however, qualifications. In British India, the Federation of Malaya, and elsewhere, it was occasionally thought necessary by the British administrations to provide themselves with powers outside the ordinary law. The troubles were not necessarily political. Armed dacoity[108] led to the Bengal regulations; and the secret Chinese societies of the Straits Settlements have always been a problem. After 1916, however, political movements, especially nationalist and communist movements, used the technique of deliberate disobedience to law in order to embarrass the British administrations. Just as there is no longer a clear line between peace and war, so there is no clear line between civil war, or rebellion, and law and order. I am, of course, not concerned with the political aspect of the problem. There are two views about President de Valera,[109] Mahatma Gandhi, Chen

[107] Authoritative text still used across Commonwealth countries on parliamentary procedures, rules, etc. Many editions have been published since the first in 1844.

[108] An Anglo-Indian colloquialism meaning banditry.

[109] Eamon de Valera, Irish political leader who agitated for independence; Taoiseach (Prime Minister) of the Republic of Ireland, 1937–1948, 1951–1954, 1957–1959; President, 1959–1973.

Ping [*sic*],[110] Sheikh Abdulla,[111] Jomo Kenyatta,[112] the leaders of the Naga rebellion,[113] and others. I take neither. I simply assert that the maintenance of law and order by the traditional and well-tried methods becomes difficult, if not impossible, if a small minority of active politicians sets out deliberately to subvert the law, especially if that small minority has active or passive support from a larger part of the population. Chen Ping, for instance, never had more than two thousand men in the Malayan jungles. There the terrain was particularly favourable to guerrilla warfare and his men had no great difficulty in getting supplies from isolated pockets of Chinese. Special powers were needed to deal with that situation, and to deal with a score of other situations in Asia and Africa, not all of them under British or other European rule. By special powers I mean powers for detention without trial, trial by military tribunals, the censorship of and the suppression of books and periodicals, curfew regulations, restrictions on public meetings, the prohibition of voluntary associations, and generally a denial of most, if not all, of the fundamental freedoms which can be found in English law.

British Governments, which have to defend themselves in the House of Commons, have always been reluctant to authorise legislation conferring special powers. With the coming of independence the local politicians seem to have less reluctance because they have, in many cases, suffered from their use. One cannot pass judgment without studying the circumstances of each country, and I think that nobody can talk in general terms about Ghana and Nigeria, Rhodesia and Malawi, Kenya and Tanzania, India and Pakistan. I know only that if one asks a specific question, such as, why suppress a periodical when one can prosecute for criminal libel or seditious conspiracy, one gets the impression that the latter had not been thought of as a possibility. It is so much easier to stop publication without proving anything. Similarly, it is so much easier to clap the suspects in gaol or banish them to remote areas than it is to prove a conspiracy. Even where there is an attempt to use the ordinary law, unconscionable methods of obtaining evidence may be used.

[110]Chin Peng was a Malayan Communist Party leader who led guerrilla attacks during the Malayan Emergency.

[111]Sheikh Muhammad Abdullah was a Kashmiri political leader who attacked princely rule in Jammu and Kashmir and defended the region's interests. He later became its Chief Minister after the Partition of India.

[112]Jomo Kenyatta, Kenyan political leader who agitated for independence; first Prime Minister of independent Kenya, 1963–1964; President, 1964–1978.

[113]This refers to movements for independence from the Republic of India of the Naga tribes in north-eastern India.

The second qualification is that frequently the parliamentary machine does not function as it does at Westminster. Constitution-makers can provide for the establishment of governments: they have not yet learned how to provide for the establishment of Oppositions. There is indeed a tendency to regard a formed Opposition, as it was called in 18th century Britain, as itself a conspiracy. Arguments, which I regard as specious, are used to justify a one-party State, as if nobody had heard of Adolf Hitler or even of Oliver Cromwell if one may include such disparate characters in one sentence. Where legislation is carried by acclamation, there is little opportunity for stressing fundamental liberties and protecting the individual from injustice. Indeed, in some countries in Africa membership of the party, and subscription to its funds, are means for securing a quiet life.

The contemplation of the problems of the newly independent countries has led to a changed view of bills of rights. The combination of a common law suffused with the principles of Magna Carta and a Parliament active in the defence of the liberties of England was thought by English lawyers to provide all that the Englishman needed, especially when every village had its Hampden[114] and every town its cohort of Pyms.[115] Emphasis, perhaps undue emphasis, was placed on the purely declaratory character of the French Declarations of the Rights of Man. The late Professor A.V. Dicey whose Law of the Constitution[116] has expressed the prejudices of many English lawyers for eighty years, pointed out that such declarations of rights could be, and frequently were, suspended. He has assumed, too, that they were extraneous to and independent of the ordinary course of the law. I have not studied enough foreign law to be sure that this is so. Probably it is not true; for one of the purposes of such a declaration of rights is to encourage legislation to give effect to the declaration when dealing with positive law.

In any case, Dicey expressly excluded the United States of America. He did not say why, but I take it that he had in mind the inability of the President or the Congress to suspend the Bill of Rights and the close correspondence between the Bill of Rights and the laws of the several States. This could be so in a Commonwealth country also, though he would be a bold man who did not provide for the suspension of constitutional guarantees in a country in which communal troubles were endemic. In the earlier Constitutions of the

[114] John Hampden, English politician who attacked the rule of Charles I during the 1620s and 1630s.

[115] John Pym, English politician who attacked the rule of Charles I during the 1620s and 1630s.

[116] A.V. Dicey, *Law of the Constitution* (London, 1885).

Commonwealth, however, the prejudices of English lawyers prevailed. The Constitutions of Canada, Australia, New Zealand, South Africa and Newfoundland (before it was absorbed into Canada[117]) contained no bills of rights, though in sec. 116 of the Australian Constitution there is a prohibition against legislation in relation to religion, and in placitum[118] xxxi of sec. 51 the power of eminent domain is conferred only "on just terms". These are potent exceptions, for it was fear of discrimination in relation to religion and to the use of the power of expropriation which led some English lawyers to think, if not of bills of rights, at least of non-discrimination clauses.

The problem which started this train of thought was that of Ireland. That problem had two aspects. First, there were the fears of the Protestant minority, whose views were strongly supported by the Unionist parties in Great Britain, that under Home Rule there would be a Roman Catholic administration and that there would be prejudice against the Protestants. Since most of the landowners were Protestants, the fear related not only to the position and property of the Protestant churches, but also to land legislation involving compulsory acquisition without compensation or with inadequate compensation. In other words, what was wanted was not merely something on the lines of the First Amendment of the Constitution of the United States but also the due process clause, at least in so far as it related to property. In the first Home Rule Bill (1885) there were limitations on legislative powers in respect of religion and corporations. In the second Bill (1893) there was also a complete due process clause. Dicey, who was active in politics as a Liberal Unionist, published a long disquisition on the restrictions on legislative power and objected that they were both inadequate and unenforceable.[119] In the third Bill, which became the Government of Ireland Act, 1914, there was only a modest non-discrimination clause in matters relating to religion. It can be followed into the Government of Ireland Act, 1920, which is the present constitution of Northern Ireland, the Constitution of the Irish Free State, and the Constitution of Ceylon, where it became a general non-discrimination clause in respect of "community", i.e. race, religion and caste.

The second aspect of the Irish problem was that constitutional government on the lines of Magna Carta and the developed common law became impossible because of the illegal activities of a relatively small minority, with whom the mass of the population in three of the

[117]In 1949.

[118]Subsection.

[119]Jennings is referring to A.V. Dicey, *A Leap in the Dark or Our New Constitution* (London, 1893), pp. 84–116.

four provinces sympathised. Trial by Jury, for instance, was impossible because few Irish juries were prepared to convict an Irishman who was merely breaking British-made laws. Even magistrates could not always be trusted to enforce the laws. In any case, we have since learned from bitter experience that, unless the general population is prepared to risk reprisals by giving information to the police, a small minority can render the administration of justice, and the enforcement of law and order exceedingly difficult. No British Government could govern Ireland, maintain law and order, and administer justice according to law, without special powers in what were called Coercive Acts. Compared with what British people are prepared to put up with in war-time, they were only mildly repressive, but legislation which concentrates on convicting the criminal necessarily restricts the liberty of the innocent and may result in injustice. The Southern Irish wanted a bill of rights for the same reason as the Americans. They had been governed by the British in a manner which they regarded as oppressive. There was, however, no flamboyant Declaration of Independence because most of the Irish politicians were prepared to accept the Articles of Agreement for a Treaty which they negotiated with the British politicians in 1921.

The Treaty, if we may so call it for short, contained the usual non-discrimination clause in order to protect the Irish Protestants; but the Constitution contained a whole collection of fundamental rights, a few of them rather odd ones. This was the first bill of rights within the British Commonwealth, but its short life was undistinguished. The war against the British turned into a civil war. Armed resistance ceased in 1923, but the Irish Republican Army did not surrender its arms or dissolve its cadres. Public Safety Acts were passed which made the old Coercion Acts look almost as mild as a Dogs Act; and they were valid because the fundamental rights never became entrenched. Even the non-discrimination clause ceased to be entrenched in 1932, when the Treaty was repealed under the Statute of Westminster, 1931.[120] In 1937 the Irish Free State was replaced by Eire, with a Constitution more attuned to Mr de Valera's philosophy.

I have dealt with the Irish experience at some length because it provided the precedent for India. Though some qualifications have to be made, the liberties of England were in general transported to India and incorporated in the Codes. At least in the Presidency towns and some other places justice was administered as freely, as openly and as equitably as in Westminster Hall. Many Indians were called to the English bar; and the Law Colleges were often the most flourishing

[120] Jennings notes 'The repeal was held to be valid in Moore v. Attorney-General for the Irish Free State, [1935] A.C. 484.'

colleges of the Indian Universities. The qualifications on the liberties of subjects of the King-Emperor were due in the first place to dacoity or secret, armed gangsterdom. They were extended after the Indian National Congress, under the inspiration of Mahatma Gandhi, started the civil disobedience movement. The problem of India was therefore very like the problem of Ireland, though on a vaster scale. In particular, there was not one minority to be protected but at least a scope, for minorities were created by religion, race and caste. The greatest of the problems, that of the relations between the Hindus and the Muslims, was never solved, in spite of the hard work put into it both by Indians and by the British politicians and administrators, between 1927 and 1946. It resulted in the creation of Pakistan.

As the prospect of Indian self-government developed after 1917 it was inevitable that the idea of entrenched constitutional guarantees, as a solution to some of the many problems involved, should develop. The Simon Commission, which reported in 1930, was against it; but in all probability Sir John (afterwards Viscount) Simon[121] was a pupil of Dicey's and in any case his Report was still-born. There was more support for the idea at the Round-Table Conferences of 1930–32. The Government of India Act, 1935, which resulted from a long travail and was in many respects a compromise between the views of Mahatma Gandhi at the one extreme and Sir Winston Churchill at the other, relied mainly on the powers of the Governor-General of India and the Governors of the Provinces; but it contained some non-discrimination clauses which might be regarded as the nucleus of a bill of rights. The Act came into force in 1937, but by 1940 it was plain that India must have self-government soon after the end of the war. Indeed, if the Indian National Congress had been as accommodating in 1940 or 1942 as it had to be in 1946 the partition of British India might have been avoided.[122] It was, however, equally plain that some substitute had to be found for the special powers of the Governor-General and the Governors. A judicious, if somewhat complicated, federal organisation with a suitable distribution of powers would help: but fundamentally the only solution was a bill of rights. In fact, a special committee of the constituent assembly had been set up before British rule ended.

The bill of rights in the Indian Constitution bears examination. It owes a little to that in the United States and rather less to the Universal Declaration of Human Rights. In the main, however, it is an attempt to formulate some of the principles of the common law with the

[121]John Simon (later Viscount Simon), British Liberal and National minister; Lord Chancellor, 1940–1945.

[122]1946 saw the 'Cabinet Mission' to India to discuss the transfer of power and the form of independent India.

necessary qualifications, and sometimes there are qualifications on the qualifications. In some lectures which I delivered in the University of Madras in March 1952[123] I was highly critical of it. It was in fact found to be unreasonably restrictive, especially in relation to modern property legislation, and it has since been amended. I think, however, that my criticisms were misconceived. It is plain from the considerable volume of case law which has developed around the bill of rights, that a body as able and as well trained in the common law as the Supreme Court of India can make use even of so complicated a bill of rights to defend the liberties of citizens. The Indian Constitution came not to destroy the common law but to fulfil it, by applying some of the eternal principles to Union and State legislation. My rather cursory study of American constitutional law had failed to demonstrate to me the proposition which is no doubt common form in this country, that the success of the American bill of rights has been due to the fact that it was, in the main, founded on the common law and that it has been interpreted by generations of judges trained in the common law in the great American law schools. The proposition applies, mutatis mutandis, to India, though the Indian bill of rights is of a very different type.

Another reason for changing one's mind was provided by events in the neighbouring Ceylon. There, all that seemed necessary, when the first drafts were made in 1943, was a fairly broad non-discrimination clause. For some reason which I have never been able to understand, the Ceylon Tamils, who have undoubtedly been discriminated against in respect of their language, have not used that clause. They seem to think that some enforcement clause is needed. Any American lawyer could tell them that that was not so, though it was perhaps necessary in India. It is probable, however, that action would have been taken if there had been a full bill of rights with an enforcement clause. It is probable, too, that some of the other pieces of legislation passed since 1956 would have been invalidated.[124] The bill of rights in Pakistan's 1956 Constitution was based on that of India, though an attempt was made to produce a less complicated text. No bill of rights could, however, have prevented a military coup d'état. The Malayan bill

[123]See Sir Ivor Jennings, *Some Characteristics of the Indian Constitution: being lectures given in the University of Madras during March 1952 under the Sir Alladi Krishnaswami Aiyer Shashitaahdapoothi Endowment* (Madras, 1953).

[124]Minorities such as Indian and Pakistani residents and the Ceylon Tamils did in fact take the Ceylon state to court (including the Privy Council) on noted occasions from 1948 onwards for discrimination on grounds of citizenship and language rights under s. 29 of the constitution, which Jennings drafted. The courts did not find in favour of these groups. 1956 was the year of the Sinhala Only Act, which made Sinhalese the sole official language. This was not seen by the courts or Parliament as contravening the constitution.

of rights was similarly based on that of India. A new factor had, however, entered in 1953. The United Kingdom had become a party to the European Convention of Human Rights and extended it to all the territories for whose international relations it was responsible. These territories included a number of countries which have since become independent. When a bill of rights was thought necessary, the Colonial Office draftsmen tended to use the European Convention, adapted to suit the language and the spirit of the common law, as the basis of their drafts.

It seems probable, however, that bills of rights will be less successful in Africa than in Asia. The politicians and the peoples of the African countries of the Commonwealth are politically much less mature than those of Asia. There are few African lawyers of long and wide experience. Independence perhaps came too slowly in Asia, but the slow development of political institutions made it possible to hope – and in India the hope has so far been fulfilled – that democratic institutions and constitutional government would be maintained. In Africa, particularly in East and Central Africa, the development began from a much more backward state and it had to proceed very rapidly if Britain was not to repeat in Africa the experience which it suffered in British India in the forties. Constitutional government under a bill of rights implies that the rights must be firmly entrenched. The founding fathers in the African countries became so dominant through their success in obtaining independence that they find constitutional amendment almost as easy as the enactment of a Dogs Act. Nor do they find constitutional government to be easy, except by making unconstitutional government formally constitutional by constitutional amendment. As recent events in Ghana have shown, even the independence of judges is in danger. The numerous African lawyers whom we in the Inns of Court are privileged to call to the English bar no doubt return to their countries with the fundamental principles of Magna Carta and the common law in their minds. They have yet to demonstrate that they can be as tough as old Coke or that they are likely to be successful if they are. Even in England the parliament men of the 1620s had to fight in a civil war in the 1640s. We owe the survival of Magna Carta and the principles of civil liberty to the Long Parliament, for even the Cavalier Parliament of Charles II could not repeal all the laws assented to by Charles I.

In one respect, probably, the British governments which secured the enactment of the independence legislation were at fault. So long as territories were colonies or protectorates, their final court of appeal was the Judicial Committee of the Privy Council which sits in Whitehall. Its handling of cases involving federal constitutions has been criticised in Canada, but its handling of cases involving civil liberty has been admirable. In the ten years from 1954 to 1963 it dealt with a dozen such cases of outstanding importance. Moreover, the fact that it invariably granted leave to appeal in any case in which a serious miscarriage of justice was alleged gave great strength to the supreme courts of the colonies. It could have been of very great assistance to a newly independent country, especially one with a new bill of rights. Independence of course implies a right to abolish appeals to the Queen in Council, and the power is conferred by the Statute of Westminster or the Independence Acts.[125] The decision of the Canadian Parliament to abolish appeals is readily understood;[126] perhaps it was unnecessary to retain appeals from India and Pakistan; in some other cases it seems unfortunate that they were not retained.

There were and are two difficulties. The one is purely technical. The Judicial Committee advises the Queen and the decision is put into operation by Order in Council. The view that independence by itself revoked the authority of the Queen in Council has been rejected by the Judicial Committee itself.[127] The procedure is, however, possible only where the Queen's writ runs. The establishment of a republic necessarily breaks the connection with the monarchy. This difficulty could easily be overcome by legislation. Indeed, it has been overcome in the case of Malaysia, which is not a republic but which has replaced the Queen by a ruler called the Yang di-Pertuan Agong. In accordance with section 3 of the Federation of Malaya Independence Act, 1957, the Judicial Committee advises not the Queen but the Yang di-Pertuan Agong, who makes the necessary order.[128] It would be quite easy to generalise this provision, but it has not been done.

The other difficulty is that the Judicial Committee sits in Whitehall and nearly all its active members are Lords of Appeal who also sit in the House of Lords. To appeal therefore involves expense. Also, the members of the Judicial Committee are unfamiliar with the conditions and even with the laws of the countries for which the appeals come to them. This difficulty could in large measure be overcome either by increasing the number of Lords of Appeal or by swearing additional members of the Privy Council who would be ready to travel by air to the capital city of the country concerned and to sit there for so long as the hearing of appeals required. Such a proposal was made by the Malayan Constitutional Commission in

[125] *R. v. British Coal Corporation*, [1935] A.C. 500.

[126] Canada abolished further appeals to the Judicial Committee of the Privy Council in 1949.

[127] *R. v. Ibralebbe*, [1964] A.C. 900, a case from Ceylon.

[128] Malaysia abolished all appeals to the Judicial Committee of the Privy Council in late 1984.

1956, but it was not accepted by Her Majesty's Government. This decision was, I believe, a serious mistake. Dicey long ago pointed out that laws are enforced not by judicial authorities but by executive authorities, and that appeals to the Privy Council would not protect the Protestant minority in Ireland if the executive authorities refused to enforce Orders in Council.[129] This would be equally true in an independent country of the Commonwealth. Indeed, when the Privy Council decided, in a recent Nigerian case, against the government of the Western Region, the Constitution was forthwith amended.[130] Nevertheless, since the jurisdiction could always be removed, in most cases by ordinary legislation and in other cases by constitutional amendment, its retention would show confidence in the Judicial Committee. Besides, no court objects to being overruled by legislation or constitutional amendment.

One advantage of having a Judicial Committee sitting locally would be that fewer English counsel and more local counsel would be employed. To appear before a board of English and Scottish judges is an education in itself; and many of the barristers so employed would themselves become judges very soon. It is essential to have good judges even when they have to administer bad laws; and too many laws in some of the independent countries conflict with cap. 29 of Magna Carta. Since the bills of rights, even those taken from the European Convention for the Protection of Human Rights and Fundamental Freedoms, derive from the common law, their interpretation should be in the hands of persons skilled in the common law. The Lords of Appeal in Ordinary are the ablest both of our common lawyers and of our civil lawyers, for the law of Scotland is founded on that of Rome. It would be necessary to retain in London enough Lords of Appeal to do the judicial business of the House of Lords, but a small addition to the number of Lords of Appeal, or in the alternative the addition of more members to the Judicial Committee, would enable Her Majesty's Government to offer to the other countries of the Commonwealth the services of some of the ablest judges of the United Kingdom. I think that the decision of 1956 was a mistake and should be reversed.

This is, however, a matter of machinery. My argument is that Magna Carta was taken to the Commonwealth as part of the common law. Not much work has been done on the common law which was exported. In many cases there are no early law reports. We do not know how and when the law libraries were built up. Even in old-established jurisdictions there are gaps. In Ceylon in 1942, when we expected a Japanese invasion, the law officers based their view of martial law on

[129] Jennings is referring to Dicey, *A Leap in the Dark*, pp. 94–102.

[130] *Adegbenro v. Akintola*, [1963] A.C. 614.

my lecture notes, because there was no set of Irish Reports in the Island. Some years later, learned counsel found that there was only one set of State Trials in the Island. It belonged to me, and so there may not be a set there now. In Pakistan in 1954 we found that even in Lahore, which had had a High Court in undivided India[,] there was a shortage of the more recondite material. These shortages were in highly developed jurisdictions. It is easy to imagine how little material there was elsewhere. I would guess – and it is a guess – that much of the law came from Blackstone's Commentaries.

Blackstone had in volume 4 a very fair summary of Magna Carta.[131] I think, however, that the summary was less important than the general tone of Blackstone's comments on the laws of England, which had to be administered by English judges in remote corners of a far-flung empire. Let me give you only one quotation:

> "... Laws, when prudently framed, are by no means subversive but rather introductive of liberty for (as Mr Locke has well observed) where there is no law there is no freedom. But then, on the other hand, that constitution or frame of government, that system of laws, is alone calculated to maintain civil liberty, which leaves the subject entire master of his own conduct, except in those points wherein the public good requires some direction or restraint."[132]

In the fourteenth and subsequent editions, published in and after 1803, this passage was followed by a long footnote written by my learned predecessor, Edward Christian, the first Downing Professor of the Laws of England at Cambridge. Its material is not of high quality, but it contains one passage relevant to my theme. Christian expresses the hope that those who acquire the most intimate acquaintance with the laws and constitution of England,

> "will always be the most convinced, that to be free, is to live in a country where the laws are just, expedient, and impartially administered, and where the subjects have perfect security that they will ever continue so; and, allowing for some slight and perhaps inevitable imperfections, that to be free, is to be born and to live under the English constitution."[133]

[131] William Blackstone, *Commentaries on the Laws of England* (London, 1765–1769), IV.
[132] *Ibid.*, I.
[133] Christian wrote this as a footnote in his 'Notes and additions' to volume I of Blackstone's *Commentaries*.

Christian displays his learning by quoting Cicero: Hanc retinete, quaeso, Quirites, quam vobis tanquam hereditatem, majores vestri reliquerunt.[134]

I quote these passages not to express approval of the nationalism implicit in them. I quote them only to show that English lawyers and British administrators, with all their faults, did try to pass on to those whom they advised and, for a time, ruled, the noble inheritance of liberty according to law. I have never met a lawyer in any part of the Commonwealth who did not think it his duty to hold fast to that inheritance. Magna Carta, at the latest count, belonged to 23 states members of the United Nations. We should, I think, encourage them to maintain its principles.

[134] 'Preserve, I beseech ye, O Romans, this liberty, which your ancestors have left ye as an inheritance.'

INDEX

Numbers in bold indicate references to pages with notes containing biographical information.